D1480079

FICTIONS OF ROMANTIC IRONY IN EUROPEAN NARRATIVE, 1760–1857

Lilian R. Furst

MACMILLAN PRESS
LONDON

© Lilian R. Furst 1984

All rights reserved. No part of this publication may be
reproduced or transmitted, in any form or by any means,
without permission

First published 1984 by
THE MACMILLAN PRESS LTD
London and Basingstoke
Companies and representatives
throughout the world

ISBN 0 333 25879 7

Typeset in Great Britain by
Wessex Typesetters Ltd
Frome, Somerset

Printed in Hong Kong

'Mit der Ironie ist durchaus nicht zu scherzen'
Friedrich Schlegel
('Irony is certainly no matter for jest')

'Irony is a disciplinarian feared only by those
who do not know it, but cherished by those who do.'
Søren Kierkegaard

PN
3500
F87
1984X

FURST, LI
FICTIONS
OF ROMANT
****
HONNOLD
 LIBRARY

Contents

Preface		ix
1	Beware of Irony	1
2	The Metamorphosis of Irony	23
3	Jane Austen: *Pride and Prejudice*, 1813	49
4	Gustave Flaubert: *Madame Bovary*, 1857	69
5	George Gordon Byron: *Don Juan*, 1818–23	93
6	Jean Paul: *Flegeljahre*, 1804–5	121
7	Denis Diderot: *Jacques le fataliste et son maître*, 1771–78(?)	159
8	Laurence Sterne: *Tristram Shandy*, 1760–67	189
9	In Search of a Theory	225
Notes		240
Selected Bibliography		261
Index		272

Preface

This book has grown out of an essay I was asked to contribute to a volume on romantic irony. In the course of writing the piece that has since appeared under the title 'Romantic Irony and Narrative Stance',[1] I became so aware of both the ramifications and the intrinsic importance of the topic that I eventually decided to develop my work into a more extensive study in which the questions raised by my initial research could be more fully pursued.

The questions are as intriguing as the complexities of the subject are daunting. How is romantic irony to be defined? Who coined and popularised the term itself? How valid is the common assumption that romantic irony began during the Romantic period and that Friedrich Schlegel was its 'father'?[2] What about its earlier manifestations in the novels of Cervantes, Sterne and Diderot, which Schlegel himself recognised as models? What is specifically romantic about this type of irony? Where does its centre of gravity lie? How does it relate to the spirit of the age whose name it bears? Such questions provoke enquiries of a more fundamental nature: What is the relationship of romantic irony to traditional irony? Is romantic irony an independent, distinctive phenomenon, or is it a variant on traditional irony? Is it a generic category unto itself? If so, are its lines of demarcation primarily historical or modal? How does romantic irony fit into the larger systems of irony outlined by such critics as Northrop Frye, Douglas Muecke and Wayne Booth? These questions in turn lead to a confrontation of the basic issues of irony: What is generally meant by irony? How does it function in a literary text? What are its possibilities – and its difficulties – as a form of discourse?

This book does not purport to answer all these questions. It aims for a clearer understanding of what romantic irony denotes in theory, how it works in practice, and the extent to which theory and practice coalesce. This entails an attempt to re-think romantic irony by envisaging the topic in a broader context, looking spatially and temporally beyond Friedrich Schlegel and German Romantic literary theory[3] and seeing it in its wider European setting in relation to earlier and contemporaneous thought and practice. By placing romantic irony in this perspective, the philosophical and literary factors crucial to the phenomenon can be identified, and an understanding of its workings can be evolved that does not depend solely on the Romantics' own often cryptic terminology.

My primary focus is on the correlation between traditional and romantic irony. For if the term 'romantic irony' is to have any signification and usefulness in literary analysis and history, its interface with normative notions of irony must be explored. I am therefore examining the distinctions between traditional and romantic irony in both the concepts advanced by the thinkers and the practices adopted by leading fiction writers between the mid-eighteenth and the mid-nineteenth century. The parameters of my study are determined by the subject itself. The mid-eighteenth to mid-nineteenth century is the period when irony became a vital concern for philosophers and also a central force in fiction. The narrative genre is chosen for the equally obvious reason that it was the main arena for the exercise of irony. *Tristram Shandy* (1760–7) is a natural starting date in so far as its innovative manipulation of irony marks an important point in the florescence of the European novel. The other works were selected because irony is crucial to the theme and mode of each. Jane Austen, Flaubert, Byron, Jean Paul and Diderot are, alongside Sterne, acknowledged as major ironists of the period, though others could well have been included. But my aim is not comprehensiveness for I am not writing a history of irony in the century after 1760. I am trying, rather, to elucidate a problem: the denotation of 'romantic irony'. For this reason a more traditional ironist such as Austen had to be considered as well as the experimenters, Sterne, Diderot and Jean Paul. For this reason also the arrangement of the works deliberately departs from the chronological sequence in favour of an order that more clearly reveals the distinction between traditional and romantic irony. It is the inner evolution of modes of irony that I want to trace, not the outer threads of literary history. And just as I have resisted a purely historical framework, so I have eschewed an overly systematic pattern lest the desire to fit individual works into a preordained schema foster distorted or biased readings. I have followed the demands of the subject by fusing the diachronic with the synchronic. My approach is predominantly pragmatic and inductive in attempting to deduce a prescriptive theory from a descriptive analysis of the concepts and, above all, the practices of irony.

It is a pleasure to express my gratitude to the institutions and the people who have actively helped this book along. The Stanford Humanities Center under the sagacious direction of Ian Watt provided the ideal balance of tranquillity and stimulation in which to complete and revise the manuscript. The John Simon Guggenheim Memorial Foundation bestowed the precious gift of free time. The University of Texas at Dallas gave me a grant from its organised research funds. I am greatly indebted to the curiosity of the many patient listeners I have had in the years that I have travelled with my lectures and my anxieties about irony. Among them five have been particularly instrumental in shaping this book: Martha Satz in Dallas, who first realised the potential of the topic; Hans Eichner in Toronto, who gave me decisive encouragement through his enthusiasm at its genesis, who continued to help me with suggestions and expert advice, and who checked my foolhardiness through his cautious objections; the late Eugène Vinaver in Canterbury, who extended to me, as ever, reassurance and understanding, and who so generously let me share his vast insights into literature; Walter Strauss in Cleveland, a brilliant and benevolent devil's advocate, whose probing clarified my ideas and whose confidence in the project sustained me through fits of doubt; and Anne Hendren in California, who led me towards the discovery of the title. Finally, my gratitude, as always, to my father for the invariable good humour with which he bears my exasperation at myself, for his sanguine common sense, and for his original and comforting comparison of the writing of a book to the process of distilling from wagonloads of pitch a microquantity of uranium.

Stanford L. F.

1 Beware of Irony

'Irony is a sharp instrument; but ill
to handle without cutting *yourself!*'
Thomas Carlyle, letter to
John Stuart Mill, 24 September 1833.

1

'Irony', Lionel Trilling tells us, 'is one of those words, like love, which are best not talked about if they are to retain any force of meaning.'[1] This is typical of the warnings issued to those approaching irony. Often the caveats resort to the imagery of dangerous ground, pitfalls and fogs, evoking the picture of an unwary pilgrim's progress. Yet the term has become one of the key concepts of contemporary critical vocabulary, as necessary to the discussion of literature as love is to the maintenance of life. Despite Trilling's and similar warnings, we must come to grips with irony, and with romantic irony too, if we are to understand modern literature.

Before venturing into the thickets of romantic irony, we need to look into the general problems of irony, to ask why in fact it poses such severe problems. Several extensive, illuminating studies of irony have appeared in recent years, notably D. C. Muecke's *The Compass of Irony* (London: Methuen, 1969) and Wayne C. Booth's *A Rhetoric of Irony* (Chicago and London: University of Chicago Press, 1974). The purpose of this chapter therefore is merely to map the terrain and to identify the pitfalls.

The *Oxford English Dictionary* gives three principal meanings for 'irony': first, 'a figure of speech, in which the intended meaning is the opposite to that expressed by the words used; usually taking the form of sarcasm or ridicule in which laudatory expressions are used to imply condemnation or contempt'; second, figuratively,

1

as 'a condition of affairs or events of a character opposite to what was, or might naturally be, expected; a contradictory outcome of events as if in mockery of the promise and fitness of things'; and thirdly, in its etymological sense, as 'dissimulation, pretence; especially in reference to the dissimulation of ignorance practised by Socrates as a means of confuting an adversary'. While these definitions clarify the connotation of the word, they stop short of explaining its common application to such writers as, say, Beckett, Kafka, or Nabokov. The second, figurative sense comes closest, except that their works show little expectation of the natural order implicit in the phrase 'fitness of things' and many signs of a paradoxical, incomprehensible dislocation. The element of contrarity so prominent in the *O.E.D.*'s definition has been attenuated, and with it the reassuring background assumption of an accepted norm. It is significant that all the examples cited in the *O.E.D.* date from before the twentieth century, the majority from the sixteenth to eighteenth centuries. Fowler's *Dictionary of Modern English Usage*, too, stresses the innate duality of irony: 'Irony is a form of utterance that postulates a double audience, consisting of one party that hearing shall hear and shall not understand, and another party that, when more is meant than meets the ear, is aware both of that more and of the outsiders' incomprehension.'[2]

If the dictionaries are rather limiting, the manuals of literary idiom are bewildering in the profusion of possibilities they offer. *A Handbook to Literature* presents irony as 'a broad term referring to the recognition of a reality different from the masking appearance'.[3] It may surface in such devices as hyperbole, understatement and sarcasm, and it may be inherent in a figure of speech, a situation, or a structure. M. H. Abrams, in his *Glossary of Literary Terms*, is more specific: 'In most of the diverse critical uses of the term "irony" there remains the root sense of dissimulation, or of a difference between what is asserted and what is actually the case.'[4] He then goes on to survey these diverse critical uses, examining verbal irony, structural irony, Socratic irony, dramatic irony, cosmic irony, and romantic irony. He also points out that 'a number of writers associated with the new criticism use "irony" in a greatly extended sense, as a general criterion of literary value'.

This 'stretching of meaning in the use of the term *irony*'[5] by recent critics has not been sufficiently recognised; however, it is a major source of the present confusion about irony. This extended meaning of 'irony' is often considered an American usage because it was most actively propagated by Robert Penn Warren and Cleanth Brooks, although it has its origins in two mid-Atlantic theoreticians, T. S. Eliot and I. A. Richards. It dates back to a lecture entitled 'Pure and Impure Poetry' delivered at Princeton in 1942, in which Robert Penn Warren called irony a 'device of reference', the frame of reference being 'to the complexities and contradictions of experience'.[6] If Warren's lecture laid the basis for the acceptance of irony in a far wider context, it was Cleanth Brooks who expounded the practical application of this new sense in an influential article, 'Irony and "Ironic" Poetry', first published in *College English* in 1948 (no. ix, 231–7) and expanded the following year for the anthology *Literary Opinion in America*[7] into 'Irony as a Principle of Structure'. This revised title is a good summary of Brooks' argument that poetry is modified by 'the pressures of a context' (p. 732) and requires 'a principle in which thrust and counterthrust become the means of stability' (p. 733). This principle is designated as 'irony', though Brooks readily concedes: 'We have doubtless stretched the term too much, but it has been almost the only term available by which to point to a general and important aspect of poetry' (p. 732). As a result of this bold extension of the meaning of 'irony', a great deal of poetry can be deemed ironic to the extent that it is governed by the dialectics of tension.[8] Brooks' adoption of the term 'irony' to denote a structural principle led first to many investigations of such irony in the arts, and later to an intense interest in the exploration of opposites, contradictions and discontinuities.[9] The conception of literature as essentially ironic was systematised by Northrop Frye in his renowned *Anatomy of Criticism* (1957). Frye not only subscribes to 'the view of many of the "new" critics that poetry is primarily (i.e. literally) an ironic structure';[10] he also offers a convincing rationale for this view:

> The critics who tell us that the basis of poetic expression is irony, or a pattern of words that turns away from obvious (i.e. descriptive) meaning, are much closer to the facts of literary experience, at least on a literal level. The literary structure is ironic because 'what it says' is always different in kind or degree from 'what it means'. (p. 81)

Frye's insistence on irony as a central determinant of literary structure is ultimately more important than his distinctions between the 'ironic mode', the 'ironic mythos', and the 'ironic age'. He holds 'that we are now in an ironic phase of literature' (p. 46), as does Wayne C. Booth whose *Rhetoric of Fiction* (Chicago and London: University of Chicago Press, 1963) expanded the role of irony in the criticism of fiction by linking it closely to the discourse of the 'unreliable' narrator.

These recent usages of 'irony' in literary criticism, though related to the dictionary definitions of the term, nevertheless represent momentous expansions of the meanings accepted before this century. It is essential to be aware of this development and of the term's aptitude for change. In talking of irony, one is not referring to a singlistic phenomenon; the term itself is protean in character. Because of 'its strange, featureless, even daimonic flexibility',[11] irony as a critical idiom tends towards diffuseness rather towards sharp focus.

The popularity of the concept in post-war criticism and the proliferation of its significations have led to a number of attempts to organise it into a systematic schema. Instead of straining for a comprehensive definition to cover all its manifestations, the newer attempts to obviate the difficulties inherent in irony aim at distinguishing and characterising different kinds of irony into a manageable order. The pluralism of irony has long been tacitly acknowledged in the plethora of descriptive tags current in critical vocabulary: verbal irony, rhetorical irony, dramatic irony, tragic irony, comic irony, satiric irony, irony of situation, structural irony, Socratic irony, cosmic irony, general irony, romantic irony, irony of fate, irony of character, metaphysical irony, self-irony, etc. These familiar labels have their usefulness in the pragmatic identification of heterogeneous uses of irony, but their worth is diminished by want of a common rationale. Some are named from the effect, some from the medium, or from the technique, or the function, or the object, or the practitioner, or the implicit attitude.

Foremost among the more systematic recent classifications are those of D. C. Muecke and Wayne C. Booth. Muecke, in *The Compass of Irony*, advocates a division into three grades: overt, covert, and private; and four modes: impersonal, self-disparaging, ingénu, and dramatised. In a review article[12] on the

Compass of Irony, Norman Knox suggests other criteria for classifying ironies. His four variable significant factors are: the field of observation; the degree of conflict between appearance and reality; a dramatic structure containing three roles – victim, audience, author; and the philosophical–emotional aspect. However, the five categories that this approach yields (tragic, satiric, comic, nihilistic, and paradoxical) are less original than Muecke's. In his monograph, *Irony* (London: Methuen, and New York: Barnes & Noble, 1970), Muecke separates verbal irony from situational irony: 'the former is the irony of an ironist being ironical; the latter is the irony of a state of affairs or an event seen as ironic'.[13] He adds that verbal irony 'raises questions that come under the headings of rhetoric, sylistics, narrative and satiric forms, satiric strategies' whereas situational irony, 'while raising fewer formal points, tends to raise historical and ideological questions' (pp. 50–1). The same broad discrimination was made earlier by A. E. Dyson in *The Crazy Fabric* where he concludes that there is on the one hand 'irony as a rhetorical technique' and on the other 'irony as a vision of the universe itself'.[14] The stylistic technique, the primary sense of the term for Dyson, consists of the 'creative manipulation of words' to conjure up 'the traps and surprises, the intellectual gymnastics, the virtuoso exuberance, the intrinsic delights' of weaving the 'crazy fabric' of literary irony. The other type of irony, which is 'more a feeling about the universe', stems from the perception of cross-purposes, of absurdity, of tragic suffering, the enigma of events that happen to us', and reproduces the 'crazy fabric of human nature itself'. The most ambitious taxonomy of ironies is offered in *A Rhetoric of Irony* where Booth draws a basic distinction between stable, readily reconstructible ironies and unstable ironies that elude reasonably definitive interpretation. On this fundamental dichotomy Booth superimposes two further opposing pairs: overt/covert, and local/infinite. These categories then admit the following permutations: stable–covert–local; stable–overt–local; unstable–overt–local; unstable–covert–local; unstable–overt–infinite; unstable–covert–infinite; and stable–covert–infinite. Booth gives no serious consideration to the position of romantic irony in his system nor to its relationship to other types of irony. Muecke devotes a whole chapter to romantic irony which he regards as an adjunct of General Irony, concerned 'principally with the ironic contradictions of art'.[15] He

underscores its source in late eighteenth-century Germany theory
by maintaining that:

> The first discovery one makes about Romantic Irony, if one
> starts out with a concept of Romanticism derived from a
> reading of the French or English Romantics and a concept of
> irony derived from the corrective ironies of La Rochefoucauld
> and Swift, Voltaire and Fielding, is that it has nothing to do
> with any simple conventional concept of Romanticism or with
> ordinary satiric or comic irony. (p. 181)

In the newest terminological complex, introduced by Alan
Wilde in *Horizons of Assent: Modernism, Postmodernism, and the Ironic
Imagination*, various stages in a scale of irony are associated with
differing phases of the modernist mentality. Thus '*mediate irony*',
which 'serves to mediate a fundamentally satiric vision, imagines
a world lapsed from a recoverable (and in the twentieth century,
generally a primitivist) norm'; 'by contrast, *disjunctive irony* (the
characteristic form of modernism) strives, however reluctantly,
towards a condition of paradox'; and 'finally, suspensive irony
(which I connect with postmodernism), with its yet more radical
vision of multiplicity, randomness, contingency, and even
absurdity, abandons the quest for paradise altogether – the world
in all its disorder is simply (or not so simply) accepted'.[16] Both the
rather arcane formulae and the attempted diachronic gradation
have too little specificity to cast much light on the problem of
irony.

2

In the case of irony its semantic history[17] – often a path of access
to the ultimate signification of a confusing term – is no great help
either for it reveals above all its innate shiftiness. In contrast to
the high esteem in which irony is held today, its original
connotation was distinctly pejorative. An *eiron* denoted in Greek a
wily, cunning person versed in every sort of unscrupulous trickery,
often symbolised as a sly fox. From this was formed *eironeia* which
was, in its early phases, synonymous with mocking pretence and
deception. As Trilling has pointed out, 'the etymology of the
world associates it directly with the idea of the mask, for it derives

from the Greek word for a dissembler'.[18] This association with the mask raises two of the crucial, recurrent questions about irony. First, is it essentially a figure of speech, manifest in such devices as understatement, blame-by-praise, i.e. saying one thing and meaning the contrary, or is it a pervasive habit of discourse and, by extension, a general mode of behaviour marked by sustained pretence of ignorance and self-deprecation? Is Socratic irony, for instance, a means of argumentation or an expression of an ontological vision? Taking it to its utmost extremes, is irony a rhetorical trope, or is it a philosophical stance? The second problem arising out of the notion of the mask concerns communication: if irony is a form of dissembling, how is the listener/reader to perceive it? How does one seen through the mask and distinguish it from the persona? How does one know that it is a mask, and that the opposite is being said to what is meant? There are no definitive answers to such questions. What is worth noting here is that as far back as the Ancient Greeks irony was already a slippery concept.

The Latin *ironia* of Quintilian and the medieval rhetoricians and lexicographers was translated into English as 'yroye' which first appeared in *Thordynary of Crysten men* in 1502. For the next two hundred and fifty years or so, as Norman Knox[19] has fully illustrated, it was used in England almost exclusively as a rhetorical device. Its two major strategies were either blame-by-praise or mockery by ironic concession which held up an opponent's views to clear light by echoing them with feigned and exaggerated approval. As a tool of ridicule during the Restoration it was so closely allied to 'raillery' as to be virtually interchangeable, 'raillery' being the common popular word for persiflage, while irony remained a relatively technical term. It was considered useful for indirect attack 'as a brief, whiplash kind of thing – a nipping taunt' (p. 177) unburdened by philosophical implications. Because it was not regarded as a weighty element of style, it was conspicuously absent from aesthetic treatises until after the mid-eighteenth century: 'throughout the entire period' (i.e. 1500–1755) 'there appeared not a single full-dress serious critical essay on the artistic principles involved in irony' (p. 141). This protracted neglect of irony as an aesthetic factor is all the more striking in contrast to the amount of attention it was to receive from the late eighteenth century onwards.

The growth of interest in irony towards the middle of the

century is a concomitant of the increasing prominence and complexity of satire. The notion of irony had become naturalised into literary discussion between about 1720 and 1730, and as satire itself evolved from the cruder methods of scoffing invective and burlesque, the subtle possibilities of irony began to be recognised as a device – still, however, as a *device* – capable of sophisticated manipulation. In such works as Swift's *A Tale of a Tub* (1704) and *Gulliver's Travels* (1726), Arbuthnot's *History of John Bull* (1727). Fielding's *Jonathan Wild* (1743), Montesquieu's *Lettres persanes* (1721) and Voltaire's *Candide* (1759), satiric fictional structures serve as a vehicle for irony, exploring its potential further than ever before.

Where then does satire leave off and irony take over, or is it vice versa? The relationship between the two is by no means as straightforward as it is generally made to seem. Any attempt to establish hard and fast lines of demarcation soon produces another graphic example of the problems encountered in containing irony within circumscribed limits and assigning it to any categoric place. Often irony is subsumed into satire, particularly by students of satire: 'irony is a form of criticism, and all irony is satirical, though not all satire is ironical'.[20] Like most generalisations, this is in need of some qualification. It would be more correct to say that in many ironies there is a streak of satire, but its extent and function is subject to large variations. Byron's *Don Juan* and Flaubert's *Bouvard et Pécuchet* are strongly satirical in thrust, aiming sharp attacks against specific, clearly visible targets and harnessing irony as a means to an end. In the novels of Jane Austen social satire, though present, is much less prominent, the acerbity of satire being dissipated by the geniality of comedy. And in Kafka's *The Castle* the element of satire against the bureaucracy, undeniably one strand of the novel, is quite subsidiary to its central import.

Apart from these quantitative reservations to the contention that 'all irony is satirical', qualitative distinctions must also be drawn between the approach of the satirist and that of the ironist. These are of cardinal importance since the differing stances reflect the divergence between the nature of satire and that of irony. Satire stems from a firm allegiance to a set of convictions; from the security of that entrenched position the satirist weighs the failings and follies of human beings. He diminishes the object of his attack by a ridicule that conveys contempt, indignation, scorn and derision, and that is often vented in forthright sarcasm. His attack is grounded in ethical standards, in a conscious discrimination between what is desirable in human conduct and what is not. In that sense the satirist is a moralist for he takes it upon himself to sit in judgement on the world without concealing his likes and dislikes. It is his self-assurance that forms the basis of his militancy. In antithesis to these trenchant value systems that prevail in satire, irony is governed by relativities. Like the satirist, the ironist often sees beyond the surface of human behaviour the grotesque and absurd forces that motivate conduct. But unlike the satirist, he does not set himself up in the authoritative pre-eminence of the judge. He does not have the absolute certainty to do that; his attitude is always ambivalent because he does not see the world in the stark colouring typical of the satirist's vision; instead he tends to admit the good *and* the bad in every alternative. Yet if satire is the harsher of the two, it is also the more buoyant in so far as its censure of human failings is balanced by an underlying faith in the potential for betterment (a pessimistic satirist without that faith would not bother to make his attack). What is more, satire yields a consistent and fairly explicit picture of the 'true' as against the 'false'. By contrast, the less immediately abrasive art of irony may ultimately be the more disturbing because its upshot is a series of open ends and contradictions. It is an inquiring mode that exploits discrepancies, challenges assumptions and reflects equivocations, but that does not presume to hold out answers.

Such indefinity permeates every aspect of irony. Even the distinction just outlined between satire and irony turns out to be more enigmatic in practice than in theory. That supreme satirist, Swift, reminds us of the precariousness of any attempt at a radical divorce between the two modes. Much of his writing – *A Tale of a Tub, A Modest Proposal*, and the first three books of *Gulliver's Travels* – is overtly satirical, directing its barbs at contemporary political abuses in a well-defined, highly coded context. As a weapon of attack Swift uses an irony that is purposeful, refined and constant, and that nearly always remains transparent and easily reconstructible. Only a reader of the utmost naîvety, ignorance and inexperience could mistake *A Modest Proposal* for a serious programme of reform. The very title, through its clever use of understatement, holds out a clue to that reversal of meaning that the reader is invited to make. For Swift's so-called 'modest' proposal 'for preventing the children of poor people in Ireland from being a burden to their parents or country, and for making them beneficial to the public' by slaughtering them at exactly one year when they provide 'a most delicious, nourishing, and wholesome food, whether stewed, roasted, baked, or boiled': this proposal is not merely *not* modest, it is monstrous to the point of obscenity. Under the mask of the commonsensical philanthropist Swift presents his plan with a straight face and such a wealth of elaborate details and financial computations as to underscore the enormity of his proposition by giving it concrete reality. Exaggeration, over- and understatement, *reductio ad absurdum*, hyperbole of every kind is handled with virtuoso control. Swift is savaging the indifference of government policies to the starvation of the poor; he does so by proposing the opposite to what he believes. His irony is a means to his end, satire. The alliance of satire and irony is equally obvious in the first three books of *Gulliver's Travels* and so are the objectives of the onslaught. The diminutive physical stature of the Lilliputians in Book One is a pointer to their spiritual and moral pettiness. In Book Two the giant Brobdingnagians show their vanity by their disdain of the glories of European civilisation as described by the dwarf-sized Gulliver. The excursion to Laputa in Book Three displays, in its ingenious exploration of a variety of scientific activities, the follies of an intellectualism adrift from common sense and feeling. Book Four, however, brings a change in character; it becomes difficult to follow the direction of the satire as the irony shifts from its subservient role as a rhetorical tool of satire into the dominant mode. Here the irony 'ceases to be a functional technique serving a moral purpose, and becomes the embodiment of an attitude to life'.[21] And that attitude is deeply ambivalent. The choice is no longer between the dismal world as it is and the ideal world as it should be, but between two equally unattractive options. The Yahoos appear as bestial creatures, antipathetic at first sight, while the Houyhnhhms, for all their alleged virtues, bear those moral and intellectual limitations that are revealed in their rejection of Gulliver. Their failings become apparent only obliquely, through a kind of blame-by-praise. But, though veiled, it is blame; Gulliver emerges perplexed, embittered, and alienated from both sides, as indeed do we. He has learned that man is not amenable to improvement, and we that satire and irony are less readily distinguishable than is commonly assumed.

The more closely one examines irony, the more intractable it proves to be. For its resistance to definition it fully deserves its Ancient Greek connotation of 'sly fox'. The normal scholarly procedures – dictionaries, handbooks, the term's semantic history, delineation by comparison to neighbouring modes such as satire – lead more to an appreciation of the problem than to its solution. From whichever angle irony is approached, it is always its elusiveness that emerges as its primary characteristic. However disconcerting, this has to be accepted as privotal to the nature of irony. If we are unable to pin down its meaning, it is because irony sets out to evade specificity.

3

This intrinsic elusiveness is a direct consequence and a reflection of the perspectivistic multiplicity of the ironist's perception of the universe. In its simple forms, irony springs from an awareness of the discrepancy between reality and appearance. But frequently the processes of irony are more complicated. For the ironist is often conscious of a choice between several possibilities, none of which has complete validity and all of which are exposed to question. After exploring every possibility, he may well find himself (and, incidentally, place us) in a labyrinth of doubts. Unlike the satirist, who lives among black and white images, the natural habitat of the ironist is in the many shades of greyness that make up the spectrum of ambivalence. To his questioning mind there are no clear and lasting answers, no serene certainties; the existence of other paths in itself undermines the authority of any one of them. Thus elusiveness, reserve, deviousness and contradiction are the hallmarks of the ironic mode. It has been claimed that: 'Whenever an ironist acquires a genuine faith and a genuine desire to establish it, he stops being an ironist and preaches'.[22] This is an overstatement, for an ironist may on occasion emerge from his ambivalences into the security of a belief without beginning to preach. But the opposition is a legitimate one in that the preacher has made a choice and publicly committed himself to a cause, whereas the ironist cannot take such a single-minded stand because he perceives alternative possibilities, any one of which might prove to encompass the truth. As a result, his philosophical vision is of contingencies, incongruities and relativities; and the linguistic medium consonant with that vision is ambiguity. Ambiguity is the very crux of irony:

> l'ironie ne se justifie que dans la mesure où elle reste au moins partiellement ambiguë: quel intérêt y aurait-il à parler ironiquement, si c'est pour immédiatement rectifier le tir en spécifiant ce que l'on veut *vraiment* dire?[23]

> (irony is justified only in so far as it remains at least partly ambiguous: what would be the point of speaking ironically if the sally were immediately rectified by the specification of what one *really* wants to say?)

The ironist therefore exists and expresses himself in ambiguities; his position, like his utterance, is perilous but exciting.

That then is the basis of the notorious elusiveness of irony. Its effect is prismatic: through hints and suggestions it arouses in the reader an inkling of latent layers of signification. As a means of literary expression its potential far exceeds the elementary reversal of meaning on which most definitions hinge. Such emphasis on reversal, on an opposite, is misleading since the subtler forms of irony draw on the art of insinuation. In place of straightforward inversion, irony prefers oblique refraction. It says not so much the *opposite* to what is meant as something *other than* is stated. There is a crucial difference between 'opposite' and 'other than': 'opposite' is limited and limiting, not least in its overtones of wanton concealment, while the modification into 'other than' opens up that latitude,[24] that spiritual freedom of movement in which irony thrives. It is 'a technique of saying as little and meaning as much as possible, or, in a more general way, a pattern of words that turns away from direct statement or its own obvious meaning'.[25] Although elusiveness is the cost of turning away from direct statement, the gain is the capacity to imply other and more than is actually said. In this respect irony represents a tremendous enrichment of literary expression, a subtle internal energy that gives access to new dimensions by extending the range of a text's referentiality. That is one of the main reasons for its attractiveness to writers and readers alike.

But if elusiveness can be exploited imaginatively as a prism of allusion, it can also become a source of danger. For ambiguity is open to misapprehension even when carefully controlled. To speak of ambiguity and control is to touch delicate concepts again. Almost any phrase can be deemed ambiguous, as Empson has taught us: 'In a sufficiently extended sense any prose statement could be called ambiguous'.[26] As an example Empson takes the apparently simple sentence, 'the brown cat sat on the red mat', and proceeds to point to the manifold difficulties of interpretation it could present. What is a 'cat'? What are the anatomical mechanisms involved in a cat's sitting? What are the laws of gravitation contained in 'on'? What is meant by 'brown' and 'red'? Empson's arguments are convincing; nevertheless, they remain in the realm of the hypothetical, as he himself concedes in his cautious phraseology: '*In a sufficiently extended sense* any prose statement *could* be called ambiguous'. Theoretically, 'the brown cat sat on the red mat' *could* be ambiguous; in practice it probably is not because most readers grasp it without hesitation and without thought about the nature of cats and colours or the laws of gravitation and feline anatomy. The ambiguity may be instilled into it from outside by the ratiocinations of a reader with a particularly analytic mind. More likely, if it strikes a reader as ambiguous, it is because of the context in which it occurs. Context is of paramount importance in any act of literary interpretation, and nowhere more so than with a possibly ambiguous, ironic utterance. So while no single element of the sentence, 'the brown cat sat on the red mat' is ambiguous taken either in itself or in relation to the other words, it may become or appear ambiguous when placed in a context that signals dubiousness to the reader.

The primacy of ambiguity in irony poses major problems for both the ironist and the reader. The ironist must control the ambiguity and establish the context without, however, prejudicing the freedom of ambivalence. While eschewing direct statement, he must phrase his oblique formulation in such a way that his deviousness does not produce mere obfuscation His is the art of the tight-rope[27] acrobat, poised dangerously between explicitness and impenetrability. Like the tight-rope acrobat in his every move, the ironist must be in control of every nuance. That control is a measure of his artistry, and also an outcome of his own ironic detachment. His ability to see beyond surface appearances presupposes disengagement, a dissociation between himself as critical observer and the objects of his observation. This detachment is the foundation of that aesthetic distance that underlies all artistic control. The extent of the aesthetic distance and the degree of artistic control may fluctuate, but the control as such remains a vital prerequisite for the practice of irony.

On this matter of control, one further distinction must be made. Artistic control of the medium is often confused with, or considered inseparable from control over the moral vision. That is not so. The aesthetic coherence which is the product of artistic control does not exclude the portrayal of an uncontrollable universe, as is shown by the works of Dostoyevsky, Kafka, and Beckett. The want of 'a secure pedestal'[28] in the metaphysical domain by no means entails the same kind of insecurity in artistic execution, although the presentation may be such as to echo the ontological disarray. Conversely, novels like those of Jane Austen and Fielding that do achieve moral clarity must not *a priori* be denied irony. Writers who uphold a particular social and moral ethos may none the less be aware of the questionability of that ethos and find an outlet for their dualistic attitude in irony. Nor is irony necessarily equivocal in its moral stance; in making discriminations between appearance and reality, false and true values, it too derives from moral and social judgements, though not with the wholehearted assertiveness of satire. Morally the ironist is conscious simultaneously of standards and of their shortcomings. But artistically he must neither falter nor waver; he must have the control to embody his binary vision in the appropriate aesthetic form.

While the ironist's task is the control of ambiguity, the reader's is that of rightly comprehending it, of correctly 'reconstructing' the latent meaning, to use Wayne Booth's phraseology. For in its elusiveness irony places insidious obstacles along the path of communication. In ironic discourse the desire for communication is paradoxically allied to a strong urge to concealment. The tension between these dual, conflicting drives is one of the mainsprings of irony. Balancing transparency and opacity, irony is like a game of hide and seek in which the object should not be too readily spotted nor so thoroughly hidden as to be irretrievable. Part of the attraction of irony lies in this playful aspect; it is an intellectual sport in which the seeking reader must take an active role, his astuteness being eventually rewarded in the triumph of understanding. A well-arranged game succeeds in establishing an indirect system of communication between narrator and reader. Irony can therefore be regarded as a secret language, a channel of communication between the initiated. Only on the surface is there that 'disconnection between the speaker and his interlocutor'[29] that Trilling singles out as a salient feature of irony. At a deeper level, beneath the apparent disconnection, there must also be a connection if the irony is to be caught. The overt information is accompanied by signals that negate it,[30] and the speaker must present both codes in such a way that his interlocutor is able to decipher them in their contradictory conjunction. For the ironist wants to try the reader's ingenuity, but not to the point of thwarting him by totally blocking access. Here again tension between dissimulation and revelation is fundamental to the processes of irony.

If, however, irony is a secret language, how are we to learn it? How can we be among the initiated? That is one of the paramount problems in dealing with irony. It is worth recalling Fowler's definition of irony as 'a form of utterance that postulates a double audience, consisting of one party that hearing shall hear and shall not understand, and another party that, when more is meant than meets the ear, is aware both of that more and of the outsiders' incomprehension'. Using different terminology, the question remains the same: How are we to be of that other party that does catch the undertones? Is it mainly a matter of intelligence, so that irony should be proclaimed the sport of an intellectual élite? Or is the perception of irony purely subjective, as is often maintained? How do we know when 'more is meant than meets the ear'? And just as important, how much more? How far should we go in interpreting irony, and how can we forestall the temptation of overinterpretation? How are radical mistakes to be avoided? To take a concrete example, when an Irishman on a grey, cool, drizzly morning comments that it is 'a soft day', is he being ironical? Probably not, but it may well seem so to the tourist who had hoped for blue skies and sunshine. The day is literally 'soft' in that the traveller will not be assaulted by extremes of heat or cold, but the drizzle may prevent him from enjoying the view. This might be ironic if the tourist had come from afar specially to see that view.

In this particular instance the key to correct understanding lies in the cultural context. Our perception of irony depends on a series of cultural norms shared by the speaker and his interlocutor. Since no sentence is in itself ironic, and conversely any sentence can be ironic, the cultural context often plays a vital role in making us decide whether irony is present, and if so, to what extent. Though the context may comprise idiosyncratic factors (such as the Irishman's assessment of his climate and the meaning he gives to the word 'soft'), tentative guidelines for the detection of irony can be formulated from a pragmatic analysis of texts deemed by common consensus to be ironic. Such an approach shows that the perception of irony is not just a subjective caprice. Texts contain coded directions for reading; it is incumbent on the reader to discover the most appropriate, i.e. that most closely in consonance with the text's own intentionality. This requires intelligence in the sense of an ear open to the undertones of a discourse. But those undertones are demonstrably woven into the text, and generally they are presented in such a form as to invite discovery. For in order to fulfil the ironist's purpose, they must be recognisable. So the ironic counter-meaning beneath the surface statement may be indicated by a variety of signals that beckon the reader to probe what is hidden. Clues of differing kinds are held out to the alert ear as hints of the presence of a subtext. These clues are so placed by a consummate ironist as to be sufficiently discreet to uphold his cover and at the same time sufficiently manifest to be elicited.

The stealthy but perspicuous strategies of an ironic narrator can be seen in the handling of Casaubon in George Eliot's *Middlemarch*. This is the record of his feelings during his betrothal to Dorothea:

> Mr. Casaubon, as might be expected, spent a great deal of his time at the Grange in these weeks, and the hindrance which courtship occasioned to the progress of his great work – the Key to all Mythologies – naturally made him look forward the more eagerly to the happy termination of courtship. But he had deliberately incurred the hindrance, having made up his mind that it was now time for him to adorn his life with the graces of female companionship, to irradiate the gloom which fatigue was apt to hand over the intervals of studious labour with the play of female fancy, and to secure in this, his culminating age, the solace of female tendance for his declining years. Hence he determined to abandon himself to the stream of feeling, and

perhaps was surprised to find what an exceedingly shallow rill it was. As in droughty regions baptism by immersion could only be performed symbolically, so Mr. Casaubon found that sprinkling was the utmost approach to a plunge which his stream would afford him; and he concluded that the poets had much exaggerated the force of masculine passion. Nevertheless, he observed with pleasure that Miss Brooke showed an ardent submissive affection which promised to fulfill his most agreeable previsions of marriage. It had only once or twice crossed his mind that possibly there was some deficiency in Dorothea to account for the moderation of his abandonment; but he was unable to discern the deficiency, or to figure to himself a woman who would have pleased him better; so that there was clearly no reason to fall back upon but the exaggerations of human tradition. (Book 1, chapter 7)

This could be read as an account of the situation from Casaubon's angle. The stilted language recalls his customary pretentious speech, suggesting his voice and his point of view. Yet its turbid extravagance encourages a critical disengagement on the reader's part. While Casaubon speculates on the possibility of 'some deficiency' in Dorothea, it does not cross his mind that the deficiency might lie in him. But that does strike the reader because the narrator has carefully prepared us for the implicit irony. In the preceding twenty pages the reader has been given ample warning of Casaubon's dry, sterile nature before the 'shallow rill' imagery of this passage. Brooke, speaking to his niece of her suitor, bluntly declares: 'I never got anything out of him – any ideas, you know' (chapter 4); Mrs Cadwallader and Celia are scathingly sceptical of the 'great soul' with which Dorothea credits her future husband (chapter 6); and his letter of proposal (chapter 5) with its insistence on the 'need in my own life' and 'your eminent and perhaps exclusive fitness to supply that need' is a skilfully managed revelation of Casaubon's immense egotism. When the narrator adds: 'How can it occur to her to examine the letter, to look at it critically as a profession of love?', she in fact spurs us as readers to do just that. So by the time we come to that description of Casaubon's feelings, we have the insight into his personality to appreciate its hidden irony. We can reconstruct the implied meaning, i.e. the deficiency in

Casaubon, behind the voiced words, i.e. the putative deficiency in Dorothea.

This example from *Middlemarch* uses both the leading methods of providing clues: the textual and the contextual. The most common textual devices are such rhetorical figures as exaggeration, hyperbole followed by anti-climax, repetition to the verge of parody, symbolic imagery, dialogue at cross-purposes, and verbal inflation. These readily spotted means, by bringing out the incongruity between matter and manner, point to the presence of an ironic subtext. Such signals tend to be most transparent when the narrative situation is relatively simple, with an assured and consistent voice firmly conducting the narration, as in *Middlemarch,* Austen's *Pride and Prejudice*, or Fontane's *Effi Briest*. The reader, trustful of the narrating voice, enters into agreeing collusion with him, sharing his perspective, privy to his knowledge, and acquiescing in his implied judgements. The irony is perceived and interpreted without difficulty. When the narrator is less reliable, the reconstruction of the intended meaning becomes increasingly vexing. The clues offered to the reader by the narrating voice in Byron's *Don Juan,* Stendhal's *Le Rouge et le Noir*, or Diderot's *Jacques le fataliste et son maître* in direct addresses, epigraphs or titles may or may not be fallacious. Once the narrating voice itself becomes suspect, the game of irony grows more complicated. These teasing narrators, however, issue their own warnings, often in serio-comic vein, of their untrustworthiness. With an unreliable narrator certain elements of the discourse assume added importance as clues to irony: tone, gesture, emphasis, proportion, pace, imagery, internal contradictions. These may furnish an evaluative commentary that enables the reader to establish the ironic perspective. In first person narratives such as *Tristram Shandy*, Nabokov's *Lolita*, or Camus' *La Chute*, which let us hear only the narrating persona's voice, internal factors have to be assessed with scrupulous care. Self-betrayals, disparities, extravagant claims, conflicting signals, paradoxes, and gaps can lead the reader to surmise an underlying equivocation and to uncover an ironic countermeaning. Such clues within the fabric of the text are 'as it were, stylistic winks' ('das gleichsam stilistische Augenzwinkern')[31] directing the reader's attention towards the ironic subtext.

Context is almost equally important in the determination of

irony. Context may refer to the microcosm within a specific work. To return to the example of Casaubon, we read the record of his feelings within the context of what we already know about his character and situation as well as about the values of the society in which he and Dorothea live. This contextual knowledge confirms that our ironic perception of him is indeed justified. In addition to this inner cadre, there is an outer one which E. D. Hirsch calls the 'generic context' or the 'intrinsic genre' in which a work is cast. He defines 'intrinsic genre' as *'that sense of the whole by means of which an interpreter can correctly understand any part in its indeterminacy'.*[32] A valid interpretation devolves from a reader's accurate recognition of the 'genre' in which a work is written, i.e. whether it is primarily comic, satirical, ironic, etc. Since the interpretation of meaning follows largely from an overall generic expectations, once the context has been ascertained, the meaning of the parts will fall into place. This is an attractive theory, but it still leaves the quandary as to how to judge that vital generic context correctly. According to Hirsch, much 'depends on the interpreter's previous experience of the shared type',[33] on what Genette calls the 'narrative *competence* of the reader'.[34] In practice, a close analysis of the early signals in a work, often in the opening paragraph,[35] will yield dependable clues as to the generic context. In *Middlemarch*, for instance, the invocation of Saint Teresa of Avila in the Prelude posits a frame of aspiration within which Dorothea's life is bound to seem an ironic shortfall. At the opening of *Pride and Prejudice, Don Juan,* and *Jacques le fataliste,* as we shall see, the generic context is rapidly set in a few strokes as remarkable for their economy as for their pertinence.

The external context must also be taken into account, and this includes besides the cultural milieu the historical moment. The political, social or philosophical background may be crucial in discerning satiric thrust and ironic nuance, as in the case of *Gulliver's Travels,* Dostoyevsky's *Notes from Underground,* or Orwell's *1984.* The relationship of 'cultural circumstances' to a concept such as sincerity has been fruitfully explored by Trilling, who insists that 'the word cannot be applied to a person without regard to his cultural circumstances'; and that the 'sincerity of Achilles or Beowulf cannot be discussed' any more than that of the patriarch Abraham. But the question of sincerity can fittingly be raised in regard to Elinor and Marianne Dashwood in Austen's *Sense and Sensibility,* or to Goethe's Werther because sincerity 'became, at a given moment in history, a new element of the moral life'.[36] Once a trait such as sincerity is incorporated into the ethical canon, the lack of that quality may be the object of satire or of irony. To ignore these historico-cultural contexts is to risk grotesque misreadings. A striking example of such a misreading has recently been documented in the Romantics' approach to *Don Quixote*:[37] they took it out of its context, overlooked the novel's satiric purpose and burlesque techniques, idealised the hero, and invested the work with a symbolism that reflected their own ideology, aesthetics and sensibility. That might be called the imposition of a burden of a present alien to a work. More often it is the burden of the past[38] that weighs so heavily as to drive a writer towards parodistic irony or self-irony.

There are thus a number of ways whereby an ironic countermeaning or subtext within the discourse may be detected. None of them is infallible, for irony must always retain its quintessential ambivalence. 'One man's Overt irony is another's Covert, as every teacher knows', Knox[39] ruefully comments; or, one man's 'soft' day is another's spoiled day. This epitomises one of the chronic problems attendant on irony: the role of personal response. However rigorous the endeavour at objective analysis, subjective input is unavoidable in the process of interpretation. The dilemma has been aptly summarised by P. Gifford in his searching article on *La Chute*: 'Precisely because irony engages the creative participation of its interlocutor, it gives scope for subjectively biased or disproportionate judgements as other modes do not.'[40] To translate this into concrete terms, the *Mona Lisa*, Muecke reminds us, 'has been interpreted both as a portrait of someone smiling ironically and as an ironical portrait of someone smiling with foolish self-satisfaction'.[41] The danger of subjective reading, of misreading, and with it of overreading is an ever threatening pitfall, for which the only corrective is constant attention to the text itself.

If subjectivity is the Scylla of reading irony, then authorial intention is its Charybdis. In interpreting signals, looking for clues and examining contexts, credence is invested in the ironist's good faith on the assumption that he intends us to understand meanings other than those explicitly stated. The criterion of intentionality has been endorsed by persuasive critics.[42] But its validity has also been severely impugned, and its authority questioned. It is particularly tricky in narrative, where it may be unclear whose intention is operative: that of the actual author or that of the narrating voice? The two must not be automatically fused, though they may coincide to an extent often hard to pinpoint. The problem of intentionality is at its most acute with the persona of the unreliable narrator, who frequently seems to intend to mislead us as readers, and who may further cloud the issue by insinuating that it is we who are unreliable readers. Leaving these complications aside for the moment, it is well to recall that the veiling of intention is integral to the practice of irony which is a willed deception. The ironist's mask of innocent ignorance may be a temporary one; the deception may be calculated to be seen through. However, a residual grain of doubt is bound to remain; in that sense, all ironists are, by definition as it were, to some degree unreliable.

Moreover, the doubt inherent in irony may grow and spread. When intentionality becomes suspect, the standard definitions of irony come to seem inadequate. The *O.E.D.* underlines the reversal of 'the intended meanings' and 'the words used'. The same dichotomy of 'intended meaning conveyed to the initiated' and 'pretended meaning presented to the uninitiated' is posited in a recent scholarly work on irony.[43] These definitions rest on certain fundamental suppositions: conscious intentionality on the part of the ironist; the existence of stable meanings; and the efficacy of words as a medium of communication between writer and reader. What happens when 'meaning', 'intention' and 'language' are themselves exposed to scutiny as to their signification? Or when they become the objects of irony? These questions lead us towards the precincts of romantic irony.

2 The Metamorphosis of Irony

> 'Jedes Ansehen geht über in ein Betrachten,
> jedes Betrachten in ein Sinnen, jedes Sinnen
> in ein Verknüpfen, und so kann man sagen,
> dass wir schon bei jedem aufmerksamen
> Blick in die Welt theoretisieren'
>
> Goethe, Preface to the *Farbenlehre*

> ('Every scrutiny turns into a contemplation,
> every contemplation into a meditation,
> every meditation into a linking, and so we
> can say, that with every attentive look into
> the world, we are already theorising')

1

For Dr Johnson irony was 'a mode of speech in which the meaning is contrary to the words'. In this terse phrase from his *Dictionary* of 1755 he subscribes to the traditional conception of irony, outlined in Quintilian's *Institutio oratoria*, as a rhetorical figure whose essence lies in *dissimulatio* and reversal. Barely fifty years later Goethe, in the preface to his *Farbenlehre* (1808), was beset by hesitations about 'Ironie', branding it a 'hazardous word'.[1] This may well be the first of those warnings often attached nowadays to the term. Its appearance in 1808 signals a change in the perception of irony since Dr Johnson's confident dictum of 1755. The connotation, usage, and aura of 'irony' underwent such a metamorphosis towards the close of the eighteenth century as to make it a hazardous notion.

The Augustans did not deem irony worthy of much respect. It

23

was a figure of speech, a vehicle for local wit, a means of adding brilliance to a discourse or of making a point strikingly. But it was not intrinsic to a work of art as a central shaping factor. Accordingly, while the Augustans gave some critical notice to a number of ways in which their irony revealed itself, they never troubled to break down its practices into principles of literary theory. The place for discussion of irony was in primers of rhetoric, and the models were almost exclusively Roman.

It was only at the turn of the eighteenth century that irony suddenly assumed a prominent position. It lagged forty or more years behind such concepts as 'genius', 'originality', and 'creativity' which had sprung into the limelight soon after the middle of the century in a cluster of aesthetic treatises from which irony was conspicuously absent. The Age of Sensibility doubtless preferred the warmth of a tender heart to the coolness of an ironic mind. When irony burst onto the intellectual scene, it was in a different place and an altered format: from the lowly primers of rhetoric it moved to the lofty tomes of speculative aesthetics, and its model switched from the Latin to the Greek, from Cicero and Quintilian to Socrates and Plato. The year 1797, with the publication of Friedrich Schlegel's *Lyceum* fragments, has been cited[2] as the turning-point in the European history of the concept of irony. Schlegel's *Lyceum* collection, together with his *Athenäum* fragments (1798) and his *Ideen* (1800), accomplished a metamorphosis of irony by presenting it in a new context and with new functions.

Friedrich Schlegel's ideas are seminal in inaugurating an innovative approach to irony that was to be of lasting importance for modern literature. He must occupy a pre-eminent place in any study of irony because he formulated an original perception of irony, to which he gave a leading role in his aesthetic theory. A bold thinker gifted with insight and imagination, a scholar with broad interests and sound Classical learning, Schlegel was a sparkling initiator rather than a patient builder of systems. His fertile mind poured out ideas in hundreds of aphoristic fragments on an astonishing variety of topics, ranging in length from a few words to several pages, and in manner from grave reflections to jesting witticisms. Writing for an élite circle, he tended to use a cryptic, idiosyncratic, compressed phraseology which presents extraordinary obstacles to interpretation. Though his doctrine is not wrought into the formal *ars poetica* customary until then for major statements of aesthetic theory, his aphorisms are interconnected into a cohesive web rich in suggestion and provocative in thrust.

Schlegel began by drawing sharp distinctions not only between differing uses of irony but also between different levels. He discriminated between what he considered the lower types of irony – the rhetorical, satirical, polemical, and parodistic – and that irony which he designated as genuine, complete, and divine in spirit.[3] The former corresponds to the Augustan view of irony, while the latter describes Schlegel's own vision. Schlegel dismisses the lower sorts of irony as cynical and tinged with viciousness, though he admits their usefulness in polemics. In an entry in his *Literary Notebooks* dating from 1798 he expresses his scorn for those who believe irony consists in knowing how many children Petrarch's Laura had.[4] The complement to this is another entry from the following year in which he emphasises that to him irony is essentially philosophical.[5] In an essay entitled *Über die Unverständlichkeit*[6] (*On Incomprehensibility*, 1800), Schlegel sets up an elaborate hierarchy of ironies: common irony; subtle or delicate irony; supersubtle irony; straightforward irony; dramatic irony; double irony; and irony of irony: From his bantering tone, his waggish examples, his accumulation of conditional verbs, his pleasure in exaggeration and deflation, it is amply evident that Schlegel's discourse is itself saturated with irony, a defence of his own irony written 'im Feuer der Ironie'[7] ('with the fire of irony'). Jesting apart, however, the dichotomy between the two levels of irony is an insistent theme throughout Schlegel's aphorisms in the closing years of the eighteenth century. What is more, it is reiterated in the writings of Tieck, Solger and Adam Müller, all of who contrast commonplace satirical irony with true artistic irony. This distinction between the former acceptance of irony and its new signification to Schlegel and his successors is the cornerstone for its metamorphosis. When Schlegel refers to 'Ironie' in his *Lyceum* and *Athenäum* fragments and in his *Ideen*, what he has in mind, unless he specifically mentions rhetorical irony, is the higher authentic type of irony, which he characterises in scattered aphorisms.

Schlegel regards this higher irony as 'das höchste Gut und der Mittelpunkt der Menschheit'[8] ('man's highest possession and his centre of gravity'). Its domain lies within the realm of philosophy: 'Die Philosophie ist die eigentliche Heimat der Ironie'[9] ('philosophy is the true homeland of irony'). Far from being just a literary device, it is endowed with 'philosophisches Vermögen'[10] ('philosophical capacity'). This means not merely that Schlegel's conception of irony has its origins in philosophy; rather it denotes the capacity of irony to confront and, ideally, to transcend the contradictions of the finite world. Again and again Schlegel dwells on the intimate association of genuine irony and philosophy: 'Bei der wahren Ironie muss nicht bloss Streben nach *Unendlichkeit* sondern Besitz von *Unendlichkeit* mit mikrologischer Gründlichkeit in Ph[ilosophie] und P[oesie] verbunden, da sein'[11] ('In true irony not only striving for the *infinite* but possession of the *infinite* must be present, linked with micrological thoroughness to philosophy and poetry'). Placed in this context, irony becomes something quite other than the mordant, half-jocular 'dry mock' it had been to the Augustans. Never before had such deep seriousness been attributed to irony. Schlegel sounds playful when he asserts in *Über die Unverständlichkeit*: 'Mit der Ironie ist durchaus nicht zu scherzen'[12] ('Irony is certainly no matter for jest'); elsewhere he expounds the same idea with a sedateness that verges on solemnity: 'Die vollendete absolute Ironie hört auf Ironie zu seyn und wird ernsthaft'[13] ('Complete, absolute irony ceases to be irony and becomes serious'). Irony is thus given a wholly new metaphysical status, and invested with an epistemological and ontological function. The philosophical stance implicit in this authentic irony has aesthetic manifestations too, perceptible in the relationship between the artist and his work. In the arts authentic irony is the equivalent to the cognitive organ that it was to Schlegel in his apprehension of the universe. The concrete forms of irony are here grounded in a distinctive ideological substructure; they are secondary to its philosophical capacity, serving not as a technical device but for the exposition of a cosmic vision.

Schlegel envisages the artist as both involved in and detached from his creation, aware of the contradictions of his endeavour, but able to transcend them. He is simultaneously committed to his work and to himself as creator. This dual loyalty determines his position and his creative procedures, and also has its precipitate in certain features of his created work. The dimension of reflection and self-consciousness is, for Schlegel, intrinsic to creativity. The artist, even as he replicates the original divine act of creation, reflects on his creation; conscious of his own creative processes and Godlike, he delights in sporting with it at will. In this way the artist is cast as the self-conscious architect of transcendence, whose instrument is the particular kind of irony outlined by Schlegel.

Through the preponderance of such irony the artist remains in a state of floating suspension (*schweben*), a sort of negative capability, that is recognised as central to spiritual life and conducive to artistic productivity. It is this belief that underlies Schlegel's affirmation of paradox as a positive value and its close association with irony. Paradox is the basis and the outcome of irony, its *conditio sine qua non*, its soul, source, and principle, as Schlegel put it in a notebook entry.[14] Hence paradox comes to be seen as the very incarnation of irony: 'Ironie ist die Form des Paradoxen'[15] ('Irony is the form that paradox takes'). To this Schlegel adds the immediate rider: 'Paradox ist alles, was zugleich gut und gross ist' ('everything that is at once good and great is paradoxical'), thereby affirming the importance of paradox as a spur to that dynamic evolutionary progression which the young Schlegel upheld with such ardour. Three core strands of Schlegel's thought on irony, i.e. the role of consciousness, the assent to mobility, and the notion of paradoxicality, are united in a key aphorism often cited as Schlegel's definition of irony: 'Ironie ist klares Bewusstsein der ewigen Agilität, des unendlich vollen Chaos'[16] ('Irony is clear consciousness of eternal mobility, of the infinite fullness of chaos'). This can only be understood holistically within the web of Schlegel's theory as a summation of his belief that the finite world is contradictory and can therefore be mastered only through the conscious floating of an ironic stance. Puzzling though that dictum may seem, not least in its tantalising brevity, it contains a view of irony illuminating for a Kafka, a Beckett, or a Cervantes. Irony is transformed into a way of seeing the world, of embracing within one's consciousness paradox and chaos.

But irony was not to be merely a passive notation of a mobile world; on the contrary, it was conceived as an active force, an instrument of transcendence as well as of perception. Together with its negative capability, it also carries a positive charge. So Schlegel maintained, 'durch sie' [i.e. Ironie] 'setzt man sich über sich selbst hinweg'[17] ('by means of it' [i.e. irony] 'one transcends oneself'). Irony is an essential tool in the dialectical process of self-transcendence. This is the context in which another famous phrase of Schlegel's has to be read: irony as the 'steten Wechsel von Selbstschöpfung und Selbstvernichtung'[18] ('constant alternation of self-creation and self-destruction'). This is frequently misinterpreted to refer simply to the breaking of artistic illusion. That may be one of its visible effects in a work of art. What Schlegel proposed, however, went far beyond a superficial play with levels of illusion. Irony, he asserted, is a permanent parabasis ('Die Ironie ist eine permanente Parekbase'[19]); it stems from the artist's critical self-detachment and unremitting self-consciousness; it denotes his complete freedom, his superiority over the work-in-progress; and it becomes manifest in the liberty with which he creates, de-creates, and re-creates. The ascending momentum implicit in parabasis for Schlegel is brought out in a notebook entry: 'Parekbase und Chor jedem Roman nothwendig (als Potenz)'[20] ('Parabasis and chorus necessary to every novel (for potentiation)'). The destructive side of irony, the 'stete Selbstparodie'[21] ('incessant self-parody'), as Schlegel called it, is only a stage in a dialectical progression towards ideal transcendental poetry of poetry. It is within this frame of reference that irony is also termed 'eine wirklich transzendentale Buffonerie'[22] ('a truly transcendental buffoonery'), for it carries a lofty purpose beneath its roguish appearance.

Schlegel's concept of irony is thus dependent on his theory of Romantic poetry as 'eine progressive Universalpoesie'[23] ('a progressive universal poetry'). In this theory irony occupies a commanding position: the dialectic of its tensions is to permeate every facet of the aesthetic artifact, shaping its outer and inner configuration, and this dynamic is to act as the propellant for the advance towards transcendence. The destructive de-creation of irony is envisaged as a vital step for the subsequent re-creation on a higher plane. The capacity for self-destruction is the ultimate measure of man's faculty for free self-determination: 'Alles was sich nicht selbst annihiliert, ist nicht frei und nichts wert'[24] ('Whatever does not annihilate itself is not free and is worth nothing').

Schlegel's theory is patently fraught with dangers. There is no doubt that he posited irony as a manifestation of supreme independence that represents a path to self-transcendence. Whether irony could in practice fulfil these expectations is another matter. Schlegel's inability to realise his aims in his novel

Lucinde (1799) can be attributed more to his own shortcomings as a creative writer than to flaws in his theory. But his conception of irony is a two-edged sword. For though irony may spring from the yearning for transcendence,[25] the shortfall from that desired state can induce a damaging sense of negativity. The possibility of such an inversion into the opposite of its intended outcome is an ever present threat. Instead of ascending in an ecstatic self-liberation, irony may provoke a descent into an agonising awareness of uncertainty. The flux of its vaunted mobility may result in acute disorientation. There is, as Beda Allemann[26] has recognised, 'etwas leicht Vexatorisches' ('something slightly vexatory') in Schlegel's concept of irony, 'die Möglichkeit eines Umschlags in die dunkle Kehrseite' ('the possibility of inversion into its dark other side'). If transcendence does not follow from irony, as Schlegel would wish, the nihilistic tendencies that Allemann discerns (pp. 99–100) could supervene. Schlegel, incidentally, soon dropped this early theory of irony, and after his conversion to Catholicism came to link irony to love.

For the reader there is another more immediate risk. Once irony is transferred from the rhetorical into the metaphysical sphere, the consequences of missing or misreading it are vastly increased. When irony is a form of witticism, as with the Augustans, ineptitude in grasping it leads to a local and limited misunderstanding. On the other hand, when irony is centrally encoded in an entire work, failure to recognise it produces a radical misinterpretation. The greater the potential of irony in its scope, range, and role in a work, the greater the attendant hazards for the reader.

While Schlegel formulated a new theory of irony allied to his postulate for Romantic poetry, he did not actually invent it. He derived his theory from the practical models he acknowledged in Socrates, Petrarch, Dante, Cervantes, Shakespeare, Sterne and Diderot. His achievement lies in his insights into the significance of their irony and in his ability to crystallise those insights into a palpable, albeit complex theory. Nor did he in fact call it 'romantic irony' in any of the writings that appeared during his lifetime. The phrase occurs four times in his private literary notebooks which were not deciphered and published until 1957. The four relevant entries[27] refer to Shakespeare, to drama, to Petrarch, and to the essence of the romantic. In the literary criticism of the German Romantics, the combination of 'romantic' with 'irony' was not common currency; Tieck, August Wilhelm Schlegel, Solger and Adam Müller simply wrote about 'Ironie', like Friedrich Schlegel, though like him they too distinguished between rhetorical irony and their particular concept of irony. Only Novalis used the phrase in reference to Goethe's novel *Wilhelm Meister*,[28] but as in the case of Friedrich Schlegel, in a private notebook not published until a century after his death in 1801. Nor does the phrase occur in Hegel's aesthetic treatises of 1835–8 despite his many attacks on irony and on Romanticism and his evidently ironic sally against the 'geniale, göttliche Ironie'[29] ('divine irony of the genius') invented by Friedrich Schlegel and 'nachgeschwatzt' ('repeated slavishly') by umpteen others. Kierkegaard does not use it either in his *Concept of Irony* (1842) where he writes about 'Irony after Fichte'. It was not until 1850 that this 'unhappy phrase' made its debut in a scholarly work, *Die romantische Schule in ihrem Zusammenhang mit Göthe und Schiller*, by Hermann Hettner, the first systematic historian of German literature. Hettner writes of that 'übermütig auflösende Willkür des Schaffens . . . die unter dem Namen der romantischen Ironie so berühmt und berüchtigt geworden ist'[30] ('exuberantly dissolving wilfulness in creativity . . . that has gained such fame and notoriety under the name of romantic irony'). In his *Geschichte der deutschen Literatur im 18. Jahrhundert* (1865–70) Hettner went on to use it freely, alluding with more verve than accuracy to 'jene vielberufene romantische Ironie, von welcher die Romantiker so viel singen and sagen'[31] ('that much vaunted romantic irony, of which the Romantics sing and speak so much'). Hettner's near contemporary, Rudolf Haym, shows greater caution and understanding in his monumental *Die romantische Schule* (1870) where he eschews 'romantische Ironie' in favour of the more neutral 'poetische Ironie'[32] ('poetic irony'). However, Haym's wise modification did not prevail, and it was the recalcitrant 'romantische Ironie' that came to haunt literary criticism.

2

Before the actual term 'romantic irony' was launched in the mid-nineteenth century, Schlegel's new perception of irony had become a topic for heated controversy. It had enthusiastic advocates and vehement opponents. Yet despite their antagonism the two camps were in agreement in fundamental approach: they envisaged irony not in a rhetorical but in a metaphysical context, not as a figure of speech but as a philosophical and aesthetic stance. This is cogent evidence of the metamorphosis that irony had undergone.

Schlegel's immediate successors among the German Romantics mostly echoed and elaborated on his principles. Adam Müller, in lectures held in Dresden in 1806, equated irony with consciousness and freedom as if the three were interchangeable;[33] asked for a German translation of the term, he averred that he could think of none better than 'revelation of the freedom of the artist or of the human being'.[34] Solger outdid Müller in his exaltation of irony in *Erwin* (1815) and in his posthumously published *Vorlesungen über die Ästhetik* (1829). Notwithstanding Solger's strictures against Schlegel's cynicism and subjectivity, his theory is in three respects strongly reminiscent of his predecessor's: the pronounced demarcation between common irony and that true, noble irony that 'fängt erst recht an bey der Betrachtung des Weltgeschicks im Grossen'[35] ('only really begins with the contemplation of the fate of the world as a whole'); the interdependence of irony and consciousness;[36] and the endorsement of irony as a philosophical stance.[37] But Solger excludes the paradoxicality so prominent in Schlegel's theory, stressing instead the divine mission of irony as a mediator between, or a transition from earthly and eternal being. Solger acclaims irony as the 'wesentlichen Mittèlpunkt der Kunst'[38] ('quintessential kernel of art'), 'die vollkommenste Frucht des künstlerischen Verstandes' ('the most perfect fruit of artistic insight'), and ultimately the 'helle Pforte zum vollkommenen Erkennen'[39] ('the shining gateway to complete understanding'). Solger repeatedly insists that artistic irony, far from being intermittent or fortuitous, is the wellspring of artistic creativity.[40] In this mystical apotheosis of irony Solger surpasses Schlegel; in aspiring to subsume all art under the aegis of irony he seems strangely to prefigure the 'new critics'.

The reaction against this virtual canonisation of irony came in the forceful reasoning of Hegel in his *Grundlinien der Philosophie des Rechts* (*Philosophy of Right*, 1833), *Vorlesungen über die Asthetik* (*Aesthetics*, 1835–8), and *Vorlesungen über die Geschichte der Philosophie* (*Lectures on the History of Philosophy*, 1837). The main thrust of

Hegel's attack is directed against the foundation of the
Romantics' concept of irony, namely Fichte's doctrine of
subjectivity. Hegel argues that the boundless vanity of the
enthroned ego undermines and displaces the authority of the
object:

> Nicht die Sache ist das Vortreffliche, sondern Ich bin der
> Vortreffliche und bin der Meister über das Gesetz und die
> Sache, der damit, als mit seinem Belieben, *nur spielt* und in
> diesem ironischen Bewusstsein, in welchem Ich das Höchste
> untergehen lasse, *nur mich geniesse.* – Diese Gestalt ist nicht nur
> die *Eitelkeit* alles sittlichen *Inhaltes* der Rechte, Pflichten, Gesetze
> – das Böse, und zwar das in sich ganz allegemeine Böse –,
> sondern sie tut auch die Form, die *subjektive* Eitelkeit, hinzu,
> sich selbst als diese Eitelkeit alles Inhalts zu wissen und in
> diesem Wissen *sich* als das Absolute zu wissen. –[41]

> (It is not the thing that is excellent, but I who am so; as the
> master of law and things alike, *I simply play* with them as with
> my caprice; my consciously ironical attitude lets the highest
> perish and *I merely hug myself at the thought.* This type of
> subjectivism not merely substitutes a *void* for the whole *content*
> of ethics, right, duties, and so is evil, in fact evil through and
> through and universally – but in addition its form is a
> subjective *void*, i.e. it knows itself as this contentless void and in
> this knowledge knows *itself* as absolute.)

This 'Konzentration des Ich in sich'[42] ('concentration of the ego
on itself') results in the opposite of what the supposedly divine
irony of the genius seeks to attain:

> Das Prinzip dieser Produktionen, die nur in der Poesie
> vornehmlich hervorgehen können, ist nun wiederum die
> Darstellung des Göttlichen als des Ironischen. Das Ironische
> aber als die geniale Individualität liegt in dem Sichvernichten
> des Herrlichen, Grossen, Vortrefflichen, und so werden auch
> die objektiven Kunstgestalten nur das Prinzip der sich
> absoluten Subjektivität darzustellen haben, indem sie, was
> dem Menschen Wert und Würde hat, als Nichtiges in seinem
> Sichvernichten zeigen. Darin liegt denn, dass es nicht ernst sei
> mit dem Rechten, Sittlichen, Wahrhaften, sondern dass an

dem Hohen und Besten nichts ist, indem es sich in seiner Erscheinung in Individuen, Charakteren, Handlungen selbst widerlegt und vernichtet und so die Ironie über sich selbst ist.[43]

(The guiding principle of these works, which can exist fully only in poetry, is again the representation of the divine as the ironic. The ironic, however, as an expression of the genius of individualism resides in the self-destruction of the splendid, the great, the excellent, and so the objective figures of art will have to represent only the principle of a subjectivity become absolute, showing all that has worth and dignity in man as null and void in its self-destructiveness. Consequently, not only is the right, the ethical, and the true not to be taken seriously; furthermore, the highest and best is reduced to nought when it contradicts and destroys itself through its appearance in certain individuals, characters and actions, and thereby becomes the ironic comment on itself.)

For Hegel Schlegel's concept of irony represents the emblem— and the scrapegoat – of his hatred of subjectivity. Censured for its reductive frivolity[44] and its irresponsible dissolution of ethical values,[45] irony is identified as 'the absolute principle of negativity'[46] in which the ego, having destroyed all external certainties, comes to bask in its self-centred consciousness.

Hegel's accusation of subjectivity against the Romantic concept of irony became the focal point of contention thereafter. It led to some curious alignments: Hegel's sympathy for Solger, for instance, stemmed from their common stand against Schlegel's subjectivity. Kierkegaard, too, sides with Hegel on this issue; in reviewing irony after Fichte, he concurs with the Hegelian view that it 'is a determination of subjectivity',[47] indeed 'the being-for-itself of subjectivity' (p. 274). Kierkegaard raises the same objection as Hegel to a subjectivity run amok: 'The ego was like the crow, which, deceived by the fox's praise of its person, lost the cheese. Thought had gone astray in that reflection continually reflected upon reflection, and every step forward naturally led further away from all content' (p. 289).[48] Kierkegaard also accepts Hegel's definition of irony as the principle of 'absolute negativity', though not for the reasons adduced by Hegel, who assailed the subjectivity of irony on the grounds that it posed a threat to the authority of the objective system. Kierkegaard's pronouncement carries all the more weight because it derives not from a doctrinaire position, but from an apparently dispassionate assessment of irony:

> Thus we have irony as infinite absolute negativity. It is negativity because it only negates; it is infinite because it negates not this or that phenomenon; and it is absolute because it negates by virtue of a higher which is not. Irony establishes nothing, for that which is to be established lies behind it. It is a divine madness which rages like a Tamerlane and leaves not one stone standing upon another in its wake. Here, then, we have irony. (p. 278)

On balance, however, Kierkegaard's posture in *The Concept of Irony* is itself ironically ambivalent. He is further from Hegel than at first seems: he takes Hegel to task for discussing irony in a tone of indignation and with contempt, specially in regard to Schlegel; yet he also emphasises that his criticism does not imply either that Hegel erred in his judgement of Schlegel, or that the Schlegelian perception of irony was not gravely flawed. Nonetheless he ends closer to Schlegel than is generally supposed, although his interest shifts increasingly from the concept of irony onto the persona of the ironist. On two major aspects of irony there is substantial accord between Kierkegaard and Schlegel. Both make the basic distinction between 'irony as a momentary expression' and 'pure irony, or irony as a standpoint' (p. 270). The former is defined by Kierkegaard in Johnsonian terms as a 'figure of speech' that 'travels in an exclusive incognito'; its characteristic is 'to say the opposite of what is meant' (pp. 264–5) so that it is, to all intents and purposes, 'identical with dissembling' (p. 272). This 'executive irony' is differentiated from 'contemplative irony' (p. 271) in quality as well as in quantity:

> Irony in the eminent sense directs itself not against this or that particular existence but against the whole given actuality of a certain time and situation. It has, therefore, an apriority in itself, and it is not by successively destroying one segment of actuality after the other that it arrives at its total view, but by virtue of this that it destroys in the particular. It is not this or that phenomenon but the totality of existence which it considers *sub specie ironiae*. (p. 271)

The total ironist, therefore, on the metaphysical plane, is

consistently ironical. Though such 'contemplative' irony springs from a perception of the discontinuities of existence, it has in itself a continuity that makes it harder to reconstruct than the intermittent 'executive' irony. Directed as it is at the 'totality of existence', it can be read only in its totality. Thus, the more thorough the irony, the scanter the indications held out to the reader. But then, according to Kierkegaard, metaphysical irony, not being engaged in a mere conceit of dissemblance, 'does not generally wish to be understood' (p. 266); indeed, the ironist may even seek 'to lead the world astray' (p. 268).

Besides this distinction between irony as a figure of speech and irony as a philosophical standpoint, there is another significant affinity between Schlegel's and Kierkegaard's views. For while Kierkegaard subscribes to Hegel's characterisation of irony as infinite absolute negativity, he realises that this is only one aspect of irony. He is certainly far more aware than the idealistic Schlegel of the dangers of an irony trapped in an annihilating scepticism. But he concludes *The Concept of Irony* by proclaiming that: 'Irony is like the negative way, not the truth but the way' (p. 340). The 'truth' and aim of irony is 'as a mastered moment', and when it attains this idea, it is the antithesis of infinite absolute negativity:

> When irony has first been mastered it undertakes a movement directly opposed to that wherein it proclaimed its life unmastered. Irony now limits, renders finite, defines, and thereby yields truth, actuality, and content; its chastens and punishes and thereby imparts stability, character, and consistency. Irony is a disciplinarian feared only by those who do not know it, but cherished by those who do. (pp. 338–9)

So Kierkegaard affirms the positive potential of irony. Its negativity is not a terminus, only a stage – 'a cleansing baptism' (p. 339) – in a cathartic process that ultimately yields 'truth'. Kierkegaard here envisages irony, like Schlegel, as a means of transcendence and self-transcendence. For both, the intent of the highest kind of irony is to raise the individual above the paradoxes that constitute the dialectic of life. Irony is simultaneously the mode of perceiving and of overcoming those paradoxes.

From the end of the eighteenth century onwards, the possibilities of irony as a metaphysical force were increasingly taken into cognizance. While theoreticians were in agreement on the philosophical nature of irony, opinion was divided as to whether it carried a positive or a negative charge. The transferral of irony from the verbal to the metaphysical domain entailed a change in its literary character too. Like the image, which underwent a parallel metamorphosis at about the same time under the impact of the same cultural constellation, irony rose from the position of servant to that of master. In its traditional role as a verbal trope it could make a limited, peripheral contribution to a work whose direction had already been determined; it was rather more than just ornamental, but less than essential. In its new guise it stood at the epicentre of the aesthetic artifact, defining not only its mode but its meaning and intent, permeating them with an ironic sense of ambivalence, mobility, and paradoxicality. This second potential of irony did not, of course, supplant its original usage. Irony as a figure of speech is a persistent resource of sophisticated discourse at all periods. But its implications as a primal source of energy in a literary work were openly avowed and fully explored only in the modern period whose roots go back into the eighteenth century.

3

The metamorphosis of irony was a product and a manifestation of a wider transformation of Western civilisation during this 'pivotal period . . . that made the turn from Renaissance to modern'.[49] It was pivotal through its searching re-assessment of the hitherto revered heritage of the Classical canon. The protracted Quarrel of the Ancients and the Moderns, despite its pedantry, was symptomatic of an underlying crisis of confidence. The spate of aesthetic treatises after 1730 reveals the upsurge of speculation about new directions in the arts. These tentative explorations of criteria for beauty and sublimity initiated the emancipation from the established models. The breakthrough came in Young's *Conjectures on Original Composition* (1759) in which the old prescript of imitation was superseded by the then startling ideal of original creation. The prominence of such terms as 'originality', 'creativity', and 'genius' shows the change of standards in the arts. The artistic revolution of the later eighteenth and early nineteenth century was the most striking indication of a radical revision of man's perception of the universe and of his relation to it and to himself.

The momentous re-orientation which took place in the second half of the eighteenth century is generally ascribed to the break away from 'the belief in the rationality, the perfection, the static completeness, the orderliness and coherency of reality'[50] that had found its supreme embodiment in the Enlightenment's schema of a continuous Scale of Being. The loss in credibility of certainties formerly buttressed by reason in philosophy and dogma in religion is the crucial 'somewhat enigmatic event'[51] that acted as a catalyst to the transition from the Classical to the modern *episteme*. The 'closed ideology', for centuries the foundation of the political, social, scientific, and metaphysical organisation of Western Europe, envisaged the world as temporally and spatially limited, and therefore amenable to the imposition of a set hierarchical order. For all its shortcomings, such an archetype fostered a sense of optimism because it made the universe appear open to rational comprehension, and ultimate truths attainable by the power of the human mind. The great monument to the 'closed ideology', the *Grande Encyclopédie* (1751–72), was designed to marshal all the definities of human knowledge into a methodical syntax. Though finally completed, it served less as an apotheosis of the code it represented than as a harbinger of its bankruptcy. For this attempt to arrange data in a logical sequence, to draw regulatory distinctions, to establish permanent values, in short, to order the universe, led instead to the confrontation of a refractory disorderliness, even though this was not then admitted publicly. It was not until a quarter of a century later that the violent end of the *ancien régime* in the French Revolution demonstrated the collapse of venerable institutions and cherished beliefs. This erosion of long standing European systems, which had been the guardians of security, forms the background for the metamorphosis of irony. The 'open ideology', nurtured by the rising young generation of Romantics, tolerated – indeed welcomed – disorder, flux, mystery, and fragmentariness as the elements of that creative chaos from which a better new world could be shaped.

The political revolution of 1789 coincided with an equally far-reaching philosophical revolution. In the preface to the second edition of the *Kritik der reinen Vernunft* (*Critique of Pure Reason,* 1787) Kant actually used the phrase 'Copernican revolution'[52] to describe the change effected by his theory of knowledge. By postulating the priority of the active perceiving knower over the inert corpus of knowledge, Kant explicitly threw open the entire question as to the bases of our knowledge of objects and the accessibility of absolute truths. Kant distinguished categorically between the phenomenal, which he believed could be known, and the noumenal, which could not. However, this discrimination hardly blunted the impact of Kant's propositions, which diminished men's faith in their epistemological capabilities. The processes of knowing were shown to be far more complicated than had been supposed, yielding fewer certainties and leaving more spaces of doubt. Kant's Copernican revolution represents an important step in the replacement of the 'closed ideology' by the 'open ideology'. The pursuit of the fixities of a finite world gave way to a probing of an infinite universe to which great areas of indeterminacy now had to be conceded. Once the reliability of knowledge had been undermined, a flood of doubt invaded men's minds, making them particularly receptive to the ambivalences of irony.

As the authority of objective judgement declined, the jurisdiction of subjective cognition expanded. It was given unlimited prerogatives in Fichte's *Grundlagen der gesamten Wissenschaftslehre* (*The Science of Knowledge*, 1794) which predicated the dependence of reality on the perceptions of the ego. Fichte went much further than Kant in sponsoring the primacy and autonomy of the ego. His transcendentalism, by considering things in relation to the perceiving subject, examines the *a priori* conditions for our experience of the world, and thereby concentrates philosophical analysis on subjectivity. When reality is reduced to the status of a non-ego posited by the ego, its claims to authenticity are shattered. In the dialectical relationship between non-ego and ego, it is the ego that has unchallenged supremacy as the fountainhead of knowledge. Fichte's sweeping idealism has a direct bearing on the metamorphosis of irony in three respects. First, his assumption of an underlying polarity between self and reality forms the paradigm for the dialectical structure of Friedrich Schlegel's theory of irony. Secondly, his apotheosis of the ego bred a self-consciousness unparalleled in its intensity at any previous period. The self became conscious of itself as a perceiving consciousness in a spiralling movement that encompassed the opposing poles of self-immersion and self-detachment. Finally, Fichte's consistent subjectivity, by stripping objective judgement of its prestige, reinforced the drift towards incertitude initiated by Kant. The processes of perception and judgement were seen to be problematical in themselves, while the validity of such concepts as 'meaning' or 'contrarity' is reduced through their subjection to idiosyncratic value referents. The ascendancy of subjectivity thus seriously prejudices the operations of traditional irony, which rests on the acceptance of a common understanding of words and ideas.

One of the consequences of the modification effected by the philosophies of Kant and Fichte in the standing of knowledge as an anterior mode of being was a subtle but vital change in the perception of language. Hitherto knowledge and language had been rigorously interwoven: 'The fundamental task of Classical "discourse" is *to ascribe a name to things, and in that name to name their being.* For two centuries, Western discourse was the locus of ontology. When it named the being of all representation in general, it was philosophy: theory of knowledge and analysis of ideas.'[53] This is the postulate that animated the so-called Port-Royal grammar, the *Grammaire générale et raisonnée* (1660; *General and reasoned Grammar*) of Claude Lancelot and Antoine Arnauld. The framework for this reasoned explanation of the parts of speech is clearly revealed in the significant title of the succeeding volume, *La logique, ou l'art de penser* (1662; *Logic, or the art of thinking*) which achieved still greater fame throughout Europe. The systematisation that is the aim of these codified universal grammars is the linguistic counterpart to that ordering of all knowledge that was the ideal of the *Grande Encyclopédie*. As the validity of objective knowledge came to be questioned, so too were the bases of language. Displaced from its previous almost automatic representative function, the word made a startling new appearance as 'enigmatic raw material'.[54] The growing scepticism and speculation through the eighteenth century about the efficacy of pre-established and received meanings and also about the assumptions underlying expression and communication is another pregnant manifestation of the wider crisis of authority characteristic of this 'pivotal period'.

The change in the perception of language is, however, harder to pinpoint than in the theory of knowledge because it occurred not with the sudden explosive impact of the works of Kant and Fichte, but in a series of treatises spread over nearly a century.

Gradual though the change may have been, its direction is plain: from the static, schematic view embodied in the Port-Royal grammar to a dynamic, developmental vision. The axiomatic certainty of 'closed' grammar gave way to the 'open' probing of emergent language theory. A major landmark in this transformation is Locke's *Essay Concerning Human Understanding* (1690) which has been deemed 'the first modern treatise devoted specifically to philosophy of language'.[55] In Book III of the *Essay*, 'Words', Locke's primary preoccupation is with the precise definition of words on the grounds that great disputes and 'errors are generally about the signification of words rather than about the nature of things' (III, x, 14). The source of the problem lies, in Locke's opinion, in the 'very unsteady and uncertain significations' (III, x, 4) attached to words which give rise in turn to 'doubt, obscurity, or equivocation' (III, vi, 40). Locke takes a pragmatic and optimistic approach, seeking to remedy an ill for which he believes a corrective to exist. He does not radically question the capacity of words to carry steady significations. His tone is that of a rational enquiry into the reasons for the failure of words to perform their assigned task; he rises to anger at vagrant uses that are a threat to intelligibility, but never to anguish about the possibility of comprehensible communication. It is not in that sense that Locke's notions about words are modern. The long range importance of the *Essay* lies rather in the connection it makes between semantic issues and the theory of knowledge. 'Semantic inquiries during the Middle Ages and the Renaissance had been intimately associated with logic and grammar. The new epistemological orientation of semantics, . . . , was first explicitly established in Locke's *Essay*.'[56] This 'new epistemological orientation of semantics' is a signal precursor of the later parallel tendency of irony. What is more, the metamorphosis of irony is directly linked to the reorientation of semantics. For when 'the name ceases to be the reward for language',[57] when 'words ceased to intersect with representations and to provide a spontaneous grid for the knowledge of things',[58] that is to say, when signification and meaning in themselves become matters of doubt, then it is no longer practical to say the contrary to what is meant in the supposition that meaning and countermeaning will immediately be understood. If words are used with uncertain meanings, as Locke saw, even rhetorical irony cannot function as the simple, stable device it is generally taken to be.

So Locke sows the first seeds of that 'linguistic relativism'[59] that was to come into full flower with Herder (1744–1803) and Humboldt (1767–1835). Locke's influence is evident in Condillac's *Essai sur l'origine des connaissances humaines* (1746; *Essay on the Origins of Human Knowledge*) which was advertised on its translation into English in 1756 as 'a supplement to Mr Locke's Essay in the Human Understanding'. For Condillac, as for Locke, the model is the mathematician's clear use of signs, although Condillac, building on both the Port-Royal principles of universal grammar and on Locke's doctrine of the origin of ideas in sensation, evolved an original theory of signs that went far beyond Locke. Condillac emphasised repeatedly the dependence of all discursive thought on the use of language, and the role of language as the medium of thought: 'Penser devient donc un art, et cet art est l'art de parler'[60] ('Thinking thus becomes an art, and that art is the art of speaking'). But the crux of Condillac's understanding of language is his interest in its origins, whereby he introduces the dimension of time into the consideration of language, and, above all, endows words with an internal energy, and, as it were, an autonomous life of their own.

The evolutionary capacity of language is the central focus of Herder's *Abhandlung über den Ursprung der Sprache* (1772; *Treatise on the Origin of Speech*). Herder's theory of speech has been described as 'at the same time a theory of perception, a theory of language, and a theory of signification'.[61] Herder in fact inverts the classical order, according to which the institution of signs rendered possible human communication; he posits the primacy of the communicating being, who defines the signs he is using. Thus the roots of language are transferred to the active subject in the same way as Fichte, in his *Wissenschaftslehre*, and Berkeley, in his *Treatise Concerning the Principles of Human Understanding* (1710), centred the processes of perception in the individual mind. This transference marks a break in the concept of language that corresponds in its thrust to the crucial turn in philosophy towards the end of the eighteenth century. In both fields the movement is from stasis to dynamism, from the acceptance of a regulatory, objective code to the assertion of a mobile, subjective mode. The most obvious and serious outcome of this innovative approach to speech is the formation of an entirely new problem area: that of understanding. A shift occurs in the locus of uncertainty: to the Port-Royal grammarians uncertainty as to what a sign might signify stemmed from a deficiency of knowledge regarding the object it intended to represent; whereas from the later eighteenth century onwards it became increasingly evident that the uncertainty might reside in the ways in which individuals use words. Like the processes of perception, the processes of communication were now recognised as far more complex and far more wayward than had hitherto been assumed.

This does not imply that the eighteenth century has a theory of meaning in the modern sense. It is well to heed Ian Hacking's warning 'of the extreme difficulty of pinning a "theory of meaning" on any philosopher of those times'.[62] However, the late eighteenth century was amply aware of the discrepancy between the sign and what it might signify, and of the hazards of language as an unreliable mediator of meaning. What begins as a critique of terminological confusions quickly grows into a disseminated unease about the ways in which language functions to convey meaning as well as about its relation to the processes of the mind, to knowledge, and indeed to the order of things. Once language comes to be regarded as fundamentally precarious, once doubt is cast on the feasibility of communicating meaning with assurance, the traditional tactics of irony, 'saying the contrary to what is meant', lose much of their effectiveness as a form of discourse. The discovery of ambiguities in all words is a potent factor impelling towards more radical and enveloping constructs of irony that mirror the essential paradoxicality of existence. The intuition of the instability of meaning paves the way for the metamorphosis of irony.

4

The dominant literary trends of the late eighteenth and early nineteenth century also encouraged the extension of irony and the change in its character. The rise of both the Romantic movement and the novel proved fertile ground for the fruition of irony.

At first sight the association of Romanticism with irony seems as strange conceptually as it is verbally. Romanticism is generally taken to denote a primary commitment to the expression of feeling, and this appears to be the opposite to the controlled detachment of irony. Yet the Romantic poets were too accomplished as poets not to realise that feeling, even at its most intense, required a certain control if it was to be turned into good poetry. Wordsworth's well-known prescript, 'emotion recollected in tranquillity',[63] was not an open invitation to a self-indulgent outpouring of feeling; it recognises the necessity for calm retrospective assessment by the shaping spirit. Nor did Wordsworth see any contradiction between his advocacy of emotion and the avowed moral intent of his poetry. The 'spontaneous overflow of powerful feelings'[64] was a means to an end: to carry 'alive into the heart by passion truth which is its own testimony'.[65] If emotion was to serve such higher purposes, its overabundance had to be curbed. Irony clearly offered one method of regulating its flow, and it was used to that end by Byron, though not by Wordsworth himself. Neither Wordsworth's poetic theory nor that of any other leading English or French aesthetician concedes any importance to irony. That was a distinctive feature of German Romantic doctrine. None the less, the demand for tranquil recollection on the poet's part suggests a stance by no means inimical to the ironist's contemplative discrimination. It would be erroneous to dismiss irony outright as alien to the Romantics' engagement in feeling, or to regard it only as a late importation, a mocking corrective to excess.[66]

Despite its absence from Romantic theory except in Germany, irony is far more integral to the Romantic perception of the world and of poetry than is usually supposed. Romanticism is the culmination of that transformation of Western culture under way during the 'pivotal period' of the eighteenth century. Its ideology is the very epitome of 'openness' in its affirmation of an infinite universe, in which flux, change and growth were the norms, and where indeterminacy, chaos, ambivalence and relativism were evaluated as positive preliminaries to a progression towards the ideal. The artistic aspirations, too, were assimilated to this vision. For this reason the Romantics reacted with vehemence against that predication of immutable laws of art that had obsessed their predecessors; they emphasised, on the contrary, its organic aspects, often adducing botanic images of germination, unfolding and flowering to illustrate the genesis of a poem. Coleridge, Wordsworth, Blake, Shelley, Hugo, Stendhal, Mme. de Staël, Friedrich Schlegel, August Wilhelm Schlegel, and Novalis all subscribed to this creed of vitalistic evolution. Friedrich Schlegel believed that the essence of Romantic poetry was that it should 'ewig nur werden, nie vollendet'[67] ('forever be becoming, never completed'). As soon as art turns from a static, finite entity into an infinitely active force, it desires not perfection but striving energy. Only through incessant movement will it attain the ideal in a self-transcendence that embraces the dialectic of opposites.

In this context it becomes apparent that the marked idealism of Romanticism is not at odds with its willingness to countenance contradiction. The polar tensions of contradiction and paradox were esteemed as productive stimulants to growth in a sequence that comprised negation as well as assertion. So irony could be placed alongside feeling as one of the major activators of Romantic art. As the mechanism for the destruction that must precede the higher re-construction, it becomes the cipher for the creative artist's autonomy, and beyond that for the upward spiral of the Romantics' hopes. Moreover, through its saturation with irony the work of art comes to have a double existence: as an independent aesthetic artifact and as a self-representation of its continuing formative processes. So it can assert *and* negate itself. The role ascribed to irony in Romantic art is therefore in consonance with its aesthetic principles, notably in the insistence on polarity and dynamism. These principles, like the concept of irony itself, reflect the attempt to delineate a form of art that devolves from a vision of the world as boundless and kinetic, and hence most fittingly conveyed in a mode aware of its own essential mobility.

Like Romanticism, though from a different angle, the novel was also conducive to the blossoming of irony. Its rise in stature about the middle of the eighteenth century is commonly connected to the emergence of the bourgeoisie and to 'the transition from the objective, social and public orientation of the classical world to the subjective, individualist and private orientation of the last two hundred years'.[68] In this respect it is a concomitant of both the outer changes in the structure of European society and the inner transformations that occurred during the 'pivotal period'. This latter aspect has recently been underscored in the contention that the increase in the novel's popularity is 'more an intimate expression in innovative form of the restless self-questioning that has characterized so much of Western culture'.[69] Whether this large claim holds for the novel as a whole is disputable. However, it certainly holds for a sub-category of the genre, the self-conscious novel, which leapt to prominence with *Tristram Shandy* (1760–7), and which has a direct bearing on the extended role of irony in fiction.

The growth of self-consciousness and its precipitate in the arts is awkward to chronicle with cogency, let alone brevity. Its aesthetic bases have been illuminated by Bernhard Heimrich's subtle book[70] on the concept of fictionality in the theory and practice of the German Romantics. He shows that its sources lay in the crystallisation of an awareness that art involves a particular kind of illusion. The understanding of this principle was still lacking in the early eighteenth century when the appeal to literal truthfulness had been the prevailing criterion. The capacity to distinguish between deception and illusion, between the faithful reproduction of reality and the aesthetic appearance of reality marks a crucial watershed in the approach to art. Heimrich dates the spread of this realisation of the innately fictional character of art to the late eighteenth century. The implications of this shift in the perception of art are momentous:

> nicht *wie* ein Roman erzählt wird, ist im Hinblick auf den epischen Fiktionscharakter, auf den ästhetischen Schein des Epischen von Bedeutung, sondern *dass* er erzählt wird; nicht *wie* ein Autor erzählt, sondern *dass* er erzählt – *dass* er erzählt, obwohl es gewissermassen gar nichts 'zu erzählen', 'zu berichten' *gibt*. So verstanden ist das fiktionale Erzählen insgesamt und von vornherein ein Fingieren des historischen Erzählens, ist es die künstlerisch-künstliche Form und hat den 'ästhetischen Schein' – des Erzählens selbst. (p. 42; italics are Heimrich's)

> (not *how* a novel is told is of importance in regard to its epic fictional character, to the aesthetic appearance of epic, but *that* it is told; not *how* the author tells, but *that* he tells – *that* he tells, although in a certain sense there is nothing 'to tell', 'to report'. Understood in this way, fictional narration is wholly and from the outset a pretence of historical narration; it is the aesthetic-artifical form, and it has the 'aesthetic appearance' – of narration itself.)

This recognition of the pretence inherent in all fictional narration breeds a consciousness of art as art on the part of the writer and the reader alike. The element of playfulness implicated in conjuring up the illusion promotes detachment from the matter and fascination with the manner of narration. The self-reflexivity that is an outcome of this stance opens up the space for irony as a mode of play with illusion and artistic form.

The concept of art as illusion is relevant to all literary genres, indeed to all the arts, but it is particularly important for narrative. On the one hand, narrative is more likely than either drama or lyric to be mistaken for true report, so to speak. On the other hand, its genetic disposition, with a teller and a listener whatever the actual 'narrative situation',[71] not only permits but strongly encourages a high degree of self-consciousness and self-reflexivity. The narrator may tell, besides his story, of himself and of the story he is telling. The extraordinary flexibility of the novel as a literary form allows it to move beyond its overt fabulation to a collateral metafictional level where its apprehension of itself as an aesthetic artifact can be voiced. The spaces surrounding the fabulation lend themselves to an elastic expansion that can accommodate interplay between the narrator and his text and/or his reader. The proportion of metafictional comment to fictive story can be varied at will, even to the point where the metafiction eclipses the fiction. And because the novel, more than any other genre, has the freedom to enlarge its spaces, it has the greatest aptitude for irony. For it is those spaces that are the opportune playground for an irony whose ambivalences are the vehicles for self-reflexion. It is indeed arguable that the novel is an intrinsically ironic genre because its form tends to foster a radical scrutiny of its own fictive constructs.

Changes in the practice of irony during the 'pivotal period' followed also from the modification of the relationship of the narrator to his audience. In the ancient epic that relationship had been ritualistic, conforming to the conventions of rhetoric, and based on the assumption of a uniform, cohesive listenership. The switch from the epic, designed for oral recitation, to the novel aimed at a solitary reader brought a fundamental alteration in the attitude of the narrator to his audience, which had become amply evident by the mid-eighteenth century and which was reinforced by a sociological shift. The readership modulated from a known collective group familiar with the canons of taste and acquiescing in them to an amorphous assortment of individuals whose reading competence could not be taken for granted and whose paths of access had to be incorporated into the narrative itself.[72]

Tristram Shandy (1760–7) and *Humphry Clinker* (1770) are the major landmarks cited by Wolfgang Iser,[73] while Goethe's *Werther* (1774) is chosen by Victor Lange[74] as the exemplar of the novel's newly personal, intimate address *ad hominen* – or, probably, *ad feminam*. The one-to-one address evinced a more immediate involvement on the reader's side. With increasing frequency he/she is required to participate actively in the coordination of events rather merely to listen passively. The 'characterized'[75] fictive reader, such as 'Madam' in *Tristram Shandy*, is turned into the narrator's accomplice in the creation of the narrative, though the alliance entails a tense combination of camaraderie and provocation. As the figure of the reader becomes more problematical, so too does that of the narrator. Aware himself of the fictive nature of his text, he is often tempted to sport with the illusion he is creating. The patterns of expectation traditional to classical story-telling are disrupted by a whimsicality that indulges irony – but that rebuffs its easy intelligibility.

The metamorphosis of irony in the later eighteenth and early nineteenth century is therefore not an isolated phenomenon nor even a particularly esoteric one. The change that irony undergoes is one facet of the broad transformation in the political face, the social structure, the philosophic tenets, and the artistic creed of Europe at that period. As such it partakes of the spirit of the age; it has filiations to factors as capacious as the ascendancy of relativistic thinking in the wake of Kant's Copernican revolution and the nascent suspicion of the unsteadiness of words; the explosion of self-consciousness following from Fichte's subjectivism; the aesthetic doctrines of the Romantic movement concerning the function of poetry, the role of the artist, and the configuration of the work; the rise of the novel and the predilection for self-reflexivity; and the altered relationship between narrator and audience. In short, the metamorphosis of irony is another intimation of the avocation of that age for questioning its heritage, reassessing its values, and fashioning an ideology in keeping with its own apprehension of the universe.

What is far more perplexing is the correlation between the new theory of irony and the literary practice of irony. The shift in the conceptualisation of irony is paralleled by roughly contemporaneous experimentation with the possibilities of irony in fiction. In fact in one respect the link between theory and practice can easily be documented in that Friedrich Schlegel

drew on Sterne and Diderot in the elaboration of his view
of irony. But whereas the theoretical metamorphosis can
confidently be dated from Schlegel's writings of 1797–1801, no
corresponding *terminus a quo* can be given for the innovative uses
of irony in fiction. *Tristram Shandy*, it is generally agreed, marks
the start of an important new phase in the novel, though it has
antecedents, not so much in the comic fiction[76] of the seventeenth
and early eighteenth century as in *Don Quixote* which Sterne
himself frequently cited. This difficulty in dating obviously stems
in part from the nature of change in the arts which tends to occur
as a gradual drift rather than as a sudden palpable deviation. The
case of irony is peculiarly complicated since the theory both
grows out of preceding practice and spawns subsequent practice.
The interdependence is so symbiotic as to defy decisive
dissociation. The position must be described as circular – or
dynamically progressive in the reciprocal fecundation of theory
and practice.

As a result, the uses of irony in fiction after the mid-eighteenth
century amount to a mottled picture. On the one hand, the early
eighteenth century model of irony, as defined by Dr Johnson,
persists into the nineteenth century and indeed to the present,
since verbal irony is an archetypal rhetorical figure (there can be
no question of its being supplanted by other forms of irony). But
from the mid-eighteenth century onwards, the type of irony
formulated by Schlegel becomes increasingly prominent in
fiction. And just as theory and practice of romantic irony
interface, so too traditional and romantic irony intertwine in the
literature of the period. However, the demography of irony is
erratic. For this reason the works discussed in the next six
chapters are treated in anachronical order in a sequence dependent
on internal rather than external temporal considerations. The
aim of these analyses of the workings of irony in a series of key
narratives is to elucidate the nature and direction of the
metamorphosis of irony.

3 Jane Austen: *Pride and Prejudice*, 1813

'it wants shade'
Letter to Cassandra Austen, 4 February 1813

1

'It is a truth universally acknowledged, that a single man in possession of a good fortune, must be in want of a wife': that opening sentence of *Pride and Prejudice* is one of the most celebrated instances of irony in European fiction. It is ironic in the Johnsonian sense of saying the contrary to what is meant. For it is not Darcy and Bingley, single men in possession of good fortunes, who are in want of wives; what is at stake, rather, is the future of the Bennet and Lucas daughters, whose lack of any fortune puts them much in want of husbands.

The possibility of reversing that initial proposition occurs to the reader long before he has witnessed the studied manoeuvres of the young women and their mothers to ensnare a husband. The discrepancy between the voiced words and their ulterior purport is signalled by a number of covert but quite unmistakable means that testify to Jane Austen's exceptional skill in the control of irony. The three weighty words, 'truth', 'universally', and 'acknowledged', create an immediate impression of security through their authoritative affirmation of absolutes; the certainty of the commonly accepted consensus of opinion acts as a disincentive to a sceptical questioning. This is evidently a society that rests on moral assumptions and norms of behaviour presumed to be shared by all right-thinking men and women. What is more, the expectation of familiarity with these conventions and assent to them is projected onto the reader too through the confidence invested in language. Jane Austen's penchant for generalisations, like her ready resort to conceptual terms, 'formulates a set of standards in such a way that they seem taken for granted, and thus it invites us to share them'.[1] The repetition of 'truth' in the second paragraph, allied now to 'so well fixed', appears to endorse the existence of a stable framework of agreement. Yet in the very moment of enunciating this 'truth', the narrator is also insidiously undermining it. The disproportion between the solemnity of 'truth universally acknowledged' and the platitude that so quickly follows it produces an effect of anti-climax which retrospectively throws the suspicion of exaggeration onto the first half of the sentence. Similarly, the overemphasis in 'must' ('must be in want of a wife') casts some doubt on the urgency of that 'want', while the abrupt drop from the lofty phraseology of the beginning to the colloquialism of the end of the sentence suggests a discontinuity of thought parallel to the break in style.

This stealthy but systematic discrediting of the overt statement is continued in the second paragraph:

> However little known the feelings or views of such a man may be on his first entering a neighbourhood, this truth is so well fixed in the minds of the surrounding families, that he is considered the rightful property of some one or other of their daughters.

Though the pivotal point is still that 'truth', its status is substantially reduced by the revelation of its subjective origins ('fixed in the minds of the surrounding families'), and its force is weakened by the disregard for 'the feelings or views' of the person who should surely be the prime instigator of action. Something is clearly amiss in this situation – and with that 'truth'. This conjecture is supported by the use of the passive ('he is considered') which diminishes the single man's standing by thrusting him into an inactive role, almost indeed that of a victim. Also, his subjection to the presumptions of 'the surrounding families' indirectly exposes once again the dominance of a biased set of opinions, and so detracts from the imperious validity of that 'truth'. The sarcastically derogatory overtones of 'the rightful property of some one or other of their daughters' – no matter which – are a fitting climax to this seemingly nonchalant but artfully manipulated overture.

In well under a hundred words then a social and even a metaphysical order of 'truth' has been both posited and subjected to discreet questioning. At the very outset of *Pride and Prejudice* the central theme is obliquely announced in the tension between acquiescence in the established system and a doubting disaffection from it. At the same time, the intellectual and artistic foundations for irony are set through the confidence invested in the transparency and communicative power of language, and through the assumption of the reader's acquaintance with the concepts and standards of this world. The widespread use of stylistic indicators of an ironic countermeaning presupposes a reader endowed with shared experience as well as a capacity for ready comprehension. The pact of community tacitly forged between narrator and reader is signalled in various ways by the narrative language. The narrator is more knowledgeable than the reader, specially at the beginning, but they subscribe to the same code and speak the same idiom. Because of this basic link, the narrator operates from the belief that the reader will know what to do with the text before him. In a world regarded as fundamentally intelligible, ironic discourse is reconstructible.

This certainly holds for the rhetoric of irony throughout the early sections of *Pride and Prejudice*, and most notably for the exchange between Mr and Mrs Bennet in the first chapter. Many of the devices of verbal irony are used here: over- and understatement, exaggeration, repetition, anti-climax, a whole chain of *non-sequiturs*, mishearings, misunderstandings, and distortions. This pattern of cross-purposes is the linguistic means of showing the psychological disparity between the marital partners; it also hints at the possibility of a deeper incongruity, namely between Mrs Bennet's heedless suppositions and Mr Bingley's intentions, which Mrs Bennet never for a moment queries, but which the reader, alert already to the context of ironic comedy, may well view from a somewhat different angle. The dual vision of irony is strongly evoked by the discordances of that conversation. And it is as if confirmed in the closing sentences of that first chapter, which balance the opening ones by renewing the direct address from the narrator to the reader, and which corroborate in comment what had been demonstrated in dialogue. The sparkling surface of verbal irony, far from being the mere play of witticisms, is the manifest cipher for the more complex network of ironies at the heart of *Pride and Prejudice*.

Often it is the simple verbal ironies that offer a pointer to further layers of contradiction, as in that early conversation between Mr and Mrs Bennet. The discongruity between the expressed sense and the real import may turn on a single word. Mrs Bennet, for example, congratulates herself on 'the felicity of her contrivance'[2] in sending Jane to Netherfield on horseback with rain impending; yet in fact that contrivance so misfires as almost to foreclose the hope of good marriages for Jane and Elizabeth through the occasion it gives for the revelation of the family's vulgarity. Or when Charlotte deems her reflections on Mr Collins 'in general satisfactory' and goes on to add that he was 'to be sure neither sensible nor agreeable; his society was irksome, and his attachment to her must be imaginery. But still he would be her husband' (vol. 1, ch. xxii, p. 122). In these instances rhetorical irony is inseparable from the underlying irony of situation. Quite small, insignificant qualifying terms may have a vital importance in opening the ironic aperture: the 'perhaps' inserted in describing Sir William Lucas' sense of his worth after his elevation to a knighthood: 'The distinction had perhaps been felt too strongly' (vol. 1, ch. v, p. 18); or the 'therefore' in the introduction of the Bingley sisters, which, through its strikingly inconsequentially, furtively provokes other interpretations:

> They were rather handsome, had been educated in one of the first private seminaries in town, had a fortune of twenty thousand pounds, were in the habit of spending more than they ought, and of associating with people of rank; and were therefore in every respect entitled to think well of themselves, and meanly of others. (vol. 1, ch. iv, p. 15)

Such little verbal signs as 'perhaps', 'therefore', 'somewhat' crop up repeatedly to halt, for a moment, the flow of the narrative – long enough for the reader to catch the insinuation of some discrepancy between the image presented and the hidden reality.

The extraordinary discretion with which Jane Austen handles these techniques attests to her virtuosity as an ironist, able to sustain the covert communion between narrator and reader with the utmost delicacy and reserve. Hers is what Genette calls 'the

purposeful attitude of the classical novelist'[3] directing the
narration with the power of knowledge. Though she remains
hidden, she is by no means absent from the narration. Despite its
unobtrusiveness, the narrating voice in *Pride and Prejudice* has a
quite distinctive timbre and a firm hold over the progression of
the narrative. The habitual recourse to direct speech is typical of
the discreet strategies of this retiring narrator. Speech becomes a
tool for ironic characterisation in the pomposity of Collins'
hollow double negatives, in the overbearing, self-satisfied dicta of
Lady Catherine, in Mrs Bennet's uninhibited garrulousness, in
Lydia's brash stridency, and in Mary's facile sententiousness. In
all these instances, the irony is readily grasped by the reader
because the narrator, while avoiding any voiced comment, has
succeeded in establishing a well-defined perspective. The context
of values, the social and philosophical vision, and the steady,
evaluating view conveyed to the reader by the self-possessed voice
narrating from behind the scenes allow for a confident
construction of meaning within the countermeaning.

2

The dialogues between Darcy and Elizabeth show the extent to
which the 'seemingly centrifugal play of irony in *Pride and
Prejudice* is dramatically functional'.[4] The dramatic force of the
irony is dependent on the preponderance of a dualistic vision
rooted in the discrepancy between appearance and reality,
particularly in the assessment of character. The discrepancy
becomes crucial to the unfolding of the plot through the limitation
of the view-point largely to that of Elizabeth from about the
middle of the first volume onwards. This is the structural
precondition for the full effectiveness of the dramatic irony.
Throughout the vicissitudes of courtship the men are seen
through the eyes of the women. Only once, early on (vol. 1, ch.
iv) is an exchange of confidences between Darcy and Bingley
reported. Their feelings remain a matter of conjecture for the
women who have no choice but to judge by appearances. Since
the reader, too, is denied access to the minds of Darcy and
Bingley, the plot is in fact made to hinge on the irony of
misapprehensions.

The work's original title, *First Impressions*, was in many ways highly appropriate because the deceptiveness of first impressions, favourable or unfavourable, is a major theme. But dualistic vision is not just a matter of occasionally mistaken judgements or biased perceptions. In *Pride and Prejudice* these occur with such frequency as to suggest an innate ambiguity in human behaviour. At innumerable points throughout the novel the protagonists – and with them, we as readers – face double images. This is most obvious in the central issue of Darcy's and Wickham's respective worth. What is perhaps less obvious but equally important is that the same basic dilemma recurs in many variants in the reiterated possibility of interpreting actions and situations in alternative ways. Generally at least two views are presented: Darcy, on seeing Elizabeth arrive dishevelled from her walk across the fields to visit her ailing sister, 'was divided between admiration of the brilliancy which exercise had given to her complexion, and doubt as to the occasion's justifying her coming so far alone' (vol. 1, ch. vii, p. 56). When Miss Bingley asks Elizabeth to walk up and down the room with her, Darcy's comment is: 'You either chuse this method of passing the evening because you are in each other's confidence and have secret affairs to discuss, or because you are conscious that your figures appear to the greatest advantage in walking' (vol. 1, ch. xi, p. 56). Reading Caroline Bingley's letter announcing the sudden departure for London of the entire Netherfield party, Elizabeth insists that her 'opinion on the subject' is 'totally different' from Jane's (vol. 1, ch. xxi, p. 118), just as she later intimates that Wickham's 'actions were capable of a very different construction' (vol. 3, ch. i, p. 288). At many points there is an element of genuine doubt as to which of the two or more explanations is the valid one. Wickham, listening to Elizabeth speak of Darcy, 'looked as if scarcely knowing whether to rejoice over her words, or to distrust their meaning' (vol. 2, ch. xviii, p. 234). As for Elizabeth's attempts to make out Darcy's character, she has to confess to him: 'I do not get on at all. I hear such different accounts of you as puzzle me exceedingly' (vol. 1, ch. xviii, p. 93). Her bewilderment at Charlotte's precipitate engagement to Collins is so intense as to provoke the petulant declaration: 'every day confirms my belief in the inconsistency of all human characters, and of the little dependence that can be placed on the appearance of either merit or sense' (vol. 2, ch. i, p. 135).

The reader may well be tempted, specially in the first half of the novel, to subscribe to that verdict of 'inconsistency'. Not only are alternative interpretations of behaviour repeatedly offered; more disconcerting, there is not a single character whose judgement is wholly and invariably trustworthy. Even Elizabeth, who ultimately emerges as the voice of good sense, is unreliable at the beginning; she is astute in her assessment of Collins and the Bingleys, but led astray by appearances – and her heart – in the case of both Darcy and Wickham. It is the cool, pragmatic Charlotte who has a sounder instinct in this regard when she warns Elizabeth 'not to be a simpleton and allow her fancy for Wickham make her appear unpleasant in the eyes of a man ten times his consequence' (vol. 1, ch. xviii, p. 90). Mrs Gardiner, too, has greater perspicacity than her niece. On the other hand, Darcy, for all his experience of human relationships, draws false conclusions about Jane's feelings for Bingley. As false, incidentally, though in the opposite direction, as Collins' suppositions about Elizabeth's reactions to his proposal. In a world beset by dual possibilities, the wise are hardly less liable to mistakes than the foolish, and no one is immune to the threat of serious blunders: these are the moral implications of the ironic vision that shapes *Pride and Prejudice.*

The human proclivity to misjudgement is vital to the design of the work. Irony here fulfils a dramatic function as a structural principle and as the mainspring of the plot dynamics. Reduced to its simplest level, the novel may be said to show the dangers of mis-taking people when they are judged first and foremost on the misleading evidence of appearances. Wickham is adjudged agreeable because he conforms to the social ritual in a pleasing fashion, going through the motions necessary to achieve a positive impression. Darcy, by contrast, though handsome in bearing and distinguished by great wealth, arouses 'disgust' (vol. 1, ch. iii, p. 10) because his manners are so 'haughty, reserved and fastidious' as to give 'offence' (vol. 1, ch. iv, p. 16). Nor does he, by his own admission (vol. 2, ch. viii, p. 175), have that easy flow of small talk in casual situations, so highly rated in a leisurely group, and so consciously cultivated by the glib Wickham. Based on such superficial social rather than moral criteria, the public evaluation of the two men is a classic example of ironic reversal as each is taken to be the opposite of his true character. The entire plot is dependent on these and similar misapprehensions, such as Darcy's misconstruction of Jane's

restraint towards Bingley. Bingley, in turn, is drawn into the web
of error through his unquestioning acceptance of his friend's
insight. Misguided conclusions from minor social interchange
lead to larger mistakes and destructive misconceptions, just as the
verbal ironies of the opening pave the way for the central
perceptual ironies at the core of *Pride and Prejudice*.
'Understanding' and 'misunderstanding', 'deceiving' and 'self-
deception', 'error', 'mistake', 'misrepresented': these are the
recurrent key-words in which the protagonists grapple with the
confusions arising out of a dualistic vision, itself a reflection of the
gulf between appearance and reality. How many times Darcy
and Elizabeth assure each other, 'you are mistaken', or
acknowledge their own mistakes to themselves before finally
correcting their 'mistaken premises' by 'good understanding'
(vol. 3, ch. xvi, p. 367). At times in their exchanges there is
double irony, when a remark intended to mean the contrary to
what it says actually hits on the truth, as in Elizabeth's early arch
comment: 'I have always seen a great similarity in the turn of our
minds' (vol. 1, ch. xviii, p. 91). Such cross-purposes in dialogue
are reminders of the fundamental misapprehensions that are the
source of the dramatic tension and the action in *Pride and Prejudice*.

3

The conspicuous verbal and dramatic ironies contain a graver
and deeper irony not so readily apparent. To call it irony of
situation is to use a somewhat misleading phrase since it usually
refers to an episode such as that towards the end of the novel
when Bingley, already betrothed to Jane, arrives in the company
of Darcy, and Elizabeth is 'forced to have that disagreeable man
all to yourself' (vol. 3, ch. xvii, p. 315). That is a comic, local,
and temporary irony of situation. But there is, too, in *Pride and
Prejudice* a potentially tragic, intrinsic irony of situation. Its focus
is marriage. Not just the bourgeois conventions of courtship in
which, as in nowhere else in books or in life, a woman of Jane
Austen's time could 'find such guarantees of distance, such
durable incongruities between form and fact, between moral
pretension and material reality, upon which to exercise and fulfil
her irony'.[5] Those courtships were presumed to lead to
satisfactory marriages. That is the hypothesis of *Pride and Prejudice*

which idealises marriage as a state eagerly sought by all women. Yet the marriages we glimpse within the novel scarcely bear out that supposition. The Gardiners, the Philips's and the Lucas's seem tolerably content, though it should be noted that we actually know almost nothing of the couples' private lives. Bingley's elder sister, Mrs Hurst, has a dreary husband; Charlotte's alliance to Collins is a calculated convenience which she cleverly arranges to occasion as little inconvenience to herself as possible under the circumstances; Lydia's foolhardy elopement with Wickham and his indifference to her hardly bodes well for their future happiness. As for the Bennet menage, it illustrates the disastrous consequences of an imprudent choice of a marital partner attractive in appearance but deficient in moral and intellectual qualities: 'Had Elizabeth's opinion been all drawn from her own family, she could not have formed a very pleasing picture of conjugal felicity or domestic comfort' (vol. 2, ch. xix, p. 236). Against the weight of all this evidence, however, we are asked to believe that Darcy and Elizabeth, Bingley and Jane will live happily ever after. These may, arguably, be the exceptions that prove the rule. Nevertheless, in the radical discrepancy between the anticipation of the marital state in this society and its realities – as far as we see them – there is a portentous irony of situation. It is an irony that arises because the characters in *Pride and Prejudice* posit, and what is more, act on the expectation of a predictable world – a world in which marriages wrought with sense and sensibility result in contentment, and in which young men in possession of a good fortune must be in want of a wife. If it were conceded that this is perhaps not so, then *Pride and Prejudice* could be read as a novel that adumbrates an ironic state of the world. But this is patently not the case.

None the less, the 'truths' on which this fictional world rests are questioned, at least to some extent. The challenge to the validity of the accepted assumptions may come from the narrating voice, as in the gently subversive presentation of the opening proposition, or it may come from characters who are themselves, consciously or unconsciously, ironists. Mary, 'who piqued herself upon the solidity of her reflections' (vol. 1, ch. v, p. 20), is quite unaware of her own irony as she consoles herself and her family with moralising banalities following Lydia's elopement:

Unhappy as the event must be for Lydia, we may draw from it
this useful lesson; that loss of virtue in a male is irretrievable –
that one false step involves her in endless ruin – that her
reputation is no less brittle than it is beautiful, – and that she
cannot be too much guarded in her behaviour towards the
undeserving of the other sex. (vol. 3, ch. v, p. 289)

Events belie Mary's contentions when Lydia is the first of the five
Bennet girls to sport a wedding ring. At the other end of the scale
to Mary is Mr Bennet's deliberately sarcastic, satirical irony, a
sharply honed defence mechanism against the onslaughts of his
wife and his silly younger daughters, 'a carapace against the plain
recognition of his own irrevocable folly',[6] certainly an assertion of
his right to independent judgement: 'I admire all my three sons-
in-law highly, . . . Wickham, perhaps, is my favourite; but I
think I shall like *your* husband quite as well as Jane's' (vol. 3, ch.
xvii, p. 379; italics are Jane Austen's) he tells Elizabeth. This is
the passage cited by Wayne Booth as an example of the
'troublesome ambiguity'[7] characteristic of irony as he recounts
his experience with 'a very bright, very sophisticated graduate
student' who had not only overlooked the ironic thrust of Mr
Bennet's comment, but had even regarded it as evidence of his
stupidity. Bright and sophisticated though that student may have
been, he could not have read the text with sufficient care, or else
he could not have failed to notice the multiple clues to the correct
reconstruction of the irony: contextual clues, such as Mr Bennet's
mordant turn of phrase throughout, his special affection for
Elizabeth, the daughter closest to him, his demonstrated scorn for
Wickham; and also stylistic clues in the phrase itself: the
exaggeration of 'admire highly', which is palpably not possible in
the case of Wickham, the understatement of 'I think' and 'quite
as well', and finally the element of doubt introduced by
'perhaps', that invites us to reconsider too.

  Far more complex than the irony of Mr Bennet is that of
Elizabeth, who is conscious of her detachment as 'a studier of
character' (vol. 1, ch. ix, p. 42) with 'a lively, playful disposition,
which delighted in anything ridiculous' (vol. 1, ch. iii, p. 12). But
she is not as much of 'an ironic spectator' nor as 'able and
prepared to judge and classify' as has been claimed by Marvin
Mudrick, who tends to identify Elizabeth too closely with Jane
Austen. 'Elizabeth', he argues, 'shares her author's characteristic

response of comic irony, defining incongruities without drawing them into a moral context.'[8] He grants that 'her youth and inexperience and emotional partiality begin to deceive her' (p. 108). This is in itself ironic. Elizabeth is an ironic spectator who is herself the victim of insufficient detachment. She cannot exclude the moral context in defining incongruities, for the framework of her thinking has been determined by the society in which she has been reared. She does, however, have an ironic dual vision in so far as she can neither espouse Mary's ponderous allegiance to prescribed societal standards without serious qualifications, nor on the other hand can she subscribe with a clear conscience to her father's eclectic individualism because – ironically – she is a nubile young woman, dependent on the approval of a society of which she cannot wholeheartedly approve. It is this dilemma that makes Elizabeth the focus of the most searching ironies of *Pride and Prejudice.*

Elizabeth comes closer than any other protagonist to a perception of the relativity of those 'truths' so confidently acclaimed. She is shaken by the erroneousness of her judgement, in which she had invested considerable pride and reliance. And she errs not once, which is, after all, only human, but twice in rapid succession and quite fundamentally in regard to both Darcy and Wickham. Through these mistakes she comes to realise not just that the estimation of society may be faulty, grounded as it is in the shaky testimony of appearances; beyond that, she experiences personally the immensity of the problem of attaining 'truth'. She learns the importance of abandoning self-deception ('prejudice') in order to engage in a constant, meticulously honest process of scrutiny that includes herself along with others. The prize for extricating oneself from ensnaring falsehood is self-knowledge, and with it, authentic knowledge of others. In working 'painfully and scrupulously through to the admission of past delusions and prejudices, and the knowledge of present feeling' Elizabeth achieves 'a sense of herself, past and present, and a sense of other people, especially Darcy'.[9]

At this point we see most clearly the depths beneath the seemingly innocuous comedy of manners. That few people correspond to the image they wish to project is borne out by the unmasking of Wickham, Collins, Lady Catherine, the Bingley sisters. It is no coincidence that 'expose' is one of the pivotal words in *Pride and Prejudice,* used both subjectively in fear of unflattering revelations, and objectively of their discovery. But these exposures of social hypocrisy remain largely within the conventional range of good and evil expected in the social spectrum. What is more, their impact is blunted by Jane Austen's recourse to comic exaggeration, to satire, even to burlesque in the portrayal of figures who form part of the familiar stock-in-trade of the genre, such as Collins and Lady Catherine. For these reasons the effect of these disclosures is in no way comparable to the disturbing inferences that must be drawn from Elizabeth's and Darcy's soundings. What they confront is not merely the hollowness of this or that individual, but the possible fallaciousness of the entire system within which they have been accustomed to make their judgements. Particularly Elizabeth, but also Darcy, must perforce examine, beyond themselves and their own capacity to discriminate, the values and standards by which they have hitherto reached those trusted conclusions that are, evidently, by no means as trustworthy as they had assumed. The 'truth universally acknowledged' forfeits the security of an absolute. This represents a much more ominous existentialist crisis than is generally ascribed to Jane Austen. It has long been readily conceded that there is, sociologically and philosophically as well as artistically, far more than meets the hasty eye in the writings of the modest little spinster, as she used condescendingly to be called. 'Jane Austen is thus a mistress of much deeper emotion than appears upon the surface';[10] 'the disparity between surface and content, between apparent narrowness and actual comprehensiveness and profundity' has become 'a commonplace of Jane Austen criticism'.[11] However, the implications of that profundity have not been fully articulated. That truth is less accessible or definitive than is normally assumed, and that judgement is considerably more precarious than is usually supposed: these admissions, though they are made obliquely, cut deep into the fabric of eighteenth century certainties on which *Pride and Prejudice* is built. In the display of alternatives in dialogue, in the dual vision of human behaviour, and in the questioning of the reigning mores from the opening proposition onwards, irony is a cogent instrument for the revaluations in which the protagonists must engage.

But that irony is as strictly delimited in its extent as in its means; the ambiguity is kept firmly under control in both the stylistic and the ontological sphere. So the final effect of the irony is far indeed from 'Proustian relativity',[12] approximating more to a 'qualified affirmation'[13] in which scepticism is balanced and checked by assent. Jane Austen does not, as earlier critics liked to maintain, take a stable and hierarchical society absolutely for granted.[14] Her novels bespeak a far more detached inclination to enquiry than such statements would suggest. On the other hand, there was a formal shape, outer and inner, to the world in which and of which she wrote. She may not always have liked everything about that shape, yet she recognised the worth of its civilised traditions, notwithstanding its perhaps undue emphasis on decorous conventions.

4

The world of *Pride and Prejudice* is, therefore, regulated by order, or more accurately, by two contiguous and interlocking patterns of order: the external, social and material order based on possessions and appearance, which is the accepted one, specially at the beginning of the novel, and which clashes in the main plot with the predominantly internal and spiritual order of personal worth. Though the social order is 'exposed' to satirising criticism, this does not imply that it should be abandoned; it forms the structural buttress of this way of life, which, despite its shortcomings, must be respected and preserved. The status quo is in need of some modification, and this can take place through the attainment of true knowledge which enables an individual of intrinsic worth both to adjust the order to himself, and vice versa. Such mutual accommodation is conceivable in the optimistic atmosphere of *Pride and Prejudice*, where the ironic contradictions are resolved in the romance of the happy ending. For what we encounter in *Pride and Prejudice* are malleable contradictions, not irreconcilable paradoxes, local and temporary disturbances, not lasting, elemental disruptions. It may be that Jane Austen 'understood deep down the alienation of *geist*'; certainly she registered 'the tension between the growing claims of the individual and those of society'. But in the last resort, 'the weight of her art hangs, literally, in the balance',[15] and it is balance that prevails. The discord between the opposing forces is not so great as to be permanently resistant to harmonious resolution. When Elizabeth sees Pemberley, she instinctively recognises the superior standards of refined taste that it represents, and so she concedes the justification for Darcy's contemptuous attitude towards her family. For his part, Darcy, through his growing appreciation of Elizabeth's sterling merits, learns to discriminate more acutely between external factors and inner values. Elizabeth's final location within the park at Pemberley has been interpreted as denoting 'the self's limitation of its power to define its own essence, the heroine's recognition of moral and social limits within which she must live'.[16] But it must not be forgotten that within Pemberley Elizabeth engages in the education of Georgiana: in other words, the reciprocal modification between social and individual ideals is envisioned as continuous and progressive. The moral order, after being challenged by the apprehension of its ironic equivocality, does at the end persist, although its authority is no longer the static complacency implicit in the opening proposition. It is a mark of Jane Austen's powers as an ironist that she is able simultaneously to question and to uphold the established organisation of her world.

This delicately controlled ambivalence permeates the language too. The cohesiveness of the vocabulary reflects the social uniformity in which the protagonists are enveloped, just as the consistency of the style echoes the assurance of its ontological basis. There is a corpus of words that are endowed with positive connotations as terms of approval and praise: for instance, such nouns as 'taste', 'esteem', 'judgement', 'benevolence', 'knowledge', 'understanding', 'simplicity', 'integrity', 'delicacy', 'steadiness', 'good-will', 'cheerfulness'; prominent among the adjectives of approval are 'generous', 'amiable', 'handsome', 'agreeable', 'respectable', 'elegant', 'sensible', 'civil', 'courteous', 'polite', 'gallant', and 'prudent'. At the opposite end of the spectrum stand words like 'folly', 'exertion', 'coldness', 'vice', 'reserve', 'ignorance', 'imprudence', 'stupid', and 'illiterate'.[17] The dialectic of these recurrent words embodies the aspirations and aversions of a particular class in a particular place at a particular period. At the same time, the use of this elaborate, almost ritualistic network of signs presupposes the stability and transparency of language. Shared concepts contained in a common vocabulary lead to ease of communication. This postulate extends from the dialogue between the protagonists within the narrative to that other dialogue between the text and the reader. In a rational, intelligible world with a right-minded way of thinking readers will correctly grasp the import of verbal expressions. A well ordered society has a correspondingly well ordered language. That is the fundamental assumption underlying Jane Austen's irony. And it holds true. Misunderstanding may reign for a while in conversations that are perversely at cross-purposes like those between Darcy and Elizabeth in the first third of the novel. But it is not only the two lovers who eventually come to a sound understanding. Long before, we as readers, though we are not yet cognizant of the precise ramifications of the plot, suspect the innate contrarity, and delight in watching its workings. When Elizabeth says: 'Mr. Darcy is all politeness' (vol. 1, ch. vi, p. 26), she intends her verdict to have the force of irony; we, however, can reconstruct its double irony out of an awareness of the surge of repressed attraction beneath the patina of conventional politeness. While the protagonists may err in a confusion of mistaken judgements and misheard comments, it is unlikely that this will befall the reader, for Jane Austen sets the generic context of comic irony from the very outset through her masterful manipulation of linguistic nuances in the expectation that these will be understood, as indeed they are. Her playing with ambiguity is not in itself ambiguous, except at those menacing junctures where a shadow of doubt is cast over the feasibility of arriving at the 'truth'.

But that shadow is decisively dispelled by the outcome of the plot, for 'truth' is in fact attained by Darcy and Elizabeth, and Bingley and Jane, and all's well that ends well, we are led to believe. The conclusion of *Pride and Prejudice* is buoyantly optimistic, illuminated by a strong faith in the advent of happiness. It is 'a generous and forgiving novel'[18] whose mood is conveyed by the prevalence of such adverbs as 'happily', 'comfortably', 'easily', 'heartily'.[19] In the marriage of Darcy and Elizabeth the two adjacent orders – the external, social, material order and the internal, personal, spiritual order – that had earlier been in conflict, coalesce into an ideally balanced union. So the novel ends with reconciliation and a good-tempered tolerance that finds symbolic expression in Darcy's expansively tactful hospitality towards the Gardiners and Elizabeth's willingness to take charge of Georgiana's education. For 'the lovers' happy-ever-after is perhaps more convincing in Jane Austen's novels than anywhere else in realistic fiction. It is something that relies on our sense of congruity in mind and feeling'.[20] That 'sense of congruity' in turn derives from the confidence that Jane Austen has evoked in the existence of a circumscribed realm of security, stability, and civilised behaviour. Within that circle the romance ending becomes fitting and therefore acceptable. The context of comedy, sketched at the beginning, though partially eclipsed for a time by the tragic potential of the plot, is forcefully re-established in the equilibrium of the resolution. It is in keeping with the conventions of comedy that *Pride and Prejudice* closes with 'a festive society . . . contained by social assumptions',[21] just as it is typical of romance that marriage represents accommodation, the sublimate adjustment of the self not only to social standards but also to 'truth'. The symmetry of the plot and its denouement in the appropriate marriages further foster the sense of a world that is metaphysically as well as socially sound.

5

Seen within this contextual frame of comedy and romance, the waning of irony in the last third of *Pride and Prejudice* appears appropriate to the point of necessity. This attenuation of the ironic vision is not a symptom of decline on the part of a tiring author anxious to tie up her story, as has sometimes been suggested. The novel does indeed lose some of its dynamic tensions when 'the close and harmonious relation between ironic wit and dramatic movement is disturbed' as the events of the final third – 'from seduction and mysterious financial transactions to reunions of lovers and weddings' – do 'seem to belong to a simpler world where outright judgements of good and bad or of happy and unhappy are in place'.[22] To maintain the intensity and depth of the irony to the end would require a complete rewriting of the novel, and, what is more, a fundamental revision of Jane Austen's perception of society and life into the sombreness of tragedy which she skirts but repudiates. Her chosen mode of comedy-romance leaves no alternative but 'the abandonment'[23] of irony towards the end.

As the misunderstandings between the protagonists, specially between Darcy and Elizabeth, are dispelled, so the tone modulates. The change is already apparent in Darcy's letter of explanation to Elizabeth after her rejection of his offensively proffered proposal (vol. 2, ch. xii, pp. 196–203): the openness of his confessional self-defence contrasts with the ironic subterfuges and masks behind which he had until then concealed his real personality. The sincere admission of mistakes and mis-judgements on both sides is coupled by an increasing directness of speech, devoid of the verbal and emotional spar-ring that had marked their ambivalent relationship of attraction/repulsion in the first third of the novel. As Darcy and Elizabeth come to a true knowledge of each other, the need for dissemblance fades, and the affectionate meeting of minds is mirrored in their cordial, forthright linguistic interaction. The few ironies that do occur in the concluding pages of *Pride and Prejudice* are largely rhetorical in nature, and are, not by chance, uttered by characters as yet unenlightened about the true state of affairs, foremost Mr and Mrs Bennet. What remains after the marriage of Darcy and Elizabeth is irony as interlocutory jousting; Georgiana is astonished to the verge of alarm by Elizabeth's 'lively, sportive manner of talking to her brother' (vol. 3, ch. xix, pp. 387–8). But it is now essentially a 'manner of talking', the frolicsome sparkle of wit without any of the jarring frictions that had found their precipitate in the sharp-edged cross-talk of their early exchanges. Darcy and Elizabeth will continue to delight in irony as a 'mode of speech', a benevolent intellectual game played in loving concert between equal partners almost as a demonstration of their mutual comprehension. Gone forever from this idyll is that irony whose dual vision opens up a chasm of irreconcilable contradiction lurking within the human condition. Its threat had loomed briefly on the horizon of *Pride and Prejudice*, but in the end all is 'light, and bright, and sparkling'.

This optimistic mood that is upheld with such determination in *Pride and Prejudice* makes the ambiguities created by irony local and temporary. Jane Austen herself, in her letter of 4 February 1813[24] to her sister Cassandra, voiced some afterthoughts as to whether her work was not in fact 'rather too light, and bright, and sparkling': 'the playfulness and epigrammatism of the general style . . . wants to be stretched out here and there with a long chapter of sense, if it could be had'; above all, she felt, 'it wants shade'. That shade is not absent from *Pride and Prejudice*; in certain aspects of the irony it is certainly adumbrated. While the verbal and dramatic ironies serve to produce the tension that activates the plot, there are also situational and metaphysical ironies that drive open apertures onto areas of existence full of 'shade'. The ironic dual vision of the searching, doubting mind – whether it be Jane Austen's or Elizabeth's – becomes the vehicle for a serious scrutiny of social standards and individual behaviour. Throughout, the portrayal is dialectically double, at once affirmative and questioning. But despite the extraordinary richness, density and variety of the ironic texture, irony does not represent 'the organizing principle'[25] of Jane Austen's art. Such a claim ascribes to her too extreme a stance. Though a detached and often critical observer of the social scene, she was far from either the bitterness of revolt or the devaluation of parody; the comic always predominates, whatever the potential 'shade' of which she – and we – are aware. So she continued to accept the norms of her society, not, to be sure, taking them for granted, but nonetheless acknowledging their intrinsic validity, albeit with the qualifications of her irony. It is this fine balance between criticism and affirmation, scepticism and faith that characterises Jane Austen as an essentially gentle ironist, knowing, good-humoured, benign and composed.

That composure is manifest in her superb control of her irony. Her sure grasp both of the values she prizes and of the artistic means at her command leads to a strategically manoeuvred and tautly organised web of ambiguities that never lose their limpidity. Jane Austen's apparent 'technique of self-effacement',[26] which earlier critics liked to emphasise, should not blind us to the effects of her constant directing presence behind the scenes. In the disposition of the dialogues and most notably in the indirect hints carried by the ironies, the impersonal author is adroitly conducting the narrative like a puppet-master pulling the concealed strings. While she does not appear overtly as the reader's Friend and Guide to dictate our reactions, her intuited presence is sufficiently palpable to establish with authority the moral angle of vision. The resultant sense of stability provides a firm base from which to interpret the many ironies. Though they are frequently multi-faceted and multi-dimensional, they do not resist confident reconstruction because they are enclosed in a dependable system of values. There is here a rightful order. It may be deranged for a while by the follies of misjudgement, and it is not wholly inconceivable that it might be irreparably dislocated. But that does not happen in *Pride and Prejudice*, nor is this negative eventuality even considered in earnest. Order is restored; our bewilderment has been no more than a passing puzzlement, far indeed from the disorientation we experience in the face of a world falling out of joint. In other words, the ironies are transparent because they are encompassed by a secure framework. Belief in an acceptable order and in the existence of 'truth' permeates every aspect of *Pride and Prejudice*: it underlies Jane Austen's use of language, her resort to conceptual terms, her readiness to generalise, and her distinctions between good and evil at an absolute level as well as in social conduct. Her writing is founded on the trust that the reader shares these convictions and will therefore move with her in understanding on both the linguistic and the ontological plane. The definity of her ideological stance, together with her control of the narrative medium, gives her work an assurance that is communicated to the reader. Within the precisely structured social and artistic organisation of *Pride and Prejudice* the equivocations of irony yield to the certainties of affirmation.

4 Gustave Flaubert: *Madame Bovary*, 1857

'Si la *Bovary* vaut quelque chose, ce livre ne manquera pas de coeur. L'ironie pourtant me semble dominer la vie.'

Letter to Louise Colet, 8–9 May 1857.

('If the *Bovary* has any worth, this book will not lack heart. But irony seems to me to dominate life.')

1

'Nous étions à l'étude, quand le Proviseur entra, suivi d'un *nouveau*'[1] ('We were in class when the headmaster came in, followed by a *new boy*'): who are the anonymous 'we' lurking at the threshold of *Madame Bovary*? These silent spectators have long intrigued readers and embarrassed critics because their presence in the first person plural is so glaringly conspicuous as the opening word of a novel known to strive for utmost impersonality. The simplest answer is that 'we' denotes Charles' schoolfellows seated in the classroom watching the new boy come in. The following pages bring four further mentions of 'us', all of which bear out this interpretation. But then 'ce curieux "nous"'[2] ('this strange "we"') disappears as unexpectedly as it had appeared, thereby heightening the mystery. For if it does indeed designate Charles' schoolfellows, what is its function in the economy of the narrative as a whole? Such a question is eminently pertinent in regard to Flaubert, whose artistic ideal was a Jamesian 'Total Relevance', and who proudly asserted that *Madame Bovary* contained not a single superfluous word,[3] that its every detail was the fruit of conscious calculation.[4] Since

69

Flaubert's claims have been substantiated by critical analysis, it seems ill-advised to venture, however apologetically, that this perplexing 'we' represents 'an error in technique' on the grounds that it is 'difficult' to discover what has been gained from this method.'[5] Nor is there a sound basis for the rebellious contention that the bewilderment *vis-à-vis* this 'we' is symptomatic 'of the *seriousness* which incapacitates so much Flaubert criticism: an attitude which induces reverence before the work of art and a refusal to entertain the possibility that it may be engaged in parody and obfuscation. For that is clearly what those first few pages do.'[6] More persuasive interpretations have been advanced: Brombert suggests that 'the collective personal pronoun *nous* evidently communicates the proper tone of childhood reminiscences' though he concedes that the 'point of view of the first scene remains puzzling'.[7] Sartre's explanation, as much biographical as literary, is that Flaubert, in using the first person plural, is intentionally putting himself on the side of the mockers by presenting his character in all his opacity from outside.[8]

The concurrence of the mockers with 'us' is a provocative hypothesis, not least because it opens up the possibility of a dualistic reading. Thus the mockers could be Charles' schoolfellows *and* Flaubert as narrator joining them. What is more, the other 'we', the implied observers/readers, also become implicated. Such a disposition sets up a fundamental tension and ambiguity – which could well have been Flaubert's purpose in beginning with that very word. The reader's inclination to identify with the 'nous' is further encouraged by their anonymity within the fiction. They are an indefinite group about whom no information is ever given, and who fade without ado. This apparent negligence is in such contravention of Flaubert's punctiliousness as to prompt the conjecture that this putative 'error in technique' has an underlying rationale. The enigmatic lacuna in knowledge as to who the 'we' are helps to foster that instinctive association on the reader's part with the unspecified first persons plural watching Charles' entry into the classroom. The reader thereby comes to share the angle of vision of both Charles' schoolfellows and the narrator. As a result, he is drawn into the narrator's perception of Charles and his world. That seemingly indeterminate 'we' is tantamount to a tacit invitation extended to the reader to participate in the narrator's point of view. It is this shared perspective on Charles that forms the basis for the understanding between reader and narrator in the opening sections of *Madame Bovary* as Charles' character and background are presented to the reader through the eyes of the narrator. By this indirect means a contract of sorts comes into being between narrator and reader, though it does not have the straightforward solidity of the assumed relationship of confidence that consistently underlies *Pride and Prejudice.* The narrating voice in *Madame Bovary* is too reticent and secretive for open gestures of positive solicitation. The contract is mooted rather than posited. Its somewhat equivocal status is of great importance for the reading of the narrative; it is sufficiently pronounced to allow for extremely delicate manipulation of the reader's apprehension and response at certain points, but sufficiently tenuous to become a source of doubt at others.

The first word of this 'almost monstrously elegant novel',[9] far from being a casual throwaway, let alone an 'error', fulfils another vital function by establishing at the outset a kind of metaperspective on the whole fictional world. That 'we' represents the outermost of the multiple frameworks surrounding the central figure, Emma. She is first seen through the eyes of Charles, but not until Charles himself, with all his lamentable history, has been seen by 'us': 'Nous le vîmes qui travaillait en conscience, cherchant tous les mots dans le dictionnaire, et se donnant beaucoup de mal' (p. 6; 'We saw him working conscientiously, looking up every word in the dictionary and taking the greatest pains'). It is his schoolmates who see him, but so do we. The effect is almost that of a cinematic camera zooming in towards the main subject, Emma, through pictures of her environment, human and physical. Her life is framed by Charles', and both are further framed by 'our', i.e. the narrator's and the reader's view of Charles. This gradual movement inwards from 'us' to Charles and onto Emma is reversed at the end when the focus returns to Charles after Emma's death, and finally shifts further out again to Homais and to an 'on' ('they') even more faceless and apocryphal than the 'nous' of the opening. The entrance through the observing 'we' has its complement in the exit through 'on'. This encircling arch between the beginning and the end of the narrative is supported by the final temporal convergence between narrated time and narrating time.[10] The closing comments about the award of the Legion of Honour to Homais are in the present tense, denoting that the events narrated have caught up with the time of narration. This emergence from story time to present time of narration completes the circle, as it were, from the beginning with its entry into narrated time to the end. The subtle handling of the time-schema therefore reinforces the metaperspective brought to bear on the fictional world. And that metaperspective interposes a space between the central action and 'us', the reader-spectators – a space that can be filled with irony.

The metaperspective also hints at a subversion of pure narrativity in *Madame Bovary*. The presence of the voyeuristic 'nous' as witnesses to the events and to the narration acts as a reminder that not only is the drama of Emma's and Charles' life being enacted, but that it is being told to 'us' as a story. Through its shock effect that surprising 'we' at the opening raises the reader's consciousness of the text as a text by triggering a series of questions: who are these 'we'? who is telling the story? and to whom? The speaker remains as anonymous as the 'we'. The questions have no answers; but the mere fact that they demand to be posed points to a dimension of *Madame Bovary* that is generally overlooked. As 'un livre sur rien'[11] ('a book about nothing') it sets out programmatically to have nothing to report, nothing to narrate,[12] concentrating instead on the creation of aesthetic illusion as if for its own sake. In this sense *Madame Bovary* is an entirely ironic construct.

2

The impetus for an ironic reading, already given in the outer casing of *Madame Bovary*, is confirmed in the inner frame, that of Charles' life up to the time of his meeting with Emma. The first chapter of *Madame Bovary* is as sure, as swift and as deft in its establishment of the ironic context as is *Pride and Prejudice*. Like Jane Austen, Flaubert rapidly expounds the major themes: inadequacy, shortfall, incongruity, and tragi-comic failure. Like Austen also, Flaubert here uses the traditional modes of verbal and situational irony with a transparency and an amplitude of clues that make the irony easily reconstructible.

Though Charles, in all outward semblance, has by the end of the chapter somehow or other clambered to the position of doctor and married man, he is also – and what is more, always will be –

the imbecilic *Charbovari* whose motto is *ridiculus sum.* The discrepancy between appearance and reality is conveyed through an interrelated cluster of narrative techniques which recur throughout *Madame Bovary* as signals for irony. In this respect the opening chapter of *Madame Bovary* is as revealing as that of *Pride and Prejudice* of the strategies characteristic of this ironic narrator. Some are relatively simple, such as the device of sentences with a marked downward trend, dropping from spacious clauses and elegant phrases to a sudden disappointing end. A sustained sequence of such sentences, as in the sketch of the career of Charles' father, suggests through the repeated syntactical let-down blunder and decline, thus undermining the character's specious surface. A similar effect is derived from the alliance of hyperbole to anti-climax; for example in the report of Charles' debauchery that results in his failure in his medical examinations:

> Il prit l'habitude du cabaret, avec la passion des dominos. S'enfermer chaque soir dans un sale appartement public, pour y taper sur des tables de marbre de petits os de mouton marqués de points noirs, lui semblait un acte précieux de sa liberté, qui le rehaussait d'estime vis-à-vis de lui-même. C'était comme l'initiation au monde, l'accès des plaisirs défendus; et, en entrant, il posait la main sur le bouton de la porte avec une joie presque sensuelle. (p. 11)

> (He got into the habit of going to cafés, and had a passion for dominoes. To shut himself up every evening in a dirty public room, to push about on marble tables the small sheep-bones with black dots, seemed to him a fine proof of his freedom, which raised him in his own esteem. It was like an initiation to life, access to forbidden pleasures; and as he entered, he would put his hand on the doorhandle with an almost sensual joy.)

The account is given in a factual manner without any explicit comment. Yet in spite of this withholding of any voiced assessment, a denigratory judgement on Charles is nevertheless strongly implied in the infantile nature of his passion for a childish game. The form that his debauchery takes encompasses in a single telling episode both the pathos of Charles' insignificance and the half-pitying, half-mocking contempt with which he is viewed.

The invention of such pregnant episodes and details is one salient aspect of Flaubert's genius as an ironist. The introduction of the Bovary family is a real masterpiece of ironic ingenuity, for everything is said, but said indirectly in the sometimes bizarre and seemingly gratuitous, but stunningly appropriate minutiae: in the famous description of Charles' anomolous cap; in the homespun, derogatory imagery applied to Charles' mother who, we are told, was aging 'à la façon du vin éventé qui se tourne en vinaigre' (p. 7; 'like a wine that, on exposure to air, turns to vinegar') as well as to Charles himself who is compared, in his study of medicine, to a 'cheval de manège, qui tourne en place les yeux bandés, ignorant de la besogne qu'il broie' (p. 10; 'mill-horse, who goes round and round with his eyes bandaged, not knowing what work it is grinding out'); in the brief, hilarious, dead-pan cameo of Charles' education by the priest 'aux moments perdus . . . dans la sacristie, debout, à la hâte, entre un baptême et un enterrement' (pp. 8–9; 'at odd moments . . . in the sacristy, standing up, hurriedly, between a baptism and a burial') or at a chance encounter by the wayside, when the conjugation of a verb would be interrupted by rain; in the farcical circumstances of Charles' first marriage, arranged in peremptory fashion by his mother who outmanoeuvres a pork-butcher, aided and abetted by priests, to boot, for the hand of a mangy but allegedly rich widow. In all these instances the wealth of circumstantial detail, which seems to be directed towards the novel's pursuit of realism, in fact serves an ulterior purpose. For besides evoking reality, the details amount to an oblique commentary on the world that is being portrayed. Through the striking incongruity of his comic juxtapositions Flaubert is able to point to the absurdity of the Bovarys' pretensions. It is a measure of his extraordinary skill as an ironic narrator that the reductive mockery is achieved wholly by indirect means.

The wealth of information accorded about Charles by an omniscient narrator to a complicitous reader in the opening chapter has a function beyond the introduction of Charles. It projects an intelligent reader privileged to share the narrator's knowledge. We know what sort of man Emma is marrying long before she makes the painful discovery. Although the full implications of the expansive history of the Bovary family in the first chapter becomes apparent only later, the reader is from the outside placed in a position superior to that of any of the protagonists. The same procedure is adopted later in relation to Emma, whom we see initially as an object through Charles' eyes, but into whose background and mind we are granted deeper and earlier insight (in chapter vi) than any of her fellow protagonists. They may only watch her actions, while we are allowed familiarity with her motivations through our insight into her consciousness. So the protagonists are condemned to ignorance, conjecture, and error about each other, whereas the reader may construe from the vantage-point of his extensive knowledge. This often leads to an ironic discrepancy between the reader's and the protagonist's interpretation of certain situations. When Charles' horse stumbles as he enters Les Bertaux, the possibility of an ill omen immediately occurs to us, though not to the unimaginative Charles. Similarly, his hesitancy to ask for Emma's hand strikes us as ironic because we know what Charles does not: that Les Bertaux is not as profitable as he assumes so that Emma could hardly hope for a better suitor; that Emma is not the asset he believes her to be; and that her father is as anxious to be rid of her as she is to escape the loneliness and boredom of the farm.

Ultimately, however, the reader's confidence in his superior knowledge is also thwarted. For in the opening chapters the narrator is luring the reader to believe in his intelligence and competence by offering him a shared perspective and the security of knowledge. The insidiousness of Flaubert's text resides in the fact that the reader's confidence is only partially justified. There are large areas of *Madame Bovary* where the irony can be reconstructed without crippling doubts. But this does not hold for the entire text. There are points where the reader finds himself as much an ironic victim as Emma and Charles, and indeed as the narrator.

3

It is from the variations in the intensity and levels of irony that much of the difficulty of reading *Madame Bovary* stems. Its irony is not concentrated on a single axis, as in *Pride and Prejudice*, nor is it univocal. Flaubert's approach is more circumspect, more devious, and far more complex. His strategy has been described as an 'épanouissement, enrichissement concentrique'[13] ('spreading out, concentric enrichment'). It is also a progressive invasion and erosion of certainties. For this reason Flaubert's irony, though less immediately explosive than Jane Austen's, is in its very stealthiness more pervasive and menacing in the long run. It is so stealthy because it evades clear-cut distinctions between transparent ironies and those whose thrust remains shrouded in doubt. While Flaubert draws on the traditional types of irony, i.e. verbal, situational, dramatic, he often does so in a non-traditional manner. The special features of his manipulation of irony are so closely linked to his distinctive mode of narration that they must be considered in relation to it.

The omniscient narrator who introduces Charles and Emma at the beginning of *Madame Bovary* gradually evanesces into the background as the narrative progresses. He does not disappear entirely, but his perceptual functions are largely transferred onto the protagonists themselves. The method has been called 'description as subjectivity' in that 'almost without exception, the point of view is that of somebody within the work itself, a character rather than the author'.[14] The widespread use of this technique entails cumulatively a different kind of narration to that of Jane Austen. While the predicaments in *Pride and Prejudice* are perceived through the eyes of the women and primarily through Elizabeth's, in *Madame Bovary* scenes and happenings are experienced through a variety of protagonists. True, in the central sections of the novel, between Emma's marriage and her suicide, it is her viewpoint that predominates and her voice that is recorded in indirect discourse. But by no means exclusively: when Rodolphe first sees Emma, his reactions to her are given, and so are Charles', and Léon's, and Justin's. Such often rapid 'shifts in point of view are Flaubert's staple technique',[15] as many critics have noted. Sometimes the point of view of several different characters is adopted successively within a few pages, and occasionally that of several characters at once. This favourite method of Flaubert's is complicated by his preference for the imperfect tense for narration, which happens also to be the cardinal tense for indirect discourse so that it may be difficult to tell exactly where authorial narration melds into the character's apprehension of a scene.

This strongly subjective method of narration has two-fold and contradictory implications for the reading of the ironies in *Madame Bovary*. On the one hand, by giving the reader direct access to the consciousness of multiple characters, it provides a great deal of information that enables him quickly to apprehend ironies beyond the ken of the protagonists. The superior knowledge gained by the reader through his insights into the minds of various characters is particularly effective in dealing with the situational and dramatic ironies which are made transparent through Flaubert's narrative strategies. For instance, Charles' innocent encouragement of Emma's outings with Rodolphe in the belief that the fresh air and exercise will do her good, and his highly ambiguous phrase, 'que sa femme était à sa disposition' (p. 166; 'that his wife was at his disposal') are glaring ironies to a reader cognizant not only of Emma's fantasies but also of Rodolphe's ruminations when he first sees her: 'Pauvre petite femme! Ça baîlle après l'amour, comme une carpe après l'eau sur une table de cuisine. Avec trois mots de galanterie, cela vous adorerait, j'en suis sûr! ce serait tendre! charmant! . . . Oui, mais comment s'en débarrasser ensuite?' (p. 138; 'Poor little woman! She gapes for love like a carp for water on a kitchen table. For a couple of gallant phrases, she would adore one, I am sure! how tender! how charming she would be! . . . Yes, but how to get rid of her afterwards?'). The shifts in the point of view reveal the facts of the character's experience and his assessment of it, and simultaneously that that assessment is at least partly mistaken.

The dramatic and situational irony that is so pronounced an element of *Madame Bovary* has its most striking embodiment in the relationship of Charles and Emma. Emma's marriage represents the ironic reversal of intention and outcome; in its incongruity it is the behavioural counterpart to saying the opposite to what is meant. For through her union with Charles Emma attains the contrary to what she had hoped, as does Charles in the grotesque fiasco of his operation on Hippolyte's foot. Far from escaping the tedium and boredom of her isolated existence in the country, she perpetuates this state. She exchanges the monotony of the wheel (implied in her maiden name, 'Rouault') for the stupidity of the ox ('Bovary').[16] In Yonville Emma finds herself imprisoned in an environment whose metaphoric flatness and aridity echo the landscape's physical features. Hers becomes a classic 'case history of frustration'[17] when, in place of the bliss, ecstasy and passion she so ardently desires and expects, she finds again and again, in adultery as in marriage, the same old platitudes: 'Emma retrouvait dans l'adultère toutes les platitudes du mariage' (p. 307). The imperfect indicates the repetitive continuousness of Emma's disappointment. So the confinement in a temporal stasis combines with the spatial restriction to the circle[18] of the village to induce a thwarting sense of inevitability. Perversely, Emma's marriage, instead of liberating her from an insipid life, finalises her inclosure into a literal and figurative dead-end.

Yet it need not necessarily have been so. Emma herself, of course, cannot see this; despite a certain elegance and refinement that raises her above, say Mme Homais, she does not have the discernment to evaluate her situation. Or rather, she is too wholly trapped in her one-sided, subjective vision and too befuddled by the sentimental claptrap she has assimilated from her reading. The humdrum reality of her life as Charles' wife falls woefully short of her expectation of bliss, passion and ecstasy, at least from her point of view. However, hers is never the only point of view. If Emma is disappointed in Charles (and in Léon and Rodolphe), so indeed is he (and they) with her. This the reader is able to appreciate because he has an alternative angle on almost every situation as a result of the shifts of viewpoint. Thus we understand that the two men who catch Emma's fancy are unsuited to her: Léon is too timid, and Rodolphe too much of a cad. Only the despised Charles has the unfailing, unquestioning, undying love for her for which she yearns. Emma does not grasp this, but we do, and we recognise the enormous irony at the core of *Madame Bovary*. Only Charles is so totally submissive to every whim of hers that he, more than Léon or Rodolphe, would for love of her have done his utmost to satisfy her. The parallel afforded by their common mediocrity and gullibility heightens the irony of the ostensible contradiction between them.

The situational and dramatic irony is perfectly transparent here; nonetheless it is more complex than first meets the eye. For the very technique that allows the reader to see the alternative view also puts onto him a burden of choice such as never faces him in *Pride and Prejudice*. Wickham is thought to be charming and proves a scoundrel, whereas Darcy, who is considered disagreeable, turns out to be a true gentleman: in each case the misapprehension is temporary, and the resolution incontestable. No such absolute clarity is attainable in *Madame Bovary*, where the mobility of viewpoint and the withdrawal of the omniscient narrator behind his protagonists' view deprives us of ultimate assurance. Emma obviously has justification for reacting against Charles, but her motivation comes from a somewhat mistaken assessment and from pursuit of a preposterous ideal. Conversely, Charles would strive to gratify Emma, but would he not lose the remnants of his dignity by yielding to her extravagant fantasies? And, given her temperament, could he – or anyone – ever satisfy her, whatever he did? The irony has a double edge; its apparent transparency is deceptive because the shifting viewpoint undercuts every position, leaving the reader suspended in an uncertainty tantalising in its resistance to resolution. The surface transparency merely opens up onto further vistas and levels of irony.

4

The irony may be double-edged even when it is used in its traditional function as a weapon of satirical attack. Throughout *Madame Bovary* Flaubert resorts to irony as a polemical device that allows him to expose the banality of provincial life and the stupidity of its inhabitants. His irony is therefore often aggressive in impetus, '*at the expense* of his characters',[19] designed to uncover their hollow pretences. This is most evident in the portrayal of nearly all the secondary characters. The disparity between the image they wish to cultivate and their actual worth is repeatedly brought out through their actions and their discourse, which are left to speak for themselves on the assumption that 'we', the viewer–readers, partake of the narrator's insight. Such irony is frequently quite simple in its transparency: Homais' diatribes show not his advanced, enlightened opinions, much less his erudition, but his foolish credulousness and his asinine lack of discrimination; Rodolphe's artificially tear-stained letter of farewell to Emma is a graphic representation of his cruel cynicism; the priest's inability to meet, or even to recognise spiritual needs is revealed in the tragi-comic cross talk with Emma and his greater concern for bewitched cows and for the parrot-like recitation of the catechism than for a soul in distress. Flaubert's choice of names for his protagonists is a further illustration of his habit of using irony as a hatchet: Charles' first wife, the scraggy widow, is called Héloïse, as if in mocking reminder of one of the great love sagas; the instrument of Emma's bankruptcy is the merchant Lheureux (Happy); the diffident Léon certainly does not have the qualities of a lion, while the dashing Rodolphe is saddled with the unromantic surname Boulanger (Baker). Emma herself is the *third* Madame Bovary we encounter in the novel, as if in perverse refutation of her quest to be unique.

But the apparent straightforwardness of such satirical irony may also conceal a secondary level of irony, that other cutting edge that rebounds on the speaker/perceiver as well as hitting the object. Here again the special form of Flaubert's irony is a direct concomitant of his technique of subjective description and shifting viewpoint. A vivid example of double-edged irony occurs in the vignette introducing Madame Homais:

> Quant à la femme du pharmacien, c'était la meilleure épouse de Normandie, douce comme un mouton, chérissant ses enfants, son père, sa. mère, ses cousins, pleurant aux maux d'autrui, laissant tout aller dans son ménage, et détestant les corsets; – mais si lente à se mouvoir, si ennuyeux à écouter, d'un aspect si commun et d'une conversation si restreinte, qu'il n'avait jamais songé, quoiqu'elle eût trente ans, qu'il en eût vingt, qu'ils couchassent porte à porte, et qu'il lui parlât chaque jour, qu'elle pût être une femme pour quelqu'un, ni qu'elle possédât de son sexe autre chose que la robe. (p. 101)

> (As for the pharmacist's wife, she was the perfect spouse, the finest in Normandy, placid as a sheep, adoring her children, her father, her mother, her cousins, weeping over the troubles of others, relaxed in her housekeeping, and opposed to corsets; – but so slow to react, so boring to listen to, so ordinary in appearance and limited in conversation, that it had never occurred to him, though she was thirty and he twenty, and they slept in adjoining rooms and spoke to one another every day, that anyone could think of her as a woman, or that she had any of the attributes of her sex other than a dress.)

At first sight this looks like a subtle, artfully controlled piece of traditional satirical irony that means the contrary to what it says. In a single long sentence two entirely disparate assessments of Madame Homais are presented. The opening compliment ('la meilleure épouse de Normandie'), that reports the consensus of

Yonville, is immediately weakened by a somewhat ambiguous simile ('douce comme un mouton'), by the implication of a certain negligence alongside her concern for others ('laissant tout aller dans son ménage'), and particularly by the linguistic and emotional shock of the incongruity of her sole ethical principle ('détestant les corsets') which ends the first part of the sentence on an anti-climactic drop. The second half, even broader in its rhetorical span, begins by reinforcing the doubts already sown through that unexpected dash that invites a reflective pause. But it is only after the build-up of the lengthy clauses with their weighty past subjunctives that the final let-down comes in the paltry, lean words 'autre chose que la robe'. The insult effects a total reversal of the initial proposition, leaving no doubts as to the worth of either Madame Homais or of the opinions of Yonville. The irony here is stable and easily reconstructible. What complicates it and adds that other edge is that this is a description of Madame Homais as perceived by Léon, not by the narrator. Obliquely it reveals a good deal not only about her but also about him: the limits of his imagination and his horizon, the languor of his sexual initiative, the mediocrity of his aspirations. A similar double irony is implicit in the description of the ball at La Vaubyessard which is experienced through Emma's consciousness. To her it is the epitome of elegance, yet several details suggest the tawdry, degenerate aspects beneath the superficial splendour, and so convey an ironic judgement both on Emma for her readiness to be dazzled by glittering appearance and on the quality of what draws her admiration.

This procedure of double-edged irony occurs throughout *Madame Bovary* and accounts for the peculiar density of its ironic texture. Nowhere is it more brilliantly displayed than in the scene that stands, fittingly, at the very centre of the novel, the agricultural fair. The movement of the narrative is halted to focus attention on the interplay of groups within a static segment of time.[20] The difference in spatial level between Rodolphe and Emma at an upstairs window and the crowd below represents the twin actions carried on in the alternation of two distinct modes of discourse: the public oratory of the market-place as against the private whispers of the secluded lovers. The bombastic eulogies of the festive ceremony act as a background to Rodolphe's ardent wooing. However, the difference between the two forms of rhetoric is far slighter than may first appear. For both are equally vacuous and equally false. Rodolphe's romantic stock phrases correspond in their spuriousness to the orators' pathetic inanities. Though the speeches from the lower level interrupt the courtship upstairs in a parodistic counterpoint, a deeper irony resides in the hidden congruity between the empty jargon of Yonville's official harangues and the counterfeit currency of its personal relationships. Rodolphe and Emma have deliberately removed themselves from – and note that they have raised themselves above – the public forum, but they in turn are unmasked as ironic victims of their own fatuous discourse in just the same way as the crowd below is beguiled by the clichés of political discourse.

Cliché is indeed one of Flaubert's most potent vehicles for irony, and again it is exploited for its capacity to be double-edged, mocking at one and the same time the speaker who uses it and the source from which it is taken. Nearly all the inhabitants of Yonville are captives of cliché: Homais with his pseudo-scientific, pseudo-scholarly mumbo-jumbo; the pious clichés of the priest as he utters platitudes in a lofty tone; Rodolphe's gushing stock-in-trade of seduction, and Léon's simpering conventionalities; above all, the ludicrous iconography of false and shoddy sentiment that takes complete possession of Emma's thoughts. The various patterns of cliché common to Yonville suggest that despite their disparity and their individuality these people belong together. What unites them is a dullness of mind that is mirrored in the stale phrases and worn images which satisfy them. And Emma, for all her ambitions and fantasies, has her appropriate place right among them.

Flaubert's double-edged irony leaves precious little unscathed by the end of the novel. There is not a single character, hardly excepting Justin and Dr Canivet, who is wholly admirable. More important, there is not a single character who can act as an organising centre of gravity, composing the world for us, after the manner of Elizabeth in *Pride and Prejudice*. No one in *Madame Bovary* has the honesty and shrewdness of Elizabeth and Darcy, nor their willingness to engage in a searching revision of their pre-conceived notions and to concede the erroneousness of their first impressions. This is what saves them from the consequences of their folly, and releases them from the dualism of an ironic dichotomy. Such redemption does not take place in *Madame Bovary* because all the protagonists are so steeped in their delusions that they cannot envisage any other standpoint. The intelligent self-scrutiny that distinguishes Jane Austen's heroes and heroines is utterly alien to Flaubert's characters who are condemned to be victims of their own blinkered vision. The detached perspective that is accomplished *within* the fictional world of *Pride and Prejudice* is the prerogative of the external 'us' in *Madame Bovary.*

In contrast to Jane Austen's faith in the human capacity for self-detachment and ameliorative reassessment, Flaubert holds out no hope of any improvement in the conditions and persons he portrays. This is inferred in the novel's overall pattern which consists of a series of repeated and increasingly severe setbacks, culminating not merely in Emma's death but in the symbolic apotheosis of mediocrity in the triumph of Homais. It is this that accounts for the sense of doom that permeates the novel and that seeps out of it like an invisible poison. The poisoning agent is Flaubert's irony which is calculated to lay bare the contemptible triviality of this world and to demonstrate the inexorability of failure. Its essentially destructive impact is in contrast to the restorative function of irony in *Pride and Prejudice.* Like Jane Austen, Flaubert uses irony for the establishment of 'truth', but his is a pessimistic truth, whereas hers is optimistic in tendency. Within the fictional world of *Madame Bovary* there are no positive values to counterbalance the ironic devastation. The clichéd illusions that are the repositories of the characters' aspirations, far from providing a worthwhile alternative to a mediocre world, are a caricature extension of it. For this reason charges of cynicism, bleakness and defeatism have been brought against *Madame Bovary.* Matthew Arnold branded it 'a work of *petrified feeling*; over it hangs an atmosphere of bitterness, irony, impotence; not a personage in the book to rejoice or console us'.[21] As it stands, the accusation is irrefutable; there is indeed nothing 'in the book to rejoice or console us'. But perhaps the book *as a book*, as a work of art, can give the catharsis lacking in its fictional realm. It may well be one of the ironies of this insidiously ironic book that its beauty as an aesthetic artifact holds out to 'us' a consoling antidote to the ugliness it depicts.

5

If intelligence is denied to the protagonists of *Madame Bovary*, it is required in very high degree of 'us', the reader-spectators. For Flaubert's irony depends almost entirely on the 'art of insinuation'[22] that he evolved. Scenes, actions, conversations are put before us in a dramatic presentation so designed that the discrepancy between appearance and reality can be deduced by the attentive eye. And it should never be forgotten that Flaubert placed at the entrance to his narrative the metaperspective of that watchful eye as if to incite us to look with care. 'Et qui est-ce qui s'apercevra jamais des profondes combinaisons que m'aura demandée un livre si simple?'[23] ('And who will ever notice the subtle combinations that so simple a book required of me?') Flaubert once asked. The answer is: 'we', alert to the tactics used to indicate the ironic subtext: the exaggerations and anti-climaxes, the blanks[24] and the repetitions, the names and the gestures, the contrasts and the clichés, the seemingly trivial details and the patterns of telling images,[25] even the tenses and the commas.[26] In all these stratagems Flaubert has recourse to the traditional means of conveying irony, though he interweaves them with the utmost finesse and endows them with an added dimension through the elaboration of a double-edged irony dependent on subjective description. Nevertheless, the basic tenor of most of his irony is traditional and amenable to reasonably confident reconstruction through 'our' intelligence.

There are, however, areas of *Madame Bovary* where these contentions do not hold and where the nature and thrust of the irony becomes highly problematical. It is in the portrayal of Emma and, to a lesser extent, of Charles that the fluctuations in ironic stance are most disconcerting. Irony blends with something akin to pity, mockery with tenderness. The focalisation[27] is so variable and the shifts of viewpoint so rapid and elusive that it is difficult to determine who speaks or from where, and to compose a scene whose salient features attain clarity in relation to each other. The most striking example of such fluctuation occurs in the scene of Emma's death. It is, as John P. Houston[28] has shown, practically impossible, even by the most scrupulous stylistic analysis, to delineate precisely between the priest's liturgical formulae as he administers the extreme

unction and the suggestive, erotically coloured phrases of
Emma's confused consciousness. This strange amalgam evokes
at one and the same time commiseration with the dying woman
and horror at her persistent infatuation with the transitory
pleasures of this world. The ironic thrust is complicated by the
double edge: Emma's emphasis on the beauties of the flesh rather
than the forgiveness of the spirit distorts the supreme religious
ceremony, while we see too how Emma, by reducing the sanctity
of the ritual to a vain parody, is emptying her death, as she had
done her life, of true inner meaning.

The ambivalences that Houston attributes to shifting
viewpoints are ascribed by Benjamin F. Bart to changes in
aesthetic distance. Through a study of the variants in Flaubert's
successive versions of his manuscript Bart traces his striving for
perfect mastery of the aesthetic distance between the narrator and
his subject, and as a corollary, for control of the reader's
response. 'When the distance remains considerable, irony is
usually present and bitter. The distance sometimes narrows,
however, and the irony becomes gentler or even disappears.'[29] In
this kinetic modulation of his narrative stance Flaubert may well
have been 'playing hide-and-seek with himself',[30] his fluctuations
reflecting his conflicting impulse to identify with Emma or to
repudiate her. From this springs an ambiguous attitude towards
Emma on the narrator's part as well as on ours, and the
consequent hesitancies in interpretation. 'What she desires –
furnishing her house, Léon, Rodolphe – may be petty, but her
desire itself – to transcend Yonville – is neither tawdry nor
wrong.'[31] While the actual objects of her dreams are
contemptible, her genuine urge to surpass the limitations of her
life does give her a certain distinction. There is an element of
pathos and even of tragedy in the fact that circumstances have
precluded her from worthier ideals to which to direct her ardour.
Again and again irony sidles into pity, negation into affirmation
in a perplexing combination unique to *Madame Bovary*.

The mechanics of this bewildering phenomenon have been
aptly diagnosed by Rainer Warning, though his language is
somewhat eliptical: 'Here ostensive dissociation is replaced by
ostensive establishment of solidarity with the medium, with the
result that it is henceforth necessary to apprehend the simulation
against the establishment of solidarity and the distance against
the simulated identification.'[32] What Warning seems to be

positing is a kind of compound and reciprocal irony between the varying positions that the narrator adopts *vis-à-vis* Emma. The persona – or, as Warning terms it, 'the medium' – is undercut as the centre of organisation. This is, of course, in keeping with Flaubert's major techniques: shifts in viewpoint, subjectivity in description and a double-edged irony. The 'ostensive establishment of solidarity', that is to say, the identification with the persona is fused with an 'ostensive dissociation', i.e. detachment, to produce a characteristically bifocal vision. The effect is then one of simultaneous solidarity and dissociation that exposes the reader to a shuttling indecisiveness.

In the last resort, however, the ebb and flow of Flaubert's irony in *Madame Bovary* cannot be explained only in terms of viewpoint, aesthetic distance, and solidarity and dissociation. Flaubert's practice cuts across these categories; that, indeed, is the hallmark of his originality as an ironist. The game that he is playing is more dangerous than Jane Austen's, and the ploys that he uses more complicated. He certainly cultivates aesthetic distance to uphold the ironist's detachment. With those characters who are the targets of unconditional attack, such as Homais and Rodolphe, the procedure is quite straightforward. On the other hand, where there is an underlying equivocation, as towards Emma, the position becomes far more delicate. Not only are aesthetic distance and viewpoint frequently modulated; even more important, they do not correspond directly to the narrator's perspective nor to 'our' metaperspective. For the point of view may be that of the persona, while the perspective is that of the narrator, and the metaperspective ours. When, for instance, towards the end of her life Emma finally comes to ask what has gone wrong: 'D'où venait donc cette insuffisance de la vie, cette pourriture instantanée des choses où elle s'appuyait?' (p. 300; 'What was the source of this inadequacy of life, this immediate rotting of everything she leaned on?') she refuses squarely to face the issue. Instead she quickly retreats once more into the comfort of her customary dreams, conjuring up 'un être fort et beau, une nature valeureuse, pleine à la fois d'exaltation et de raffinements, un coeur de poète sous une forme d'ange, lyre aux cordes d'airain sonnant vers le ciel des épithalames élégiaques' ('someone strong and beautiful, a man of valour, passionate yet refined, the heart of a poet in the form of an angel, with a bronze-stringed lyre playing elegiac epithalamia to the heavens'). The words, the thoughts, the viewpoint are here patently Emma's; on one level, therefore, the identification with the persona has been accomplished. But at the same time, on another level, through our recognition of the familiar code of her sentimental clichés, there is an evaluating detachment from her. The coolly appraising intelligence comes from the superior gaze of the watching 'us', while the intoxication with feeling comes from her. Such separation of subjective viewpoint and objective perspective is unusual, to say the least, and particularly the persistence of an independent metaperspective alongside the persona's viewpoint. Flaubert is able to achieve this through his initial positioning of 'nous' in the role of spectators that is sustained throughout the narrative. This is the ultimate source of the fluctuations of his irony towards Emma. The 'anonymous author' does indeed 'sneak in and out of his characters' heavy stupidity',[33] letting their voices be heard and appearing to empathise with them. But these deft 'slides' ('glissements')[34] that make up Flaubert's 'art des modulations'[35] only become unique in alliance with the concurrent maintenance of an external perspective. In effect Flaubert 'is asking us to accept two separate literary conventions at once, and to change from one to the other when it suits him'.[36] Alternatively, it could be claimed that Flaubert actually evolves a new form of precarious ironic narration. Between the viewpoint of the speaking persona and the perspective of the seeing narrator and the perceiving reader lies the space for irony.

A fine example of Flaubert's practice is his presentation of Charles' and Emma's daydreams as they lie awake side by side one night (pp. 207–9). The reveries are narrated successively, each in turn from within the mind of the dreamer, with no link other than the position of the two dreamers. In spite of their physical closeness to each other, no word or touch is exchanged between them, an outer lack of contact that reflects the emotional gulf revealed by their contrasting daydreams. The parallelism underlines the disparity, each enclosed fantasy acting as a foil to the other. The antithesis is all the more striking because of the specificity of the opposing pictures. Charles paints a homely domestic scene as he envisions his daughter coming home from school in an ink-stained apron, carrying her lunch-basket, later growing up to resemble her mother, the two of them looking like sisters in their big straw hats, then helping in the house, embroidering slippers for her father, and some day marrying a good man with a steady business. His hopes are modest, and his anxieties, primarily financial in origin, realistic. Meanwhile Emma is in her thoughts roaming the world in the arms of her lover, discovering from mountain-tops splendid domed cities, floating in gondolas, or swinging in hammocks, in a setting with all the right sensual trappings: bells, fountains, guitars, palm-trees, flowers, scents, and exotic fruits. The extravanganzas of her images are echoed in the pretentiousness of her high-flown, long-winded rhetoric which stands out sharply against Charles' short, simple phrases. The thoughts are from the consciousness of the characters, while the response is ours. Charles' genuine attachment to his daughter elicits warmth despite the humdrum nature of his desires. Sympathy for him and for Berthe is heightened by the dramatic irony of hindsight through the later discovery that Charles' humble dream is as doomed to be thwarted as Emma's sensational fancies. Towards her scenario the reaction is one of conditioned scepticism: the galloping horses, the mountains, the strong silent lover, etc. are dismissed with a mixture of exasperation and condescension and just a little pity as the dreary paraphernalia of her perverted mind. Her limitations are as severe as Charles'; though he appears to be the 'contraire absolu'[37] ('absolute contrary') to her passionate, imaginative temperament, beneath the apparent incongruity of this union lurks a kind of ironic congruity. These are insights that spring from the external perspective brought to bear on the two daydreams. Both characters are illumined from within, and both evince a curious blend of contempt and compassion. The ambivalence of the narrator's stance is projected onto 'us'. The difficulty of reading stems not from the inadequacy of our intelligence to the task but from the conflicting signals emanating from the ironic duality of the irony. The double-edged irony characteristic of *Madame Bovary* is sharpened at points into an ironic undercutting of its own ironies.

This pervasive ambivalence is fostered by the capacious use of indirect discourse throughout the text. Flaubert does not question the basic efficacy of language to convey meaning; his notoriously obsessive quest for the *mot juste*, the perfect turn of phrase, belies any doubts of that kind. However, he does explore the potential of language for creating ambiguity, especially in indirect discourse. Indirect discourse precisely serves Flaubert's purpose through its dualistic charge: it allows extreme closeness to the persona's consciousness while appearing to be 'the exact equivalent, on the linguistic plane, of this withdrawal of the author from the work'.[38] In other words it attains stylistically what Warning would call 'ostensive establishment of solidarity' *and* 'ostensive dissociation', i.e. identification and detachment. Flaubert derived 'remarkable advantage . . . from this ambiguity, which permits him to make his own language speak this both loathsome and fascinating idiom of the ''other'' without being wholly comprised or wholly innocent'.[39] It is through indirect discourse that the alliance of subjective viewpoint and objective perspective can best be maintained. The irony at Emma's expense becomes operative in two tiers, as it were: directly through the accumulation of romanticised clichés, the exaggeration, specially of emotive factors, the redundancy of detail, the amplification of triviality. These belong officially to Emma, but indirectly they spark a reaction in the reader who is made aware of the capriciousness of her aspirations and the misguidedness of her values. A mocking judgement of Emma is implicit in the perspective, though the viewpoint merely purports to reproduce her thoughts. The ironic intent on the narrator's part is palpable but covert. The lines of demarcation between the speaking subject and the reporting narrator become blurred because Flaubert habitually resorts to the imperfect tense for narration and this coincides with the dominant tense of indirect discourse. As a result the character's reverie and the report of it are not clearly separated from each other so that it is by no means certain whose word we are being asked to accept. It is in this respect, in this elision of viewpoint and perspective that Flaubert makes such distinctive use of indirect discourse. The switch from direct to indirect discourse has been likened[40] to the focusing of a telescope for closer or more distinct vision. What happens in *Madame Bovary* is an apparently contradictory symbiotic fusion of closeness and distance as if our two eyes were looking through opera-glasses with two different kinds of focus. The double edges of this irony then come to be turned against the reader too.

6

Is Flaubert's then an 'uncertain irony', 'a version of what is often called Romantic irony'?[41] Culler backs these claims by asserting

that the text of *Madame Bovary* resists reading by breeding
constant suspicion:

> We do not know who speaks or from where. The narrator is
> depersonalized, in that we cannot give him a character which
> would explain and hold together the moments of his discourse.
> We have, in short, a written text, which stands before us cut off
> from a speaker.[42]

Flaubert, he concludes, is so insidious – and so effective – because
his text challenges the interpretative process of constructing
meanings by linking the novel to other forms of experience:

> His realism provides firm links with an empirical world and
> draws the reader into a process which appears very familiar,
> only to expose him to the drama of the sentence and to the
> demystification of his role in making sense of the text.[43]

Culler's contentions are worth quoting because of their bearing
on certain facets of *Madame Bovary*. In relation to Emma and, to a
lesser degree, to Charles, Flaubert's irony is uncertain, and his
text does breed suspicions that resist definitive interpretation. Is
Emma a 'Female Don Quixote'[44] whose 'odyssée amoureuse'[45]
('odyssey of love') is a parodistic echo of a heroic quest? Is she a
victim of her environment and upbringing, a searching soul
frustrated in her desire to surpass the meanness of her
surroundings? Is she admirable by virtue of harbouring such
desires? Or despicable for letting her head and her heart be
turned by the synthetic tinsel of gaudy romance? Similarly, does
ridiculous '*Charbovari*' deserve to be derided for his plodding
dullness, his gaucherie, his flaccidity? Or should he be esteemed
for his generosity, his enduring love for his wife and daughter, his
ingenuousness? In the presentation of these figures Flaubert's
irony moves into indeterminacy by fluctuating between two
conjoined images without final indications as to which we are to
take as the 'correct' one. The shiftiness of the text in indirect
discourse seems deliberately designed to preclude authoritative
answers. The succession of conflicting signals saps the reader's
assurance, leaving him to face an enigma that defies resolution. It
may well be, as has often been suggested, that these fluctuations
of Flaubert's irony towards his central figures are a reflection of

his own wavering stance. The irony would then be at the narrator's expense too as he pokes fun – or rather, censures – his own inclination to empathy with the Bovary attitudes by subjecting them to a curious alloy of mockery and tenderness. Be that as it may, the dialectic of the irony in which Emma and Charles are embedded is not to be resolved. If there is sufficient evidence in the text to support a multiplicity of readings, there is also sufficient dubiety to question them. But that is one of the sources of this text's lasting fascination. *Madame Bovary* displays a high degree of internal organisation, yet it is such as to thwart the reader's efforts to organise it for himself – at least in certain areas.

The mobility of the text in regard to Emma and Charles should not, however, lead to the assumption that *Madame Bovary* represents 'a version of what is often called Romantic irony'. The fragility of the viewpoint is counteracted by a firmness of perspective that is closer to the certitudes of Jane Austen than to the relativism of the Romantic ironists. It is not so much that Flaubert envisages an inherently ironic universe as that he brings an ironic perspective to bear on a despised part of it. The function of his irony is negative: exposure, deflation, mockery, and rejection, but this denunciatory posture in itself gives a base of sureness. So there is no leeway of doubt as far as Homais, Rodolphe or Bournisien are concerned. The context and manner in which they are portrayed amounts to an incessant, unmistakably taunting critique. Through the orchestration of decor and incident, the selection of detail and imagery, the emphases and omissions, the management of contrast and pause, the rhetorical tone in direct and indirect discourse, an ironic assessment of Yonville and its inhabitants is instilled into the portrayal. For despite the variability of the viewpoint, ultimately it is the narrator's perspective that prevails, and his position is one of certainty except in regard to Emma and Charles.

Perhaps the most astonishing aspect of *Madame Bovary* is the way in which the narrator asserts his perspective while remaining seemingly absent from his text. Flaubert has succeeded in this novel in fulfilling his aesthetic ideal: 'être dans son oeuvre comme Dieu dans la création, invisible et tout-puissant; qu'on le sente partout, mais qu'on ne le voie pas'[46] ('to be immanent in the work, like God in his creation, invisible and omnipotent; to be everywhere felt and nowhere seen'). He is so invisible as to have provoked mistaken comments about 'the absence of a controlling narrator'.[47] In fact the narrator controls his own absence, choosing anonymity for his artistic purposes but not abdicating control. On the contrary, while he never intervenes in an obvious manner, he is present in every detail, in every word, in every single line as the animator of this entire fictional world that he makes 'us' see. And he is also always in guiding control of the reader's response, even when that response is one of indefinity or puzzlement. The fiction of the narrator's absence from *Madame Bovary* is like an ironic joke perpetrated by his ever vigilant controlling presence.

However, the semblance of the narrator's absence permits the elaboration of a sustained ironic discourse apparently independent of a recognisable speaker. In this respect *Madame Bovary* differs markedly from *Pride and Prejudice* where the consistency of the narratorial voice is an assurance of its continuing presence. Its absence is a fiction and a deception in *Madame Bovary* for the author-narrator retains supreme control. But in a complicated interplay of simulated positions he conceals his own voice behind that of the persona whose speech he assumes in a kind of ventriloquism that takes the form of indirect discourse.

Such sustained, encapsulated ironic discourse is one of the main methods that Flaubert devised to shift immediate responsibility from an identifiable narrator. It fulfils the same purpose as the separation of viewpoint from perspective: as a veil for the uncertainties that disturb an irony that is by and large fairly transparent. For much of *Madame Bovary* Flaubert is working from a base of secure, albeit negative knowledge, exposing and deflating with a satirical irony confident of its superior understanding. He exploits the possibilities of such irony to their utmost limits in the subtlety of his narrative techniques and particularly in the strategy of double-edged ironies. Such double-edged irony is already a step towards a more radically doubting and questioning irony of uncertainty. Flaubert crosses its verge, but he avoids confronting it by devising ways to blunt its impact. Emma remains an enigma, not a paradox, in a world that can be evaluated with certainty.

5 George Gordon Byron: *Don Juan*, 1818–23

> 'A paper kite which flies 'twixt Life and Death'
>
> (Canto 14, stanza viii)

1

'I maintain that these illicit kinds of book are far more interesting than the proper books which respect illusions devoutly all the time', Virginia Woolf asserted in *A Writer's Diary*.[1] According to this eclectic but illuminating division, *Pride and Prejudice* and *Madame Bovary* belong among the 'proper' books since they consistently respect fictional illusion even though they question societal illusions. Byron's *Don Juan*, on the other hand, ostensibly and, it would seem, joyously falls into the category of the 'illicit' for it bucks against illusions on various levels: against the illusions portrayed within the fiction, and against the very illusion of fiction. At both these levels irony of differing sorts is the major instrument to undo illusions. The eventual outcome of this systematic dismantling of illusion is a vision of the world devoid not merely of illusions but also of certainties.

The illicit note is sounded right at the outset of *Don Juan* when the first stanza of the first canto begins with the blatant proclamation: 'I want a hero'. Despite the familiarity it has acquired, this opening still retains its capacity to shock through its unconventionality, its unpredictability, its wanton departure from expected narrative norms. Virgil, with his prototypical 'Arma virumque cano', had announced a settled subject with programmatic definity and a staid self-assurance in the function of the narrator. The validity of making such assertions is exposed to some question in the ironically deceptive overture to *Pride and*

Prejudice. However, even though the 'truth' enunciated there proves in need of qualification, the narrator nevertheless appears in full control of the unfolding narrative. Byron's 'I want a hero' is so radically disturbing because it removes the sustaining illusion of authorial authority, and though this may in itself be just a wilful ploy, an indirect method of self-advertisement, its momentary impact is one of bewilderment, of a narrator and a reader equally adrift in a sea of indeterminacy.

Yet that startling declaration is a wholly appropriate entrance to the idiosyncratic work it heralds. Its iconoclasm sets the tone and mode of the ensuing text. Its emphasis on the processes of creativity points forward to the tension between the progress of the story and the strategies of story-telling that is the dominant feature of *Don Juan*. From the first phrase onwards the narrator of *Don Juan* is highly conspicuous, in contrast to the covert, unobtrusive puppet-master of *Pride and Prejudice* and the invisible creator of *Madame Bovary*. Here the act of telling is not only public, ebullient and ostentatious, but an integral and important aspect of the narrative. Plot, commentary and digression are at times so closely intertwined as to defy separation. For this reason, so as to maintain a maximum freedom of movement, too settled, i.e. too confining a narrative contract is avoided. Through that 'I want a hero' a relationship of sorts is set up between the narrator and the reader, though it is different from the trusting closeness in *Pride and Prejudice* or the shared perspective in *Madame Bovary*. For 'I want a hero' is not aimed primarily at the reader; his turn will come later on the many occasions when 'the Bard' will issue an immediate appeal to him:

> But for the present, gentle reader! and
>   Still gentler purchaser! the Bard – that's I –
> Must with permission, shake you by the hand,
>   and so – 'your humble servant, and Good-bye!'
> We meet again, if we should understand
>   Each other; and if not, I shall not try
> Your patience further than by this short sample –
>   'T were well if others followed my example.[2]

Such direct engagement of the reader does not take place in 'I want a hero' which is more of a self-exhortation than an address to others. At most, by musing aloud, by voicing his needs audibly, the story-teller lets us overhear. We are allowed, perhaps even invited, into his workshop and behind the scenes as the narrative is being devised. The link between narrator and reader, that alliance in collusive knowledge necessary for irony, is thereby adumbrated. The improvisational stance encourages a more casual and, as it were, reciprocal relationship with the reader than the austere withdrawnness of a Flaubert because the improviser's inspiration devolves from his consciousness of the audience's response. The atmosphere of intimacy is further fostered by the narrator's use of a speaking voice, his projection into the role of oral story-teller. As a ' "colloquial" poet' Byron 'is one who retains the feeling of the *colloquium*, the free give and take of easy conversation'.[3] That phrase, 'the free give and take of easy conversation', aptly summarises the nature of the narrative contract between story-teller and listener in *Don Juan*: it is personal, fluid, and open, less formal than in *Pride and Prejudice* and less conspiratorial than in *Madame Bovary*. Its liberty is a source of its great flexibility as well as of its gnawing uncertainty.

Besides the conversation with the reader, there is a second continuing exchange in *Don Juan* which is central to the structure and intent of the entire work, and that is the narrator's self-dialogue with himself as a creative artist. On the one side stands 'the Bard' giving 'a dramatic performance'[4] to an assembled audience, and every so often stepping off the stage to drop an aside either on the drama or on his own performance. This situation in itself already predisposes to a dualistic perception and hence is conducive to an ironic running commentary alongside, yet still within, the main fiction. In addition to this, on the other side, stands a distinct persona, '*Me* – the present writer of / The present poem' (7, iii, p. 227) engaged in a constant, intense scrutiny of his work-in-progress. But who is this 'Me'? who is the 'I' that wants a hero? In other words, whose is the narrating voice in *Don Juan*? It is, of course, tempting simply to equate the narrator with Byron. There are ample grounds for assuming that the narrating 'I' is a self-dramatisation: in many respects the narrator's background corresponds to Byron's, and in the English cantos he draws freely on Byron's own experiences of and reactions to English society. However, the overlap between the narrator and Byron, even on the level of experience, is only partial. The visit to the harem, for instance, is invention. 'The fictive Byron and the empirical Byron are and are not the same';[5]

or, to put the relationship into sharper focus: 'the author Byron is
creating in the narrator an alter ego or mode of consciousness'[6]
that often coincides with himself in experience, outlook and tone,
but that nonetheless retains its freedom as a fictive self-
creating persona. The distance between Byron and the narrator is
never defined or articulated. So an element of uncertainty hovers
over this narrating voice, adding mystery to its semi-anonymity.
Yet at the same time that voice does maintain its own
consistency. It is, admittedly, a paradoxical consistency because
its essence lies in its quirkiness, its capacity for endless surprise
and apparent inconsistency. Far from concealing his
uncertainties, as does the narrator of *Madame Bovary*, the voice
narrating *Don Juan* flaunts his uncertainties about the
development of his narrative as evidence of his superior power
over the microcosm of the fiction.

The narrator's actual identity is less important than his
insistent and intrusive presence in the forefront of narration. For
the initial 'I want a hero' is a first indication of the metafictional
aspect of *Don Juan*. The fact that the narrative begins not with the
customary exposition but with a reflection on the story about to
be fashioned is a key signal of that displacement of the story by
story-telling characteristic of *Don Juan*. The dominant focus of
interest is in effect shifted from the narrative to the making of the
narrative, and with it the primary line of communication is not
between the narrator and the reader but between the narrator
and his narrative-in-progress. Consequently the reader becomes
something of an eavesdropper. The position is by no means clear-
cut, for this narrator, though an improviser, always aware of his
audience and in need of response, is also a reflective artist critical
of his disposition of the narrative. There is a parallel dualism in
his irony. In contrast to the irony of such 'proper' narrators as
Jane Austen and Flaubert, which operates almost exclusively
through and within the fiction, that of Byron and his kindred
authors of 'illicit' books, Jean-Paul, Diderot, and Sterne, has a
further dimension. In *Don Juan*, there is beyond the irony within
the fiction an irony of fiction. That is what is intimated in that
half-searching, half-flippant opening 'I want a hero', and that is
why it strikes us as half-beguiling, half-alienating.

2

The hero on whom the narrator settles in 'our ancient friend Don Juan' (1, i, p. 10). He is selected, tongue in cheek, with a touch of condescending humour in preference to Condorcet, Clootz, Desaix, La Fayette and

> many of the military set,
> Exceedingly remarkable at times,
> But not at all adapted to my rhymes. (1, iii, p. 10)

If the reason for the choice of Don Juan seems in itself somewhat ironical in view of *his* ill-rhyming name, this subservience of the hero to considerations of rhyme forcefully and comically underlines the priority of the writing over what is written.

The 'ancient friend' is in any case treated rather summarily. After a brief reference to his legendary career, which places him in the context of the Don Juan myth –

> We have all seen him, in the pantomime,
> Sent to the Devil somewhat ere his time (1, i, p. 10)

– he appears in his traditional setting, Spain, but as a virgin lad of sixteen! Byron's inversion of the Don Juan figure[7] from the customary erotomanic predator into an ignorant, immaculate youth 'of saintly breeding' (4, xix, p. 139) corresponds virtually to the Johnsonian concept of irony as reversal. Instead of being a heartless, compulsive seducer of women, this Don Juan is a helpless prey, not moved by the upsurge of his own sensual appetites, of which he has no inkling, but victimised by the lust of others, and often caught in a complicated network of social relationships beyond his grasp. It is his very innocence that leads repeatedly to the irony of the situations in which he lands. He is first beguiled by the 'determination' (i, lxxxi, p. 27) of Julia, the older, experienced woman who deftly takes the initiative. Then he is nursed and nourished, cherished and loved by Haidée. With Gulbeyaz once more it is he who 'had caught/Her eye' (5, cxiv, p. 186): her dominion over him, and with it the role reversal into actively pursuing female and passively pursued male is externalised when he is attired in women's clothing and lodged in the seraglio. Again and again this same pattern recurs, from his imperious mother onwards, as Juan is manipulated by a series of strong-minded women, to whose forced attentions he submits without reflection, calmly letting the world have its way and the women theirs. 'As a libertine,' W. H. Auden[8] laments, Byron's 'Don Juan, who sleeps with only four women, and then either because they take the initiative or because they happen to be around, makes a poor showing beside the Don Giovanni of the opera's "Catalogue Aria".' He does indeed blunder from one to the other by chance, not by design in any sense of the word. In Russia, as ever, 'the Sovereign was smitten' (9, lxxvii, p. 294): in England Lady Adeline 'felt on the whole an intense interest' (15, xxviii, p. 409) and so apparently did the Duchess of Fitz-Fulke (16, cxxiii, p. 454). The irony of situation has an element of parody through the repetition and also through the ludicrous simplicity of the women's automatic response to the youth's dumb good looks. He, by contrast, generally stays relatively detached, feeling at most 'much flattered by her love' (9, lxxvii, p. 294) or motivated by 'Self-love' (9, lxviii, p. 292). Throughout these adventures, 'fundamentally he remains the same pleasant and courageous young man whose follies are due to circumstance, to sentiment and to mistaken idealism rather than to anything vicious in him'.[9] Not that he is himself without heart: he is certainly touched by Haidée, and protective to little Leila, 'a pure and living pearl' (10, li, p. 308), his counterpart in innocence. But the only woman on whom his choice falls is Aurora Raby (16, xii, p. 428), and that spontaneous attraction seems – ironically – to go no further than a wistful sigh on his part. For his fate is contrary to what is expected of a Don Juan: 'Juan, instead of courting courts, was courted – ' (10, xxix, p. 303). Even at the very end of the poem he still has his 'virgin face' (17, xiii, p. 457) though it is 'wan and worn' (17, xiv, p. 457) as he trembles in fear of the ghost who is, after all, no summons from Hell, but only the 'full, voluptuous . . . bulk . . . of her frolic Grace – Fitz-Fulke!' (16, cxxiii, p. 454). The implicit contrast with the cynical bravado of Don Giovanni as he stoically faces his due punishment emphasises the gulf between Byron's 'Poor little fellow' (1, lxxxvi, p. 29) and his mythic prototype.

Through such reversals of the traditional Juanesque situations the central ironic theme of *Don Juan*, i.e. the discrepancy between appearance and reality, is explored in a comic guise. This is as intrinsic to the descriptions of the social scene in Russia, Turkey, and England as to the portrait of the non-heroic hero. To set this 'poor little fellow' up against the legendary Don Juan is a means of underscoring the disparity between what is and what seems. The upside down rendition of the seducer's progress produces point and counterpoint simultaneously by never letting us forget that both the stock story and its opposite are being told. Parallel though perhaps less fully articulated examples of a similar technique are found in Jane Austen's *Northanger Abbey*, which is and is not a Gothic novel, and in Diderot's *Jacques le fataliste et son maître*, which is at once a sentimental novel and its rebuttal. Since Byron exploits the materials of a popular myth rather than the conventions of a literary genre (as in *Northanger Abbey* and *Jacques le fataliste*), the impact of his version is heightened through the reader's immediate familiarity with the standards against which he is tacitly being asked to measure this particular vision. To that extent Byron is, even in so 'illicit' a work as *Don Juan*, using irony in a quite traditional way to say and show the contrary to what is meant. His Don Juan is no Don Juan in the accepted sense. Through his flagrant shortfall from his role, he is drastically cut to size, albeit in a good-humoured fashion. Byron's irony may be as reductive of Don Juan as Flaubert's is of Emma Bovary (or even more so), but his stance towards his naïve hero is consistently affectionate and his tone bantering, in contrast to Flaubert's ambivalence and bitterness. That 'continual banter and mockery', as T. S. Eliot realised, 'serve as an admirable antacid to the high-falutin which in earlier romances tends to upset the reader's stomach'.[10] By means of that 'antacid' of irony *Don Juan* 'strips off the tinsel of *Sentiment*'.[11] So one of the functions of its irony is to separate grandiose emotionalising from sardonic humour, romance from realism, semblance from truth – not 'truth universally acknowledged' with a capital 'T' and an aura of the absolute, as might exist for Jane Austen, but a modest and relative truth, nonetheless for all its modesty more authentic than that of romance.

3

By recasting the Don Juan myth into 'a modern subject' (4, vi, p. 136) set firmly around 1790, Byron has turned a legendary tale into a vehicle for the social comment that dominates the later cantos. After canto 7 young Juan begins to lose his resemblance to the picaro he had originally been to serve instead as 'a lens for focussing and illuminating the actions of others'.[12] In canto 13 he appears only marginally as the house-guest of Lord and Lady Amundeville, whose country estate rituals form the principal subject. As Juan moves out of the romance realms of Spain, Turkey, and Russia through his whirlwind tour of Europe into the contemporary English scene, his role in the structure of the work is modified. In the closing cantos, written in 1822–3, almost five years after the opening ones, there is a perceptible change in pace and tempo. So much so that one critic conjectures that 'it is not quite misleading to speak of "two *Don Juans*" '.[13] This extreme though cautiously worded opinion alludes to the common view of *Don Juan* as a narrative that starts in the ironic mode and modulates into satire.

Byron himself lent substance to this interpretation when he wrote to John Murray in December 1822: '*Don Juan* will be known by and bye, for what it is intended a *Satire* on *abuses* of the present states of Society – and not an eulogy of vice.'[14] The context and thrust of this declaration are of the utmost importance. Although the emphasis seems to fall on '*Satire*' and '*abuses*' because Byron underlined these words, his ulterior aim was not to characterise *Don Juan* as a satire, but rather to defend his work against the charges of indecency that were being levelled against it. Byron's purpose becomes clearer from the rest of that letter which is less frequently cited than the phrase about '*Satire*': 'it may be now and then voluptuous: I can't help that. Ariosto is worse; Smollett – ten times worse; and Fielding no better. No Girl will ever be seduced by reading D. J.: no, no; she will go to Little's poems and Rousseau's romans for that, and even to the immaculate De Stael; they will encourage her, and not the Don, who laughs at that, and – and – most other things'. When Byron's description of his work as a '*Satire*' is returned to its context, a different perspective emerges. Granted that his defence may in itself have been a subterfuge; granted that Byron may not have weighed the import of the term. Nevertheless there are grounds for reserve here.

Given that caveat, it must also be conceded that there is undeniable evidence for a reading of *Don Juan* as satire. Few critics nowadays would go as far as the categoric contention:

'Lord Byron was primarily a satirist',[15] although even so subtle a mind as Karl Kroeber envisages *Don Juan* chiefly as a satire, maintaining that in the last cantos 'we find his irony to be no longer merely a weapon of attack but also a means of illuminating. His satire is no longer abusiveness; it becomes a means of evaluation'.[16] That, I think, is open to question, as is Lovell's thesis that 'Byron repeatedly used irony as a qualifying device within the larger frame of his satire'.[17] The opposite is more likely the case.

The arguments in favour of satire are strongest in certain areas. The Dedication, for example, is 'a brilliant, self-contained satire in the Augustan manner'.[18] Similarly, the accounts of the siege and the battle (in cantos 7 and 8) are unmitigated attacks on the vileness of warfare and the savagery of man to man that exclude the ambivalences of irony. In regard to the portrayal of English society the situation is less simple. Byron was motivated by 'an acute animosity' which 'sharpened his powers of observation'[19] and fed his lashing tongue. He examines the basic institutions and social arrangements of upper-class life: conventional marriage, the workings of the law, politics, courtship and love. In every instance, 'what he holds up to ridicule is some attempt to restrain life, to force and bind it into some narrow, permanent form'.[20] For what Byron abhorred was 'the mathematical' (1, xii, p. 12) in all its aspects as control, rigidity and consequently sterility, the opponent of that freedom of spirit to which he aspired as a poet and as a human being. His celebration in *Don Juan* of the growth, openness, expansion and abundance inherent in life necessarily entailed an attack on stasis, retrogradation, closed minds and systems, bigotry, and sterility. His onslaught against confining restrictions certainly has the vehement passion associated with satire.

But despite his contention:

> For like an agéd aunt, or tiresome friend,
> A rigid guardian or a zealous priest,   .
> My Muse by exhortation means to mend
> All people, at all times, and in most places (12, xxxix, p. 344)

– despite this explicit contention, the corrective impulse fundamental to satire is not uppermost to Byron. Again the context – the comically unpleasant similes of the first two lines and the hyperbole of the last – significantly limits the force of the central claim. Byron's 'Muse' has the insight to perceive the complexities and confusions of men's behaviour and the indignation to inveigh against the '*abuses* of the present states of Society'. What is missing, however, is the restorative vision that would recreate some positive values to replace the falsehoods and hypocrisies that are exposed and rejected. No such alternative is ever implied, no moral definition takes place, and there is no sign of any underlying belief in ends and goals, let alone in the mendability of the world. In this respect Byron is much closer to Flaubert than to Jane Austen. In all the many places visited in *Don Juan* the human condition is shown to be – *mutatis mutandis* – disorderly and vicious. Even the island idyll *à la* Rousseau is rudely and tragically disrupted after a brief spell of harmony. While Byron's 'negative penetration'[21] is brilliantly successful in piercing the frauds and deflating the devices of pretence, he can champion in its stead nothing other than an incoherent freedom.

Though the impotence of the satire in *Don Juan* must ultimately be linked to Byron's vision, its immediate source is the inadequacy of Juan himself to carry the ethical and intellectual weight that would be required to fulfil a satiric purpose. His lack of moral fibre and the total absence of ratiocination on his part are fatal drawbacks in the later cantos – at least in so far as they are to be read as satire. The passivity that was appropriate and even necessary for the inversion of the Don Juan legend becomes a liability within the framework of satire. Juan is merely the blunt recipient of events, always accommodating to a situation with a survivor's instinct, never stopping to assess, to reflect, or indeed to wonder. The contrast with those other famous travellers in foreign lands, with the nimble, reasoning wit of Usbek in Montesquieu's *Lettres persanes* or with Swift's Gulliver brings out Juan's feebleness as the carrier of satire.

Just as Juan drifts in inertia, the narrating voice hovers in the ambivalences of irony. His is not the confident self-assertion of the world-improving satirist who can set himself on a pedestal to judge others. Seeing that the righteous are no better than he, and knowing that there are no infallible remedies for the ills of the world, he can at most rebel and attack. *Don Juan* therefore has the semblance of satire, but not its essential moral core. Beneath the satiric surface there is a deep substratum of ironic uncertainty. It may well be, as Roger Salomon has so shrewdly ventured, that Byron 'realized in *Don Juan* that the narrative role of satirist or moralist is a form of heroic endeavor (literary knight-errantry, so to speak) subject to the same strong ironic qualification as other forms of heroism'.[22] Accordingly both the central figure, Juan, and the various social organisations through which he is propelled are – to borrow another vivid phrase from Salomon – 'immersed, so to speak, in the solution, half acid, half formaldehyde, of irony'.[23] It is that questioning, exposing, debunking irony that holds together the multiple facets of *Don Juan.*

4

Within the fiction then irony is used in the traditional Johnsonian sense to imply the contrary to what seems overtly to be said, and thus to show the disparity between appearance and reality. The customary literary and rhetorical devices of the mode are exploited with extraordinary linguistic inventiveness in an often dazzling display of wit. The recurrence of the same ironic features throughout the seventeen cantos is indeed a stronger unifying factor than the rather colourless figure of the picaresque hero.

The basic ironic structure of *Don Juan*, dependent on the inversion of the Don Juan legend, is reinforced by the glaring contrast between this Juan's perpetual naïvety and the sated cynicism typical of his mythic namesake. Plain John Johnson, 'clever' and 'cunning' in his sense of self-preservation, is an obvious foil to that 'mere novice' (8, xxxv and xxxvi, p. 254) who scrapes by more through good luck than good calculation. The fleeting juxtaposition with Johnson fulfils the same function as the sustained antithesis between the hero and the narrator. The ardent freshness of youth is set off against the disillusioned worldly-wisdom of middle age in the disjunction between the innocent, romantic, experiencing protagonist and the reflective, ironic, experienced narrator. As a secondary ironic substructure this supplements the primary Don Juan configuration, though the two evolve by different means; the first uses the myth as a constant yardstick, while the second hinges on a series of time-frames whereby Juan's present, i.e. the period of the story

(1789–91) is in counterpoint with the narrator's present, i.e. the actual period of writing (1818–23) and to some degree also with various phases of the narrator's past.

This dual ironic structure supports a long sequence of ironies of situation, many of them springing from Juan's involvement with women. Other instances are unrelated to this leitmotif, as if to suggest that the ironies dogging Juan are, in their ubiquity, typical of human existence. Thus, to take two widely divergent examples: the island idyll with its fairy-tale atmosphere is inserted into the sardonically tough environment of piracy; in an entirely different setting of apparently utmost civilisation Juan is robbed at the very moment he is singing the praise of England's law and order (11, x, p. 318).

Even more prominent than these ironies of situation is the pervasive rhetoric of irony which has been amply documented and analysed.[24] The ease and verbal ingenuity of the narrating voice that prides itself on 'conversational facility' (15, xx, p. 408) belies the virtuoso degree of control beneath that seemingly careless rattling on. It is as if 'the narrator, not the hero, possesses the hurricane energy of Don Giovanni, which, redirected from sex into art, is expressed in the hectic and irregular sportive velocity of the language'.[25] He delights in every kind of linguistic gymnastics: puns, epigrams, double meanings, renovated clichés, astonishing metaphors and breathtakingly clever rhymes. For ironic contrast he makes strikingly effective use of incongruous juxtapositions, often combined with a pattern of hyperbole and anti-climax that drops its characteristic shock in the second half of the pairing:

> He learned the arts of riding, fencing, gunnery,
> And how to scale a fortress – or a nunnery. (1, xxxviii, p. 18)

> – He was the mildest mannered man
> That ever scuttled ship or cut a throat; (3, xli, p. 116)

> Let us have Wine and Women, Mirth and Laughter,
> Sermons and soda-water the day after. (2, clxxviii, p. 99)

> Their union was a model to behold,
> Sincere and noble, – conjugal, but cold. (14, lxxxvi, p. 400)

Sometimes the irony resides in the order of the pairing, implying a sly comment on the priorities and values of Juan's world:

There's nought so much the spirit calms
    As rum and true religion; (2, xxxiv, p. 66)

Until each high heroic bosom burned
    For cash and conquest (7, lxiv, p. 240)

In many of these examples the ironic impact is intensified by the close alliance forged between the incongruous elements by the rhyme. It may be the brief play of an internal rhyme:

But Juan was a bachelor – of arts,
    and parts, – and hearts (11, xlviii, p. 326)

or an extended conceit:

Oh! ye immortal Gods! what is Theogony?
    Oh! thou, too, mortal man! what is Philanthropy?
Oh! World, which was and is, what is Cosmogony?
    Some people have accused me of Misanthropy;
And yet I know no more than the mahogany
    That forms this desk, of what they mean; – *Lykanthropy*
I comprehend, for without transformation
Men become wolves on any occasion. (9, xx, p. 282)

Here the rhyme acts as a tool for an ironic undermining as sarcastic fun is made of 'Theogony', 'Philanthropy' and 'Cosmogony' through the alliteration with 'Misanthropy', 'mahogony' and 'Lykanthropy', a tour de force of reductive associationism. Equally spectacular is the handling of the final couplet of the *ottava rima* stanza: normally the first six lines rush forward to the expected security of a summarising resting-place in the couplet; whereas in *Don Juan* that summary, instead of bringing the anticipated closure, unties the stanza in the ironic reversal of its stinging tail:

In thoughts like these true Wisdom may discern
    Longings sublime, and aspirations high,
Which some are born with, but the most part learn
    To plague themselves withal, they know not why:
'T was strange that one so young should thus concern
    His brain about the action of the sky;
If *you* think 't was Philosophy that this did,
I can't help thinking puberty assisted. (1, xciii, p. 30)

The traditional practices of irony are inventively adapted and expanded to suit the purposes of *Don Juan*. Yet by and large, for an essentially 'illicit' book, the ironic procedures are remarkably 'proper'.

5

What makes *Don Juan* 'illicit' above all is its irony *of* fiction. Apart from the ironic undercutting to which the hero and society are subjected within the fiction, there is another tier of irony extraneous to the fictional action, at the expense of the processes of narration. And just as the Don Juan myth serves as the fulcrum of irony within the fiction, so there is a parallel context for the irony of fiction in the conventions of the epic form. *Don Juan* thus has two normative frames – the Don Juan myth and the epic form – both of which are fractured by irony. Their function within the economy of the work as a whole is precisely as a springboard for irony, and as an implicit standard against which to assess its disruptive inroads.

Don Juan is called 'this Epic' (16, iii, p. 426), and again and again, from the first canto to the last, conspicuous references are made to its alleged epic character as repeated reminders of the genre in which it purports to be written. The narrator emphasises this already in the exposition of intent:

> My poem's epic, and is meant to be
> Divided in twelve books; each book containing
> With Love, and War, a heavy gale at sea,
> A list of ships, and captains, and kings reigning,
> New characters; the episodes are three:
> A panoramic view of Hell's in training,
> After the style of Virgil and of Homer,
> So that the name of Epic's no misnomer. (1, cc, p. 54)

In the middle he assures us that he is keeping his word:

> Reader! I have kept my word, – at least so far
> As the first Canto promised. You have now
> Had sketches of Love – Tempest – Travel – War, –
> All very accurate, you must allow,

And *Epic*, if plain truth should prove no bar;
  For I have drawn much less with a long bow
Than my forerunners. Carelessly I sing,
But Phoebus lends me now and then a string.
                          (8, cxxxviii, p. 276)

Through these reiterated appeals to 'the ancient epic laws' (5, clix, p. 196) and through the patently unjustifiable claims to conform to them, the evident disregard for those conventions is in effect being advertised. The boldest instance of this tactic comes at the opening of canto 3: 'HAIL, Muse! *et cetera* – ' (3, i, p. 107), a travesty of the traditional invocation which, like the frequent allusions to Horace, Virgil, Aristotle and the Classical canons, serves to draw attention to the boisterous infringements of those norms.

I'll call the work 'Longinus o'er a Bottle,
Or, Every Poet his *own* Aristotle'. (1, cciv, p. 55)

Byron is 'his *own* Aristotle' in turning the customary epic conventions upside down. *Don Juan* does not have a hero of imposing stature; it does not show deeds of great valour performed with superhuman courage; it does not have a style of sustained elevation; nor is it recounted with objectivity. It deals with the perennial epic themes, 'Love–Tempest–Travel–War,–' (8, cxxxviii, p. 276) and pays lip-service to the acknowledged formulae such as the invocation to the Muse, but only to capsize them into burlesque. Burlesque, derived from the Italian word 'burla' meaning 'ridicule', is here taken as consisting 'in the use or imitation of serious matter or manner, made amusing by the incongruity between style and subject'.[26] This applies exactly to Byron's ironic handling of epic matters: the hero of *Don Juan* is a passive youth manipulated by a succession of scheming women; his deeds of valour are submission to whatever befalls him; the style substitutes colloquial familiarity for loftiness, and there is not the slightest pretence of objectivity. Even the intrusion of supernatural forces into the action, in the guise of the ghost, is a humorous burlesque, for that apparition is none other than 'the phantom of her frolic Grace – Fitz-Fulke' (16, cxxiii, p. 454). It is doubtful whether Byron really 'set out deliberately to write an anti-*Iliad*',[27] as has been asserted. Perhaps it is more accurate to call *Don Juan* 'both a romantic epic and a realistic satire'[28] – both, or neither, or rather none of these, for it so resolutely resists the usual literary categories.[29] One attractive solution is to envisage *Don Juan* (as I have chosen to do) as the 'metrical Novel' that Wordsworth recognised as a favourite species of narrative in his day.

Besides the conventions of epic, its actual practices are also subverted by irony. The narrative is characterised not by epic formality and coherence but by endless 'unsettling disruptions'.[30] The classical strictness of plot with its chain of cause and effect is abandoned for a loosely linked, freely associative process of accretion; *Don Juan* 'is not a poem that develops, it is a poem that is added to'.[31] That it was written in fits and starts is well-known; Byron was literally exploring the nature of his work as he went along. When asked in 1819 whether he meant to continue it, he answered bluntly: 'how should I know?'[32] Two months later he seems to be elaborating on that brusque phrase when he writes to his publisher: 'You ask me for the plan of Donny Johnny I *have* no plan – I *had* no plan – but I had or have materials. . . . If it don't take, I will leave it off where it is, with all due respect to the Public. . . . Why Man the Soul of such writing is its license – at least the *liberty* of that license, if one likes.'[33] The license to add, to juxtapose, to digress, to comment at will contravenes the austerity of the epic prescript in which local episodes and descriptive excursions must be subordinate to an architecture purposeful in its internal cohesion. Whether *Don Juan* has aesthetic self-consistency and unity is a matter of debate. Its easy-going principles of organisation are the antithesis to the stringent functionalism of *Madame Bovary*, where every detail, every word, almost every comma has its allotted part to play. The 'springy random haphazard galloping nature'[34] of its method of narration involved an enormous risk in its iconoclastic defiance of narrative norms and expectations. Yet it was for that very quality, for having discovered 'what one has looked for in vain – an elastic shape which will hold whatever you choose to put into it'[35] that Virginia Woolf admired Byron.

That elasticity is highly conspicuous in the language of *Don Juan*, whose combination of the conversationally offhand with the elaborately rhetorical is a stinging affront to the epic ideal of unbroken loftiness. The narrator does indeed 'rattle on exactly as I'd talk' (15, xix, p. 408), the '*Improvvisatore*' (15, xx, p. 408) without peer, stringing his tale together with 'and so' and 'but then', and interspersing it with flippant bavardage. This so-called 'medley' style, which Byron noted quite early in Ariosto and later derived from Pulci, gave him the liberty for which he yearned: the liberty of that license manifest in the inconsequences, the outrageous rhymes, the colloquialisms, the experimentation with the *ottava rima* stanza. The import of this medley style has evoked much speculation as to Byron's intentions: is this a conscious rebuttal of Coleridge's ideal of organic form?[36] or an expression of his opposition to Pope's and Fielding's world view?[37] or an acknowledgement 'that the complex and varied "nature" external to the poet is not fully knowable and therefore not subject to his mastery'?[38] or, more simply, another facet of his rebellious mockery of epic orderliness? These alternatives are not mutually exclusive. On the contrary, they reveal the kind of fortuitousness, the awareness of multiple options – and of ironic ambivalences – that Byron so successfully evoked in converse to the well regulated certitudes of the epic.

Ultimately it is not just the conventions, the practices and the art of the epic that are ironically subverted in *Don Juan*, it is the whole meaning of epic and its system of values. Byron's work has been deemed an 'Epic of Negation':[39] it is down-to-earth, unheroic, with an aimless protagonist who is devoid of any mission and whose depature into the world is marred by the need for flight from disgrace as well as by sea-sickness. The Dedication to Southey, the official spokesman for the English poetic establishment, is, in its bitterness towards false prophets, a startling reversal of the usual epic rhetoric. The Horatian epigraph too, 'Difficile est proprie communia dicere', has been interpreted as 'granting the impossibility of treating his polished patricians as traditional epic heroes'.[40] In attempting the epic genre in the early nineteenth century Byron must have realised the conflicting demands of imitation and originality. His solution was to resort to irony, in itself a doubled-edged weapon. For on the one hand it allowed him to make a creatively original use of imitation; on the other, however, it denoted an implicit avowal of his self-consciousness as a writer – a surprising and paradoxical concession on the part of one who cultivated demonstrations of spontaneity. It is here, in the tension between spontaneity and self-consciousness, that a central axis of the irony of *Don Juan* is to be found.

6

The narrator's incessant reflections on his writing are eloquent evidence of his ingrained self-consciousness. The keynote is sounded immediately in that opening phrase, 'I want a hero', and in the rejection of various possible heroes because their names are 'not at all adapted to my rhymes' (1, iii, p. 10). Throughout *Don Juan* the flow of the narrative is repeatedly interrupted and the illusion broken by parenthetical excuses about the rhyme:

> (The rhyme obliges me to this; sometimes
> Monarchs are less imperative than rhymes) – (5, lxxvii, p. 178)

> (I needs must rhyme with dove,
>   That good old steam-boat which keeps verses moving
> 'Gainst reason – Reason ne'er was hand-and-glove
>   With rhyme, but always lent less to improving
> The sound than sense) – (9, lxxiv, p. 294)

There is obviously a certain comic self-irony in the fact that a rhymer of such dizzying inventiveness should so often be lamenting the 'extremity of my rhyme's distress' (14, lxxv, p. 397). These complaints and excuses, like the striking manipulation of language through puns, foreign borrowings, and slang, are continual reminders that a device is being used for the making of a literary artifact. Through the narrator's consciousness of the processes of writing, the reader too comes to perceive the fiction as an artistic fiction being created in his presence. That is the effect also of the comments on the grammatical constructions:

>   few are slow
>   In thinking that their enemy is beat
> (or *beaten*, if you insist on grammar, though
>   I never think about it in a heat.) (7, xlii, p. 236)

and on the metaphors:

> I hate to hunt down a tired metaphor (13, xxxvi, p. 364)

or on the similes:

> My similes are gathered in a heap,
> So pick and choose – (6, lxviii, p. 215)

The language is constantly calling attention to its own powers
and limitations. In this sense *Don Juan* can rightly be called 'a
linguistic performance . . . poetic language as *action,* as *process*'.[41]
As a medium of communication the language of *Don Juan* is endowed
with the utmost flexibility. It is the plaything of the narrator who
sports with it at will, twisting, turning, and contorting words and
phrases. Such handling of language implies no great respect for
its canons, but no real distrust in its efficacy either. Words are
instilled with whatever meaning suits the moment, evidently on
the assumption that the reader will have the agility to go along
with these capers. But never is the reader allowed to forget for
any length of reading time that a text is here being made before
his eyes, and that its design as well as its wording is wide open to
change at the whim of the creator-narrator.

As a result of this narrative strategy, the reader is drawn into
the problems presented by the writing process, and at the same
time driven to detachment from the tale he is reading. This
paradox projected onto the reader runs parallel to a similar
contradiction implicit in the text where the reiterated, self-
conscious references to the writing-in-progress appear to
contravene the narrator's vaunted spontaneity. It becomes
apparent that if improvisation is a matter of inspiration, it is not
without its own peculiar difficulties.[42] The narrator's 'Muse is a
capricious elf' (4, lxxiv, p. 151); so much so that the perplexities
of creativity form one of the salient themes of the writing. For this
reason, as Hazlitt[43] already recognised, *Don Juan* is 'a poem
written about itself'. Although the subject is treated in a jocular
tone, there is nonetheless an undertow of anxiety. For, as Walter
Jackson Bate[44] has impressed on us, the poets of the late
eighteenth and early nineteenth century (and even more so their
successors) were faced with such a burden of irreconcilable
demands – for 'originality', for 'sincerity', for loyalty to past
tradition – as to drive them to a self-conscious irony as a defence
mechanism. The irony which in Jane Austen and Flaubert is
turned outwards against the characters is in Byron, Jean-Paul,
Diderot and Sterne directed inwards onto the writer himself as he

reflects on his own work. So irony, which had traditionally been intrinsic to the fiction, assumes a metafictional dimension as an extraneous questioning of the text and of the very possibility of writing at all.

In *Don Juan* the two types of irony co-exist. The narrator functions, like Jane Austen and Flaubert, as a superior possessor of hidden knowledge to expose obliquely the protagonists' limitations and shortcomings. In this role, as the older, experienced, somewhat wry but largely sympathetic observer of Juan's antics, he remains relatively discreet, even if he is far from the God-like invisibility to which Flaubert aspired. Along certain stretches, when the plot becomes particularly gripping, as in the shipwreck (canto 2) he disappears behind the action. But then he will suddenly drop the mask and step out of the narrative to become highly visible as he speaks in another voice, that of the first-person narrator. What he is in fact doing is to don a second, different mask, that of the rattle-brained chatterbox. This persona, with his vociferous and intrusive 'I', is that of the improviser shaping the narrative. It is he who presents and arranges the story, unifying it through his tone, his timing and his presence that is 'Changeable too – yet somehow "*Idem semper*" ' (17, xi, p. 457). There is nothing that he enjoys more than teasing his reader, telling him: 'Perhaps you think, . . .' for one whole stanza only to hit back at the beginning of the next with: 'You're wrong' (3, xl and xli, p. 116). He loves to surprise and shock, to play the *enfant terrible*. More than the putative hero this is the figure who stands in the foreground of *Don Juan*, attracting the greatest attention. Yet he is basically 'as much a mock-hero as his youthful protagonist, with the distinction, however, that he is self-conscious rather than naive'.[45] For his art as an improviser feeds on 'a consciousness of his own powers, his own elocution – the wondering and applauding audience, – all conspire to give him confidence',[46] as Byron himself put it. He stands therefore in full view *beside* the story, unlike such traditional ironists as Jane Austen or Flaubert who were behind or within the narrative. By contrast, the self-conscious ironist watches himself at work, enacting the rite and at the same time evaluating his performance. He becomes both subject and object, creator and critic, and in this dual role he discloses the ambivalences of his own product with as much acuity and rather less tolerance than he shows towards the ineptitude of his hero:

But I am apt to grow too metaphysical:
    'The time is out of joint,' – and so am I;
I quite forget this poem's merely quizzical,
    And deviate into matters rather dry.
I n'er decide what I shall say, and this I call
    Much too poetical: men should know why
They write, and for what end; but, note or text,
I never know the word which will come next. (9, xli, p. 286)

The narrator's self-consciousness is the instrument for the second
tier of irony in *Don Juan*, where the fiction *qua* fiction comes under
constant scrutiny. The innocent world within the fiction is thrust
into a relative and indeed endangered position through the
pointers to its fictionality. So the metafictional irony limits the
force of the representation, while simultaneously making it
transparent as a representation, thereby indicating its additional
status as an aesthetic entity.

7

The essentially fictive nature of the tale is underscored by the
digressions which keep on breaking the illusion in a manner that
would he wholly inadmissible in a 'proper' book. The narrator
does begin by apologising for this 'fault' of his:

But let me to my story: I must own,
    If I have any fault, it is digression,
Leaving my people to proceed alone,
    While I soliloquise beyond expression;
But these are my addresses from the throne,
    Which put off business to the ensuing session: –
Forgetting each omission is a loss to
The world, not quite so great as Ariosto. (3, xcvi, p. 131)

But as the narrative unfolds, no attempt is made to conceal or
correct this 'fault'. On the contrary, the reader's attention is
again and again drawn to the narrator's wanderings either by
such phrases as 'But I'm digressing' (3, cx, p. 134), or 'Kind
reader! pass / This long parenthesis' (6, lvi, p. 212), or 'I'm "at
my old lunes" – digression' (13, xii, p. 358) or alternately by the
narrator's own exhortations to himself to return to his tale: 'But

let us to the story as before' (5, xxxix, p. 170), 'But to resume' (5, lxii, p. 175), 'To our theme' (11, vii, p. 317), 'And now to business' (12, xxiii, p. 341). The digressions disrupt the Don Juan story not only dramatically but also stylistically through the conversational voice of the whimsical story-teller, and temporally through the intrusion of the present time of narration into the past of narrated time. In many instances the substance of the digression can be related thematically to the narrative strand as it grows by free mental association. However, the primary function of the digressions is not to serve as comment on, or elaboration of the Don Juan material, but rather as a continual reminder of its standing as fictive material.

The digressions, therefore, distance the reader from the tale as the narrator's thoughts are interposed between him and the protagonists. Often digression within digression takes us even further from the action and makes us almost forget it because the digression can be more interesting than the plot: 'But to my subject – let me see – what was it? – ' (3, lxxxi, p. 125). In the long run the Don Juan story, already seriously undermined by the ironic inversion of the myth, is drastically reduced in importance in the economy of *Don Juan* as a whole.[47] Through the ironic treatment of the legend and equally much through the displacement of the plot by digression, the overt content of *Don Juan* is, as it were, depreciated. The entire centre of gravity is shifted. The narrator telling the story, beginning with that 'I want a hero', seems at first a framework of the Don Juan tale, just as the 'we' at the opening of *Madame Bovary* formed a frame for the narrative of Emma's life and death. But in *Don Juan* appearance is at odds with reality, in form as well as in theme. In fact the form itself of the work becomes a vital demonstration of its theme. For the narrator dislodges the hero; the frame is more riveting than the picture it contains, and *Don Juan* is truly 'a poem written about itself' – not in the pejorative sense in which Hazlitt meant it but in the modern connotation of metafiction. The Don Juan story is relegated to a subsidiary position, hardly more than a pretext for engaging in the act of narration, while the real focus is on the creative process, on which the improviser dwells with such pressing insistence. Accordingly he favours the openness of the undirected digression because it gives him the space and the time to reflect, to meditate, to reconsider, to create experimentally, and to re-create.

What then is one to make of this radical reversal which turns *Don Juan* into an 'illicit' book? Is it just a frolicsome game? Sometimes the narrator is certainly 'having intellectual fun',[48] and his irony is a playful teasing as in his sudden assertion in canto 12 (liv, p. 348): 'But now I will begin my poem'. It is hard (though critics have occasionally attempted it) to see this as anything other than an ironic joke. Mostly, however, beneath the witty capers there is a substratum of earnest. 'In mine irregularity of chime' (15, xx, p. 408) the narrator is, by his defiance of narrative norms, asserting his freedom of self-expression as an artist. To take 'at least the *liberty* of that license, if one likes'[49] represents an active protest against the social and literary restrictiveness that is under attack in *Don Juan*.

But if this is 'intellectual fun', it is also intellectual torture. For the disruption of norms entails, too, the erosion of certainties, just as improvisation, while capturing life's fluxional nature, begets also a disconcerting sense of the insecurity of things. The jolting discontinuity of *Don Juan* is a disturbing indication of the fundamental instability of the narrative as of the universe. The narrator's presence, far from functioning as an authoritative organising centre, actually generates disorder. The firm authorial control, an artistic and moral necessity to Jane Austen and to Flaubert, is cast off by the Byronic narrator. This does not mean that he lacks command over his creation. It is hardly warranted to conclude that 'Byron dramatizes successive failures of the will to control and direct a sequence of events in such a way as to bring it to order, and he includes among these a significant and continuous failure of his own.'[50] What is dramatised in *Don Juan* is not a personal or artistic failure on Byron's part, but his perception of the world as resistant to control and defiant of orderliness. What is embodied in the shattering of illusion, the self-conscious intrusions, as well as the digressions, is the fragility of the fictive microcosm in its subjection to the haphazardness of the macrocosm.

8

The irony of *Don Juan* thus opens out in ever widening concentric circles. It starts within the fiction with an inversion of the Don Juan myth which illustrates the discrepancy between appearance and reality endemic to human existence. This dominant ironic theme is reflected in the mode of narration in its infraction of specific epic canons and in its demonstrative violation of narrative conventions. These concrete manifestations of the derangement of the expected order lead to a third sort of ironic disarray at the ontological and epistemological level.

To Byron 'what is here' on this earth, as he put it in *Childe Harold's Pilgrimage* (4, cv) is a vast spectacle of incongruences that testify to the uncertainty of all things. Mobility is a recurrent and key feature of *Don Juan*: the mobility of the hero ready to be controlled by any will imposed on him; the mobility of the women eager to follow the impulse of the moment; the mobility of the narrating voice as it improvises its 'epic', and the mobility of aesthetic form in accommodation to its creator's changing fancy. The impression of flux springs alike from the bizarre succession of accidental linkages within the action and from the fortuitous movement of the text as a whole. Its temporal shuffling, together with its spatial vagrancy, is symptomatic of the pervasive restlessness of a realm in which human relationships are no more stable than physical objects. The careful disposition of the perspective and the premeditated design, so important to *Pride and Prejudice* and to *Madame Bovary*, are matters of indifference to *Don Juan*. This is generally attributed to its improvisational character: 'it was essentially an improvisation, its purpose and its direction shifting and veering and evolving according to the whims and needs of the particular moment at which it was being written. Obviously this is a fundamental reason why it has been such an exasperatingly slippery poem to pin down'.[51] Certainly, slipperiness is an outcome of improvisation; however, this in turn is a precipitate of Byron's underlying scepticism. *Don Juan* cannot be pinned down because Byron could not and would not pin anything down. Pinning down is tantamount to mathematical confinement. Its opposite is mobility, and mobility is achieved in *Don Juan* to a large extent by that endless flow of ironic qualifications that prevent any state or statement from ever becoming definitive. The rapid multiplication of perspectives produces on the one hand an exhilarating awareness of freedom, but on the other an ominous sense of disorientation. Hence the frequent complaint that *Don Juan* lacks direction, that its structure, imagery and diction convey the 'irreconcilable encounter of conflicting attitudes and points of view'.[52] To reconcile the contradictory elements is the aim of such interpretative approaches as that of George Ridenour[53] who proposes the myth of the Fall as a means of organising *Don Juan* into a manageable coherence. According to Ridenour, 'the basic problem of *Don Juan* for the modern reader' amounts to the question: 'is *Don Juan* a chaos or a unity?' (p. 21). The alternative is fallacious insofar as a work of art may derive its unity from the principle of chaotic disorderliness governing it; for disorder may in itself be a form of order. What is more, the perception of ontological disorderliness and the assent to aesthetic disorderliness as a reflection of such a perception are not to be condemned as negative attributes – or else we would have to dismiss a large part of twentieth century literature, art, and music. *Don Juan* seems chaotic only so long as efforts are made to press it into the kind of order that is foreign – and anathema – to it, the very order in fact against which it was protesting. It resists reduction into a rational, comprehensible grid of explanation in the same way as it spurns established designs. In this context its pervasive, multi-faceted irony is of paramount importance as a cipher for its subversive repudiation of accepted systems, mythological, social, and literary.

If the ontological difficulty is embodied in the form of *Don Juan*, the epistemological dilemma is explicitly voiced as a gospel of incertitude that is first sounded in the opening declaration and that grows more strident in the latter half of the work. After copious illustrations of the mutability of all relationships, the unreliability of all judgements, and the fluidity of all positions in the human tragi-comedy, the crowning question is put point-blank:

> When we know what all are, we must bewail us,
> But ne'ertheless I hope it is no crime
> To laugh at *all* things – for I wish to know
> *What*, after *all*, are *all* things – but a *show*? (7, ii, p. 227)

'To laugh at *all* things', 'to under-rate and scoff' (7, iii, p. 227) is the only way to handle a quandary that is regarded as beyond solution. This is neither to belittle the gravity of the problem nor to advocate casuistical freedom or unresponsive disengagement, except that such a stance is the sole option 'in this scene of all-confessed inanity' (7, vi, p. 228). ' "To know that nothing could be known'' ' (7, v, p. 227) brings the inevitable recognition of 'the nothingness of Life' (7, v, p. 228), of a world without 'Truth, the grand desideratum' (7, lxxxi, p. 244), or faith, or any of the absolute, transcendental beliefs that buttress ethical values and social institutions. What is adumbrated here is the abyss of negativity, and the references to Socrates, Plato, Newton, Solomon, as well as to religious teaching, place the crisis in its appropriate context of seriousness. That it is nonetheless shrugged off with the facetious jest that all these authorities 'knew this life was not worth a potato' (7, iv, p. 227) is not so much a sign of levity as of resignation in the face of an impenetrable enigma. In the later cantos the note of cynicism deepens:

> '*Que sçais-je?*' was the motto of Montaigne,
> As also of the first academicians:
> That all is dubious which man may attain,
> Was one of their most favourite positions.
> There's no such thing as certainty, that's plain
> As any of Mortality's conditions;
> So little do we know what we're about in
> This world, I doubt if doubt itself be doubting. (9, xvii, p. 281)

Finally, towards the close, the narrator concedes that he has given up, leaving the 'mystery' 'to those who are fond of solving doubt' (16, lxii, p. 441), and in the penultimate stanza of the entire work: 'I leave the thing a problem, like all things: – ' (17, xiii, p. 457). In a universe of unpredictable incongruences, ironic sensibility has had to modulate at every point whatever emotional or intellectual commitment might be made until only ambivalence, paradox, and irony itself are left.

This aspect of *Don Juan*, so long repressed by the many critics intent on squeezing the work into some comforting schema, has been trenchantly confronted by Michael G. Cooke, who concludes that 'Byron is creating the recognition of disorder where it has been blinked or denied, exploring the terms of a truer fidelity to the demands and interdictions of our knowledge, our judgements, our aspirations'.[54] Thus 'the whole of *Don Juan*' represents 'a multiform statement of obligatory irresolution'.[55] This 'obligatory irresolution' is close to the paradoxicality that Friedrich Schlegel posited as the philosophical foundation of literary irony. The problem of doubt and knowledge, skirted by

Jane Austen and happily dissolved in a rainbow of romance, is a
baffling impasse for Byron, to whom infinite doubt is the only
authentic form of truth.

Baffling, irksome, perhaps even sad and rather frightening;
but this does not make *Don Juan* 'a sad and frightening poem'.[56] It
may well 'skirmish endlessly against protean falsehood' 'without
a flag to fight under, without goal or reward',[57] with a
pragmatism that distances it from satire. But while its irony is the
hatchet for demolition (as in *Madame Bovary*), it serves too as a
rescue ladder to climb out of the crumbling edifice. For the
detachment of the ironist in his capacity to see the ambiguity of
all phenomena can induce that balance, however precarious,
between laughter and despair that is the characteristic timbre
of Byron's narrating voice. So the irony that makes him see
through the various pretences of the world to the core of
doubt also enables him to transmute the nihilism into something like Friedrich Schlegel's 'transzendentale Buffonerie'[58]
('transcendental buffoonery'). In this way irony acts as a force of
reconciliation that sanctions and nurtures the exercise of a
consistent – ironic – attitude towards a universe whose
inconsistencies invalidate all systems.

> But if a writer should be quite consistent,
> How could he possibly show things existent?
>   (15, lxxxvii, p. 423)

Since 'things existent' are inconsistent, the writer must needs
renounce the aim of establishing a consistent order in his fiction.
Instead, he must accede to the reigning mutability, yielding to it
in the shifts of a sharp, impish irony which is the idiom most
commensurate to a world ruled by sheer contingency.

In *Don Juan* irony is, therefore, at the heart of the work. It is the
theme as well as the mode of writing. And just as Byron uses a
medley of styles and covers a medley of topics, so also he has
recourse to a medley of ironies: the rhetorical irony of verbal wit,
the dramatic irony of structural reversal, the metafictional irony
of the self-conscious narrator, and the philosophical irony of
incertitude. Besides the simpler kinds of irony that involve only
two points – what seems and what is – *Don Juan* encompasses
more complex ambiguities that derive not merely from the
tension between two alternatives but from the cognition of an

infinite series of possibilities that reveal a multiplicity of perspectives which may complement each other, or cancel one another out. The act of definition, accomplished positively in *Pride and Prejudice* and negatively in *Madame Bovary*, remains in abeyance in *Don Juan*, where irony prevails as indeterminacy.

The formal and philosophical open-endedness of *Don Juan* is a curiously apposite comment on its 'illicit' nature. The persistent strength of its ironic vision inhibits neat enclosure into any finite pattern. Doubt undermines whatever is written, but even in the process of destruction it leaves space for further buoyant reconstruction. That *Don Juan* comes to no conclusion either in regard to its aesthetic shape or to its cognitive position is a testimony equally to despondency and to hope.

6 Jean Paul: *Flegeljahre*, 1804–5

> 'Der Dichter muss selber seine Handschrift
> verkehrt schreiben können, damit sie sich
> im Spiegel der Kunst durch die zweite
> Umkehrung leserlich zeige.'
>
> *Vorschule der Ästhetik*, #39

> ('The post must himself must be able to
> write his script in reverse, so that it should
> appear in legible form through the second
> inversion in the mirror of art.')

1

Who was Jean Paul anyway? The question is by no means as idle
as it may seem, nor is the answer simple. For 'Jean Paul' is the
most frequent but not the only name adopted by a German prose
writer born in 1763 and christened Johann Paul Friedrich
Richter. His first work, *Grönländische Prozesse* (*Greenland
Lawsuits*) appeared in 1783 under the signature 'R', while the
next, in 1789, *Auswahl aus des Teufels Papieren* (*Selections from the
Devil's Papers*) was signed 'J. P. F. Hasus'. Since both these
were topical satires, the anonymity may have had a practical
motivation. In the early 1790s he transmuted the native Johann
into its French equivalent, Jean, in homage to Jean Jacques
Rousseau whom he admired both as a poet and an educator, an
exemplar of that fusion of heart and head that was his own ideal.
It is under this modification of his given name that he is generally
known (he is listed in library catalogues under 'Richter'). But he
further differentiated between his everyday and his literary
persona by using just Jean Paul for the latter. Thus he was in the

habit of signing personal letters 'Richter' and poetic epistles 'Jean Paul'.[1] And it was as Jean Paul that he published a series of distinctive narratives beginning with *Schulmeisterlein Wutz* (*Schoolmaster Wutz*) and *Die unsichtbare Loge* (*The Invisible Lodge*) in 1793.

Yet the first edition of the *Flegeljahre* of 1804–5 gave Jean Paul Friedrich Richter as the author. Perhaps he opted for this form in this case because the novel was originally conceived as the 'Geschichte meines Zwillingsbruders'[2] ('story of my twin brother'), that twin being his poetic, i.e. Jean Paul, half. Later in the evolution of the work a figure was introduced who had abandoned his name – and, not by chance, it had been Friedrich Richter – in order to accept a legacy along with the testator's name; he in turn bequeaths his fortune to one of the twins on condition that he eventually assume his old name, Friedrich Richter. This play on names continues; according to an early sketch, the twins were to write a novel together under the title *Das Buch der Richter* (*The Book of Judges*). These puns and jokes, whimsical though they seem, raise searching questions about identity and judgement.

The profusion of Jean Paul's pseudonyms, far from being an idiosyncratic game, expresses an awareness of the vexatory plurality of the self; this fluctuating perception of his own persona and role signals an urgent concern with the essence of being and, specifically, with the dichotomy between appearance and reality as embodied in the relationship of persona to name. Jean Paul's intense consciousness of himself as an entelechy is documented in his startling account of an early childhood experience:

> An einem Vormittag stand ich als ein sehr junges Kind unter der Haustüre und sah links nach der Holzlege, als auf einmal das innere Gesicht 'ich bin ein Ich' wie ein Blitzstrahl vom Himmel vor mich fuhr und seitdem leuchtend stehen blieb: da hatte mein Ich zum ersten Male sich selber gesehen und auf ewig.[3]

> (One morning, as a very young child, I was standing by the door of the house and looking to the left towards the wood-loft, when all of a sudden the inner vision 'I am an I' burst like lightning from heaven before me and became fixed ever since like a shining ray: my I had seen itself for the first time and for ever.)

What is evoked here is not just the budding of self-consciousness, but the beginning of an exponential consciousness of his own self-consciousness. This is the origin of that conspicuous self-reflexivity which forms the mainspring of his writing, animating its shapes as distinctively as its contents. The volatility of his name is the outer indication of that inner multiplicity, to which Jean Paul repeatedly testified. 'Mir ist immer in meinem Bewusstsein, als wär ich doppelt, als wären zwei Ich in mir: ich höre mich im Innern reden'[4] ('I always have the consciousness of being double, as though there were two I in me: I hear myself speaking within'). This personal epiphany is sublimated in his *Vorschule der Ästhetik* (*Preschool to Aesthetics*) into an attribute of the creative genius whose special 'Selbstbewusstsein' ('consciousness of himself') is described as 'ein ganzes Sichselbersehen des zu- und des abgewandten Menschen in zwei Spiegeln zugleich'[5] ('total self-vision of the person turned towards and away from himself in two mirrors simultaneously'). The preoccupation with seeing, with doubles, and with mirrors, recurrent motifs in Jean Paul's work, is already connected here to the recording of self-consciousness. The linguistic reminder of this fascination comes in the manifold, sometimes curious combinations with the prefixes 'Selbst' and 'Selber' ('self'), obvious manifestations of Jean Paul's absorption 'with self-knowledge and self-evaluation, with self-deception, with his own writing, and with the syndrome of self-annihilation'.[6]

Such extreme awareness of self leads not only to a heightened creative consciousness, but also to a menacing self-doubt; for the ego perceived in the mirror may after all be nothing more than an illusion in an illusory universe. And if the 'I' can become the primary object of its own contemplation, conversely the objective world may be assimilated and even dissolved in a wholly subjective image. The distinction between appearance and reality, between illusion and truth, so well defined to Jane Austen's steady, ordering gaze, becomes blurred within Jean Paul's pervasive and invasive self-consciousness. It is his vision of the self in relation to itself and to the universe that is the decisive determinant of his irony.

2

Appearance and reality, illusion and truth meet in the figure of the narrator in the *Flegeljahre*. None other than a certain J. P. F. Richter is appointed by the executors of Van der Kabel's will to chronicle the heir's progress towards fulfilling the conditions imposed on him. The second chapter of the novel, which details the acceptance of this commission together with the terms of payment and the plans for the prospective work, is signed J. P. F. Richter. It is, of course, tempting simply to identify the narrating voice, the writer of a chronicle he proposes to call *Flegeljahre*, with the German writer born in 1763 who actually published a novel entitled *Flegeljahre* in 1804–5. Such an amalgamation is in fact encouraged by the biographical information in the fictive J. P. F. Richter's letter, such as date, place, family status, all of which coincide with the data of the historical personage Jean Paul Friedrich Richter. The two share many characteristics, including their literary style, their opinions on many matters, and even their birthplace.[7] Like Byron, Jean Paul creates a fictive narrator who is, and is not, himself. The figure is more fully characterised than in *Don Juan*, and becomes the focus of a good deal of ironic jousting as the relationship between the internal fictive narrator and the external actual author is repeatedly skirted. The similarity of their names and biographies clearly points to some overlap between them, but the extent of their identity or dissociation is never articulated. Sometimes they are made to seem quite distinct, especially when the fictive narrator refers rather derisively, as he does on several occasions, to satires by a certain Jean Paul. On the other hand, the chronicler's *Vorlesungen über die Kunst* (no. 50, p. 261) are a reflection of Jean Paul's *Vorschule der Ästhetik*, which suggests an affinity between them. The situation is further complicated when the fictional protagonists within the chronicle also allude to Jean Paul, and in just as contradictory a manner. One of the twins confesses to having devised the anonymous *Grönländische Prozesse*, thereby equating himself with Jean Paul; next he makes a scathing comment on the conjunction of the jocular and the serious 'wie in J. P . . .'s Werken' (no. 54, p. 297; 'as in the works of J. P . . .') which would seem to divorce him from Jean Paul, but eventually his own writings are rejected for their resemblance to those of that 'Kuckuck Jean Paul' (no. 61, p. 355; 'that cuckoo Jean Paul'). It becomes extremely difficult to sort out the precise interconnections between the various writers in the *Flegeljahre*: the figure known as Jean Paul, who is presumably the actual author, the fictive chronicler J. P. F. Richter, and the twins who are themselves writing. Perhaps we are not even meant to separate them, but to confront and accept the fusion and confusion of identities.

The reiterated references to the existence of the writer Jean Paul are, however, by no means gratuitous exercises in self-reflexivity. They serve to counteract the temptation to coalesce the fictive narrator with the actual author by distancing the present chronicler, J. P. F. Richter, from that Jean Paul who is presented as a somewhat notorious literary personality. A tense ambivalence prevails between the compiler of this story – 'der Verfasser dieser Geschichte' (no. 2, p. 20), as he often describes himself – and the 'real' author who has conjured up the entire fiction and is external to it. The chronicler is a kind of mirror image of the author, a 'närrisches Selbstporträt'[8] ('waggish self-portrait'), the incarnation of Jean Paul's belief that the humorist is 'sein eigner Hofnarr und sein eignes komisches italienisches Masken-Quartett . . ., aber auch der Regent und Regisseur dazu'[9] ('his own court-jester and his own quartet of masked Italian comedians . . ., but also his and their ruler and director'). Such a concept is even more apposite to the ironist than to the humorist; the ironist acts on the appearance of things, though as the detached manipulator he is simultaneously activating the whole charade. In its use of a persona who bears the author's name and features but who functions wholly within the parameters of the fiction, the *Flegeljahre* offers an original variant on the ironic narrator. The result of this stratagem is the establishment of 'eine–fiktive – Subjektivität'[10] ('a – fictive – subjectivity'). So the answer to the question: 'Who is telling the story?'[11] in the *Flegeljahre* must be dualistic: a fictional character called J. P. F. Richter who is himself part of the total fictional invention of an extraneous narrator who chose the name Jean Paul for his literary persona. This cryptic partial projection of the author's self into the narrating voice suspends the narrative of the *Flegeljahre* in an indeterminate and indeterminable space, the ideal location for the exuberant play of irony.

The aura of uncertainty enveloping the narrator is heightened by the chronicler's own vacillations as to his intent. He seems to consider it his brief to compile a biography of the heir, Walt. In this respect his work in progress, entitled *Flegeljahre*, fuses with Jean Paul's *Flegeljahre* which bears the sub-title 'Eine Biographie'. In the fifth chapter J. P. F. Richter traces the 'Vorgeschichte' ('Pre-history') of Walt who does, by and large, remain the centre of interest. But the biography does not get very far, and the first three parts submitted to the work's sponsors evidently evoke disappointment, for Kuhnold, the spokesman for the executors of the will, writes to the chronicler: 'Unsere Biographie soll doch, der Sache, der Kunst, der Schicklichkeit und dem Testament gemäss, mehr zu einem historischen Roman, als zu einem nackten Lebenslauf ausschlagen' (no. 56, p. 318; 'Our biography should, in accordance with its import, with art, with seemliness, and with the will, turn more into a historical romance than a bare outline of a life'). This demand casts some doubt onto the existential status of the manuscript, and indirectly raises also the question as to the generic affiliation of the narrative. It is no more a fictive biography than a *Bildungsroman*, despite its echoes of Goethe's *Wilhelm Meister*. Vult's sarcastic suggestion that Walt could feature as the hero of a novel to be called 'Tölpeljahre eines Dichters' (no. 56, p. 316; 'A Poet's Years of Ineptitude') has a wry appropriateness. More so indeed than the actual title *Flegeljahre*[12] which could conceivably be a slyly ironic comment on the text. For the action spans not years but six months, and the gentle Walt has nothing of the noisy adolescent 'hobbledehoy' generally associated with *Flegel*. 'There is no English word that gives correctly the meaning of *Flegeljahre*', notes the American translator[13] who spurns Carlyle's rendering, *Wild Oats*. She herself opts for *The Twins* on the grounds that Jean Paul's friends referred to the book as 'Die Zwillinge'. Her solution, though it has the virtue of directness, drastically reduces the innate ambivalences of the German, as does her entire translation, which concentrates on the fable and eliminates the by-play as if it were a dispensable frivolity and as if the fundamental ironic tension between the fictive narrator and the actual author did not exist at all.

The fictional existence of the J. P. F. Richter within the novel is emphasised by his involvement with other personae of the story, particularly his disputes with the city council of Haslau, his employers. Twice in the later stages of his work he sends extensive letters of complaint about the treatment meted out to him and the difficulties inherent in his undertaking. The second missive receives a negative reply from the executors of the will. These letters have a twofold and contradictory effect. Through the sub-plot of his wrangling with his patrons the chronicler J. P. F. Richter is more closely integrated into the plot of the *Flegeljahre*. However, these altercations bring a sudden break in the main narrative thread, an abrupt change in the tone and level of the discourse. Throughout his narration the chronicler takes the liberty of interspersing his record of events with various comments of his own. For instance he adds: 'Hier sollte Zeit sein, das Axiom einzuschichten, dass überhaupt die Menschen mehr in Viertelstunden, als in Stunden gelernt' (no. 5, p. 34; 'This should be the point to interject the axiom that people have altogether learned more in quarter hours than in hours'); or: 'Es ist vielleicht der Mühe wert, zu bemerken, . . .' (no. 41, p. 222; 'It is perhaps worth noting that . . .'). Such rather pompous phrases are recurrent reminders of the presence of a narrator mediating the story to the reader. But those letters to the city council of Haslau are very different in kind from these random observations, for they are concerned primarily with the chronicler's own business, that of telling the story. He laments bitterly the restrictions placed on his freedom as a creator by the contemporary dislike of sentiment and by the circumstances of his position 'wo ich bloss nur nachschreibend zusehen muss' (no. 50, p. 267; 'where I have merely to watch and record'); he expresses anxiety about the length of his opus which already comprises fifty chapters in three volumes and seems likely to run to another five hundred in umpteen volumes; above all, he is distraught at the nature of the material he has to handle: 'guter Gott, welche eine der verwickelsten Geschichten, die ich kenne! . . . Allerdings, verehrlichster Stadtrat! hat eine solche Geschichte noch kein Dichter gehabt' (no. 50, p. 266; 'good God, what a most complicated story of any I have known! In truth, most venerable city council, no poet has yet had such a story'). These reflections on the narrative-in-progress contain a two-tiered irony. The chronicler, surveying his narrative with sceptical detachment, is distanced from the fictional happenings into which he would seem to be drawn by his address to the city council. His present time of writing further separates him from the past events of the chronicle. This metafictional layer of the

Flegeljahre acts as a buffer zone, where the outermost reality of the historical author and the present reader interchanges with the innermost kernel of the illusion. As chronicler, J. P. F. Richter is encapsulated within the total fiction, although his self-conscious metafictional ruminations serve equally to sever him from, and to link him to, the central action. And finally in yet another stratum of irony, the chronicler's exasperation at the complications of the story he has to tell is shared by the reader of the *Flegeljahre* at the narrative with which he has to grapple.

Where in fact is the reader placed in this odd arrangement? The fictive narrator occasionally alludes to him or her, advising him in one instance to keep the clauses of the will to hand (no. 55, p. 306) or voicing the hope that female readers will not take offence at Vult's behaviour (no. 27, p. 152). In the footnotes[14] too, scattered through the *Flegeljahre*, the fictive narrator communicates directly with a characterised reader, often in a whimsical show of friendship under the guise of additional information. Notwithstanding these addresses, the reader's role is conceived as an essentially passive one. In a revealing and typically humorous picture, he is perched in an apple-tree, along with members of ten Imperial German Reading Circles ' – da ja alle Leser durch ein Fenster in die Stube sehen – ' (no. 8, p. 44; ' – since all readers peep into a room through a window – '). In other words, he is banished into the position of a silent voyeur. And the size and shape of the window through which he peeps is determined by the fictive narrator who functions as the controlling agent and sole intermediary between the outer macrocosm of the reader and the inner microcosm of the narrative. It is through J. P. F. Richter's fictive subjectivity that the reader perceives the protagonists and the action. This represents a major modification of the communicative base, namely 'eine Subjektivierung alles Erzählten . . ., dergestalt, dass kein Sachverhalt mehr als objektiv gegebener erscheint, sondern als vom Erzähler und durch den Erzähler gestalteter'[15] ('a subjectivisation of all that is narrated . . ., to such an extent that no situation appears any longer as objectively posited, but as shaped by and through the narrator'). The view is essentially a mediated one, in which the reader is a quite remote spectator. What is more, the possibility of a distortion innate to this mediated view is suggested in the numerous images of lenses that magnify, minimise, or otherwise – like the chronicler? – are unreliable refractive prisms.

Such a narrative disposition is in sharp contrast to the collusive understanding between the alert reader and the arch narrator in *Pride and Prejudice*, and to the perspective 'we' share with the invisible narrator in *Madame Bovary*. In the *Flegeljahre* the reader is at the mercy of the fictive narrator.[16] The narrator has a more pressing obligation to his present employers than to any prospective readers. His interest is directed more to the progress of the chronicle, to the responses of the city council, and to future criticisms of reviewers than to the reactions of readers. His contract with the executors of the will is very specific, whereas that with the reader is highly elusive. Amidst the private jokes and esoteric references of this self-oriented narrator, the uninitiated reader is made to feel something of an intruder as well as a victim. His reading experience creates a sense of irritation to which earlier critics and more recent ones[17] alike have openly alluded. The annoyance is caused by the position of eavesdropper to which the reader is relegated. The privilege of active participation in the process of ironic communication accorded to him in *Pride and Prejudice* and in *Madame Bovary* is withheld in the *Flegeljahre*. The primary dialogue here is not between the reader and the narrator, but between the narrator and the narrative he is fashioning. His enthrallment with the protagonists, the oddities of the tale, and the ardours of his own task overrides concern for the reader. He comes across as a narcissistic personality wholly immersed in his own doings. With such an enigmatic and recalcitrant narrator no contract of confidence can be entertained. Because of the insecurities inherent in his own precarious dangling between appearance and reality, the fictive narrator of the *Flegeljahre* cannot provide a firm anchor. His intrinsic shiftiness precludes that delineation of clear distinctions necessary for the resolution of irony. So the persona of the chronicler forms the pivot of the irony central to the *Flegeljahre*, where the constant presence of a loquacious narrator, far from giving reassuring guidance to the reader, has the paradoxically opposite effect of increasing our perplexity *vis-à-vis* the text. It is in these undefined spaces between the author and the narrator, and between the narrator and the reader that irony has the latitude in which it flourishes.

3

The beginning of the *Flegeljahre* is deceptively innocent: 'Solange Haslau eine Residenz ist, wusste man sich nicht zu erinnern, dass man darin auf etwas mit solcher Neugier gewartet hätte – die Geburt des Erbprinzen ausgenommen – als auf die Eröffnung des Van der Kabelschen Testaments' (no. 1, p. 11; 'Since Haslau has been a princely residence, no one could recall any event – except the birth of the crown-prince – that had been awaited with such curiosity as the opening of the Van der Kabel will'). This straightforward introduction, with its obvious cultivation of suspense, seems to herald a traditional tale into which we are drawn through the appeal to our curiosity. The story of Van der Kabel's will in fact forms an additional framework beyond that of the chronicler. The sequence is anomalous: the text starts on the reading of the will, and it is in compliance with one of its clauses that a writer be appointed to record the execution of its conditions. But in the second chapter, in J. P. F. Richter's letter accepting this commission, we learn that he had already written that first chapter which he encloses with his letter. Thus the device of the chronicler takes precedence within the fiction, although chronologically and actually it follows on that of the will. This sub-plot of the will was, according to Eduard Berend's account, incorporated into the plan for the *Flegeljahre* quite late as a 'perspektivistischen, alles ordnenden Punkt'[18] ('perspectivistic, ordering centre'), as a cohesive scaffold to unify the diversified strands. It does not fulfil that purpose; it soon disappears from sight, and only a couple of the will's conditions are ever completed, another two remain incomplete and five unattempted. So the opening of the novel proves to be a red herring, teasing the reader just as Van der Kabel teases his presumptive heirs in a will that cannily combines joke and gravity. He leaves his pew in church to the local Jews, his house to the first person capable of shedding a tear for him, and naught to his relatives because he knows from their own assurances that they esteem his humble person more highly than his large fortune ('weil ich aus ihrem eigenen Munde weiss, dass sie meine geringe Person lieber haben als mein grosses Vermögen' – no. 1, p. 12). A strong streak of transparent irony informs both the moral situation and the verbal formulation; Van der Kabel chooses to take as literal what has been said contrariwise. Although its function in the novel as a whole is slight, this initial episode of the will is appropriate as an overture to the *Flegeljahre* in its sardonic humour and, above all, in its rapid discreditation of the normative expectations that had been aroused. It is an early oblique clue to the irony ingrained in the text.

The interdependence of the two preliminary frames shows the labyrinthine structure of the *Flegeljahre*. Just as the fictive narrator is entwined with the actual author, so the motif of the will is interwoven with that of the chronicler. Such encapsulation is characteristic of the design of the *Flegeljahre*; it is as evident in the reduplicative patterns of its characterisation as in its arabesque forms. As J. P. F. Richter himself puts it: 'Ein Autor gibt lauter Nüsse aufzubeissen, welche dem Gehirne gleichen, das nach Le Camus ihnen gleicht, und die also drei Häute haben; wer aber schält sie ab? –' (no. 50, p. 264; 'An author gives us nuts to crack, which are like the brain that, according to Le Camus, is like them, and that have three skins; but who is to peel them? –'). This striking image extends an invitation to peel the 'skins' of the *Flegeljahre*, the preliminary frames, so as to 'unshell' the core: the tale of the twins, Walt and Vult, Walt's unexpected legacy, the reunion of Vult with Walt, Walt's passing friendship with Klothar, the twins' common love for Wina, their joint work on a novel, and their final separation. This story in turn spawns a series of outgrowths, the internal counterparts to the outer frames of the will and the chronicler. The inner circles consist largely of the twins' writings. Walt's idyll of the life of a Swedish pastor, his 'polymeters', Vult's 'digressions', a number of letters and the journals kept by both. Most of these inserts into the chronicler's narrative are destined for the 'Doppelroman' ('double romance'), on which the twins are eagerly at work in the latter part of the *Flegeljahre*. So there is a fictive novel within the narrative that forms the actual novel read by us, and it is written by a pair of writers whose lives are being recorded by the fictive narrator invented by the actual author. To complete the box-within-a-box-within-a-box arrangement, the twins' novel, too, might have been entitled *Flegeljahre* if Walt had not rejected this proposal of Vult's as too 'conspicuous' ('auffallend') and 'strange' ('wild – no. 14, p. 75). Their novel interfaces with the narrator's chronicle in the same way as the fictive narrator himself interplays with the actual author and as illusion and reality are constantly interlaced with each other throughout the *Flegeljahre*. Even the times of writing are entangled, the twins putting their novel together as J. P. F. Richter compiles his chronicle. The convolution is deliberately underscored, and the irony of the situation disclosed, by the narrator's periodic dismissal of certain material as belonging to *their* book, not his. The lines of demarcation between the various narratives-in-progress in the *Flegeljahre* are as fluid as those between narrator and author. The 'skins' surrounding the fiction are porous, unlike the hard shells that enclose the fictional worlds of *Pride and Prejudice* and of *Madame Bovary* in a categoric separation of illusion and reality. The firmer the perspective both within the fictional realm and at its boundaries, the more secure is the reader's basis for the reconstruction of irony.

The tortuosity of Jean Paul's fictional organisation has provoked accusations that his works are 'ästhetische Ungeheuer'[19] ('aesthetic monstrosities'), examples of that 'Formlosigkeit'[20] ('formlessness') and of that unruliness[21] to which the German Romantic novel was prone. Though the practice of using frameworks was common and the form of the 'Arabeske'[22] much favoured, even Friedrich Schlegel, despite his admiration for Jean Paul, expressed astonishment at his inability to tell a story well or to shape a neat phrase.[23] Jean Paul's work was long considered a literary curate's egg, fit to be read only once the grain had been gleaned from the mass of chaff.[24] As a corrective to this fragmentary approach, recent critics have gone to the opposite extreme by trying to prove the total aesthetic unity of the *Flegeljahre*. Hermann Meyer, for instance, sees in the concept of antithesis its integrative archetectonic principle.[25] Illuminating though such a reading may be, it cannot altogether escape the rigidity of formalistic systematisation. Its dangers are illustrated by Meyer's pupil, Peter Horst Neumann,[26] whose determination to ferret out the recondite meaning of every detail and to fit everything into a perfect pattern results not only in a network of cabalistic significations but in a veritable betrayal of the true character of the *Flegeljahre*.

The criticisms of 'formlessness' and, curiously, also the opposing efforts to squeeze the *Flegeljahre* into conventional shapes stem from an entrenched – though unvoiced – assumption of the existence of a 'proper' form for a narrative, with an orderly sequence of beginning, development, and conclusion, and with

clarity and respect for fictional illusion. To these proprieties Jean
Paul defers even less than Byron. 'Wie ungern ich blos erzähle'[27]
('How I dislike pure narration'), he wrote in an autobiographical
sketch, where he confesses explicitly: 'Ich kann durchaus keine
Freude an reinem Erzählen finden'[28] ('I cannot find any pleasure
whatsoever in pure narration'). In a letter to his friend, Friedrich
von Oertel he is even more outspoken: 'Ich hasse doch, sogar im
Roman, alles Erzählen so sehr, sobald nicht durch die
Einmischung von 100,000 Reflexionen und Einfällen die alte
Geschichte für den Erzähler selber eine neue wird'[29] ('I so much
hate, even in a novel, all narration, if the old story does not
become a new one for the narrator himself through the admixture
of 10,000 reflections and ideas'). Jean Paul's departure from the
traditional narrative paradigm was, therefore, a matter of
deliberate choice, growing at least as much out of personal
predilection as out of his regard for Sterne. It is in this light that
the *Flegeljahre* must be viewed: as an alternative construct that is
essentially open, ambivalent, self-referential, and ironic in
nature.

As an ironic construct, its most distinctive hallmark is the
multiplicity of its dimensions and levels. The frames and the
outgrowths are enmeshed in each other in so complex a web as
almost to defy unravelling into its separate strands. This tightly
knotted fabric contrasts with the texture of *Don Juan* where the
metafictional stratum is kept largely apart from the mythical
elements; each in turn is exposed to the narrator's irony, but he
remains constant, even if only in his persistent presence and in
his very inconstancy. The organisation is simpler and more
transparent than in the *Flegeljahre* which opens out in an expansive
array of spatial vistas. In place of the linear progression of *Don
Juan* with its temporal succession of picaresque episodes, the
Flegeljahre spreads digressively in a lateral manner. Additions are
made by a cumulative process that bears the marks of
improvisation, particularly towards the end. Though every
strand is linked to and dependent on what has gone before, the
relationship is that of an image to its reflection in a mirror. This
explains in part the repetitive, *déjà vu* effect of the *Flegeljahre*; we
have indeed seen things before, perhaps from a different angle or
on a different level. The fictional world that is created by such a
perspectivistic, self-reflexive technique is radically other than that
of *Pride and Prejudice* where the sub-plots (Bingley and Jane,

Wickham and Lydia, Collins and Charlotte) stand in a rational relation to each other as an intellectually perceptible reiteration of the same experience of courtship and marriage. In the *Flegeljahre* too the same experiences and motifs recur in the various dimensions: creativity, appearance and reality, friendship and deception. However, the interconnections are primarily associative and as if by chance, suggesting a universe at the mercy of contingency rather than governed by any syntactical principles. What is more, in an ordered world with definite moral and social values, irony can emanate from the perspective of a discriminating observer-narrator, as in *Pride and Prejudice* and in *Madame Bovary*. Whereas in the syncretic flux of the *Flegeljahre*, the source of the irony lies not in a single point but in the multiplicity of the laywers, each of which encases and thereby qualifies and relativises the validity of the others. So the irony devolves from and resides in the text's very instability.

4

It is in this context that the 'intermittierende Erzählungsform'[30] ('intermittent manner of narration') assumes a special significance as the most prominent indicator of the ironic import of the construct as a whole. The 'interruptive' narration, far from showing Jean Paul's inability to tell a story well, is in fact 'das notwendige Mittel für die Verwirklichung ihrer Totalität'[31] ('the necessary means for its realisation as a totality'). The disruptions have an aesthetic and an ontological function. The continuous surprising shifts from one mode of discourse to another serve as perpetual reminders of the existence of alternative dimensions. When the reader is most deeply absorbed in the tale of Walt's friendship with Klothar or his courtship of Wina, he is abruptly jerked to another level by the insertion of perhaps a passage from Walt's journal which, we are told, must be carefully kept for inclusion in the twins' novel. Even more radical disturbances are effected by the appearance of the chronicler with his woes. Such dislocations have a purpose, and they go beyond merely drawing attention to the business of story-telling. Jean Paul is not concerned with metafictional questions to the extent or in the way that Byron is. He does not aim primarily to underline the character of his representation as fictional representation. The chronicler's presence does, of course, distance the central fable of the twins, and reduces its authority through its dependence on the voice of the intermediary. But that 'intermittent manner of narration' has the effect of reducing the authority of each and every strand in the fabric of the novel. As a result of the incessant shifts from one facet to another, no single thread is allowed to attain lasting dominance, not even the chronicler himself who sometimes fades from sight for considerable stretches, only to re-assert himself suddenly with renewed vociferousness. Nothing is ever certain in the *Flegeljahre*, least of all the disposition of the narrative. Just as every strand germinates successively from the previous one: the twins' novel from their reunion, their reunion from Walt's inheritance, the inheritance from Van der Kabel's will, the will from the chronicler's account (or vice versa?); so, retroactively, each element is seen to have displaced and, above all, qualified the relative importance of its antecedents. The deliberate interlineation of such a network of diverse but reciprocally dependent pieces leads to an innately ironic construct whose operative principle lies in its very mobility, its basic refusal to commit itself to any single voice, to any single view, to any single perspective.

This fundamental ambivalence determines also the continuing tension between the maintenance of the work's fictionality and the breaking of the illusion. This dualism surfaces already in the persona of the narrator who is, and is not, identical with the author. Although the chronicler's interventions are the most blatant interruptions of the fictional façade, they are not the only ones. Walt's and Vult's attempt at a novel raises many of the problems confronting writers, including the difficulty of finding a publisher. The chronicler readily declares his sympathy with their predicament. His feuds with reviewers coincide with Vult's, while his tolerance towards Walt's sloppy proof-reading is motivated by his own incompetence in this task. Throughout the *Flegeljahre* therefore, as the processes of writing in their various stages are repeatedly mentioned, a strong consciousness of a creative enterprise is fostered. However, this does not oust the story, as in *Don Juan*, where the tactics of the writer are of more enduring interest than the exploits of the hero. In the *Flegeljahre*, on the contrary, partly because of its endless surprises and bizarre twists, the plot does manage to hold the curiosity aroused in the opening episode. Despite the unconventionality of his narrative strategies, Jean Paul does not jettison or negate the norms of the genre with the radicality of a Sterne. Rather, he modifies and stretches its parameters to accord with his own inclinations. His handling of narrative does indeed amount to a 'komische Individualisierung'[32] ('comic individualisation') but not to an 'ironische Travestierung' ('ironic travesty') which presupposes a more destructive impulse than is apparent in the *Flegeljahre*. The irony stems from the contradictory combination of the fiction of reality with the reality of fiction. It is the simultaneity and interpenetration of these two opposing modes that creates the particular tone and texture of the *Flegeljahre*. This mingling of 'anachronistic' and 'avant garde' narratorial patterns may well testify to Jean Paul's transitional position in the emergence of authorial autonomy.[33]

The fluctuations in narrative mode are matched by the mutability of the perspective. The firmly directed gaze of an external observer, the buttress of *Pride and Prejudice* and of *Madame Bovary*, is conspicuously absent from the *Flegeljahre,* as is the familiar, recognisably personal note of the narrator of *Don Juan* and of *Tristram Shandy*. The chronicler of the *Flegeljahre* is something of a chameleon, changing voice and shifting perspective with histrionic empathy. This is most apparent in regard to the twins, with both of whom he identifies. His use of their letters and journals, inserted as direct quotations, facilitates the adoption of the viewpoint and style of different protagonists. For example, the concert in the section 'Musik der Musik' (no. 25) is first evoked in lyrical terms through the experience of Walt. It is with Walt that we enter the concert hall, see the orchestra and the audience, and feel the surge of the music (pp. 139–42). Then in the interval, in one of those lightning shifts typical of the *Flegeljahre*, an 'Extrablatt' ('extra leaf') of Vult's contribution to the joint novel is briefly interposed. Entitled '*Vox humana – Konzert*', its scathing sarcasm expresses a drastically different view of the social aspects of concert-going to Walt's idyllic emotionalism. The same kind of contrast recurs in the twins' conflicting memories of their childhood (no. 58, pp. 329–38). In a bewildering pluralism of images Walt is perceived through his own eyes, through those of his brother, of his benefactor, of his hostile rivals, and of the chronicler. No single image predominates, nor is any invested with greater validity because the fictive narrator himself is not in possession of a secret 'truth' such as the narrator of *Pride and Prejudice* holds in regard to Darcy and Wickham. That base of certain knowledge is the foundation for the transparently ironic games that can be played with a reader with whom a tacit understanding has been established. Whereas the chronicler of the *Flegeljahre* is himself still in search of truth, and none too confident that it can be found in any absolute sense. For this reason he cannot assume a definitive stance. Instead, he surveys the characters and actions from all angles, including the 'Wurm- und Froschperspektive'[34] ('worm's and frog's eye-view') of the footnote, without reaching any conclusions or resolutions. His apologia would be that he is merely the chronicler appointed by the executors of the will, and not a free agent with full responsibility for the interpretation of the happenings. Significantly, no such person exists in the economy of the *Flegeljahre*, the fictive narrator acting as an effective shelter for the actual author, who can with impunity abdicate authority over his work through the interpolation of a nescient narrator who is only a partial self-projection.

So the mobility characteristic of the structural organisation of the *Flegeljahre* affords a key to its essence. The shiftiness of the text, a frequent source of irritation for readers, is in fact its central axis. Dissonance is at the heart of the *Flegeljahre*: 'die Dissonanz erweist sich als Strukturgesetz der Erzählweise Jean Pauls'[35] ('dissonance proves to be a structural principle of Jean Paul's manner of narration'). Dissonance as a structural principle does not, of course, mean disorganisation, nor does it justify the practice of excerpting 'beautiful pieces' for anthologies. For those pieces, in all their discontinuity, belong together; the contradictions, the interruptions, the dislocations have no need to be tactfully explained away because they constitute the particular format of this narrative. Its unity is neither simple nor classically epic; nevertheless, its elements do coalesce, albeit into an unorthodox and paradoxical entity. The form that Jean Paul evolved has aptly been described as that 'eines einheitlichen, aber desintegralen Kunstwerks'[36] ('of a unified, but disintegral work of art'). Such a form is not atomistic, but it is innately ironic: ironic not in the Johnsonian sense of saying the opposite to what is meant; rather, it is ironic in the Schlegelian sense of representing within itself the eternal agility and paradoxicality of the universe.

Jean Paul, unlike Jane Austen, Flaubert, or even Byron, does not *use* irony for artistic (and moralistic) purposes. His *Flegeljahre is* ironic in its internal tensions, in its involuted shape, in its ambivalences, in its perspectivism, and in its self-conscious self-reflexiveness.

5

It is at the 'Wirtshaus zum Wirtshaus' ('inn to the inn') that Vult proposes to his twin brother his plan for a joint novel. The inn has a sign on which is painted nothing 'als wieder ein Wirtshausschild mit einem ähnlichen Schild, auf dem wieder das gleiche stand' (no. 12, p. 63; 'than another inn-sign with a like sign, on which the same was depicted again'). Registering at the inn,

> Vult setzte mit einem angeketteten Schieferstift auf den Schiefer mit Schiefer – so wie unser Fichtisches Ich zugleich Schreiber, Papier, Feder, Tinte, Buchstaben und Leser ist – seinen Namen so; 'Peter Gottwalt Harnisch, K.K offner geschworner Notarius und Tabellio, geht nach Haslau.' Darauf nahm ihn Walt, um sich auch als Notarius selber zu verhören, und seinen Namen und Charakter zu Protokoll und zu Papier zu bringen.
>
> Erstaunt sah er sich schon darauf. (no. 13, p. 65)

> (Writing with the attached slate pencil on the slate with the slate – like our Fichtean I is simultaneously writer, paper, pen, ink, letters and reader – Vult inscribed his name thus: 'Peter Gottwalt Harnisch, Imperial publicly sworn notary and Tabellio on his way to Haslau.' Then Walt took it in order to register himself as notary and to record his name and profession on protocol and paper.
>
> To his surprise he saw it there already.)

The solipsistic Fichtean I finds a fitting outlet in Vult's frolicsome scheme:

> Was kann ich nun dabei machen? Ich allein nichts; aber mit dir viel, nämlich ein Werk; *ein* Paar Zwillinge müssen, als ihr eigenes Wiederspiel, zusammen einen Einling, *ein* Buch zeugen, einen trefflichen Doppelroman. Ich lache darin, du weinst dabei oder fliegst doch – du bist der Evangelist, ich das

Vieh dahinter – jeder hebt den andern – alle Parteien werden befriedigt, Mann und Weib, Hof und Haus, ich und du. (no. 14, p. 73)

(What can I do then? I alone can do nothing; but together with you, a great deal, namely a work; *one* pair of twins must, as their own reflection, together create a single entity, *one* book, a superb double romance. I will laugh in it, you will weep or soar – you will be the evangelist, and I the animal behind him – each will raise the other – all parties will be satisfied – man and wife, master and servant, I and you.)

Such episodes reveal once again that reduplication, that same tendency to multiply and encapsulate typical of the structural organisation of the *Flegeljahre*. Its dominant motifs – the doubles, mirrors, echoes, and masks – are further evidence of that proliferating perspectivism innate to an ironic vision that perceives a multiplicity of appearances at once, envisages the potential for 'truth' in each of them, but cannot conclusively opt for any one of them as the sole carrier of an absolute truth. Truth and illusion are as closely linked as twins, mirror images, or echoes, the 'real' indistinguishably fused with the other. So doubles, contradictions and uncertainties are the incongruously congruous expressions of a universe that is *a priori* ironic.

The twins embody the prototype of such complex doubling. Their names symbolise[37] the conjunction of their identity in that they are two versions of the same name: the first child is called Peter Gottwalt (Peter God's Will) while the surprising second, greeted with '*was Gott will*' (no. 5, p. 33; '*what God wills*') is designated by the Latin *Quod Deus vult*. Walt and Vult are mirror images of each other: one is fair and delicate, whereas the other is dark and energetic; in a village where the right side belonged to a prince and the left to a nobleman, one is a 'Righter' and the other a 'Lefter' – the bed having been moved between the births across the room through which the boundary runs! Where the gentle Walt sees the idyllic aspects of life, the forceful Vult is aware of its harsher facets. Yet it is Walt who becomes a notary and Vult a flutist. This discrepancy hints at the interchangeability between the twins. Though Walt remains a dreamer with 'gar kein Geschick zu Welthändeln' (no. 11, p. 56; 'no aptitude whatsoever for worldy affairs'), Vult conceals beneath his sharp tongue a capacity for tenderness, specially towards his brother. His instrument is, significantly, the *flute traversière*, the transverse flute developed in the seventeenth century and so named because it was held out transversely to the player's right rather than straight out from the mouth, like the *flute à bec*. In its agility as in its fragility it is the appropriate instrument for Vult, and its transverse position perhaps suggests the oblique nature of Vult's often ironic comments. His flute is occasionally the vehicle for his irony, as in the luscious, yearning background accompaniment to Walt's meeting with Klothar which he has arranged and from which he, the displaced twin, is excluded. Generally, however, his flute is a 'Zauberstab, der die innere Welt verwandelt' (no. 13, p. 66; 'a magic wand that transforms the inner world'); a Mozartian 'Zauberflöte' (no. 59, p. 349; 'magic flute'). Thus Vult, the sceptic, is the fountainhead of enchantment, while Walt, the idealist, stands in unceasing danger of disillusionment; they represent a double person in contrasting, yet complementary form. The literal and metaphoric interface between the two is brought out in one of the strangest incidents in the *Flegeljahre* when Walt on his travels comes across an arresting drawing:

Walts Auge fiel auf eine Quodlibetszeichnung, auf welcher mit Reissblei fast alle seine heutigen Weg-Objekte, wie es schien, wild hingeworfen waren. Von jeher hielt er ein sogenanntes Quodlibet für ein Anagramm und Epigramm des Lebens, und sah es mehr trübe als heiter an – jetzt aber vollends; denn es stand ein Januskopf darauf, der wenig von seinem und Vults Gesicht verschieden war. Ein Engel flog über das Ganze. Unten stand deutsch: 'was Gott will, ist wohlgetan'; dann lateinisch. 'quod Deus vult, est bene *factus.*' Er kaufte für seinen Bruder das tolle Blatt. (no. 42, p. 227)

(Walt's eye fell on a quodlibet drawing, on which nearly all the objects of his day's travel had, so it seemed, been wildly tossed with a sketching pencil. He had always considered such a so-called quodlibet an anagram and epigram of life, and regarded it in a muted rather than jubilant way – now more than ever; for it showed a Janus-head, much like his and Vult's face. An angel hovered over the whole portrayal. Underneath was written in German: 'what God wills is well done'; then in

Latin: 'quod Deus vult est bene *factus.*' He bought the queer picture for his brother.)

The Janus-head on this drawing denotes the symbolic amalgamation of the twins. That the artist who has drawn it is the very brother, in disguise, for whom Walt buys it, intensifies through an irony of situation the basic vexatory ambivalence.

The quodlibet sketch concentrates many of the salient features of the *Flegeljahre* in a single revealing figure: the exponential sequence, the self-reflexive doubling, the interpenetration of truth and illusion. These are the major manifestations of the ironic perception of the ontological order (or disorder) of things. They crop up throughout the *Flegeljahre*, sometimes in quite minor forms: in the enclosure of a letter within a letter, in the chapter title 'Musik der Musik' (no. 25), in Walt's wish for 'zwei Ichs . . ., um mit dem einen spazierenzugehen, während das andere mit der Feder sass' (no. 16, p. 87; 'two I's . . ., so as to go for a walk with one, while the other sat pen in hand'), or in comic cumulations such as the picture of 'ein Paar Paare Verliebter' (no. 56, p. 317; 'a pair of pairs of lovers') to describe Walt and Raphaela, Vult and Wina. But the cardinal incarnation of such internal analogy is the twins' 'double romance' which is both a facsimile and a reversal of the narrative from which it springs. Its reduplicative propensity as a reflection of J. P. F. Richter's chronicle is implied by the suggested title, *Flegeljahre*, by the similar alternation of elegiac and caustic strains in the two texts, and by the inclusion of certain letters, journals, digressions, and Walt's verses as components of *both*. The dichotomy in the twins' novel is summarised in its title: *Hoppelpoppel oder das Herz (Scramble-mammble[38] or the Heart)*, the first word of which is an alliterative formation. This fictive romance purports to overcome its own dualities: its twin authors were to be united in a single work about one hero who succeeds in finding friendship. This is the complementary opposite to the *Flegeljahre*, in which one chronicler writes about two brothers, neither of whom attains spiritual harmony with another being. The novel within the novel 'dient der immanenten Selbstdeutung der *Flegeljahre*'[39] ('serves for the immanent self-interpretation of the *Flegeljahre*'). Characteristically it does so in two contradictory ways by acting both as a reiteration and a rebuttal. Its function is therefore ironic in more than one sense; it is ironic in the traditional Johnsonian manner by being the opposite to what it appears, i.e. not a repetition of the *Flegeljahre*; and it is also ironic in what has been defined as the Romantic understanding of the concept: 'eine besondere Form der Spiegelung, in der gerade der Gedanke in sich selbst gespiegelt eine neue Anschauung wiederherstellt'[40] ('a particular form of mirroring, whereby the thought induces a new perception through its mirror image'). Despite the mockery to which the self-consciousness of the Fichtean 'I' is exposed in the inn to the inn with the sign within the sign, the *Flegeljahre* is a half humorous, half serious incarnation of the workings of that very principle of progressive self-reflexivity.

It is because of its bearing on this central principle that the motif of the mirror is so prominent in the *Flegeljahre*. As a means of reduplication and reflection, involving some degree of distorting departure from simple reproduction, the mirror is a crucial instrument in the play of perspectivism. It is partnered by the echo, the aural counterpart to the mirror's responsive effects. Like the mirror, the echo returns a semblance that may resemble the original to a greater or lesser extent. Here again the fluidity of this universe becomes manifest as the doubling of the mirror/echo glides imperceptibly from truth to illusion, from the certainty of a definitive image or tone to the uncertainties of a mobile pluralism. Just as the pattern of the *Flegeljahre* consists of labyrinthine congeries of frames within frames, so its world abounds in mirrors and echoes from its main themes – the twins, the chronicle and the 'double romance' – down to its smallest details. For instance, as Walt enters a room, he notices 'die Papiertapeten statt des ihm gewöhnlichen Tapetenpapiers – die drei Spiegel – die Kommode-Beschläge mit Messing-Masken' (no 47, p. 246; 'the papered walls instead of the more usual wallpaper – the three mirrors – the chests ornamented with brass-masks'); or there is a 'Vergrösserungsspiegel' (no. 32, p. 180; 'magnifying mirror'), or figures seen 'in doppelten Spiegeln' (no. 22, p. 128; 'in double mirrors') that parallel the notion of a 'gegenseitiges Echo' (no. 35, p. 196, footnote; 'reciprocal echo'). Klothar, the prisoner of his narcissistic vanity, is described as 'ein Bilddiener seines Spiegelbildes, ein Spiegel seiner Pfauenspiegel' (no. 18, p. 107; 'an idolator of his own image in the mirror, a mirror of his peacock reflection'). These reflections and echoes always carry an insinuation of error, or at least allude to the absence of an assured, verifiable reality. For how can the faithfulness of the reflection or the echo to its source, much less the ultimate validity of either be assessed? The echo can act like an idealising magic flute; the world can be 'encompassed in magic mirrors' ('rings umher voll Zauberspiegel gestellt'; no. 7, p. 43). Or the reflection can be comically reductive, as in the entries Walt glimpses in a child's exercise-book, where the elements of his name, 'Gott – Walt – Harnisch' ('God – Rule – Armour') are matched with 'Hammel – Knorren – Schwanz' (No. 41, p. 222; 'Sheep – Bone – Tail'). Who is to know which image, which note is the 'true' one?

6

The mirror and the echo both raise the question as to the trustworthiness of subjective perception. This entails more than merely the personal tendency to be 'bezaubert' ('enchanted'), like Walt, or 'entzaubert' (no. 18, p. 107; 'disenchanted'), like Vult. What is at stake is the capacity to distinguish between the true and the illusory, to 'see' aright. So the theme of sight and of perception is intimately linked to the motif of the mirror in the *Flegeljahre*. At the very beginning J. P. F. Richter expresses the hope that his book will be a useful manual 'weil jedes Werk der Darstellung so gut aus einem *Spiegel* in eine *Brille* muss umzuschleifen sein, als venetianische Spiegelscherben zu wirklichen Brillengläsern genommen werden' (no. 2, p. 22; 'because every work of representation must be fit to be re-tooled from a *mirror* to a pair of *spectacles*, just as fragments of Venetian mirrors are used for actual lenses'). The distortion of the magnifying lens is introduced literally in the 'Vergrösserungsglase' (no. 61, p. 355; 'magnifying lens') in which the flea may appear hardly different in size from the elephant, and metaphorically in the '*Vergrösserungslinsen* des Herzens' (no. 25, p. 142; '*magnifying lenses* of the heart') that can effect a similar transformation of feeling. Physical and, even more so, moral modes of subjective perception are shown to be as unreliable, indeed as deceptive as mirror images. It is Vult, who has the greater experience of human affairs and the deeper insight, who feigns blindness. Conversely, Walt, the seeing but deluded twin, speaks of the ubiquity of illusion without really grasping it: 'Wir ziehen immer nur einen Theater-Vorhang von

einem zweiten weg und sehen nur die gemalte Bühne der Natur'
(no. 23, p. 134; 'We keep on raising one theatrical curtain after
another, and see only the painted stage-scenery of nature'). That
comment, made in a conversation with Klothar, is left without
response: 'Keiner antwortete recht dem andern' ('Neither really
answered the other any further'). Nor is any answer given on the
two occasions when the innate perversity of optic perceptual
processes is discussed: 'Wie kommt's, . . ., um auf Sehende zu
kommen, dass alle Bilder im Auge verkehrt sind, und wir doch
nichts verkehrt erblicken?' (no. 22, p. 130; 'Speaking of the
sighted, . . ., how come that all images are reversed in the eye,
and yet we do not perceive them in reverse?'); and again:
'Warum wird denn das einzige Bild im Auge nicht mit
umgekehrt? – Warum greifen operierte Blinde nichts verkehrt? –
Was hat denn das Hautbildchen mit dem innern Bilde zu tun?'
(no. 23, p. 130; 'Why then is the sole picture in the eye not
reversed too? – Why do the blind, whose sight has been restored,
not grasp in reverse? – What in fact has the surface image to do
with the inner image?'). These apparently random questions
touch on dilemmas central to *Flegeljahre*: the waywardness of
perception, the inversions of irony, and the essential
precariousness of any attempt to discriminate between the
illusory appearance and the hidden reality.

The concealment of reality behind appearances is epitomised
in the disguises that play such an important part in the *Flegeljahre*.
Vult is first not recognised by his twin from whom he has been
long separated; later he deliberately hides in a series of
masquerades so as to accompany the vulnerable Walt as an
unseen protector in his travels. Walt in turn is persuaded to go to
his meeting with Klothar dressed up as a nobleman in order to
pander to the latter's snobbery. The climax of the mystification –
and of the plot – comes in the elaborate masked ball, where all the
protagonists surrender their identity to a play with illusion. The
confusion is capped by the exchange of masks and of costumes
between Walt and Vult at the instigation of Vult, who had
determined to use this opportunity to discover whether Wina
loved Walt or him: 'auf dem Larventaz entlarv' ich' (no. 62, p.
364; 'at the masked ball I shall unmask'). He succeeds in
wresting from the reticent Wina, who takes him for his twin, her
love for Walt, knowledge which he must for ever keep secret. 'So
schloss der Larventanz voll willkürlicher Verhüllungen endlich

mit unwillkürlichen von grösserer Schwere' (no. 63, p. 373; 'So the masked ball with its voluntary concealments finally ended on involuntary ones of greater gravity'). The symbolic import of this scene is unmistakable: only through the double disguise of the crossed masks can the truth be uncovered. Its wider implications are spelled out in Wina's comment: 'So mag wohl einem höhern Wesen die Geschichte des Menschengeschlechts nur als eine längere Ball-Verkleidung erscheinen' (no. 63, p. 369; 'So to a higher being the history of mankind may well seem nothing other than an extended masked ball').

Human history as a long masquerade; individual identity as an unstable entity, liable to all manner of modification through the gratuitous refraction of the self as well as the calculated intervention of disguise; appearance and illusion as so interpenetrant as to render truth at best relative, at worst unattainable; the possibility of error and deception as omnipresent ('die *Möglichkeit* solcher Täuschungen' – no. 38, p. 211); the sensation 'als wenn sich die Welt rückwärts drehte' (no. 46, p. 242; 'as if the world were turning backwards'): these signal a radically ironic universe marked by ambivalences, reversals of the norm, dislocations of perspective, in short, the harbingers of paradoxicality. In these insights Jean Paul's vision is the antithesis to that of Jane Austen, and the contrast is only sharpened by their contemporaneity. The ontological and social order implicit in *Pride and Prejudice* fosters a firmness of perspective and hence an irony of discrimination that ultimately resolves the initial ambiguities into explicit certainties. Jean Paul, on the other hand, is conscious of facing the chaotic potential of an interminable 'Widerschein ins Unendliche' (no. 12, p. 63; 'reflexion into the infinite'). Even though the chronicler inveighs against 'die jetzige Philosophie des Witzes' (no. 12, p. 63; 'the present day philosophy of wit'), his text, and Jean Paul's too, are supreme examples of that 'Schein des Ernstes, um den Ernst des Scheines oder den ironischen zu treffen'[41] ('semblance of gravity in order to achieve the grave or ironic semblance'). Semblance and gravity are wholly intertwined, like truth and illusion, and irony occurs at their intersection as a kind of cosmic humour.[42] While a conclusive, universally accepted line is drawn between semblance and gravity in *Pride and Prejudice,* in the *Flegeljahre* the boundaries are indeterminate as the two constantly infiltrate one another. In a realm of mirrors and echoes there is no respite of

security, not even in the voice of the narrator, who is himself as
mercurial as the shifting world he portrays. He is like Walt who
tries to set the clock right and 'kehrte die Umkehrung um' (no.
41, p. 222; 'reversed the reversal'). Only he does this so often
that in the end we no longer know what is right and what is
reversed.

7

The same sense of disorientation is also fomented by Jean Paul's
aberrant use of language. Its idiosyncracies elicited baffled
response from his contemporaries already. Madame de Staël,
perhaps for once herself at a loss for words, described it in an
adjective that has dogged Jean Paul ever since: 'très-bizarre'.[43]
Goethe considered it an example of 'Orientalität',[44] while
Heine roundly denounced it as 'baroque' and 'unpalatable'
('ungeniessbar').[45] This assortment of terms denotes a style that is
conspicuous, florid, and strange. Yet in its marked preference for
doubled, pluralistic forms, it is the appropriate linguistic
counterpart to the novel's layered structure and mirror motifs.

The basic principle governing the language of the *Flegeljahre* is
polarity. 'Besagter Jean Paul habe ferner oft den Leser ins
Dampfbad der Rührung geführt und sogleich ins Kühlbad der
frostigen Satire hinausgetrieben'[46] ('The said Jean Paul is
alleged, furthermore, to have led the reader on many occasions
into the steambath of sentiment and to have driven him out
immediately into the cold shower of icy satire'). In this much
quoted self-analysis, which summarises the criticisms directed
against him and also again testifies to his dualistic sense of self,
Jean Paul half humorously concedes the innate contradictoriness
of his style. The two-toned voice, the affective and the astringent,
is literally split in the *Flegeljahre* into the lusciousness of Walt and
the acerbity of Vult. Each acknowledges the need for the
complementary other: Vult envisages himself as the Sancho
Panza of realism alongside Walt's quixotic idealism (no. 14, p.
75), while Walt too recognises that life must be shared 'zwischen
Gesang und *Prosa*' (no. 35, p. 197; 'between *poetry* and *prose*'). A
whole series of wry pronouncements insists categorically on the
necessity for both modes and for the dualistic perspective
produced by their alternation: 'die Poesie ist ja doch ein Paar

Schlittschuhe, womit man auf dem glatten reinen kristallenen Boden des Ideals leicht fliegt, aber miserabel forthumpelt auf gemeiner Gasse' (no. 15, p. 85; 'poetry is, after all, a pair of skates, with which you can fly with ease over the smooth, pure, crystalline surface of the ideal, but thump about wretchedly on a common street'). Or again: 'In der Tat braucht der Mensch bei den besten Flügeln für den Äther doch auch ein Paar Stiefel für das Pflaster' (no. 41, p. 221; 'Indeed, besides the best wings for the ethereal heights, one also needs a pair of boots for the lowly pavement'). The language of the *Flegeljahre* has both wings and boots in its stylistic 'Hoch- und Tiefebene'[47] ('upper and lower level'). The ecstatic musings of Walt, prompted by nature, music, or his feelings, form the upper level which is best illustrated in his lyrical evocation of the 'Idyll of a Swedish Pastor'. The discourse of this lofty side is sonorously high-flown, emotionally laden, and strongly associative. As for the lower level, the boots on the common street are those of Vult, whose cynical commonsense finds vivid expression in an energetic outpouring of pithy colloquialisms spiced with comic pictorial images. These two tones are separate but juxtaposed in the conversations between Walt and Vult, in their letters, in the excerpts from their respective journals and other writings intercalated in the text of the *Flegeljahre*. The complicated design of the narrative, through its liberal openness to such insertions, gives the reader immediate experience of each facet. In its heterogeneity, the discourse of the *Flegeljahre* is a brilliant incarnation of the dissonance that is its thematic and structural core.

The chronicler is able to adopt either tone, though his own voice, in his letters and comments, is noticeably closer to Vult's than to Walt's. His affinity with the waspish Vult is most apparent in the mischievousness of his eclectic imagery which effects a drop from the upper to the lower level. During the reading of Van der Kabel's will, for instance, the book-dealer, Passvogel, is described as looking 'wie ein Hund, der das Brechmittel, das ihm der Pariser Hundarzt Demet auf die Nase gestrichen, langsam ableckt' (no. 1, p. 14; 'like a dog who slowly licks off the emetic put onto his nose by the Parisian veterinarian Demet'). The proximity of the chronicler's idiom to Vult's has important implications for the ironic thrust of the *Flegeljahre*. For the similarity of their language suggests a kinship of vision. To identify J. P. F. Richter unilaterally with Vult would be mistaken because he has empathy with Walt too and speaks in his mode also. But usually his stance tends to merge with Vult's, and this forms the basis for his irony at the expense of Walt's rhapsodically evoked castles in the air which are exposed as the mere mirages they are. Walt's confident expectations of a fine romantic adventure, for example, are ridiculed through a reductive juxtaposition: it would not have astonished him 'falls ihm etwa eine Fürstentochter einmal ans Herz gefallen wäre, oder der fürstliche Hut ihres Herrn Vaters auf den Kopf' (no. 13, p. 66; 'if perchance a prince's daughter had suddenly fallen upon his heart, or her father's princely hat upon his head'). Walt's ready accommodation to the contingencies of existence, the chronicler explains,

> kam aber nicht bloss von seiner angeborenen Milde, überall nur die übermalte, nicht die leere Seite der Menschen und des Lebens vorzudrehen, sondern auch von jener göttlichen Entzückung und Berauschung her, womit besonders Dichter, die nie auf Reisen waren, einen von Träumen und Gegenden nachblitzenden Reisetag beschliessen; die prosaischen Felder des Lebens werden ihnen, wie in Italien die wirklichen, von poetischen Myrten umkränzt, und die leeren Pappeln von Trauben erstiegen (no. 13, p. 64)

> (stemmed not only from that innate gentleness that made him focus everywhere only on the embellished and not the empty aspects of people and of life, but also from that divine enthusiasm and intoxication with which especially poets on their first travels end a day still aglow in their minds with dreams and vistas; the prosaic fields of life become for them, as they really are in Italy, wreathed with myrtles, and the bare poplars encircled with vines).

The idyll is here disrupted through the detached comment of a knowing narrator. This is the closest approximation in the *Flegeljahre* to the traditional practice of irony in uncovering the discrepancy between truth and illusion.

Such transparency is, however, rare. Generally the irony latent in the language of the *Flegeljahre* is not what is commonly known as verbal irony, i.e. saying the contrary to what is meant, or obliquely indicating by discreet clues the disparity between appearance and reality. Appearance and reality are here so fluid as to preclude the stable irony of discrimination which is based on firm distinctions. The ironic effect of Jean Paul's language is considerably more devious and recondite in its source: it derives from the discongruity between the notorious agglomerations and the fragmentation resulting from them. For the outcome of the extraordinary ingatherings is, perversely, the contrary to expectation, namely a perceptual dispersal.

Jean Paul's predilection for a luxuriant profusion of words and images is very evident in the *Flegeljahre*. Language is a medium where he can give free rein to what he himself called his 'fataler *frère terrible*, die Phantasie'[48] ('unruly *frère terrible*, imagination'). The verbal prolixity, as a register of the multiplicity of the universe, represents the stylistic equivalent to the tendency to lateral spread in the structural pattern of the *Flegeljahre*. In characteristically serio-comic vein Jean Paul wrote a treatise on compound words: *Über die deutschen Doppelwörter: eine grammatische Untersuchung in zwölf alten Briefen und zwölf neuen Postskripten* (*On German Compound Words: A Grammatical Analysis in Twelve Old Letters and Twelve New Postscripts*). He examines the rules governing those verbal twins, triplets and quadruplets 'mit welchen allein, wie bekannt, Charaden zu erzeugen sind, durch Tisch- und Bett-Scheidung und Wiedertrauung des Doppelwortes'[49] ('with which alone, as is well known, charades can be conjured up through board- and bed-separation and remarriage of the double-word'). He delights in piling up such preposterous combinations as 'Fürstenschlafkammerthürhüter',[50] making 'wahrhaft babylonische Vergleichstürme'[51] ('veritable Babylonian towers of comparison'), and stringing together the most outlandish nominal and conceptual lists:

> Ich berühre darin die Vaccine – den Buch- und Wollenhandel – die Monatsschriftsteller – Schellings magnetische Metapher oder Doppelsystem – – die neuen Territorialpfähle – die Schwänzelpfennige – die Feldmäuse samt den Fichtenraupen – und Bonaparten – das berühr' ich, freilich flüchtig als Poet. (no. 2, p. 21)

> (I shall touch therein on vaccination – the book and wool trade – writers for monthly periodicals – Schelling's magnetic

metaphors or double system – – the new territorial markers – the fines for remissions – fieldmice together with caterpillars – and Bonaparte – I touch on that admittedly only fleetingly as a poet.)

The utter nonsensicality of this ludicrous jumble elicits a dumbfounded astonishment. These accumulations, devoid of assonance, alliteration or rhyme, signify the defiance of all canons of rationality through a capricious poetic wit.

A similar sense of bewilderment is provoked by the weird collection of items in Van der Kabel's cabinet of curiosities. For each chapter that he delivers the chronicler is rewarded with one piece which is named alongside the chapter-title: no. 1, 'Bleiglanz: Testament' ('A Vein of Lead: The Will'); no. 23, 'Congeries von mäusefahlen Katzenschwänzen: Tischreden Klothars und Glanzens' ('Congeries of mouse-gray cats'-tails: Table Talk of Klothar and Glanz'); No. 4, 'Mammutsknochen aus Astrakan: Das Zauberprisma' ('Mammoth Bones from Astracan: The Magic Prism'); No. 57, 'Regenpfeifer: Doppel-Leben' ('Winter Plover: Double Life'); No. 17, 'Rosenholz: Rosental' ('Rosewood: Rose Valley'); No. 15, 'Riesenmuschel: Die Stadt – chambre garnie' ('A Gigantic Shell: The City – furnished Lodgings'). In some of these pairs, a certain consonance is discernible between the object and the chapter to which it belongs, as in the last two; in a few, the correlation appears to be ironic, as in the first two; but the vast majority, particularly in the latter part of the novel, have little relevance to each other.[52]

These agglomerative techniques, far from fostering the move towards wholeness, breed, on the contrary, the anxiety of disjunction. The sheer quantity and variety is so overwhelming as to induce a feeling of estrangement when the excess of words and images obscures the meaning, acting as a cover, like the masks worn by the protagonists and the pseudonyms adopted by the author. The surface abundance conceals an inner decomposition, the dissolution of the world into an unrelated mass of details. The appearance of amalgamation does not coincide with the reality of disintegration. Metaphorically even more than literally this is a 'Gedankenstrichstil'[53] ('style made up of dashes') whose disruptive impact can be likened to that of a surrealist[54] painting. It jumps unpredictably from one object to another in a rhythm reminiscent of the rabbit's 'hoppeln' ('erratic little leaps'). Its compulsive mobility, that 'Paroxysmus der Bewegung'[55] ('paroxysm of movement') is yet another manifestation of that perspectivism that shies from the fixity of a single image or expression in favour of inexhaustible alternatives.

The upshot of this agitated multiplicity is not to encompass the world, but to fragment it. The grotesque juxtapositions bring disparate elements alongside each other but not together. As Friedrich Schlegel already noted: 'Richter experimentirt bloss ohne darzustellen; er armirt die Objekte und setzt sie in Contact'[56] ('Richter merely experiments without representing; he mobilises objects and puts them into contact'). These mobilised objects, because they do not fuse or even interlock into cohesive units, underline the disjointedness of things rattling around at random. The lengthy metaphors in particular are startling not for the connections they establish, but as paradigms of dissociation. Their momentum is the ironic opposite to their customary function since they puzzle instead of illuminating. The language of the *Flegeljahre* makes the things it describes opaque, not clear; it veils meaning. Though the question of its efficacy as a means of communication is not directly addressed, an indirect answer is contained in its practices which constitute a barrier to understanding.

Jean Paul's language dis-arranges and deranges the homely German provincial environments in which the narratives are set. Its discontinuities are symptomatic of the chaotic absurdity of a world swayed by contingency. It causes a shock not as immediate as, but in the last resort more searing than the dislocations in *Don Juan*, where the narrator's manipulating hand and ruminating voice always remain clearly in evidence. As he disposes his material, calculates his effects, and looks to his reception, it is he who is assuming responsibility for his narrative. In the *Flegeljahre*, on the other hand, the narrator retreats into the role of a recording annalist, abjuring responsibility for his tale to the point where he laments the undertaking commissioned of him. The ironies and reversals are not devised and instilled by the narrator, as in *Don Juan*; instead, they are innate to the fabric of his material, and the role of his discourse is simultaneously to articulate and to conceal them. In the carnival of life – and of this text – death 'finally pulls off the dancers not only their masks but their faces' (no. 37, p. 207; 'am Schlusse den Tänzern nicht nur die Larven abzieht, auch die Gesichter'). This sinister image evokes the frightening chasm beneath the game of life and of this text. That ultimate reality is screened through the mask of appearances. In the text of the *Flegeljahre* it is language that has the function of the mask.

8

The mask is never wholly lifted in the *Flegeljahre*, the discrepancy between appearance and reality never resolved. The novel's enigmatic ending has provoked considerable dispute as to whether it is finished, or whether a continuation was intended. While earlier critics, such as Frey, regret its incompleteness, more recent analysts, notably Bosse[57] and Neumann, argue that it is complete as it stands. Schweikert maintains that the character of the work is such that it 'musste notwendigerweise Fragment bleiben'[58] ('had of necessity to remain a fragment').

In its avoidance of either the happy end or the catastrophe, the close of the *Flegeljahre* is inconclusive. Yet in its last chapters it is patently heading for calamity. The final split between Walt and Vult is symbolised in the dissolution of their communal living arrangements; the idyll of their shared quarters ('Einquartierung' – the pun in the German is hardly translatable); 'wie ein Vögelpaar *ein* Nest oder Quartier bewohnen' (no. 55, p. 311; 'like a pair of birds inhabit *one* nest or dwelling'), is of short duration. After the revelations at the masked ball, Vult hastily packs his things and leaves, without his brother even realising what is happening: 'Noch aus der Gasse herauf hörte Walt entzükt die entfliehenden Töne reden, denn er merkte nicht, dass mit ihnen der Bruder entfliehe' (no. 64, p. 380; 'Walt heard the fleeing notes float up from the street with rapture, not noticing that with them his brother was fleeing'). Those last words of the *Flegeljahre* leave little doubt as to the negativity of the denouement. Whether the dualism between Walt and Vult is overcome on a higher level in sublimated form in the joint romance on which they are engaged during their cohabitation of their 'Doppel-Käfig' (no. 55, p. 311; 'double-cage'): that is a moot point. The harmony absent in the real world is, according to German Romantic theory, attainable in the work of art.[59] Though we are given to understand that *Hoppelpoppel oder das Herz* was eventually published, we have insufficient and unreliable information as to its nature, so that once again we are left in a state of uncertainty.

The cryptic but decidedly sombre ending is indicative of the tendency of the *Flegeljahre* as a whole. The ultimate release into knowledge of the truth, or even into true knowledge, never takes place. A distinction is drawn between those limited areas, such as the law, where definitive truth is deemed accessible (no. 20, p. 117) and the wider, more complex forum of philosophical enquiry where fallaciousness is regarded as virtually inevitable (no. 23, p. 132). In its succession of errors, misapprehensions and misconstructions, the *Flegeljahre* offers a graphic illustration of this pessimistic assumption. The mistakes range the whole gamut from the comical to the grave: from Walt's phonetic mishearing of 'cher père' as 'Scher-Bär' (no. 22, p. 129; 'dear father' as 'shear bear') and his heedless misreading of 'e' and 'c', 'f' and 's', '6' and '9' in his proofs (no. 59, p. 340) to his serious misjudgement of Klothar, in whom he idolises, as Vult so forcefully puts it, 'nur schlechte abgeschmierte Heiligenbilder deiner innern Lebens- und Seelenbilder' (no. 56, p. 316; 'mere badly daubed icons reproducing your soul's inner images'). Walt's projection of the ideal onto a worthless person has its ironic counterpoint in his failure to recognise the sterling worth of his own brother. Such misprisions become increasingly common as the novel progresses, reaching their climax in the disguises and mis-takings of the masked ball. 'Versprechen' (literally, 'mis-speaking') is partnered by 'verhören' (literally, 'mis-hearing') to result in a confusion of miscommunication at cross purposes: 'Wina missverstand wieder sein Missverstehen' (no. 59, p. 343; 'Wina again misunderstood his misunderstanding'). What begins as a comedy of errors turns into a tragedy of mis-knowledge, 'des Verkennens' (no. 50, p. 265). The German term *verkennen*, in its combination of *kennen* (to know) with the particle *ver* to denote the shift into misconception, has no direct equivalent in English. It is the perfect word to summarise the unhappy stalemate at the end of the *Flegeljahre* when Walt has bestowed his friendship on Klothar, and Wina has confessed her love for Walt to the 'wrong' twin in the costume of the other. Only Vult, who has dropped his pose of blindness, has insight into the ironic perversity of these reversals when he writes in his parting letter to Walt:

Wir beide waren uns einander ganz aufgetan, so wie zugetan ohnehin; uns so durchsichtig, wie eine Glastür; aber Bruder, vergebens schreibe ich aussen ans Glas meinen Charakter mit leserlichen Charakteren: Du kannst doch innen, weil sie umgekehrt erscheinen, nichts lesen und sehen, als das Umgekehrte. Und so bekommt die ganze Welt fast immer sehr lesbare, aber umgekehrte Schrift zu lesen. (no. 64, pp. 374–5)

(We two were as wholly open as we were close to each other; as transparent to each other as a glass door; but brother, it is in vain that I write my character outside on the glass door in legible letters: you, on the inside, to whom they appear in reverse, can read and see nothing other than the reverse. And so the whole world nearly always gets very readable but reversed script to read.)

This eternally reversed script of mis-knowledge is the antithesis to the confident recognition of true knowledge in *Pride and Prejudice*, where the ironies of misjudgement are positively resolved as appearance becomes distinguishable from truth. In the *Flegeljahre*, on the contrary, because such concepts as appearance, truth, and reality are perceived as fluid, the ambivalences resist resolution. For this reason, 'Jean Paul kann das Spannungsverhältnis' [Sein/Schein] 'nicht auflösen, sondern nur gestalten'[60] ('Jean Paul cannot resolve; merely depict the tension' [between appearance and reality]). This non-resolution is exemplified in Walt, a static character, as steeped in his illusions at the end as he had been at the beginning. Unable to learn, to 'see', to discern, he remains unredeemed, in contrast to Elizabeth and Darcy who do develop the better judgement that enables them to rise above their initial prejudices. The two novels represent differing views of the world and of human nature, and consequently also of the temper of irony. To the optimism of Jane Austen it is transitory and solvable; to the darker, more deeply doubting vision of Jean Paul it is ingrained and indecipherable. Just as there are no simple constructions in the language or design of the *Flegeljahre*, so there are no affirmative reconstructions of an ulterior 'true' meaning. The movement of the *Flegeljahre* is the opposite to that of *Pride and Prejudice*: further and further into the obliquities of irony rather than out of them into the clarity of certitude.

A world that is, as it were, permanently and inescapably reversed, can best be tolerated with humour. Humour is indeed central to Jean Paul's work. But in the *Flegeljahre* it is not the liberating means of self-transcendence, the 'grosses Erziehungsmittel zur geistigen Freiheit'[61] ('great medium of elevation to spiritual greatness') that it is generally claimed to be. The 'Komik des irren Durcheinanders'[62] ('comedy of the droll pell-mell') is very much to the fore for sure. However, though the jocular aspects of situations are often explored, as when Walt and Vult in their communal habitat and communal poverty become 'jeder der Almosen-Pfleger des andern' (no. 57, p. 322; 'each the alms-keeper of the other'), such surface badinage, far from suppressing the tragic undercurrent, brings it into sharper relief. For the humour of the *Flegeljahre* is not of a benevolently conciliatory kind; it has a biting edge of bitterness. Vult's parting letter, despite its wit, shows the anguish of a man thwarted in his desire to give affection, and driven against his will more deeply into the isolation of the 'Schmollgeist' (no. 18, p. 103; 'sulky spirit'). His humour, like Jean Paul's, becomes simultaneously an expression of, and a cover for his scepticism; it is a black 'gallow's humour' (*Galgenhumor*) that delights in the grotesque and the paradoxical because it finds in distortions and reversals of the norm the format most consonant with its particular perception of the universe. As reflections of the contradictoriness of a world whose script is in reverse, the grotesque and the paradoxical become the preferred shapes of the ironist's humour.

Irony, then, is not an instrument applied for a specific purpose in the *Flegeljahre*. It does not have the function of a constructive corrective, as in *Pride and Prejudice*, nor is it a strategem for demolition, as in *Madame Bovary* and in *Don Juan*. Because of its volatility the irony of the *Flegeljahre* has been dismissed as 'kaum wahrnehmbar'[63] ('barely perceptible'). It is certainly most elusive, not manifesting itself in its simpler forms as a verbal trope or as a dramatic device. There are a few instances of such irony, but they are not of primary importance in the *Flegeljahre*.

The real difficulty with the irony of the *Flegeljahre* is that it is itself, in an appropriately ironic fashion, paradoxical: it is so hard to pin down not because it is either scant or subsidiary, but, on the contrary, because it is so pervasive and commanding. It is immanent to the core of the work rather than ostensible on its surface. The world portrayed in the *Flegeljahre*, with its doubles, mirrors, masks, layers and agglomerations, is a self-contradictory and constantly shifting realm of paradoxicality. It can neither be arranged into its proper order, as can that of *Pride and Prejudice*, nor mastered from the vantage-point of a single, knowing perspective, as in *Madame Bovary*. It is a world not so much of disorder as of non-order. Truth, identity, reality, and narration too dissolve in an indeterminacy that admits alternatives without reconciling them. So nothing is definite, everything possible: the frames are not closed, the plots not concluded, the relationships not clarified. The inverted script is reversed not just once but again and again until its message can be read only as a cipher for what must be called 'undecidability'.

The irony of the *Flegeljahre*, therefore, though less immediately visible than that of *Pride and Prejudice*, *Madame Bovary*, or *Don Juan*, is more intrinsic to the text and also more radical in the literal sense of the word: at its root, at its very kernel. For this is not a localised irony directed against certain characters or certain features of society; it animates the text in its totality and in its every facet as a fictional system. The ironic handling of narrative form goes far beyond the largely jocular play with the various levels of discourse in *Don Juan*. Once the perception of paradox becomes the very axis of the narrative, the novel is turned into 'ein durch Widersprüche sich vorwärts treibendes Weltpanoptikum'[64] ('a world panopticon propelling itself forwards through its own contradictoriness'). Irony is the shaping artistic force of the *Flegeljahre* in the same way as it is the determinant factor of its ontological vision. It is so basic to the work that it could be termed a genetic irony. In this respect it comes close to Solger's view of irony as 'künstlerische Dialektik'[65] ('artistic dialectic') and to Cleanth Brooks' 'irony as a structural principle'. However, in its origins and in its ramifications, the irony of the *Flegeljahre* surpasses even these broad categories. Its nature can best be understood through Walter Benjamin's fundamental discrimination between irony of content ('Stoff') and that other type of irony which he denotes as 'Ironisierung der Form'[66] ('ironisation of form') and which he regards as the crux of German romantic irony. The former is presented as negative, subjective, and destructive, while the latter is positive, objective and constructive (p. 491). Whether such an implicit value judgement can be substantiated is another question, for this seems to me one of the points where German Romantic practice diverges from its theory. Be that as it may, Benjamin's distinction is extremely important in its identification of one kind of irony that operates essentially *within* the parameters of the fiction, and another that extends beyond the limits of the fictional world to encompass the text in its entirety. The former type of irony is indigenous to 'proper' books, while the latter prevails in 'illicit' books, to revert to Virginia Woolf's terminology. Benjamin cites Jean Paul's 'zerfetzte Romane' (p. 49; 'ragged novels') together with Tieck's dramas as the clearest examples of the second type of irony, as incarnations of the 'paradoxen Versuch . . ., am Gebilde noch durch Abbruch zu bauen' (p. 492; 'paradoxical attempt . . ., to continue building the artifact through rupture'). This striking image delineates an irony that transcends the boundaries of the artifact by continuing the cycle of self-creation and self-destruction in an unending succession, impelled by its own inner dynamism. This sort of irony is adumbrated in *Don Juan* in the metafictional thrust that is one strand of its irony. It comes fully into its own in the *Flegeljahre*, where the irony becomes, to adopt Heimrich's tentative formulation, 'meta-ironic in conception'[67] and metaphysical in implication. What it loses in concrete palpability, it gains in the enormous power latent in its progressive paradoxicality.

7 Denis Diderot: *Jacques le fataliste et son maître*, 1771–78(?)

> 'Peut-être que cela était-il vrai,
> peut-être que cela était-il faux:
> que sait-on?'
>
> ('Maybe that was true, maybe that
> was false: what does one know?')

1

The opening of *Pride and Prejudice* is striking, of *Madame Bovary* intriguing, of *Don Juan* startling; but that of *Jacques le fataliste* is downright provocative:

> Comment s'étaient-ils rencontrés? Par hasard, comme tout le monde. Comment s'appelaient-ils? Que vous importe? D'où venaient-ils? Du lieu le plus prochain. Où allaient-ils? Est-ce que l'on sait où l'on va? Que disaient-ils? Le maître ne disait rien; et Jacques disait que son capitaine disait que tout ce qui nous arrive de bien et de mal ici-bas était écrit là-haut.[1]

> (How had they met? By chance, like everyone else. What were they called? Does that matter to you? Where were they coming from? From the nearest place. Where were they going? Does one know where one is going? What were they saying? The master was saying nothing; and Jacques was saying that his captain used to say that all the good and the ill that befalls us down here was written up there.)

The shock effect of this brusque beginning amounts to a verbal,

159

psychological and ontological assault on the reader. What is heralded is a text that has been described, in a modest understatement, as 'an odd book as well as a complex one' that 'almost invariably irritates'[2] on a first reading, and continues to do so. For the questions remain unanswered to the very end, resisting the fictive reader's repeated, explicit efforts, in bursts of impatience, to raise them again: 'Mais, pour Dieu, l'auteur, me dites-vous, où allaient-ils? . . . Mais, pour Dieu, lecteur, vous répondrai-je, est-ce que l'on sait où l'on va? Et vous, où allez-vous?' (p. 83; 'But for God's sake, author, you say to me, where were they going? . . . But for God's sake, reader, I'll answer, does one know where one is going? You, do you know where you are going?'). The surging curiosity aroused by the initial questions is never satisfied; definitive information never comes as questions are countered either by further questions or by frustrating non-answers (e.g. 'From the nearest place'). Normative narrative expectations are continually disappointed by this systematic denial of the simplest basic facts such as the master's name, and the destination and purpose of the journey. If the act of naming conventionally confers stable meaning, the persistence of anonymity suggests mystery and groping uncertainty. Besides the master, the narrator too remains nameless as a curiously shadowy but vociferous presence; and even Jacques himself has only a kind of generic first name and no surname. The questions that introduce *Jacques le fataliste*, apart from illustrating its characteristic strategy, announce a world in which the security of knowledge is beyond grasp.

The absence of answers and of names creates a space of indeterminacy that encompasses the narrative situation. The questions, because they remain open, spawn other questions: whose is the speaking voice? and who are the 'you' that are addressed? A dialectic is inaugurated between a fictive narrator and a contrived reader or readers that constitutes a major dynamism of the text. Yet despite the prominent role these personae play, none of them – any more than Jacques or his master – is physically or morally delineated with the precision accorded to such subsidiary figures as Mlle Duquênoi and Hudson. For instance, whether the narrator withholds information in order to incite the reader's participation, or whether he himself is not in the know either, stays a matter of conjecture. Both postulates are intimated in the course of *Jacques le fataliste* in typically ambiguous fashion. From the interrogational mode of its opening only two inferences can be drawn with any assurance: that the relationship between narrator and reader is a tense, almost adversary one, and that this in turn engenders the suspicion hovering in and over the entire text.

The adversary relationship between fictive narrator and reader stems from the narrator's quizzical stance. He is so patently and outrageously unreliable that the source and the effects of his unreliability become, as it were, independent objects of fascination. He is evasive, elusive, mercurial, verbosely eager to tell his tale, but at the same time quick to rebuke and rebuff his audience for alleged recalcitrancy. A will-o'-the-wisp of duplicitous wit, he is recognisably an ironist of the type whose constantly amended statements are designed to defy reconstruction into firm meaning. His signals to the reader are characterised by incessant fluctuations and surprising reversals: 'Cela est très beau. – Assurément! et d'après cette action héroïque, vous croyez à Gousse un grand fonds moral? Eh bien, détrompez-vous, il n'en avait pas plus qu'il n'y a dans la tête d'un brochet. – Cela est impossible. – Cela est.' (p. 102; 'That's fine. – Certainly! and judging by this heroic action, you credit Gousse with moral solidity? Well, shed your illusions, he has no more than is in a pike's head. – That's impossible. – That is.'). He delights in teasing the reader, alternately chiding him for his imputed impatience and then abruptly turning to fault his placidity: ' – Mais Jacques et son maître? Mais les amours de Jacques? Ah! lecteur, la patience avec laquelle vous m'écoutez me prouve le peu d'intérêt que vous prenez à mes deux personnages, et je suis tenté de les laisser où ils sont . . .' (p. 102; ' – But what about Jacques and his master? But what about Jacques' amorous adventures? Oh reader, the patience with which you are listening to me shows how little interest you take in my two characters, and I am tempted to leave them where they are . . .').

This wayward oscillation between cajolery and censure clearly militates against the development of a stable relationship. To put it bluntly, this narrator reveals himself to be untrustworthy. His shiftiness is the central axis on which the narration of *Jacques le fataliste* performs its astonishing girations, and it is also the primary site of its irony. Granted that the dialectical dialogue between the narrating voice and the fictive reader 'functions as a principle of irony and relativism',[3] the ironic dislocation emanates first and foremost from the narrator. It is he who is the embodiment of a roguish scepticism that undermines, retracts, and destroys whatever it has just posited and created. Because of his mediating intervention between story and reader, *Jacques le fataliste* has an erratic framework; its norm is the chronic turbulence generated by its volatile narrator. Its narrative disposition differs significantly from the mutual confidence between narrator and reader in *Pride and Prejudice* and from the shared perspective in *Madame Bovary*. Even in *Don Juan* the narrator, for all his bantering, is on an intimate footing with the reader, beckoning him to laugh *with* him *at* the hero and the work in progress. In *Jacques le fataliste*, however, the link between narrator, text and reader, if not actually dissolved, as Herbert Dieckmann[4] maintains, is gravely complicated by the refractive distortions of an ironic narrator, whose overt sporting with his fictive reader precludes a trusting rapport. The capers of this ironic narrator debar not only a steady contract between the telling voice and the perceiving mind, but also direct access to objective information about Jacques, his master, or their journey for either the fictive or the actual reader. Everything we hear has had to pass through the filter of the narrating persona, and who knows how capriciously selective or impishly slanted his account is?

The reiterated questions throughout *Jacques le fataliste* thus represent the verbal precipitate of the text's continuing state of flux, while the lack of a settled framework is indicative of the breaks in its system of values. As a result, *Jacques le fataliste* is pervaded by a haunting tone of irony, a disquieting feeling that the reader – fictive and actual – is being led on and on, as indeed we are, but is left without any base from which to interpret with confidence. No ironic counter-meaning can be implied in contrast to established norms because the norms themselves are tantalisingly vexatory. Although the traditional rhetorical strategies of irony – hyperbole and anti-climax, *non-sequiturs* and contradictions, cross-communication, etc. – are much in evidence from the opening onwards, there is no authoritative context to which to relate them. Even the clues often prove misleading or equivocal. Such is the case with the word *hasard* (chance), the first noun in the text, which recurs again immediately as the last noun at the end of the initial dialogue between Jacques and his master, so that it enframes the opening episode as if in prefiguration of its significance for *Jacques le fataliste.* Yet its import remains ambivalent. Does the prominence of 'chance' alert us obliquely to the prevalence of a force that contravenes the voiced ascendancy of a predestined fate? or is 'chance' to be seen as a manifestation of that fate? or is this a complicated double irony,[5] designed to lead the reader astray? The multiple alternatives, all potentially valid, but none achieving the status of undisputed definity, induce a sense of disorientation, of floating in an unstable universe. When the context is flux and the norm is doubt, irony resists reconstruction.

By the time we reach the only categoric assertion in the opening paragraph, namely 'que tout ce qui nous arrive de bien et de mal ici-bas était écrit là-haut' ('that all the good and the ill that befalls us down here was written up there'), we are sufficiently dazed by the series of questions and non-answers to be uncertain whether to accept this affirmation or to query it too. It comes as the climax of the only extended phrase in the paragraph, but its authority is sapped by its place at the end of a word-of-mouth chain ('Jacques disait que son capitaine disait' – 'Jacques was saying that his captain used to say'). Is the overt message to be taken at its face value, or is it to be read as an ironic reversal of its true meaning? The interrogational form and the syncopated style of the beginning could be taken to signal a covert countermeaning; the illogicality, disorder and inconsequentiality of the discourse seem in contradiction to the explicit thesis of an orderly and inevitable sequence of cause and effect governing the world. However, the possibility cannot be ruled out that this may in itself be an elaborate masking deception. No possibility can ever be ruled out in *Jacques le fataliste*; the fictive and the actual reader are actively encouraged to entertain every conceivable hypothesis. The turbulent mobility of *Jacques le fataliste* forecloses any absolute conclusions. The dualisms, tensions, and dilemmas emanating from its intrinsic indeterminacy are the manifestations of its rampant irony.

2

With disconcerting abruptness, after the preliminary exchanges between the fictive narrator and his contrived . reader, and between Jacques and his master, Jacques all of a sudden breaks

out in a curse of the inn-keeper and his inn. Because he had got
drunk on the inn's poor wine, he had forgotten to water the
horses; this had made his father so angry that he had given
Jacques a sound hiding. Out of spite and vexation Jacques had
joined a regiment passing through on its way to a battle, where he
had sustained a wound that was tended by a young woman with
whom he fell in love. Thus, he explains, it is with the
inexorability of 'les chaînons d'une gourmette' (p. 36; 'the links
in a curb-bit') that the inn's poor wine had led to his being lame
and in love. This preposterous string of associations illustrates
Jacques' belief in that 'suite d'effets nécessaires' (p. 218;
'succession of inevitable causes and effects') that is the essence of
his philosophical stance of fatalism. At the same time it hints at a
certain latitude for free will in so far as Jacques does, after all,
make his own decision to enlist. Whether falling in love involves
volition or not is a moot point. Be that as it may, this
introductory example of the workings of fatalism suggests an
ironic critique of the concept through the sheer incongruity of its
farfetched overstatement. At its first appearance, the two central
issues bearing on its place in *Jacques le fataliste* become apparent:
its innate ambivalence as a metaphysical theory and, even more,
as a practical guide to conduct, and, in addition, the force of
irony to which it is exposed.

As an ontological and epistemological system, fatalism
harbours serious inconsistencies. The difficulty pivots on the
discord between the laws of necessity and the claims of freedom in
a world where events are seen alternately as belonging to a
necessary order and as unfolding with a capricious freedom. On
the one hand, predictability is the consequence of the necessary
enactment of what has been 'écrit là-haut' ('written up there') on
some mysterious 'grand rouleau' ('great scroll'). On the other
hand, our ignorance of what is in fact predicated and our
uncertainty as to what may follow from any given chain of causes
and effects can be seen as the equivalent of some personal liberty.
The 'ironic ambiguity of the fatalistic formula' has been aptly
summarised by Aram Vartanian: 'fatalism can pertain either to a
necessary concatenation of events, hence implying their
predictability, or contrariwise, to a fortuitous series of events,
with the suggestion of their unpredictability'.[6] In other words,
fatalism can denote a rigid predetermination, or it can accept flux
as a necessary corollary. Within the system, the quandary turns

most acutely on the role of chance, of that *hasard*, on which *Jacques le fataliste* opens, obviously not by chance! Is the contingency of chance contrary to the doctrine of fatalism, or should its evident incursions into human life be regarded as an incarnation of necessity, an expression of what is 'written up there'?[7] To take a concrete instance, when Jacques' runaway horse twice in succession gallops off towards the gallows, is this because the horse is in some way 'inspiré' (p. 93), cognizant of the fate prescribed for Jacques on the great scroll? or is this merely one of those 'hasards singuliers' (p. 78; 'strange chances') in which human experience abounds? On a practical level the puzzle is resolved when the horse turns out to have belonged previously to the hangman, and to be following its homing instincts. But on the philosophic plane enigma continues to hang over *Jacques le fataliste*. Because of the paradoxicality of its metaphysical base, the text is grounded in quicksand. Its contextual frame of reference, being itself devoid of certainty, cannot function as a sound determinant of standards. Its norm is marked by an overriding irony: the unexpected is indistinguishable from the expected in a system that envisages everything as predetermined, yet that must perforce admit chance as the expression of an unknown destiny. So *Jacques le fataliste* rests – or rather, shifts – on an innate dualism. The 'geheime Doppelbödigkeit'[8] ('hidden double-grounding') of its irony resides in its conceptual core.

In the light of these doctrinal ambiguities, Jacques' easy-going accommodation with the fatalism inculcated into him by his captain is more readily comprehensible. He is attempting to come to grips with the problem he repeatedly encounters in his endeavour to remain faithful to the creed he has been taught. Since a totally consistent fatalism proves untenable, he makes his own little compromises; for example, he views chance not as a wilful independent agency, but rather as a disclosure of fate in the sense: what will be will be. He is most severely perplexed when he falls in love:

Est-ce qu'on est maître de devenir ou de ne pas devenir amoureux? Et quand on l'est, est-on maître d'agir comme si on ne l'était pas? Si cela eût été écrit là-haut, tout ce que vous vous disposez à me dire, je me le serais dit; (p. 40)

(Does one have the mastery to fall in love or not to? And when one is in love, does one have the mastery to act as though one were not? If that had been written up there, all that you are ready to tell me, I would have told myself;)

The involuntary act of falling in love can be converted into a controlled action of free will only through voluntary submission to all that is 'écrit là-haut': 'notre consentement à une loi nécessaire' (p. 212; 'our assent to a law of necessity') is, he argues with rather flimsy reasoning, the sole path to liberty. Jacques' muddled sophistry underlines the fallacies in the tenet he is trying to uphold even as he wends his slippery way through its intricacies:

> Le calcul qui se fait dans nos têtes, et celui qui est arrêté sur le registre d'en haut, sont deux calculs bien différents. Est-ce nous qui menons le destin, ou bien est-ce le destin qui nous mène? (p. 46)

> (The reckoning made in our heads, and that kept in the account up there are two quite different reckonings. Is it we who guide destiny, or rather is it destiny that guides us?)

These are among the questions that go unanswered in *Jacques le fataliste*. Jacques never attains clarity as to where he stands in regard to fatalism, nor do we for that matter. However, while theoretically proclaiming his complete subservience to his captain's teachings, empirically he relies on his own judgement in each particular situation, thereby retaining a considerable degree of freedom. And whatever happens through his actions is *post festum* declared a clear example of the fulfilment of what had been 'écrit là-haut' anyway. He cheerfully admits, 'je suis inconséquent' (p. 204; 'I am illogical'), maintaining for all practical purposes a guarded neutrality: 'Je ne crois ni ne décrois' (p. 43; 'I neither believe nor disbelieve'). Accused by his master of having his head stuffed with paradoxes, he replies: 'Et quel mal y aurait-il à cela? Un paradoxe n'est pas toujours une fausseté' (p. 90; 'And what's wrong with that? A paradox isn't always a falsehood'). In the last resort the espousal of paradox is the only way to live with fatalism.

The pattern of contradiction is incarnate in the relative positions of Jacques and his master too. For it is Jacques, the nominal adherent of fatalism, who reasons on the supposition of necessity while acting on the assumption of freedom as the occasion demands, whereas the master, who attacks Jacques' 'impertinent dicton' (p. 43; 'impudent axiom'), i.e. that everything is 'écrit là-haut', in fact turns out to be an 'automate' whose actions follow so predictable a course that he is perturbed by the slightest departure from his routine. The divergence in their attitudes is vividly revealed by their contrasting idiom. Jacques' is colourful and energetic, spiced with neologisms, borrowings from foreign languages, medical terminology, country dialects and army slang, while the master's is a curiously disembodied, anonymous voice, whose staid speech is laden with clichés as if he were repeating what had already been said, or reading from the orthodox script of the 'grand rouleau'. From the title onwards, it is the servant who takes precedent, who possesses the greater gusto and inventiveness as well as the greater eloquence in argumentation. Notwithstanding the axiom that he who takes a master is 'jamais libre' (p. 210; 'never free'), Jacques promptly browbeats his master into conceding that he is indispensable to him ('que je vous suis essentiel' – p. 211), leaving him no choice but to submit 'à la loi d'un besoin dont il n'est pas en votre pouvoir de vous affranchir' (p. 211; 'to the law of a need from which it is not within your power to free yourself'). The relationship of Jacques and his master represents a reversal of the customary social hierarchy. It is also, incidentally, a reversal of the literary paradigm from *Don Quixote*. These ironic inversions of normative expectations suggest, cumulatively, an insidious dislocation of the overtly posited order. Submission to what is written up there on the great scroll may be impressive as an ideology, but the refractory and anomalous quirks of human existence frustrate every attempt to apply it methodically.

Jacques le fataliste therefore hinges on a doctrine riddled with inconsistencies and paradoxes. What is more, that doctrine is presented in such a way as to bring out its ironic ambivalence. The fundamental thesis that everything is already written up there on some great scroll is expounded time and again with the relentless insistence of an advertising slogan. Some incidents seem to confirm it, such as the episode of Jacques' brother, Jean, and his companion who happened to be in Lisbon at the time of the earthquake. In answer to his master's enquiry as to their reason for going there, Jacques says. 'Chercher un tremblement de terre, qui ne pouvait se faire sans eux; être écrasés, engloutis, brûlés, comme il était écrit là-haut' (p. 81; 'To seek out an earthquake that couldn't take place without them; to be crushed, engulfed, burned, as it was written up there'). Jacques acquiesces in predestination with humorous resignation, whether it be his brother's death, his own arrest (p. 325), the knock on his head (p. 106) or his wretched cold (p. 218). The incongruity of his mechanical recourse to his motto amounts to a comic reduction of its worth. Nor are his beliefs well founded, for he holds them at second hand from his captain, who never appears in person, and who is shrouded in mystery. The dubiousness of the theory is exposed in the protracted and reiterated discussions between Jacques and his master. These could serve as paradigmatic evidence for Friedrich Schlegel's contention: 'Die Romane sind die sokratischen Dialoge unserer Zeit'[9] ('Narratives are the Socratic dialogues of our time') because they are the scene for a radical, ironic, dialectical scrutiny of common assumptions.

Through its precariousness, the doctrine of fatalism forms the second epicentre of irony in *Jacques le fataliste*, the persona of the narrator being the first. Irony is here the focal theme as well as the dominant mode. It is an integral and compound irony, far removed from the transparent ploys of the verbal trope. Its mainspring is not just an obliquely assertive opposition to a prescriptive norm that is deemed questionable or misguided. Its menacing implications derive from the covert postulate which animates the entire narrative: that certainty is unattainable.

3   *

The lack of sure standards, the unreliability of evidence, the uncertainty of all judgements, and the discrepancy between expectation and outcome: these are the recurrent motifs of *Jacques le fataliste*. On the most mundane level, not even pedestrian objects are exempt from the general untrustworthiness of this shaky universe: a dog may be mistaken for a person, while a coffin may prove a container not for a corpse but for contraband. Things are rarely what they seem: a paragon of piety turns out to be a whore, a best friend a treacherous villain, two duelling enemies bosom friends, and one of the most decent persons Jacques has ever met the hangman. Apart from such misconstructions as arise from misapprehensions or from intrigue and calculated deception, there is a deeper moral ambiguity that vitiates human judgement. It is given cryptic embodiment in a number of the subsidiary figures: is Gousse's peculiar behaviour utterly crazy or remarkably wise? How are Le Pelletier's actions to be interpreted? Was Jacques' conduct in giving so much of his money to a needy woman a 'belle oeuvre' (p. 125; 'good deed') or a 'sottise' ('folly')? The master, from a conventional moral position, praises Jacques for his beneficence, whereas Jacques realises his foolhardiness from the hindsight of the practical consequences – that he was promptly attacked by robbers who assumed, again quite mistakenly, that any man capable of such generosity must have considerable resources.

These seemingly minor incidents are of great importance because they address one of the central issues of *Jacques le fataliste*: that of mistaking 'le vrai pour le faux, le faux pour le vrai' (p. 99; 'the true for the false, the false for the true'). This is the typical pre-occupation of all ironic plots in so far as they pivot on the disparity between semblance and reality. In a predominantly optimistic context, such as that of *Pride and Prejudice*, the perplexity can be resolved by reference to the clear-cut distinctions of a firm and widely accepted scale of values. In the fluid and relativistic context of *Jacques le fataliste*, on the other hand, the confusion of true and false is an incessant pitfall into which the reader may slide as easily as Jacques and his master because moral standards are as wavering as the contractual framework and as the metaphysical creed. Even the foundations of evidence are shown to be dubious when the word of mouth chain is the primary means of transmission of information. Jacques picked up his belief in fatalism from the sayings of his captain. The landlady is ready to tell the adventures of two of her guests 'tout comme leur domestique l'a dite à ma servante, qui s'est trouvée par hasard être sa payse, qui l'a redite à mon mari, qui me l'a redite' (pp. 127–8; 'exactly as their servant told it to my maid, who happened by chance to be her countrywoman, who told it to my husband, who told it to me'). The chanciness of the entire process is underscored by the apparently casual inclusion of the clue word, 'hasard'. The riskiness of forming a judgement on such tenuous evidence is corroborated by the circumstances in which Le Pelletier's story is told. Its intricate encapsulation puts it beyond the reach of direct assessment; it is placed within a narrative within a narrative within a narrative. Jacques is telling his master about his captain with whom he was at an inn in Orleans when he heard 'une espèce d'orateur, le barbier de la rue' (p. 90; 'a kind of orator, the local barber') launch on *his* eye-witness account of Le Pelletier. But how much credence is to be attached to the memories of 'a kind of orator', or for that matter to the gossip of servants, or even of the landlady who seems educated beyond her station, yet who adamantly refuses to divulge her personal history? What we face in *Jacques le fataliste*, alongside a capricious fictive narrator and a controversial dogma, is an untrustworthy epistemology. With a sly irony the narrative casts aspersions on its own reliability, thereby further undermining the reader's already impaired confidence in his ability to interpret with any measure of assurance.

The difficulty, perhaps impossibility, of distinguishing true from false and of correctly evaluating moral dilemmas is the crux of the three extensive interpolated tales about Mme de la Pommeraye, Hudson, and Saint-Ouin. Their common motif is the deceptiveness of human conduct. In every instance the protagonists are themselves victims of unforeseen turns of events that come about through the unexpected reactions of their foes. Mme de la Pommeraye suffers an ironic reversal when she seeks revenge on her unfaithful lover by manipulating him into a marriage with a woman 'digne de vous' (p. 191; 'worthy of you'). The woman she has selected and trained for her machinations is a consummate hypocrite, an ex-prostitute now masked in chaste piety. The verbal irony of that phrase 'worthy of you' prepares for the ultimate irony of situation when the duped marquis finds greater happiness with his 'unworthy' wife than with the virtuous Mme de la Pommeraye: 'En vérité, je crois que je ne me repens de rien, et que cette Pommeraye, au lieu de se venger, m'aura rendu un grand service' (p. 195; 'In truth, I believe that I do not regret anything, and that that Pommeraye, instead of wreaking vengeance, has done me a great service'). Contrary to calculation, the marriage that was planned as a mesalliance is a singularly congenial match. The same crass discrepancy between intention and outcome marks the two parallel tales of Hudson and Saint-Ouin, which also deal with vice and virtue, and attest to the falsehood of surface appearances. Both involve astonishing reversals when Richard is trapped by Hudson, and the master deluded by Saint-Ouin. As in the case of Mme de la Pommeraye, the ironic turning of the tables suggests, beyond the arbitrary nature of social processes, human susceptibility to the bizarre and fortuitous, and the sheer waywardness of life. The psychological contrariness and inconsistency of the characters in *Jacques le fataliste* is the opposite to the consistent behaviour, whether for good or for ill, of Darcy, Bingley, and Wickham in *Pride and Prejudice.*

That steadiness on their part, together with the specific moral standards prevalent within their fictional world, enables the reader, like the protagonists themselves, to form positive or negative judgements once the reality behind the appearance has been uncovered. For that reality is stable; the social appearance may be temporarily misleading, but as soon as the mask is removed, there are no further surprises, disguises or even doubts. The opposite happens in *Jacques le fataliste:* 'Nous marchons dans la nuit au-dessous de ce qui est écrit là-haut' (p. 119; 'We walk in the dark beneath what is written up there'), Jacques tells his master, and we the readers are in much the same position in relation to the text we confront. Lacking both a dependable narrative contract and a secure normative system of values, we become increasingly aware of the insidiousness of ethical discriminations and interpretative readings. The minor interpolated tales about Gousse, Le Pelletier, Jean and Père Ange, and M. de Guerchy show again the absence of comprehensive solutions to moral problems or even of widely applicable principles. Each predicament is unique and not amenable to precedent. Moreover, actions and characters are often endowed with several conceivable meanings which are held in suspension. Like Jacques and his master, the reader faces a contradictory set of happenings, and it falls to him to figure out the most probable interpretation from among the multiple possibilities. Is Mme de la Pommeraye at least partially justified in her act of revenge on her faithless lover, or is she a despicable creature who gets her just deserts? Similarly, is Saint-Ouin perhaps less monstrous than he seems if he still remains loyal to Agathe after ten years? These alternatives are left open to the reader who is thereby forced into the same continual revaluation of empirical reality as Jacques and his master.

These persistent ambivalences can lead only to paradoxical non-conclusions: the unattainability of definitive verdicts; the relativity of all inferences; the enigmatic nature of human conduct; the questionability of all criteria; and the want of a

logical chain of cause and effect. The actual happenings in *Jacques
le fataliste*, as well as the text, represent an ironic refutation of its
theoretical fatalistic model of an inevitable sequence of cause and
effect. The action and movement of the narrative demonstrate
the unpredictability of existence, while its philosophical dogma
proclaims its predictability. The earthquake of Lisbon, that so
shook mid-eighteenth century Enlightenment minds, is a potent
countersymbol – and a threat – to the alleged inviolability of the
'grand rouleau'.

4

Jacques' invocation of that great scroll and what is written up
there runs through *Jacques le fataliste* like a choral refrain. It acts as
a constant reminder of the underlying philosophical dilemma and
as an ironic cipher of its obscurity. Neither Jacques nor the
master nor the narrator nor the fictive or the actual reader is ever
able to fathom the formula. In the 'little scroll' of this narrative,
its fallibility as a guide to conduct is exposed to an irony that
creates an internal anti-text in counterpoint to its overt text. Text
and anti-text are symbiotically fused, but in such a way that the
ironic countertext emerges through the devices whereby the
narrative purports to present the text while actually insinuating
the contrary.

   The treatment of the theme of the 'grand rouleau' is a good
example of the tactics adopted in *Jacques le fataliste*. The verbal
formulation and hence the idea of a 'great scroll' has covert ironic
force as 'an incongruous blend of opposites, an eccentric *alliance
du mots*'; since *rouleau* comes from the Latin diminutive *rotullus*,
i.e. little scroll, the discrepant combination with *grand* 'serves to
bring philosophy down to the patchwork uncertainties and antics
of Jacques and his master'.[10] Similarly, the repetition of the key
phrase 'écrit là-haut' to the point of parody reduces the theory it
enunciates to absurdity through its drastic schematisation and its
insertion in ludicrously inappropriate circumstances. In like
manner, Jacques' reiterated appeals to what 'mon capitaine
disait' ('my captain used to say'), supposedly to back the
authenticity of his assertions, has the contrary effect of
accentuating the derivative dubiousness of Jacques' ideas.
Occasionally *double entendre* is brought into play, as in the word

'ciel' (p. 132; 'heaven') which the narrator uses metereologically to refer to the rain that is delaying the journey, and which Jacques interprets as denoting providence.

Generally, however, the sporadic and limited reversals of verbal irony are superseded by a sustained rhetoric of paradox that depends less on specific strategies than on overall syntactical patterns. The marked predominance of interrogatives is the concrete expression of the questioning tone of *Jacques le fataliste*. Time and again the progress of the narrative is halted by a torrent of questions, usually addressed either by the fictive narrator to his contrived reader or vice versa. The interrogative is equally important in the conversations between Jacques and his master. The same sense of uncertainty as emanates from the questions is fostered by other stylistic traits: the high incidence of conditional tenses; the frequency of equivocating constructions such as 'Je ne crois ni ne décrois' (p. 43; 'I neither believe nor disbelieve'); the recurrence of 'peut-être' ('perhaps') in the open alternatives of 'peut-être que oui, peut-être que non' (p. 135; 'maybe yes, maybe no'). Also, the pronounced preference for dialogue, with its undulating give and take rhythm, is an almost physical embodiment of incessant movement. This is what Spitzer[11] has so aptly called the 'style of mobility', and its mobility is that of the hermeneutically closed self-referential text as it turns on its own axis. By its obdurate refusal to admit any steadfast affirmations, it implicitly subverts referentiality through its *de facto* denial of a consistent reality. Its haphazard motion demonstrates the inadequacies of language to convey coherent meaning as it scuttles on its precipitous rush onwards without ever allowing a respite of calm, let alone of certitude: 'Le quiproquo général de l'existence ne peut se traduire qu'en un quiproquo du langage'[12] ('The general quid pro quo of existence can only be translated into the quid pro quo of language'). The restless flux of the rhetoric of paradox captures the contradictoriness central to *Jacques le fataliste*.

Like its language, its organisational format, too, is an image of paradoxicality. The tale of the journey acts as a skeletal backbone to which are attached the adventures of the road and the experiences of the characters, as in the traditional *voyage philosophique*. But this journey is devoid of aim in either concrete or spiritual terms. Its commanding motto, 'Est-ce que l'on sait où l'on va?' ('Does one know where one is going?') suggests not only the waywardness of this particular journey, but the futility of setting goals. There is certainly a satirical edge[13] to this inverted treatment of a common literary theme, but the primary impact of the inscrutable journey is as a striking symbol of uncertainty. Considered as a structuring device in *Jacques le fataliste*, this journey produces not the shapeliness of departure, travel, and arrival, but the sinuosities of a fortuitous meandering. Far from functioning as a way of lending meaning, it is so enigmatic a pursuit as to raise doubts whether it has any meaning at all.

The randomness of the journey is a paradigm for the shakiness of all structures in *Jacques le fataliste*. The haphazard, the temporary, the improvisational: these are the hallmarks of a textual tissue whose disjointedness is a material substantiation of the ontological dilemma portrayed. Dialogues between varying sets of protagonists are interspersed with narrative from sundry voices in a fragmented fabric that is a dislocation of the internal logic of the narrative process. It is the principle of discontinuity that governs this discourse which can best be described as 'décousu'[14] ('hacked up'). It jumps without warning from the exchanges of the fictive narrator with his contrived reader to the doings and discussions of Jacques and his master on their journey. On the way Jacques is to give an account of his 'amours' ('amorous adventures'), but though this is started several times, it is postponed over and again, displaced by occurrences on the road, such as the encounter with the robbers, the passing of the funeral procession, the meeting with other travellers at the inn, whose often rambling life-stories are further interpolations, as are Jacques' tales of his brother, of his captain, and so forth. Every tale in turn spawns yet more excrescences, each leading into the next in a labyrinthine involution. The sudden leaps from one strand to another and back to the commentaries of Jacques and his master, and of the fictive narrator and reader produce a 'roman en lambeaux'[15] ('novel in shreds'), a tangled skein of threads, one supplanting the other with the unpredictability of chance. For like the questions that remain unanswered, the threads are left hanging whenever a new element breaks in that must itself yield to another incursion from a different quarter, or perhaps give way to an unexpected doubling back to a unit long since abandoned and almost forgotten. The contour is that of an arabesque; the individual episodes are not self-contained, as in *Don Juan*, nor are the various time-levels clearly distinguishable.

Narrative time and time of narration overlap when the fictive narrator invites the contrived reader to pass the time while Jacques and his master are asleep or otherwise occupied by listening to *his* tales. The switches between present fictive time, past fictive time, past perfect fictive time, and time of narration intensify the sense of kaleidoscopic movement engendered by the rapid interflow of the multiple strands. So narration comes to assume a precarious form in a world of chance and uncertainty, partaking of the universal flux, of that 'ewigen Agilität'[16] ('eternal mobility'), the creative chaos which is the source of cognitive irony.

Nowhere is this mobility as visible as in the countless interruptions of the narrative. They have in fact been counted, with totals ranging from 158 to 180 breaks and resumptions[17] and twenty-one inserted stories. Besides the major fractures at the shifts from the plane of the narrator and reader to that of Jacques and his master or to one of the tales, there are umpteen minor disruptions. The restiveness of Jacques' horse twice disturbs his recital, while the landlady is cut short no fewer than eleven times as she is launching on the story of Mme de la Pommeraye by the servants' importunate queries. These apparently banal interruptions are often regarded as the attributes of a mimetic realism; but they have quite another importance also as evidence of the systematic use of interruption as a narrative mode. For in *Jacques le fataliste* the interruptive becomes the norm, disarticulating the textual fabric and thwarting the viability of the fictional illusion. The interruptions are so numerous that cumulatively they have the effect of questioning the possibility of sustaining the conventions of illusion at all. This methodical subversion of fictional illusion amounts to a radical structural irony. The ironic demolition is immanent to the very strategies chosen for the purposes of narration. The act of narration becomes as controversial in *Jacques le fataliste* as its philosophical creed. Irony is thus embedded in its central core, not projected from the external, evaluating perspective of a discerning, detached observer, as in *Pride and Prejudice* and *Madame Bovary*. *Jacques le fataliste* admits no definitive vantage points: of perspective, of time, of belief, or even of social hierarchies, from which to organise the disparate, opaque, and often incongruous happenings that occur. The act of narration itself, in its dishevelment, reflects the confusion of the world as it appears phenomenally. The fragmentation of the text is a mirror of contingency and a metaphor of arbitrariness. The narrative is as liable to accidents as Jacques and his master on their journey, and also as unsure of its destination or meaning. Each construct is deconstructed and reconstructed, frequently with an abrupt leap backwards or forwards in its temporal scale. Nothing is predictable other than unpredictability itself.

The dominant pattern of *Jacques le fataliste* is an artistically cohesive disorder. It resists the many ingenious scholarly efforts[18] to subdue its exuberance into a neat order. It is not so much that a form is here devised to convey formlessness,[19] as that a literary format is elaborated whose eccentricity is the congruent coefficient of its essentially ironic casuistry. The dissonant twists and turns of the discourse give palpable shape to an ontological haphazardness. The aesthetic configuration of *Jacques le fataliste*, like its metaphysical vision, is composed of the perpetual tensions of an irony consistent only unto itself.

5

Jacques with his 'écrit là-haut' is not the only voice with a repetitive stereotype catch-phrase. The fictive narrator has his formula too as he keeps proclaiming that 'il ne tiendrait qu'à moi' ('it would be entirely up to me') to do this or that: 'il ne tiendrait qu'à moi de vous faire attendre un an, deux ans, trois ans' (p. 36; 'it would be entirely up to me to make you wait a year, two years, three years'); 'il ne tiendrait qu'à moi, que tout cela n'arrivât' (p. 47; 'it would be entirely up to me that all this should not happen'); 'il ne tiendrait qu'à moi de donner un coup de fouet aux chevaux' (p. 97; 'it would be entirely up to me to start the horses up with a lash of the whip'); 'il ne tiendrait qu'à moi d'arrêter ce cabriolet' (p. 278; 'it would be entirely up to me to stop this carriage'). That phrase expresses a belief that is the antithesis to Jacques' ostensible submission to fatalism; the narrator is asserting his mastery over the narrative he is shaping.

The narrator's claim to freedom is one of the cardinal themes of *Jacques le fataliste*. Again and again in his addresses to the fictive reader he goes out of his way to underline his controlling position:

Qu'est-ce qui m'empêcherait de marier le maître et de le faire
cocu? d'embarquer Jacques pour les îles? d'y conduire son
maître? de les ramener tous les deux en France sur le même
vaisseau? (p. 37)

(What would prevent me from marrying the master off and
making him a cuckold? from packing Jacques off to the isles?
from sending his master there? from bringing them both back
to France on the same boat?)

Often the narrator boasts of his kindness to the reader by what he
is sparing him: 'Vous concevez, lecteur, jusqu'où je pourrais
pousser cette conversation . . .' (p. 41; 'You realise, reader, just
how far I could pursue this conversation'). At other times he
wields his power by teasing threats: 'Que cette aventure ne
deviendrait-elle pas entre mes mains, s'il me prenait en fantaisie
de vous désespérer!' (p. 38; 'What would this adventure not
become in my hands if I were to take it into my head to
exasperate you!'). At several points he explores at some length
the alternatives open to him in directing the plot:

> Telle fut à la lettre la conversation du chirurgien, de l'hôte et
> de l'hôtesse: mais quelle autre couleur n'aurais-je pas été le
> maître de lui donner, en introduisant un scélérat parmi ces
> bonnes gens? Jacques se serait vu, ou vous auriez vu Jacques
> au moment d'être arraché de son lit, jeté sur un grand chemin
> ou dans une fondrière. – Pourquoi pas tué? – Tué, non.
> J'aurais bien su appeler quelqu'un à son secours; (p. 71)

> (That was, word for word, the conversation between the
> surgeon, the innkeeper and the landlady: but what a different
> complexion would I not have been able to give it by
> introducing a villain among these good people? Jacques would
> have seen himself, or you would have seen Jacques being
> dragged from his bed, cast onto the highway or into a bog. –
> Why not killed? – No, not killed. I would surely have known
> how to call someone to his help;)

Or again:

> Lecteur, qui m'empêcherait de jeter ici le cocher, les
> chevaux, la voiture, les maîtres et les valets dans une

fondrière? Si la fondrière vous fait peur, qui m'empêcherait de les amener sains et saufs dans la ville où j'accrocherais leur voiture à une autre, dans laquelle je renfermerais d'autres jeunes gens ivres? Il y aurait des mots offensants de dits, une querelle, des epées tirées, une bagarre dans toutes les règles. Qui m'empêcherait, si vous n'aimez pas les bagarres, de substituer à ces jeunes gens Mlle Agathe, avec une de ses tantes? (pp. 295–6)

(Reader, who would have prevented me here from throwing the coachman, the horses, the coach, the masters and the servants into a bog? If a bog frightens you, who would have prevented me from bringing them safe and sound into the town where I could run their carriage into another into which I would put some drunken young fellows? There would be abusive words, a quarrel, drawn swords, a brawl in keeping with all the rules. Who would prevent me, if you do not like brawls, from replacing those young people with Mlle Agathe and one of her aunts?)

Such hypotheses fulfil several functions in *Jacques le fataliste*: they suggest a certain improvisational quality, an arbitrariness of the text open to development at the whim of the narrator, as in *Don Juan*; they betoken the fictive narrator's latitude to play at will with both his fiction and his reader, and, by implication, the author's liberty to do the same; and finally, they appear to demonstrate that the fictive narrator possesses the freedom that is denied to Jacques. While Jacques laments, 'Savez-vous, monsieur, quelque moyen d'effacer cette écriture?' (p. 40; 'Do you know, master, of any means to wipe out this script?'), the fictive narrator constantly declares his capacity to do just that. Within the circle of fatalism, art serves 'comme dernier et inaliénable refuge de la liberté, . . . comme un anti-destin en quelque sorte'[20] ('as the final and inalienable refuge of freedom, . . . as a kind of anti-destiny').

In those interjections into the narrative, the fictive narrator is flaunting his autonomy over his text. These flagrant departures from the conventions of story-telling call attention to his independence, to his right to be as idiosyncratic as he pleases in the conduct of his tale. It is with glee that he keeps emphasising his unorthodoxy: 'Il est bien évident que je ne fais pas un roman, puisque je néglige ce qu'un romancier ne manquerait pas d'employer' (p. 47; 'It is quite obvious that I am not writing a novel, because I disregard what a novelist would not fail to exploit'); and again: 'mais ceci n'est point un roman, je vous l'ai déjà dit, je crois, et je vous le répète encore' (p. 74; 'but this is not a novel at all, I have already told you that, I think, and I repeat it once more'). He ascribes his infraction of prevailing usage to his aim of recording 'la vérité' (p. 47; 'the truth') instead of writing 'une fable' ('a fabulation').

This advocacy of realism is, in part, a satirical attack on the outrageous plots of eighteenth century tales of adventure. But the effect of this programme is decidedly ironic for it leads to breaks in the fictional illusion in the name of realism. The accepted methods for creating the illusion of a fictional reality are pointedly contravened in *Jacques le fataliste* for the sake of faithfulness to reality. To maintain a smooth surface of fictional illusion is tantamount to a betrayal of real life by art; conversely, disruptions of the illusion intensify the sense of reality because they result in a text that is mimetically closer, in its very discontinuity, to the contingencies of human experience. Such a procedure, however, not only subjects the conventional practices of narration to an ironic scrutiny. By extension it also queries the meaning of 'truth' and 'fabulation' in narration, and beyond that, in a wider context, of 'reality' and 'illusion'. The outcome of this narrative strategy is a sharp paradox: for the breaks in illusion, the digressions, the interruptions that intensify the semblance of reality simultaneously heighten the awareness of artifice. Empirical reality and fictional reality are played off against each other as the existential status of fictional reality is constantly thrown into question. This is what Benjamin describes as 'Ironisierung der Form'[21] ('ironisation of form') and what Heimrich calls 'Fiktionsironie'[22] ('irony of fiction'). In *Jacques le fataliste* that ironic undermining of the entire artifact comes from a voice within the fiction, i.e. from the fictive narrator. The dialectic of creation and negating critique, that emanated in *Don Juan* and in the *Flegeljahre* from narrators who stood at the periphery of the fiction and who were and were not identical with the author, is in *Jacques le fataliste* made an integral part of the fiction through the transference of the function of construction and destruction to a fictive persona. So the metafictional element comes to occupy a pivotal position, dominating the fiction and jeopardising its viability. Its role is more eclectic and more crucial than in either *Don Juan* or the *Flegeljahre*.

There is, moreover, a further paradox that derives from the inordinate fragmentation of the textual fabric which casts rather an ambiguous light on the narrator's claim to freedom. The signals of authority in the narrator's boasts of his controlling autonomy conflict with the random mobility of the narrative. Is there an imperious mind directing the narrative from a position of superior knowledge, or do the subversive dislocations divulge its ultimate wantonness? In what sense is there in *Jacques le fataliste* 'an *intelligence du Récit* experimenting with means of ordering narrative materials which will not do excessive violence to the essential disorderliness of ordinary discourse, of human psychology, of the chain of events and circumstances in most lives'?[23] Only in so far as that *intelligence du Récit* is that of Diderot, the author. For it is *not* that of the fictive narrator who turns out to share the epistemological impasse common to the characters he is portraying. On many occasions he has to confess: 'je ne sais' (p. 38; 'I don't know'), or: 'J'ignore ce qui se passa dans l'auberge après leur départ' (p. 47; 'I don't know what happened at the inn after they had left'). He is certainly not omniscient, nor, it becomes evident, as wholly in command as his vaunted 'il ne tiendrait qu'à moi' would make it seem. He even has to admit categorically in one instance:

> La voilà remontée, et je vous préviens, lecteur, qu'il n'est plus en mon pouvoir de la renvoyer. – Pourquoi donc? – C'est qu'elle se présente avec deux bouteilles de champagne, une dans chque main, et qu'il est écrit là-haut que tout orateur qui s'adressera à Jacques avec cet exorde s'en fera nécessairement écouter. (pp. 157–8)

> (Here she is installed again, and I warn you, reader, that it is no longer within my power to send her away. – Why not? – Because she comes with two bottles of champagne, one in each hand, and it is written up there that any speaker who addresses Jacques with this exordium will of necessity get a hearing.')

In this jocular concession, the restrictions on the narrator's own liberty are revealed. He too is subject to the prescriptions of the 'great scroll' which can limit his power to create, destroy, and recreate at will. So the 'little scroll' of *his* text becomes, in its vulnerability to chance and in its unpredictability, another illustration of fatalism. The fictive narrator faces the same problem of freedom and necessity as Jacques, and despite his cocky affirmations of his capacity for self-determination, he discovers little by little, as do we, that his narrative is not entirely in his power. In an intrinsically ironic process, he discloses in the course of his own discourse that the true state of affairs is the contrary to what he asserts. Towards the end, when he comes upon 'une lacune vraiment déplorable dans la conversation de Jacques et de son maître' (p. 265; 'a really dreadful gap in the conversation between Jacques and his master') the script, down here and up there, reaches a point of crisis. 'Qu'allons-nous donc devenir? – Ma foi, je n'en sais rien' (p. 264; 'What's to become of us then? – Upon my faith, I don't know'). As his text goes its own way, the fictive narrator himself is forced into a submission to indeterminacy that is in ironic self-contradiction to his initial arrogation of sovereignty.

The accidents that befall this story in the telling testify to more than playful capers of a gamesman-narrator. The act of narration is subtly unmasked as an ironic performance that demonstrates the opposite to what it purports. The fictive narrator proves a betrayer betrayed, an ironist who is at the same time the object of an irony beyond his control. If he has 'das Wissen, dass er nicht wisse',[24] which has been cited as the hallmark of the complete ironist, he is not prepared openly to admit it. That is left to the authorial *intelligence du Récit* as it fashions a text that is a brilliant image of the disorderliness of the universe.

6

And what of that 'homme questionneur' (p. 83; 'questioning fellow') the fictive reader, who is so prominent in *Jacques le fataliste*: what is he to make of his fate? It is fraught with perplexity because of his extensive dependence on a narrator who is obstinately unwilling to answer questions. Only gradually does it emerge that his recalcitrancy is not so much a matter of unwillingness as of inability to answer because his base of knowledge is so exiguous.

Jacques le fataliste, like *Don Juan* and the *Flegeljahre*, has a visible

and highly audible narrator. However, his copious harangues do
nothing to facilitate communication with his readers, fictive or
actual; on the contrary, instead of clarifying and mediating, as he
pretends to do, he obfuscates and alienates. So the effect of the
narrator's addresses to his readers is the ironic opposite to
expectation: 'What at first strikes us as a gesture of dis-
alienation, a mediation between text and audience, seeking to
reconcile each to each, is in fact a gesture that invites a mounting
irony'.[25] The overt presence of a voluble narrator does not foster
a trusting understanding between the narrating voice and the
reading mind. The collusive entente linking narrator and reader
in *Pride and Prejudice* and in *Madame Bovary* is scuttled in *Jacques le
fataliste* by the narrator's temperament and tactics. He is an
ironist whose method is to manipulate, mystify and confound the
reader, and the pressures that he exerts on his fictive reader
impinge on the actual reader too. But in a further twist of an
ironic situation, the actual reader eventually discovers what the
fictive reader may or may not suspect: that this ironist is himself
not in possession of sufficiently comprehensive knowledge to
function as the clever mentor he would like to seem. His
mystifications are in part at least a cover for the shortcomings of
his own understanding. With this sophisticated narrative
disposition a new dimension of problems – and of ironic
deception – is introduced into the relationship between narrator
and reader. The process of story-telling is not only one of the
salient themes, as it is in *Don Juan* and in the *Flegeljahre*, but itself a
major locus of irony.

The fictive narrator's stance towards his reader is marked by
baffling fluctuations of distance, tone, and manner. By exercising
an autocratic authority over the reader, he is putting on a show of
his power so as to disguise his own impotence in the face of an
impenetrable universe. The reader becomes the object and the
victim of the narrator's changing moods. At times he is
benevolently confiding: 'Lecteur, à vous parler franchement,
. . .' (p. 261; 'Reader, to be open with you, . . .') or: 'Je vous
supplie, lecteur, de vous familiariser avec cette manière de dire'
(p. 60; 'I beg of you, reader, to familiarise yourself with this form
of expression'). More often he provokes the reader, toying with
his curiosity, attributing to him bursts of anger and impatience,
teasing and rebuking him, and continually reminding him of his
subjection and his liability to error. This strategy is designed to

frustrate, bewilder and confuse him, destroying his belief in his capacity to understand: 'De quelque côté que vous vous tourniez, vous avez tort' (p. 261; 'Whichever way you turn, you are wrong'). Through his vagaries, the narrator comes to function as a principle of chance and unpredictability for the reader, who is himself thus directly exposed to a variant of the predicament of fatalism. He is reading not within the parameters of an articulated system of values, as in *Pride and Prejudice,* nor from an established perspective, as in *Madame Bovary,* but in the precarious context of the kaleidoscopically shifting perspectivism that arises out of the discrepant signals of the mercurial narrator. Such a mode of narration compounds ironies in an infinite progression where every meaning is queried or negated by conflicting countermeanings. Access to definitive meaning is blocked in a construct such as *Jacques le fataliste* which quivers from the shocks of its own convulsiveness. Its mobility not only forecloses every haven of fixity which might serve as a base for interpretation, but goes so far as to insinuate the hopelessness of striving for definitive meaning.

So the reader is made to face an unending dilemma in the task of reading. The narrator, instead of guiding and leading him, often befuddles and misleads. At several points he nonchalantly puts forward an array of alternatives: 'Entre les différents gîtes possibles, dont je vous ai fait l'énumération qui précède, choisissez celui qui convient le mieux à la circonstance présente' (pp. 58–9; 'Between the various possible lodgings that I have enumerated for you just before, choose that which best suits the present circumstances'); go along with Jacques or with his master, but beware in either case because you will run into predicaments (p. 59); 'De ces deux versions, demain, après-demain, vous choisirez, à tête reposée, celle qui vous conviendra le mieux' (p. 201; 'Of these two variants, you will choose tomorrow or the day after, when your mind is rested, whichever suits you best'). By giving the reader a choice, the narrator is apparently endowing him with freedom. But it is a debatable freedom because it is severely circumscribed and in practice it amounts to a burden. For its effect is to throw the onus onto the reader who in turn is thrust back into the turmoil of the text. In *Jacques le fataliste,* 'ce n'est plus le lecteur qui s'empare de l'oeuvre, mais l'oeuvre qui s'empare du lecteur'[26] ('it is no longer the reader who takes possession of the work, but the work that takes possession of the reader'). The reader can take possession of *Pride and Prejudice* through his confident understanding of its prevailing order. *Jacques le fataliste*, by contrast, evades conclusive grasp; the reader can never fully master it because its indeterminacy takes possession of him.

The abdication of 'positive direction'[27] from the narrator is predicated on the bestowal of a certain freedom on the reader. This has farreaching consequences for him. In making his choices, it falls to him in each instance to enter into a pragmatic consideration of the dividing line between truth and error, reason and unreason, message and misprision. His undertaking is vitiated by the absence of any firm lines of demarcation, the relativity of all judgements, and the fluidity of every position. As a result, he is 'left in a querying state' ('in einer Fragestellung belassen'[28]). And while defence mechanisms against narrative discontinuity may in time be acquired, there is no equally effective protection against the ontological fragmentation it presents and represents. The ironies inherent in the communicative situation of *Jacques le fataliste* lead back into the heart of its paradoxicality.

7

Le lendemain ils arrivèrent . . . – Où? D'honneur je n'en sais rien. – Et qu'avaient-ils à faire où ils allaient? – Tout ce qu'il vous plaira. Est-ce que le maître de Jacques disait ses affaires à tout le monde? Quoi qu'il en soit, elles n'exigeaient pas au-delà d'une quinzaine de séjour. Se terminèrent-elles bien, se terminèrent-elles mal? C'est ce que j'ignore encore. (p. 316)

(The next day they arrived . . . – Where? Upon my honour, I don't know a thing about it. – And what was their business where they were going? – Whatever you wish. Did Jacques' master speak of his affairs to everyone? Be that as it may, they did not require more than a couple weeks' stay. Did they end well, or did they end badly? That I don't know either.)

The ending of *Jacques le fataliste* is like its beginning; even after the journey, its destination and purpose remain in the dark. We never get to know what happened to Jacques' captain, nor to Richard and Hudson, nor to the marriage of the marquis, nor to Jacques' for that matter. Entrances and exits, like beginnings and endings, are erratic and inscrutable in a world of contingencies. Everywhere there are gaps, enigmas, ambivalences, and questions, particularly in the non-end of the end. The *perpetuum mobile* of *Jacques le fataliste* does not come to rest in a quiescent closure. Rather than ending, it just stops:

> Et moi, je m'arrête, parce que je vous ai dit de ces deux personnages tout ce que j'en sais. – Et les amours de Jacques? Jacques a dit cent fois qu'il était écrit là-haut qu'il n'en finirait pas l'histoire, et je vois que Jacques avait raison. Je vois, lecteur, que cela vous fâche; eh bien, reprenez son récit où il l'a laissé, et continuez-le à votre fantaisie ou bien faites une visite à Mlle Agathe, sachez le nom du village où Jacques est emprisonné; voyez Jacques, questionnez-le: il ne se fera pas tirer l'oreille pour vous satisfaire; cela le désennuiera. (pp. 325–6)

> (As for me, I am stopping because I have told you all I know about these two characters. – What about Jacques' amorous adventures? Jacques has said a hundred times that it was written up there that he would not finish the story, and I see that Jacques was right. I see reader, that this vexes you; so, take up the narrative where he left off, and carry on according to your own fantasy, or pay a visit to Mlle Agathe, find out the name of the village where Jacques is imprisoned; see Jacques, question him: he will not need much urging to fulfil your wish, that will relieve his boredom.)

Jacques and his master disappear as unexpectedly as they had appeared, while the reader is given the option of setting out on some mysterious quest of his own. As for the narrator, he simply washes his hands of the whole matter.

The philosophical and psychological position at the end of *Jacques le fataliste* is much the same as at the beginning. Although some physical movement has taken place because they have 'arrived', there is none of the development associated with the *voyage philosophique*, no 'process of maturing or coming to terms with society',[29] no palpable climax, let alone any resolution. The pattern of *Jacques le fataliste* is like that of *Le Neveu de Rameau*: 'cyclic, epicyclic and retrograde'.[30] If it makes any advance at all, it is towards increasing uncertainty as its progressive irony erodes the possibility of definity. It ends at the opposite pole to *Pride and Prejudice,* where the duplicity of irony wanes with the establishment of assured truth. In *Jacques le fataliste* irony is intensified through the proliferation of alternatives. No fewer than three different endings are outlined, each in itself open-ended, as if either to mock the desire for an ending, or to suggest the endlessness of the problems raised in story-telling as in life.

The three endings are ushered in by an unprecedented kind of breach in the narrative illusion. In a parenthetical notation of the passage of time, an unspecified 'éditeur' (p. 326) suddenly intrudes, who refers to the work in hand as 'les mémoires' and 'le manuscrit' (pp. 326–7). This is not the fictive narrator stepping out of his frame to comment on his own text. The late and unexplained appearance of this new persona introduces another stratum of mystification into *Jacques le fataliste,* provoking misgivings as to its existential status: is this an edited manuscript, including plagiarisms from *Tristram Shandy,* as the second of the endings claims? or is it an independently invented fiction? or the true relation of experience? The implication is that this text being written down here is as impervious to certainty as that other text 'écrit là-haut'. With characteristic equivocation, *Jacques le fataliste* breaks off on a paragraph that hints the likelihood of still further perplexities after Jacques' marriage; this world of chanciness holds out little prospect of living happily ever after. But this too is left open: 'Je n'en sais ce qui en est' (p. 330; 'I don't know about that'). The only unqualified facts at the termination of the narrative are that Jacques put his trust in what was 'écrit là-haut' (which, as we know by then, is very disputable), and that he went to sleep (which may be true).

These stings-in-the-tail of the non-end wittily catch the impasse of *Jacques le fataliste.* It defies closure because it is philosophically and aesthetically locked into a quandary that cannot be resolved and can only be portrayed in its very paradoxicality. The primary means for the literarary representation of paradox is – as Friedrich Schlegel recognised – irony. The irony of *Jacques le fataliste* can be seen as an expression of its author's philosophical scepticism, of a terminal reluctance to fix on any final single view. So Diderot has been called 'le romancier des possibles'[31] ('the novelist of possibilities') for whom narration becomes a way of exploring the alternatives of life, thought, and art. But *Jacques le fataliste* is more than merely a 'chef d'oeuvre de non-engagement'[32] ('masterpiece of non-commitment') because it does make a commitment, if only to uncertainty. It is a masterpiece of paradoxical irony that deconstructs every system of order to leave no proposition other than its intimation of doubt at all levels: ontological, moral, and aesthetic. Anything may be possible, nothing is sure: it is this perception of perpetual flux as the normal state of human existence that is conveyed in the text's never ending and never answered questions. *Jacques le fataliste* is indeed 'self-negating'[33] but in almost the same breath, as it were, it re-creates itself with unabated energy. This is yet another aspect of that ironic paradoxicality that is its governing principle, and that makes it a model of romantic irony.

In *Jacques le fataliste* various kinds of literary irony – verbal, situational, structural, communicative – become the artistic correlatives of the central metaphysical irony. Through the use of irony as the incarnation of paradox, vivid tangible shape is given to the mutability of existence and the elusiveness of truth. These abstract concepts take the concrete form of a perspectivism that admits all alternatives and settles for none; as such it represents the translation into graphic terms of the indeterminacy of human life. In place of the either/or tensions, generally between appearance and reality, of traditional irony, which are amenable to resolution within a referential framework of a stable reality, this type of irony offers a series of multiple choices without definite, let alone correct, solutions. Where the frame of reference is a reality perceived as essentially shifting, or a pattern of introverted self-referentiality, the absolutes of truth are engulfed in the confusion of appearance and reality.

The network of philosophical and aesthetic irony in *Jacques le fataliste* is far removed indeed from the limited verbal device that irony signified in the conventions of rhetoric. Here irony denotes a mode of thought and of expression that assents to the relativity of all positions, including the antithesis with the thesis in a scrutiny so radical as to transcend the traditional dialectic. In the last resort, this irony exposes itself to its own irony in the avowal that everything is perhaps a game: 'Quoi! c'était un jeu?' (p. 323; 'What! it was all a game?'), Jacques' master exclaims in surprise and indignation. Human existence is acknowledged and represented as a kind of sublime sport, and so is the act of writing. It is the ultimate, triumphant irony of *Jacques le fataliste* that it goes on deconstructing and reconstructing itself as an exuberantly serio-comic game.

8 Laurence Sterne: *Tristram Shandy*, 1760–67

' – My good friend, quoth I – as sure
as I am I – and you are you –
– And who are you? said he. – –
Don't puzzle me; said I.'
Tristram Shandy, vol. 7, ch. xxxiii

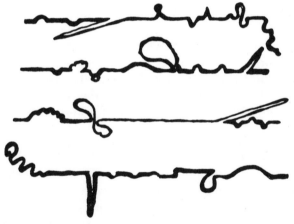

These were the four lines I moved in through my first, second, third, and fourth volumes. – In the fifth volume I have been very good – the precise line I have described in it being this:

Tristram Shandy, vol. 6, ch. xl

1

With *Tristram Shandy* doubt and equivocation arise even before
the first word of the narrative. Who devised its full title, *The Life
and Opinions of Tristram Shandy, Gent.*? Tristram, the fictive
author, or Sterne, the actual author? Perhaps it should be
attributed to Tristram since he himself refers to 'the story of my
LIFE and my OPINIONS'.[1] But was it also Tristram who chose
the epigraph from Epictetus? There is really no way of knowing.
Between the Dedication to Pitt, which is unquestionably Sterne's,
and Tristram's opening 'I wish' stretches a disquieting area of no
man's land that invites speculation and induces uncertainty. This
neutral space is replicated in those blank pages, dashes, asterisks
and the device of aposiopesis for which *Tristram Shandy* is
notorious. While stimulating reader participation, these vacuums
also provide within and beyond the text room for further
hypotheses of the kind that characterise Tristram's thinking.
Such open spaces, temporally as well as narrationally, are the
very element of *Tristram Shandy*, and it is these interstices that are
the breeding-ground for the ambivalences of irony.

One large and perplexing gap that becomes apparent at the
outset and persists to the end is that between the fictive and the
actual author. Obviously it is Laurence Sterne who creates
Tristram Shandy the writer of his Life and Opinions. Yet though
we may smile at the naïvety of the earliest reviewer who praised
'the droll Mr Tristram Shandy' as 'a writer infinitely more
ingenious and entertaining than any other of the present race of
novelists',[2] in practice it is far from easy to dissociate the fictive
from the real author. Sterne appears without disguise only in the
initial Dedication to Pitt, in a supplementary Dedication to
Viscount Spencer that precedes volume 5 (p. 238), and, most
interestingly, in five footnotes[3] in which he annotates or corrects
what 'Mr Shandy' has written, thereby clearly revealing his
responsibility as the presenting editor of Tristram's memoirs.
Generally, however, he remains concealed behind the persona
Tristram Shandy, though his commenting intrusions in those
footnotes indicate that the two are not identical. This
reduplication of the author in effect thrusts us into a curious
double role as readers simultaneously of Tristram Shandy and of
Laurence Sterne. Here there would seem to be a likely source for

that dual vision that would permit an assured interpretation of ironic alternate meanings. But this is not the case in *Tristram Shandy*. Except in those Dedications and footnotes on the outer margins of the narrative, Sterne's perspective is not discernible beside that of his creation, as is that of the narrator in *Don Juan* distinct from his hero, or of J. P. F. Richter, the chronicler of the twins' tale in the *Flegeljahre*. In *Tristram Shandy* the enframing contrivance is an intact, integral part of the fiction, in which only Tristram, not Sterne, addresses us directly. Although we, of course, know of Sterne as the originator of the artifact, we are at most occasionally and dimly aware of his background presence. As we heed to Tristram's voice, we have none of that benevolent, discreet guidance extended to us in *Pride and Prejudice*. We are in fact stranded in the position Booth has so graphically described when 'the author has decided to go away and send no letter'.[4] This is, as Booth concedes, a 'troubling' narrative situation, and, moreover, one that precludes definitive reconstruction of irony. For while the text emits clues and signals as to Tristram's irony, primarily in his rhetoric, such irony is, like Elizabeth's at Darcy's expense in *Pride and Prejudice*, internal to the fictional realm. Irony of the fiction, on the other hand, emanates in *Tristram Shandy* from that indeterminate expanse between fictive and actual author, and it is from there that we as readers must operate. It is an insecure and uncomfortable spot without any *terra firma* from which to take our bearings.

With the introductory words of Tristram's tale the nature of the intrinsic equivocation undergoes a change. His 'I wish' dispels doubts as to the identity of the writer but heralds others of a different sort. For this 'I wish', which will re-echo throughout *Tristram Shandy* not only from Tristram's mouth but also from Toby's, Trim's, and Walter's – this 'I wish' leads into a world of conjecture, desire, and fantasy. Its tentativeness is in striking contrast to the affirmative assertion: 'It is a truth universally acknowledged . . .' that lays the foundation for *Pride and Prejudice*. Whereas that dictum links the narrative to public standards, this 'I' removes Sterne's to a private inner space of personal 'Opinions'. That *Tristram Shandy* is 'a history-book, . . . of what passes in a man's own mind' (vol. 2, ch. ii, p. 61) has often been pointed out. Of utmost importance is the angle from which that history is told; for we experience what passes in Tristram's mind through the record of his own consciousness. If it was, as Lanham maintains, 'the application of the older narrative techniques to the new *subject* of realistic narrative, the private life'[5] that shocked Sterne's contemporaries, in retrospect that position is reversed; now it is less the subject than the subjectivity of *Tristram Shandy* that seems its most remarkable feature.

Sterne has not merely made the narrator the theme of his own book; he has made his mind its scene and its organising epicentre. Through his triple role as infant, as adult protagonist, and as writer, Tristram is omnipresent. The doings of Walter, Mrs Shandy and Toby are related, and implicitly subordinated, to his vision when he constantly refers to them as 'my father', 'my mother', and 'my uncle'. The narrative is thus to an extreme degree internalised, for the entire fictional world presented in *Tristram Shandy* is encompassed within a single consciousness. Though Tristram may tell of what passed in Walter's or Toby's mind, in fact he is not entering their minds in the manner of an omniscient narrator; he is reporting *his* perception of what he assumes to be passing in their minds. Whether Tristram's autonomous 'I' is ever able to grasp an outer reality is a moot point; it seems rather as if this 'I' goes on floating in its self-created amniotic fluid into which it assimilates external phenomena but from which it cannot emerge. Tristram and his narrative remain captive to that enveloping 'I', and so do we as readers. We cannot, for example, see and evaluate Walter or Toby directly; our view is solely through the eyes of Tristram, through the mediation and at the remove of his 'I'. Nor can we judge the degree to which those eyes are distorting, to which he is a reliable or unreliable witness. We have nothing other than his words and his evidence; as he himself acknowledges: 'Let us leave, if possible, *myself*: – But 'tis impossible, – I must go along with you to the end of the work.' (vol. 6, ch. xx, p. 311).

This consistent, radical subjectivity of the narrating stance in *Tristram Shandy* has important consequences for the reader's capacity to discern and reconstruct irony. Our reading of the text is conditioned and determined by two inescapable factors: that we are entrapped between overlapping narrators, Sterne and Tristram; and that we are confined within Tristram's mind. The freedom of discrimination essential to the comprehension of an ironic countermeaning is impaired by this distinctive narrative set-up and by the very particular point of view we are made to share. The 'I' of the self-advertising narrator represents here not just a technique or a device; it is the source of a fundamental problematic, literary and philosophical, for by limiting our horizon, it debars any immediate access to reliable knowledge. Tristram's 'I', as it looms over the entire narrative, imprints its unmistakable stamp, casting a shadow which is, despite its jocular aura, quite menacing. For 'der ausschliessliche Anspruch des Erzählers auf die überlegene Wirklichkeit des eigenen Bewusstseins'[6] ('the narrator's exclusive claim to the superiority of his own consciousness') marks a turning-point, and possibly a crisis, in the art of narration. The axis shifts from communication – overt or covert – with a reader to the introverted exploration of mental states and processes. In practice this means that the narrator is more in colloquy with himself than with any implied reader. And as soon as the narrator's principal commitment is towards his own consciousness, the reader is banished to an outer perimeter of the narrative, where he languishes alone as an uninitiated spectator. Writing becomes an egocentric activity that pays no more than lip-service to the reader, however loud the lip-service may be, as if in compensatory concealment of the lack of true contact. The collusive entente between narrator and reader, which is the precondition for the assured comprehension of irony, tends to wane in proportion to the growing complexity of the narrative strategy.

In *Tristram Shandy* the set-up is further complicated by the tensions inherent in Tristram's own position. He too, like the reader, is the victim of ironic ambiguities, of which he is aware but which he tries to disguise. He faces the difficult task of representing himself as a multi-level persona in his book, balancing the self-detachment of self-presentation with the self-analysis of self-assessment. He is both character and narrator,[7] an actor in the story he is telling and the object of his own contemplation. So he appears at once as an infant controlled by parents and servants and as the controlling animator of the entire scenario. It is a curious result of this two-fold continuity that 'Tristram is not born of his parents; in a strange way they are born of him',[8] or perhaps it would be more accurate to say that they mutually bear each other. For Tristram functions simultaneously as the experiencing and the telling 'I', as the remembered and the remembering figure. One bizarre outcome of this double-take is that he is actually dying while being born. Between the two poles lies his life, the 'Life' that he is supposed to be chronicling. Yet here again there is a paradox, for his life is mysteriously and sadly empty, devoid of 'adventures' and even of the domesticity of wife and children. The gap that is his life is filled by Toby's martial career and *amours*. Such life and adventures as Tristram does have – the accidental mashing of his nose and other parts – are socially hardly mentionable. This leads to further ambivalence in so far as the telling of his life implies a social act of communication, specially in the format that Tristram chooses, that of conversational utterance. Appropriating the 'double prerogative of narrator and commentator, of observer and material witness, of writer and philosopher',[9] Tristram cloaks his embarrassment in buffoonery. Nevertheless his stance is necessarily a precarious one as he endeavours to convey the unspeakable facts of his life while avoiding offensive explicitness. His mask is that of 'the giddy and flexible entertainer, always dynamically involved with his audience and his material, in danger every moment of losing the sympathy of the one and his control over the other'.[10] His apparently naive, delirious monologue turns out to be a self-conscious performance. And once the reader begins to realise this, the character of the speaker, one time-honoured touchstone of rhetoric, becomes dubious and shifty. The scene is set for the more intricate enigmas of irony.

The elusiveness of the narrator in *Tristram Shandy* is matched only by his magnetism. 'I wish', he muses, 'I wish either my father or my mother, or indeed both of them, as they were in duty both equally bound to it, had minded what they were about when they begot me.' This is one of the oddest beginnings ever invented. By embarking on his life-story with a consideration of the circumstances of his conception, Tristram immediately thrusts his narrative out of the orbit of normal expectation. His wish induces a disorientation far greater than the 'I want a hero' in *Don Juan*, which disrupts the *narrative* process, whereas here it is the most private *human* creative process that is abruptly exposed to public scrutiny. Tristram's wish is the expression of the esoteric non-logic of a mind liberated of all conventional restraints and ready to make inconsequential leaps of the imagination. The gentle hesitancy of its tone emphasises the enormity of its contents. For all its poignant wistfulness it throws the accepted natural order wholly out of joint, not simply through Tristram's voyeuristic prying into his parents' marital bed, but rather through the underlying implicit assumption that the individual can impose his will on the world by the force of his mind. It is no casual usage of a word when Tristram says that his parents should have 'minded'. This is tantamount to a denial of the validity of outer reality, which is here subjected to the shaping powers of the personal imagination. By subverting the laws of nature, Tristram's wish destroys the familiar ontological schema, which he replaces with a flimsy, idiosyncratic order. It is the individual sensibility, however quirky, that creates the rules of the system in *Tristram Shandy,* and its criteria are the imperatives of an eccentric psychology. The wish of the opening sentence thus postulates the potential for the unlimited reversibility of all the generally recognised bases of human existence. Its deranging iconoclasm is the opposite to the reassuring affirmation of moral axioms and social codes at the beginning of *Pride and Prejudice.* The unexpected is the only standard of expectation in *Tristram Shandy.* Its spaces, its gaps, its subjectivism, its ambiguities, and its profession of the topsy-turvy as its governing principle all point to the fragility of its universe and of its artistic edifice. Everything in *Tristram Shandy* may be other than what it seems.

2

This becomes fully evident in the narrator-reader relationship. At first glance this might appear one of the less controversial aspects of *Tristram Shandy.* The first-person narrator is disposed, indeed anxious, to engage his reader's benign response. He offers him many assurances of his good faith and credibility with such phrases as: 'you may take my word', and 'Believe me, good folks'. At least half of *Tristram Shandy*, according to Ian Watt's[11] reckoning, is taken up with these direct addresses by Tristram to his audience. His rapport with his reader has been characterised as one of 'friendship'.[12] Certainly he is eager for the reader's attention, and, beyond that, for his active participation in the unfolding of the tale. The rhetoric is designed to impress on the occasionally lazy reader the need for a lively creativity on his part. The technique of insinuation, the famous aposiopesis, is one common goad to provoke co-operation by exciting curiosity, just as the blank page may serve as a concrete invitation: ' – call for pen and ink – here's paper ready to your hand. – Sit down, Sir, paint her to your own mind – ' (vol. 6, ch. xxxviii, p. 330). These transparent devices to implicate the fictive reader in the action of Tristram's story have a further function in fostering in the actual reader a consciousness of himself as reader that partners the writer's unremitting awareness of himself as a writer.

However, beside the reader who is internal to the fiction and 'who actually becomes a character in the novel',[13] there is another who is external to the fiction. This reduplication of contrived and real reader corresponds to the doubling of fictive and actual author; just as Sterne writes of a writer writing, so we read of readers reading. But though the external reader is superimposed on the internal and at times concurs in his reactions to Tristram's pleas and admonitions, the two by no means coincide. In counterbalance to his involvement in the narrative, the external reader also maintains a detachment from it. Apart from following the action alongside the internal reader, he is in a position, too, to watch Tristram's manipulation of his contrived reader. For the actual reader is distinct from the fictive reader, who is entirely the product of Tristram's invention, in his capacity to distance himself from the action and from the narrator's manoeuvres. He has the independence of judgement that enables him to see what is going on and at the same time to see through it. In other words, he possesses that dual perspective that is the foundation for irony.

This dichotomy between the internal and the external reader is of vital importance for *Tristram Shandy*. Surprisingly it has been largely overlooked. 'The text itself . . .', Preston[14] for instance maintains, 'forms the basis for a relationship; it is what reader and narrator share'. Certainly it is what the contrived reader and the fictive narrator share because this captive fictive reader's responses are literally dictated by the puppeteer, Tristram. On the other hand, the actual reader, who faces the text from outside the fiction, can evaluate and construct it from his own angle of vision in a manner denied to the contrived reader. So the actual reader, while 'sharing' the text with the narrator and being drawn in by some of his tactics, can at the same time take cognizance of its essential slipperiness and the lack of assurance it affords to those who – to borrow its own imagery – use both ears: 'whilst I satisfy *that ear* which the reader chuses to *lend* me – I might not dissatisfy the other which he keeps to himself' (vol. 7, ch. xxi, p. 353).

Whether Tristram's contrived reader has two ears is open to question. He repeatedly mishears, misunderstands, misinterprets, jumps to the wrong conclusions, makes mistaken associations. But for this we have only Tristram's word, his constant reprimands and his assiduous corrections of the alleged misreadings. In fact the fictive reader, though strong as a presence, remains shadowy in outline. His image is vexatory: male ('Sir'), female ('Madam'); singular ('your worship'), plural ('your reverences'); 'curious and inquisitive' (vol. 1, ch. v, p. 4), yet 'impatient' (vol. 5, ch. xxxv, p. 278); 'inattentive' (vol. 1, ch. xx, p. 40), yet endowed with a good memory (vol. 4, ch. xvii, p. 212); often deemed incapable of understanding (vol. 1, ch. xviii, p. 35; vol. 3, ch. xvii, p. 137), yet capable of imaginative input (vol. 2, ch. xi, p. 77; vol. 6, ch. xxxviii, p. 330).

As equivocal as his persona is his relationship to the fictive narrator. On the surface it is one of cordial warmth, in contrast to the contentious tartness in *Jacques le fataliste.* Tristram shows concern for his reader as he explains his procedures, encourages and reassures him: 'don't be terrified, madam, this stair-case conversation is not as long as the last' (vol. 4, ch. xx, p. 232); he warns him about 'a devil' of a chapter (vol. 5, ch. iii, p. 245), cajoles him to persevere (vol. 5, ch. xli, p. 283), and even indicates when it is permissible for him to skip or sleep, and when he must pay attention (vol. 5, ch. vii, p. 253). But despite this apparently close and amiable collaboration, he does not give as much guidance as would seem. He maintains at the outset that he has been 'so very particular already' for the sake of those readers 'who find themselves ill at ease, unless they are let into the whole secret from first to last' (vol. 1, ch. iv, p. 3). 'Very particular' he may indeed be in the sense of offering massive detail on small matters; 'let into the whole secret from first to last': this the reader never is, neither the fictive nor the actual reader. On the contrary, Tristram loves to mystify, to lead on, to drop hints, or asterisks – in short, to leave the reader in a state of uncertainty. He often refuses to answer questions, preferring to retreat into his recital, and he shuns responsibility by sheltering behind characters and events. Consequently he does not develop any intimate, confiding alliance with his audience, let alone establish any steady contract. In a *double entendre* that reveals the tragi-comedy of his position, he confesses that only 'with an ass, I can commune for ever' for 'I understand thee perfectly' (vol. 7, ch. xxxii, p. 367). With human beings his tone is on many occasions begging or apologetic, as he pleads for a tolerant hearing or even

for 'help' (vol. 9, ch. xx, p. 440). Gradually it becomes clear to
the actual reader with his two ears that Tristram's insistent
addresses are a form of public rhetoric, and that his handling of
the fictive reader is a facet of his showmanship. A show of genial
self-confidence is put on as much for his own benefit as for his
reader's. For he tries to hide from himself and from his listener
that he cannot fulfil his promises, that he gets nowhere with his
tale, that he is quite unable to lead or direct in this journey
through the maze of his mind because he himself cannot find the
way. Having culled the reader's trust, he cannot live up to the
expectations he has fostered. It is even doubtful whether he
accomplishes his vaunted goal to write 'against the spleen', 'to
drive the *gall* and other *bitter juices* from the gall bladder, liver and
sweet-bread of his majesty's subjects' (vol. 4, ch. xxii, p. 218) by
laughter since the contents of his tale with its four deaths, many
misadventures, and his own decline, is far from cheering.
Tristram's volubility, his animation, and his will to optimism
screen out these sombre aspects of his tale. While not deliberately
duplicitous, he is both evasive and cunning as a narrator. By
cultivating a seemingly intimate relationship with his contrived
reader, he is in fact drawing him into an ironic game in which the
reader becomes an accomplice to, and a dupe of, deception as
well as of self-deception on Tristram's part. Ultimately the
narrator's proffered friendship yields only puzzlement and
discomfort to a reader who has been inveigled into patience,
participation, and perseverance and who is, for all his pains, left
in the dark.

The actual reader fares little better, for we too are at the mercy
of the fictive narrator's conflicting signals. Though we may
perceive the innate shiftiness of the narrative situation, we have
no means to overcome it. Instead of enjoying the narrator's
confidence, as in *Pride and Prejudice* and *Madame Bovary*, we are
relegated here to the position of unacknowledged eavesdroppers.
Granted that the problem of evaluation is intrinsic to first-person
narratives; as Lowry Nelson has put it, the reader is 'on his own
and left balancing the evidence as given and evaluated by his
first-person fictional collaborator, who happens under the
circumstances to be his only source'.[15] But, as Nelson goes on to
argue in regard to *Moll Flanders*, there can be 'a sort of contractual
understanding between author and reader that transcends the
self-knowledge of Moll'.[16] Such a contractual understanding is at

best fleeting in *Tristram Shandy*, subject itself to the teasing mobility that pervades the entire work. The restless movement of the eternal present recording the activity of Tristram's consciousness leaves neither time nor space for the reader's deliberations. In the kaleidoscopic verbal and situational commotion no stance is ever sufficiently fixed to provide a reasonably lasting basis for interpretation.

So the actual reader, like his fictive counterpart, is involved in an unceasing process of reassessment and readjustment. This concerns not only the happenings within the tale, but also the personality of the teller. It may well be that 'willingly or grudgingly, fully or partially, trust him we must'[17] because we have no choice; yet in fact we can't and we don't trust him. We doubt the reliability of the information he transmits; we wonder how he came to know certain things, and, above all, we speculate whether he is presenting things as they were, or as his imagination perceived them. As Helene Moglen has pointed out, 'Tristram's weakness for histrionics, revealed in his liberal use of apostrophe and invocation, places his honesty in a questionable light'.[18] His constant need to correct himself and, even more, his inconsistencies evoke an image of confusion that further reduces confidence in his trustworthiness. Our options, however, are scant since any dialogue between actual narrator and reader can occur only through the mediation of the fictive narrator's self-representation.

Occasionally there is a palpable discrepancy that opens up a chink for an alternative view. The most important centres on the matter of power. It is Tristram's reiterated boast that his is the will that controls the protagonists and the reader: ''tis enough to have thee in my power', he tells his 'gentle reader' (vol. 7, ch. vi, p. 340); more petulantly he asserts his jurisdiction over his mother by abruptly declaring: 'In this attitude I am determined to let her stand for five minutes' (vol. 5, ch. v, p. 250), and his omnipotence over his whole artifact by giving free rein to his momentary whim: 'A sudden impulse comes across me – drop the curtain, *Shandy* – I drop it – Strike a line here across the paper, *Tristram* – I strike it – and hey for a new chapter!' (vol. iv, ch. x, p. 203). Here there is firm ground for discriminating irony: beyond the irony that takes place between the fictive narrator and his creation as he plays with his protagonists, his contrived readers and his plot, there is an additional level of irony

at Tristram's expense as we realise that the truth is the contrary
to what he says. His will does not control and shape his narrative;
it seems almost to have a will of its own, to be as susceptible to
contingency as Tristram himself is. His physical impotence is the
symbol of his lack of power. Through the erratic, inconclusive
course of Tristram's narrative, the actual narrator, Sterne,
indicates to us the irony of Tristram's claim. Behind Tristram's
back, so to speak, a secret collusive intimation passes from the
hidden author to the reader, as in *Pride and Prejudice* and *Madame
Bovary*.

This is the exception rather than the rule in *Tristram Shandy*.
Generally we are hostages to the first-person narrator. Having
two ears, we are conscious of the ironic game that is going on, but
we do not have sufficient clues to reconstruct any meaning with
definity. This is the major reason for the vague malaise which
besets readers of *Tristram Shandy*, the uneasy sense, as in Kafka
or Beckett, of ineffable implications that are felt but cannot be
specified. This method amounts to 'warfare with the reader'.[19] It
is a cross between a guerilla campaign and a sparring match, in
which the text seems teasingly to defy us to read it. In the end it is
the reader who is made to feel unreliable. For when the author-
narrator is a mischievous adversary rather than a sound partner,
co-operation between reader and narrator is perforce replaced by
the reader's solitary, largely unaided effort. Irony becomes not a
matter of reconstructing a covert intended meaning but of
confronting a bewildering multiplicity of possible meanings.
What began as a pretty innocuous intellectual game turns into a
disorienting experience of vertigo. The impact of *Tristram
Shandy* has been vividly captured by Virginia Woolf: 'our sense of
elasticity is increased so much that we scarcely know where we
are. We lose our sense of direction. We go backwards instead of
forwards'.[20] In effect we are circling in search of a categoric
meaning where the text is driving us to acknowledge the existence
of a plurality of meanings; we are looking for standards of
judgement in a work that takes oddity as its norm; we long for
closure as we stare into the open spaces. We have no authoritative
guide to direct us with discreet promptings. For the highly
audible and visible narrating persona has, despite his vociferous
presence, a tenuous and problematical relationship with his
audience. He is a showman, intent first and foremost on his own
performance and on the impression he is making; that is to say,

more concerned with himself as narrator than with his narrative. Here we have one of the great paradoxes – and stumbling-blocks – of the art of narration: where the narrator appears closest to the reader, he may be most distant. A surface friendliness may be the ironic mask for a far-reaching alienation. Thus, extensive though Tristram's account is of his Life and Opinions, we remain outsiders, bemused spectators, 'in a manner perfect strangers to each other' (vol. 1, ch. vi, p. 6). Our participation is an illusory and our reading as flawed as that of the fictive reader. What is more, Tristram takes delight in fostering this state of uncertainty: 'Sir, I am of so nice and singular a humour, that if I thought you was able to form the least judgement or probable conjecture to yourself, of what was to come, in the next page, – I would tear it out of my book' (vol. 1, ch. xxv, p. 57). But on what grounds should 'Sir' – or we – accept at face value even so explicit a statement from the pen of a master-ironist?

3

Such extreme scepticism is supported by the rhetoric of *Tristram Shandy* whose jagged physical surface points to the pitfalls and the brittleness of language as a means of communication. It offers irrefutable evidence for Tristram's contention that it is 'the unsteady uses of words' that is 'the true cause of the confusion . . . and a fertile source of obscurity' (vol. 2, ch. ii, p. 62). So the rhetoric, 'alienating and seductive',[21] as much a focus of irritation as of fascination, becomes the illustration and the incarnation of the equivocation that is central to *Tristram Shandy*. The language, the syntax, and even the punctuation bring the reader into a direct encounter with the turbulence it both presents and represents. And it is inescapable because this peculiarly fitful use of words, in an irony singularly appropriate to *Tristram Shandy*, is the only element of consistency. The sole constancy of *Tristram Shandy* lies in its very inconstancy.

The one narrating voice is heard by the fictive and the actual reader alike, but what we perceive may differ substantially from the interpretation imputed to 'madam'. This discrepancy of response is one of the primary spaces for irony in *Tristram Shandy*. Particularly those instances where the fictive reader is chided for misreading or for jumping to wrong conclusions afford an opportunity to alert the actual reader to the correct understanding, though the irony may be a compound one in that the fictive reader's – possibly bawdy – construction may after all be the right one, however strenuously Tristram tries to head it off. Through such complicated manoeuvres the rhetoric becomes an important vehicle for irony in *Tristram Shandy*.

All the traditional stylistic devices of the ironic mode are used freely: hyperbole followed by anti-climax, comic overstatement, blatant *non-sequiturs*, incongruous comb:nations and self-evident misstatements. But these tropes, though common in *Tristram Shandy*, are almost incidental, and certainly subsidiary. The major stratagems are at once more gross and more original, the favourite resources being *double entendres*, puns, innuendoes, suspensions, asterisks, aposiopesis, and sundry typographical capers. All these fulfil the same function: to deprive language of its denotative simplicity and to open it up to other possible meanings. Words themselves are made duplicitous, dubious, 'unsteady' by a subversive process of extension. The most famous instance of this technique is with the totally innocent word 'nose' which is loaded with sexual overtones by a devious art of suggestion that manages to insinuate exactly what it purports to deny:

> I define a nose, as follows, – intreating only beforehand, and beseeching my readers, both male and female, of what age, complexion, and condition soever, for the love of God and their own souls, to guard against the temptations and suggestions of the devil, and suffer him by no art or wile to put any other ideas into their minds, than what I put into my definition. – For by the word *Nose*, throughout all this long chapter of noses, and in every other part of my work, where the word *Nose* occurs, – I declare, by that word I mean a Nose, and nothing more, or less. (vol. 3, ch. xxxi, p. 159)

By this so-called 'definition' 'to avoid all confusion', confusion and ambiguity are skilfully nurtured, and this is done again brilliantly with 'whiskers' (vol. 5, ch. i, p. 240), 'Cover-d-way' and 'Backside' (vol. 2, ch. vi, p. 72), and even with such neutral terms as 'means', 'matters', 'things', 'it', 'affairs', 'faculties', whose very vagueness allows them to be laden with insidious implications. The same procedure governs aposiopesis, suspensions, asterisks, dashes, blanks: these are spaces which the reader is invited to fill by the creation of his own meaning. The technique is as risky as it is clever; it misfires if the reader cannot discover a meaning; but if the meaning he discovers is scabrous, the responsibility is his.

The rhetoric of *Tristram Shandy* thus enriches the spectrum of ironic communication. 'For irony, . . ., has passed from the verbal nuance to a still wider range of suggestiveness. It exists now in gesture and mime, as far as the printed page can be adapted to these things.'[22] On the other hand, this expansion, coupled with the belief in the essential unsteadiness of words, leads also to far greater complexity in the nature of ironies. *Tristram Shandy* has been deemed 'annoying and sometimes infuriating because not only are things not what they seem; they are not the opposite of what they seem either'.[23] The simpler irony of reversal, such as predominates in *Pride and Prejudice*, is superseded by a progressive deconstruction of meaning. While the traditional ironist 'dodges between the innocuous letter of what he says and the subversive spirit of what he means',[24] the romantic ironist darts about in a labyrinth of hypothetical meanings, none of which can be equated with 'what he means' because he maintains an awareness of the plurality of meanings and therefore does not settle on any single one as definitive. His perception of the world and, most important, of language as in a state of flux differentiates him decisively from the traditional ironist who believes that words can be used in a steady format to convey a specific meaning. Only the postulate of the stability of language in its denotative as well as in its emotive capacity warrants the assumption – basic to *Pride and Prejudice* and *Madame Bovary* – that the reader will be able to reconstruct the covert intended connotation of a message encoded in irony. Once language, on the contrary, is seen as 'unsteady', the comprehension of meaning inevitably becomes uncertain and open-ended. This is one of the major reasons why confident reconstruction is virtually excluded in *Tristram Shandy*. The shiftiness of the linguistic base militates against that hierarchical ordering necessary to the understanding of irony. The rhetoric of *Tristram Shandy* embodies in the sphere of language the same fundamental indeterminacy inherent in the perplexing narrative situation with its dual writers and two-fold readers.

The syntax and the tempo of the prose heighten the sense of

indefinity through their extreme mobility. The abrupt
transitions, the inordinate exploitation of the dash, the rapid
shuffling of interrogation and correction, the conversational
casualness all contribute to the impression of chaos and
incoherence. Whatever is posited in one phrase is restricted,
modified or amended in the next; the text of *Tristram Shandy* never
rests into fixity literally or figuratively. Even the physical
components of the book create a confused motion that militates
against the establishment of a steady perspective. The favoured
grammatical elements: the optative 'I wish', the alternative 'or',
the reservation 'except', the relative clause qualifying what has
preceded it – these testify to the precariousness of every
statement. As in the style of the *Flegeljahre*, the sheer abundance of
Tristram Shandy tends to obscure rather than clarify; the minute
concentration on the precision of the microcosmic detail serves
ironically to highlight the sprawling blurred expanse of the
macrocosm. The involuted, apparently aimless flow is objectified
in those quirky squiggles (vol. 6, ch. xl, p. 333) which are at once
'Tristram's cardiographs of consciousness'[25] and the epitome of
the text he is shaping. In *Tristram Shandy* the fractured
hyphenated style 'demonstrates the impossibility of merely literal
meaning; for by means of the very extravagant, foolish syntax
attitudes shift and redefine one another'.[26] Language is being
queried through and in its own practices.

The fluidity of meaning and its interconnection with 'the
unsteady uses of words' is shown in the strange verbal and mental
associations that all the main protagonists habitually make.
Though the effect is comic, the implications are serious. For each
figure has his own personal, frequently idiosyncratic trains of
thought on which he drifts away from the accepted understanding
of words and ideas. The best example is Toby with his fixation on
war-games; to him the 'auxiliaries' on which Walter holds forth
denote not verbs but troops, while 'radical moisture' suggests
ditch-water, and 'radical heat' brandy (vol. 5, ch. xl, p. 282).
Quite ordinary words too, such as 'bridge' and 'train', are liable
to be misunderstood as a result of mistaken or merely odd
associations.[27] Through the repetitive network of misapprehensions the pervasiveness of cross-communication is
strongly implied. Every individual, by endowing words with
private connotations, comes to speak a language inaccessible to
others. The multivalence of words is another symptom of the

fragility of a fictional world in which there are no secure points of reference that transcend the subjective vision.

In this sense the problem of the dysfunction of language is crucial to *Tristram Shandy*. Sterne was familiar with Locke's *Essay Concerning Human Understanding*, to which reference is made in *Tristram Shandy*. In book III of the *Essay* Locke elaborated his innovative view of words as signs for ideas. While by no means unaware of the potential danger of such a theory, Lock maintains by and large a sanguine optimism. By comparison, Sterne harbours a far deeper scepticism about the prospects of ' "getting something across", whether it is missiles or people or meanings'.[28] His witty use of graphic devices – blank pages, a black page, a marbled page – is an attempt to circumvent conventional methods of expression. But these are hardly sufficient grounds for turning Sterne into a crypto-modern writer obsessed with the inadequacy of words and the limitations of language.[29] His reservations about language are counteracted by an exuberant pleasure in words. His fictive narrator is surely one of the most loquacious ever invented, delighting in verbal gymnastics of astonishing agility. If *Tristram Shandy* is about the dysfunction of language, it is also about its hyperactivity. The two, far from being mutually exclusive, are poised in an ironic tension that imparts to *Tristram Shandy* its particular flavour. In its language as in its narrative situation *Tristram Shandy* is a prolonged contradiction of its overt posture: in the same way as the first-person fictive narrator does not maintain any authentic relationship with his contrived or actual reader despite his insistent presence, so none of the manifold conversations – between Tristram and the contrived reader, between Walter and Toby, Walter and his wife, etc. – achieves any true communion. The almost overwhelming mass of words belies – or covers – an unaccountable inner lacuna. Tristram says a great deal about his 'Life and Opinions', but in the end, what essential facts are really known about him? and what is the upshot of Toby's affair with Widow Wadham? or of Mrs Shandy's long listening at the chink? Beneath the resonance of the rhetoric there is a space of silence; for the irony of the language is that it reveals, in the very effort at verbal exchange, that there is no exchange because each individual is enclosed within the private confines of his own understanding of words. This fragmentation is the antithesis to the common language shared by the protagonists of *Pride and*

Prejudice, whose unproblematic grasp of words and concepts is the basis for their confidence in the truth of knowledge and its attainability. When words are basically 'unsteady', they are less usable as the medium for irony because they are in themselves already embodiments of an ironic principle. Language in *Tristram Shandy*, for all its brilliant profusion, is fallible to the point of fallaciousness.

4

Towards the end of the first volume, Tristram begins to tell Madam of the wound that Toby sustained at Namur, and then suddenly breaks off, thwarting her curiosity by dodging her imputed queries: 'The story of that, Madam, is long and interesting; – but it would be running my history all upon heaps to give it to you here. – 'Tis for an episode hereafter; and every circumstance relating to it in its proper place, shall be faithfully laid before you' (vol. 1, ch. xxi, p. 48). The questions raised here extend well beyond the particular episode of Toby's wound: is there in fact a 'proper place' for things in *Tristram Shandy*? and by what or whose criteria is the 'proper place' to be determined? Such questions have a direct bearing on any consideration of the organisation of *Tristram Shandy*. For a recognition of its norms must precede exploration of its ironic departure from, or reversal, or subversion of that implicit norm.

However, difficulties immediately arise: by what norm is *Tristram Shandy* to be measured? The generic context that should serve as a yardstick is so blurred that it cannot be invoked as an authoritative standard. Are *The Life and Opinions of Tristram Shandy, Gent.* to be read as a biography, compiled by Laurence Sterne, or as an autobiography being written by Tristram? The peculiar dual texture forces an inclusive and inevitably ambiguous answer. Should the work be regarded as a burlesque? or an improvisation? and what is the place of the digressions in the total disposition? Through the admission of Tristram's 'Opinions', the work's scope is so vastly expanded as to warrant the inclusion of everything that passes through his mind, even his so-called 'digressions'. For 'madam', the fictive reader, these matters are settled by Tristram, who is the final arbiter within the fiction; for the actual reader the answers are by no means so

simple. Indeed, here once again, he finds himself in an alarming
quicksand that denies him a sound footing. Ingenious solutions to
this predicament have been put forward, notably by Richard
Lanham who sites *Tristram Shandy* in the framework of games of
pleasure as an *'ilinx* (games involving loss of balance, the
sensation of vertigo – drugs, for example, or a ride on a roller
coaster)'.[30] The game could also be described as the deployment
of a progressive irony that undermines, almost systematically,
each and every postulate only to replace it with a further one that
will in turn be scuttled in a volatile sequence that captures the
evanescence of human existence.

This is the irony that shapes the entire design of *Tristram
Shandy*. It consists of overlapping, superimposed components that
encroach on each other and displace one another as if in
competition for the reader's – and the narrator's – attention.
There is no separation into distinct units, as in the incidents of
Don Juan's adventures, nor any ordering of the various levels of
fiction as in the *Flegeljahre*. What is characteristic of *Tristram
Shandy*, on the contrary, is the perpetual state of flux. No single
fictional strand ever remains in unchallenged ascendancy; what is
the centre of gravity? the story of Tristram's life? or of Toby's
amours? or of the writing of Tristram's autobiography? The
continual breaks, the fluctuations in time and space with the
abrupt switch from one focus to another induce a dizzying sense
of turbulence. The movement of *Tristram Shandy* has aptly been
characterised as 'indirect, parabolic, hyperbolic, cycloid';[31]
Tristram summarises it more simply but no less puzzlingly: 'In a
word, my work is digressive, and it is progressive too, – and at
the same time' (vol. 1, ch. xxii, p. 52). The paradoxicality of this
double, self-contradictory motion is justified by the nature of the
story which obliges him 'continually to be going backwards and
forwards to keep all tight together in the reader's fancy' (vol. 6,
ch. xxxiii, p. 325). The work expands in this seemingly wayward
manner because it can progress forwards only by digressing
backwards into Tristram's memory. Its structure is governed by
an inner irony that determines its architectonics. Digressiveness
is in fact an integral and necessary part of this peculiar novel's
economy. The earliest to perceive this was Coleridge who noted
in jottings for a lecture given 24 February 1818 that 'the
digressive spirit is not wantonness, but the *very form* of his
genius'.[32] With his imaginative insight Coleridge places Sterne in

the lineage of Cervantes and alongside Jean Paul Richter; he denotes their common features as 'humour', 'ironical wit', and a 'delight to end in nothing, or a direct contradiction'. What Coleridge recognised was that an artistic principle governs the apparent capriciousness of *Tristram Shandy*. Its name is not 'Muddle', as E. M. Forster[33] averred, but irony in the Schlegelian sense. The configuration of *Tristram Shandy* is that 'gebildetes künstliches Chaos'[34] ('shaped artificial chaos') that Schlegel was to extol as the ideal romantic form of narrative.

Such conceptual irony must be distinguished from dramatic irony. Dramatic irony structures plot through the pattern of contrasts and reversals internal to the work. Conceptual irony is intrinsic to the fabric of the work, to its narrative strategies, to its overall organisation as well as to its language. Because it is literally ingrained in the fabric itself as a pervasive determinant, it is not amenable to resolution in the same way as dramatic irony, which is more local, temporary, and limited in its manifestations. And, paradoxically, because of its very centrality, conceptual irony proves more resistant to identification than the ironies closer to the surface and therefore more readily visible, such as the rhetorical or the situational. Extended into a wider format, this distinction amounts ultimately to a differentiation between irony as a device and irony as a *Weltanschauung*, between those works, on the one hand, that *use* irony for a specific purpose, such as plot dynamics, or characterisation, or satire, and, on the other hand, those that *are* ironic. *Pride and Prejudice* is the prototype of the one, and *Tristram Shandy* of the other.

One outlet for the conceptual irony of *Tristram Shandy* is in its wholesale sabotage of narrative conventions. Tristram's preface pops up without warning in the middle of the third volume when he has 'a moment to spare' with all his heroes off his hands (vol. 3, ch. xx, p. 140); two chapters are skipped (vol. 9, chs xviii and xix, pp. 438–9) and inserted later; a chapter of ten pages is missing (vol. 4, ch. xiv, p. 219); protagonists are left standing on the stairs or abandoned in the kitchen for pages and hours on end while more urgent business intervenes until they are suddenly recalled and brought back into the story. These flamboyant affronts to narrative syntaxis transmute the straight line of traditional story-telling into those errant squiggles that Tristram draws (vol. 6, ch. xl, p. 333). By seeming to aim for the straight line, by including a preface, by pretending to aspire to regularity, the incongruity of the text's irregularity is further emphasised. Yet Sterne is more than merely one of the 'zany jugglers of narrative convention'.[35] The mishaps, interruptions, digressions that beset the narrative are ciphers for the contingencies of existence. The text, too, is subject to accident and susceptible to the unpredictability of life; 'if nothing stops us in our way' (vol. 1, ch. x, p. 15) is its rueful, poignant and ironic motto. The innumerable stops, delays, detours and entanglements are an image of the inconsequential, illogical world of *Tristram Shandy*, in which there is no 'proper place' for things.

Nor for that matter is there a proper time. The dislocation of plot order has as its corollary a glaring discontinuity in the time sequence. The action swings constantly not only from Tristram's present time of writing to the past of his memory, but well back into the pre-history of the protagonists. The total length of fictional time amounts, according to Mendilow's calculations,[36] to three-quarters of a century on the shortest reckoning; other critics arrive at a much longer time-span, dating the events to the years between 1644 and 1766.[37] Whichever is the case, the impression is one of utmost confusion: temporally the narrative has no beginning, middle or end. In fact it closes four years before Tristram's birth, on whose conception it opened; in the meanwhile, in a series of intersections, interpolations and superimpositions, it leaps back and forth from the present to various disconnected segments of the past. What makes this technique so disconcerting is not the temporal multi-dimensionality as such, nor even the jumbling that gives causes after effects, conclusions before happenings; it is rather the absence of any discernible basic linear chronology to which the time-shifts can be related. There is no central point of reference from which the flashbacks and excursions can be arranged and mastered. As a result, the individual incidents appear more like fragmentary spots of time than as parts of a continuum.

Time is thus made relative, shifting, and personal; it is largely removed from the outer objective measure of chronos to the inner subjective realm of duration. Tristram's two journeys to France, many years apart, are telescoped in his mind as if into one: 'I have been getting forwards in two different journies together, and with the same dash of the pen – for I have got entirely out of Auxerre in this journey which I am writing now, and I am got half way out of Auxerre in that which I shall write hereafter' (vol. 7, ch. xxviii, p. 362). This is one of several instances when the fictive narrator explicitly draws attention to problems of time. In the middle of the fourth volume, for instance, he takes stock of his progress:

> I am this month one whole year older than I was this time twelve-month; and having got, as you perceive, almost into the middle of my fourth volume – and no farther than to my first day's life – 'tis demonstrative that I have three hundred and sixty-four days more life to write just now, than when I first set out; so that instead of advancing, as a common writer, in my work with what I have been doing at it – on the contrary, I am just thrown so many volumes back – was every day of my life to be as busy a day as this – And why not? – and the transactions and opinions of it to take up as much description – And for what reason should they be cut short? at this rate I should just live 364 times faster than I should write – It must follow, an' please your worships, that the more I write, the more I shall have to write – and consequently, the more your worships read, the more your worships will have to read. (vol. 4, ch. xiii, p. 207)

The discrepancy between time remembered, time of writing and time of reading is underlined here. What is more, the time of reading itself, the 'hour and a half's tolerable good reading since my Uncle Toby rung the bell' (vol. 2, ch. viii, p. 73) has a dual connotation since it refers in the first place to Tristram's fictive reader but can apply to the actual reader too. External, mechanical time has therefore been replaced in *Tristram Shandy* by a multifaceted, relativistic and ironic sense of time that plays the past off against the present, mathematical time against experiential time, reading time against fictional time.

The manipulation of time in *Tristram Shandy* produces a two-fold and contradictory effect: a disorientation, almost a feeling of vertigo, arising from the scurrying transition from one temporal segment to another; yet also a haunting apprehension of circularity and indeed of statis. Between Toby's first 'I wish . . . you had seen what prodigious armies we had in Flanders' (vol. 2, ch. xviii, p. 104) and his reiteration of the identical phrase (vol. 3, ch. i, p. 112) some eight pages intervene and far more than 'a minute' (vol. 2, ch. xix, p. 104) as Tristram inserts what 'should have been told a hundred and fifty pages ago' and launches into an account of his father's opinions. The repetition twice of 'What prodigious armies you had in Flanders' by Walter (vol. 3, ch. ii, p. 113, and vol. 3, ch. vi, p. 116) together with the triple reprise of 'Any man, madam' (vol. 3, ch. v, pp. 115–6) suggests that the narrative is, as it were, becalmed; it re-echoes the same phrases, retreads the same ground, and in spite of its rhetorical energy it finally gets nowhere. It is by no means coincidental that it ends four years before it began. In the wholly ironic structure of *Tristram Shandy* 'proper place' and proper time have become conditional notions.

5

There is still a further dimension of irony in *Tristram Shandy*. It is not only Sterne, the actual author, who is an ironist; the fictive narrator, too, is endowed with a self-questioning ironic intelligence that engages in an incessant scrutiny of the autobiography he is writing. Through the portrayal of an immensely self-conscious writer at work, an internal metafictional irony is woven into *Tristram Shandy*. The arrangement is considerably more complex than in *Don Juan*, where the ironic commentary on the work-in-progress comes from a source external to the fictional myth, from an author who stands beside his artifact and who addresses his scathingly humorous critique to his readers as well as to himself. In *Tristram Shandy*, by contrast, the ironic commentator is a persona within the fiction, and it is he who subverts his own narrative by his perpetual breaks in the fictional illusion. This is the context in which the intruding narrator becomes 'a force so disruptive that it transforms the very nature of the work'.[38] That transformation occurs through an intensification and a compounding of irony that has the effect of increasing the distance – and the alienation – between the text and the reader. For Tristram's reflections on his writing are primarily a dialogue with himself; at most he extends to his fictive reader the semblance of an apologia or an exhortation. It may be no more than a semblance since he is a showman playing games and cultivating illusions with his tale. As the actual reader takes cognisance of Tristram's dubiousness, he becomes more and more of a sceptical outsider to the narrative process. Not being trusted by Tristram, he in turn grows untrusting. So Sterne's invention of an ironic gamesman as narrator creates a kind of immanent irony that represents a quantum leap in ironic narration.

The immediate impact of Tristram's keen awareness of himself as a writer comes as a threat to the viability of his fiction. He destroys what he creates through his innumerable references to its fragile fictional status. There is hardly a page of *Tristram Shandy* without an overt mention of 'my story', 'my work', 'my book', 'this volume', what is to come in 'the next chapter', the disturbance caused by 'the door harshly opening in the next chapter but one' (vol. 3, ch. xi, p. 131), what future chapters are being planned (including a chapter on chapters!). The typographical tricks, too, serve as teasing reminders of the printed nature of the entire enterprise. Tristram even portrays himself physically at the time of writing, sitting at his desk 'this 12th day of August, 1766, in a purple jerkin and yellow pair of slippers, without either wig or cap on' (vol. 9, ch. ii, p. 423) or 'in the most pensive and melancholy frame of mind, . . . dropping thy pen, – spurting thy ink about thy table and thy books' (vol. 3, ch. xxviii, p. 156). He envisages himself more as a writer than as an actor in the happenings he is recording. This is hardly surprising since he is either not yet born or an infant at the time he is chronicling, while his present reality is the act of composition. His self-consciousness leads to a continuous anxious assessment of his performance and progress. The hypothetical account of his Life and Opinions is punctuated and punctured by a running critical review of his own methods of narration, the difficulties facing him as a writer and the means whereby he hopes to overcome them.

Yet in endeavouring to bolster the credibility of his text, Tristram is in fact undermining it by drawing attention not merely to the predicaments of composition but also to the essential fictionality of the illusion he is conjuring up. The world of Walter and Mrs Shandy, Toby and Widow Wadham comes across not as a self-sustaining entity enclosed in a well-wrought capsule (as, for instance, the worlds of Elizabeth and Darcy, of Charles and Emma) but as an articulated authorial construct. This does not, of course, imply that the world of Walter and Toby lacks imaginative vitality; that vitality, however, is the outcome of Tristram's creative effort in evoking it. Intervening between that world and the reader – fictive and actual – there is not only a palpable distancing, but also a pronounced refraction through the mediating presence of Tristram, whose vision generates that other removed fictive world within the fiction of *Tristram Shandy*. The recurrent allusions to the business of writing are insistent representations of Tristram's role as author and of the fictionality of his artifact. What is more, the concentration on the techniques of writing, for example on the metaphorical aspects of a phrase, foster in the reader a concomitant consciousness of his involvement in the act of reading. The prominence of this metafictional element, allied with the interruptive mode of narration, results in a fundamental shift of emphasis in *Tristram Shandy*. Its story is not just 'in part the story of its telling';[39] the telling of the story-telling becomes so dominant and invasive as to overshadow and virtually oust the story itself. The overt content of *Tristram Shandy* – the lives of Walter, Toby, Le Fever, even Tristram himself – may be likened to branches growing out of the main supporting trunk which is the drama of the birth of this text. Instead of telling the story traditional to the novel, *Tristram Shandy* depicts the processes of shaping the novel. Like Tristram himself in the early volumes, the narrative is in *statu nascendi*. In place of the polished, finished product, the smooth fabric of illusion of *Pride and Prejudice* and *Madame Bovary, Tristram Shandy* offers a glimpse of the turmoil in the narrator's workshop. That this workshop is itself fictive, i.e. an invention of Laurence Sterne, is another facet of the multiple play with illusion. The text's prodigious self-reflexiveness is the expression of a progressive irony that takes an impish delight in sapping the foundations of its own edifice.

The same ironic obliquity is characteristic of the act of communication too. Presumably Tristram labours so long and hard at the mechanics of composition in order to convey a meaning or at least to impart some information about his life and opinions. He does no such thing. The facts of his life are of such an embarrassing nature that from the outset he is torn between the urge to disclose and the necessity for discreet reticence. His obsession with the problems of presenting his material becomes a screen and a substitute for his avowed undertaking. In the absence of other commitments, writing comes to be the major adventure of his life. But then the writing that was intended to serve a concrete purpose turns into an end unto itself. His preoccupation with the triumphs and perils of creativity eclipses his original desire to tell his life and opinions. The act of telling in and for itself has primacy over both the living experience on which it is based and also over the tale it is supposed to produce. Absorbed in his own manipulations, the narrator turns his gaze inwards onto himself as a creative being and onto the work he is fashioning. His orientation is towards himself rather than towards the reader, who is extraneous to the central drama that is being enacted between the writer and his text.

What happens to Tristram in this respect is a paradigm for what happens in *Tristram Shandy* as a whole. The story is so disrupted and so reduced in importance as to be subordinate to the circumstances of its evolution. Metafiction here overtakes fiction. It is this that makes *Tristram Shandy* the prototype of ironic reversal in the art of narrative. It tells of itself. In so doing, it destroys itself in the very moment of creation. It denies the reader all the props requisite for confident reading by negating any firm contours, any fixed points of reference, any secure positions or any consistency except its own inconsistency. What it holds out to the reader are the shifting uncertainties of an irony that thwarts and excludes definity.

6

The contingencies that beset the reader, like the accidents that befall the narrative, parallel the mishaps that dog Tristram's life. In its mobility, its 'digressive and progressive', 'backwards and forwards' movement, *Tristram Shandy* is itself the tangible incarnation of the unpredictability which rules its fictional world. For this is, as Virginia Woolf recognised, 'a world in which anything may happen'.[40] It is a world that acknowledges 'what nonsense it is, either in fighting, or writing, or any thing else (whether in rhyme to it, or not) which a man has occasion to do – to act by plan' (vol. 8, ch. xxiii, pp. 406–7), that hates 'your *ifs*' (vol. 1, ch. xii, p. 19) but that accepts '*happenings*' as 'a matter of contingency, which might happen, or not, just as chance ordered it' (vol. 8, ch. xix, pp. 400–1) and that submits, however reluctantly, to the 'unforeseen stoppages' (vol. 1, ch. xiv, p. 26) which are man's inescapable lot when chance, lucky or unlucky as the case may be, together with time, are 'the powers . . . which severally check us in our careers in this world' (vol. 9, ch. i, p. 422).

From the point when Mrs Shandy interrupts her husband at the most inpropitious moment with '*a silly question*' (vol. 1, ch. i, p. 2) about that other regular domestic ritual of winding up the clock, Tristram's entire life is an illustration of the laws which govern the Shandyan universe. He is the 'sport of small accidents' (vol. 3, ch. viii, p. 118) in a series of bizarre reversals. Because of a false alarm the previous year, Tristram's mother had forfeited her legally sanctioned right to confinement in London, so that Tristram is born in the country, where Dr Slop's ineptitude results in the mashing of his nose. Because of his frailty he has to be baptised in haste, and owing to Walter's tardiness and Susannah's distraction he is christened with the one name his father abhors. Because Trim had removed certain vital parts of the sash-windows as building materials for Toby's fortifications and nothing was ever repaired in the ramshackle Shandy home, Tristram suffers the 'misadventure' (vol. 5, ch. xviii, p. 264) of a fortuitous circumcision when the window drops at another inopportune moment. And finally because of the slow progress made by his father in compiling the *Tristra-paedia*, his growth outstrips the manual whereby he is to be educated, and 'the misfortune was, that I was all that time totally neglected' (vol. 5, ch. xvi, p. 263). These are ironies of situation when the opposite – or something other – occurs to what might reasonably be expected. They are so common in *Tristram Shandy* as to coalesce into a pattern of perversity in which it becomes natural to anticipate the reverse of what might in the normal course of events be foreseen. For the Shandy family is so prone to 'cross-reckonings' (vol. 4, ch. vii, p. 201) that the coat-of-arms emblazoned on its coach has a '*bend sinister*' (vol. 4, ch. xxv, p. 220) as if to denote 'the sinister turn, which every thing relating to our family was apt to take'. The 'confusion' occasioned by a 'jumble of cross accidents' (vol. 7, ch. xxxvii, p. 372) comes to be the customary (dis)order of this singular household. Surprising turns and wholly contrary outcomes recur with a frequency amounting almost to unfailing regularity. So much so as to contain the tacit but strong implication of a universe turned topsy-turvy because it operates under the aegis of an ontological irony.

Ontological irony has the effect of debarring any

systematisation whatsoever. Even to assume the prevalence of reversal is to impose a format on a world whose foremost characteristic is its defiance of rational reckoning. Possibilities go on remaining open in *Tristram Shandy*: with ineradicable optimism and against all odds Toby continues to build his fortifications, Walter to evolve his grandiose schemes, and Tristram to write his book. 'Every thing in this world', Walter maintains, 'is big with jest, – and has wit in it, and instruction too – if we can but find it out' (vol. 5, ch. xxxii, p. 276). That 'if' is simultaneously the great hope and the great impediment in *Tristram Shandy*; it supports the protagonists' buoyant faith in potentiality, but only to frustrate ultimate attainment. Tristram's early hesitant phrase: 'if nothing stops us in our way' (vol. 1, ch. x, p. 15) comes to have an ominous ring, for this is a narrative which not only itself is constantly stopped in its way, but which also takes for its theme the ironic stoppages that halt and hinder human beings on their way through life.

Denied though they are for ever the possession of that positive certainty that resolves ironies in *Pride and Prejudice*, the protagonists of *Tristram Shandy* nonetheless manage to live quite cheerfully by acceding to a state of negative capability. In so far as there is a norm in *Tristram Shandy*, it is equivocation, the suspension of certainty in an open space filled with multiple possibilities:

> Whether *Susannah*, by taking her hand too suddenly from off the corporal's shoulder (by the whisking about of her passions) – broke a little chain of his reflections –
> Or whether the corporal began to be suspicious, he had got into the doctor's quarters, and was talking more like the chaplain than himself –
> Or whether . . . .
> Or whether – for in all such cases a man of invention and parts may with pleasure fill a couple of pages with suppositions – which of all these was the cause, let the curious physiologist, or the curious any body determine – (vol. 5, ch. x, pp. 255–6)

Such teasing tactics of prevarication are used again and again in *Tristram Shandy*; often, as in this instance, they have a comic impact through the inflation of small dilemmas into impenetrable predicaments. The comic hyperbole, however, masks a tragic impasse, i.e. that assurance has been dislodged by 'suppositions'. The erosion of knowledge into doubt is graphically shown in Tristram's account of Toby's disability:

> Now as all the world knows, that no effect in nature can be produced without a cause and as it is as well known, that my uncle *Toby* was neither a weaver – a gardener, or a gladiator – unless as a captain, you will needs have him one – but then he was only a captain of foot – and besides the whole is an equivocation – There is nothing left for us to suppose, but that my uncle *Toby*'s leg – but that will avail us little in the present hypothesis, unless it had proceeded from some ailment *in the foot* – whereas his leg was not emaciated from any disorder in his foot – for my uncle *Toby*'s leg was not emaciated at all. It was a little stiff and awkward, from a total disuse of it, for the three years he lay confined at my father's house in town; but it was plump and muscular, and in all other respects as good and promising a leg as the other.
>
> I declare, I do not recollect any one opinion or passage of my life, where my understanding was more at a loss to make ends meet, and torture the chapter I had been writing, to the service of the chapter following it, than in the present case. (vol. 8, ch. vi, p. 384)

Beginning with the confident appeal to a publicly accepted sequence of cause and effect – not quite, admittedly, 'a truth universally acknowledged' – Tristram slips further into 'equivocation', supposition, 'hypothesis' and contradiction until he confesses his 'understanding . . . at a loss to make ends meet'. The failure of logic and reason in the face of an inconsequential world is a corollary of ontological irony.

What is remarkable about *Tristram Shandy* is the good-humoured equanimity with which it acquiesces to a pretty sombre vision of human existence. As Dyson has commented, 'the materials for satire exist in plenty, but the will to satire is nowhere to be found'.[41] Or only very intermittently and in attenuated form, as for example in the grotesque portrayal of the scholarly disputation in Slawkenbergius's Tale (vol. 4, p. 190). By and large, the purposefulness and the venom of satire are alien to Sterne; he espouses rather the relativism of irony, aware of ubiquitous incongruities, yet tolerant towards them. An acute sense of the disproportions that typify the jumble of the Shandyan living and thinking space is revealed in the strange couplings of disparate particles, outlandish in the discrepancy between their levels. The embryo 'HOMUNCULUS' is immediately deemed 'as much and as truly our fellow-creature as my Lord Chancellor of England' (vol. 1, ch. ii, p. 2); Tristram's role as chronicler of 'the affairs of the kitchen' is likened to that of Rapin, the illustrious French historian of England (vol. 5, ch. v, p. 250); and Trim voices the solemn – and ludicrous – axiom that 'there is nothing so awkward, as courting a woman, an' please your honour, whilst she is making sausages' (vol. 9, ch. vii, p. 428). The unlikely verbal and conceptual combinations of *Tristram Shandy* denote a world so out of joint as to resist rational explanation. Coleridge was surely right when he characterised Sterne as one of those writers 'who delight to end in nothing, or a direct contradiction'.[42] The unending paradoxicality of a world shaped by an ontological irony was for Sterne not a source of anguish, as it is for most modern writers, but of hilarity, albeit a 'sad hilarity'.[43] For he remains a child of the eighteenth century even when he foreshadows the concerns of the age of anxiety.

7

'Did Sterne complete Tristram Shandy?'[44] is the title of a provocative article. The answer given is in the affirmative on the grounds that 'from the beginning, Sterne planned the structure of the book as an elaborate and prolonged contradiction of the title-page' (p. 544), that it is literally a cock and bull story consisting 'of the substitution of one story-thread for another – Toby's for Tristram's' (p. 545). Clever though this argument is, it addresses a question inappropriate to *Tristram Shandy*. The real issue is whether a narrative that does not merely portray but actually embodies uncertainty can and should be completed; must it not of aesthetic and philosophical necessity remain up in the air? In its concluding exchange:

> L . . d! said my mother, what is all this story about? –
> A COCK and a BULL, said *Yorick* – And one of the best of its kind, I ever heard. (vol. 9, ch. xxxiii, p. 457)

Tristram Shandy is given a summary, not an ending. It arrives at a provisional halting-place, not a terminal point, when it stops without the finality of closure. The definity implicit in conclusion is alien to the equivocation central to *Tristram Shandy.* Both its perception of the universe as a product of contingency and its associated literary form as process literature prohibit the type of neat resolution that is feasible within either the optimistic assumptions of *Pride and Prejudice* or, alternatively, the pessimistic ones of *Madame Bovary.* In its open-endedness *Tristram Shandy* is more akin to *Don Juan* and to *Jacques le fataliste.* None of these works can repose in a comfortable trust in 'truth universally acknowledged'; in place of the security of the finite closure, there is an infinite quest in an unbounded space. 'Endless is the Search for Truth!' (vol. 2, ch. iii, p. 64) could well be the motto (and perhaps the message) of *Tristram Shandy.* Indeed, its scepticism extends even further in its insinuation that truth may ultimately be unattainable:

> 'Tis a pity, cried my father one winter's night, after a three hours painful translation of Slawkenbergius, – 'tis a pity, cried my father, putting my mother's thread-paper into the book for a mark, as he spoke – that truth, brother *Toby*, should shut herself up in such impregnable fastnesses, and be so obstinate as not to surrender herself sometimes upon the closest siege. – (vol. 3, ch. xli, p. 173)

From the concession that truth may be beyond reach to the suspicion that it may be a mirage or an illusion is only a small step. Whether that step is taken in *Tristram Shandy* is debatable; like most of the text's major issues, this remains enveloped in indeterminacy. Clearly, no majestic truth exists here possessing the absolute validity of that posited in *Pride and Prejudice* – truth with a capital 'T', so to speak. The truths in *Tristram Shandy* are modest, limited, and frequently questionable. Tristram, for instance, claims certitude in matters generally not amenable to such sureness: 'I was begot in the night, betwixt the first *Sunday* and the first *Monday* in the month of *March*, in the year of our Lord one thousand seven hundred and eighteen. I am positive I was.' (vol. 1, ch. iv, p. 4). The proof that he advances by his pseudo-reasoning references to family habits, departures and returns 'brings the thing almost to a certainty' (vol. 1, ch. iv, p. 5), he

insists. But his circuitous, digressive ratiocinations, together with
the tenuous nature of the evidence he adduces, have the contrary
ironic effect of raising serious doubts as to the authenticity of his
knowledge. This comical, apparently trifling incident in the
opening pages sets the pattern for *Tristram Shandy*. Each
protagonist is passionately convinced of the truth of his
knowledge; however, the knowledge is purely subjective, the
product of an idiosyncratic mind, and based not on verifiable
evidence but on intuitive convictions which may be delusions.

The foremost example of this syndrome is Walter Shandy. 'I
am convinced,' he proclaims to Yorick, 'that there is a North-
west passage to the intellectual world' (vol. 5, ch. xlii, p. 284). He
is just as convinced, on equally gratuitous grounds, that the
gateway to enlightenment is through 'the use of *Auxiliaries*' whose
function is 'at once to set the soul a going by herself upon the
materials as they are brought her; and by the versability of this
great engine, round which they are twisted, to open new tracks of
enquiry, and make every idea engender millions' (vol. 5, ch. xlii,
p. 284). The processes that Walter here extolls are ironically
exposed in Toby's misunderstanding of 'Auxiliaries' which he
associates with troops, not verbs:

> 'But the auxiliaries, Trim, my brother is talking about, – I
> conceive to be different things. –
> – 'You do?' said my father, rising up.
>
> (vol. 5, ch. xlii, p. 285)

There could hardly be a more telling illustration of the
subjectivity of the mental spaces that the characters in *Tristram
Shandy* inhabit. Such eccentricity of vision is most strongly
emphasised in regard to Walter:

> his road lay so very far on one side, from that wherein most
> men travelled, – that every object before him presented a face
> and section of itself to his eye, altogether different from the
> plan and elevation of it seen by the rest of mankind. – In other
> words, 'twas a different object, – and in course was differently
> considered. (vol. 5, ch. xxiv, p. 268)

This holds no less for Toby, or for Tristram himself; they too
'saw all things in lights different from the rest of the world' (vol.
6, ch. xxvi, p. 316). It is in this context that the epigraph to

Tristram Shandy must be invoked: 'It is not things that disturb men, but their judgements about things.' Men's judgement is shown to be grossly fallacious, and consequently understanding either of an extraneous object or between individuals intrinsically fallible. Every attempt at comprehension through logic fails, from Tristram's enquiry into the origins of his misfortunes to Walter's efforts to relate happenings systematically to their causes.

If judgement, intuitive as well as rational, is deceiving, on what can men rely? 'For we *trust* we have a good Conscience' is the theme of the interpolated sermon (vol. 2, ch. xvii, pp. 88–101). 'Surely', is its postulate, 'if there is any thing in this life which a man may depend upon, and to the knowledge of which he is capable of arriving upon the most indisputable evidence, it must be this very thing, – whether he has a good conscience or no.' (vol. 2, ch. xvii, pp. 89–90). This is promptly translated by Dr Slop into: 'I am positive I am right.' But 'conscience is nothing else but the knowledge which the mind has within herself' (p. 90); it is 'not a law: – No, God and reason made the law, and have placed conscience within you to determine' (p. 101). The sermon in effect proposes a two-tiered ontology: the controlling level is that of God and reason, the source of the law; secondary to them is the personal conscience, intuitive in its workings. Whether conscience is 'a matter of *trust*' or whether it can be 'a matter of *certainty*' (p. 90) is the pivot of the sermon. The preacher's arguments in favour of certainty are confounded by Dr Slop's simplistic apprehension: 'I am positive I am right'. Conscience is shown, in ironical contradiction to the thrust of the sermon, to be a matter of trust, in practice a matter of sheer subjectivity. Since God is invisible in *Tristram Shandy*, reason faulty, and the law erroneous, the only recourse is to trust in conscience, and that is, in the last resort, as untrustworthy as judgement.

'No wonder' then, as Walter laments, 'the intellectual web is so rent and tatter'd as we see it; and that so many of our best heads are no better than a puzzled skein of silk, – all perplexity, – all confusion within side' (vol. 2, ch. xix, p. 108). The world of *Tristram Shandy* is 'beset on all sides with mysteries and riddles' (vol. 9, ch. xxii, p. 441). As Tristram tells 'madam':

we live amongst riddles and mysteries – the most obvious things, which come in our way, have dark sides, which the quickest sight cannot penetrate into; and even the clearest and most exalted understandings amongst us find ourselves puzzled and at a loss in almost every cranny of nature's works; (vol. 4, ch. xvii, p. 212)

The protagonists of *Tristram Shandy* are inevitably 'puzzled' and 'at a loss' because they can interpret the world only 'as we see it', in the light – or the obscurity – of a subjective perception. The novel admits no criteria, no norms, no logic and no order external to its enchanted circle, and the radius of that circle is drawn by the 'I' of the fictive narrator. Sterne has devised the perfect way to represent the solipsistic inner space of subjective consciousness.

In so doing he also produced the most radical example of literary irony not only in the eighteenth century but possibly in the entire canon of Western literature (though this claim might be disputed in regard to Joyce's *Finnegans Wake*). In its literary form and in its ontological vision *Tristram Shandy* demonstrates the impossibility of what it purports to be doing: of writing a story, of communicating meaning, of capturing definity. As such it is an ironic self-portrayal whose very failure denotes its success, for it is the comic incarnation of a tragic paradox.

Yet the irony of *Tristram Shandy*, despite its intensity and its importance, is peculiarly difficult to analyse. Attempts to pin it down seem to arrive at only partial descriptions. This holds for Dyson's view that the irony 'turns out to be Sterne's way of mirroring the odd complexities of real life';[45] for Moglen's contention that: 'The overriding irony of the work derives from the relation of the apparent confusion of form and theme to the actual structural and conceptual order';[46] and for Rolle's thesis[47] that *Tristram Shandy* shows man at the extreme of his contradictoriness, and that its irony resides in the attitude of the fictive narrator who relativises every position he assumes by envisaging its opposite too. All these are valid assessments, but none of them grasps the core of *Tristram Shandy*'s highly distinctive irony. It is too dense and too multivalent to be reducible to a single neat formulation. It cannot be attributed to this or that specific feature because it so thoroughly pervades the entire text; it seems to be nowhere special because it is *everywhere*: in the ambiguity of the empty spaces, in the subjectivity of the time-scales, in the reiterated reminders of the unsteadiness of words, in the problematical relationships between narrators and readers, in the incessant pointers to the fictionality of the fiction being created, in the dominance of contingency, and in the insubstantiality of the private versions of truth. The keystone to *Tristram Shandy* is the perception of the relativity of all things, just as its ultimate unity lies in its flexibility.

In effect what Sterne has created – and this is the crux of *Tristram Shandy* – is an ironic context. A state of perpetual flux, aesthetically as well as philosophically and linguistically, is its controlling factor; so much so that it absorbs into its endless mobility the very bases of judgement. There is no pedestal of security either in the persona of the narrator, or in a sequential time-schema, or in the development of plot, or even in the haven of language or typography from which the reader may take stock so as to exercise his powers of discrimination. When the fixity of perspective is replaced by the multiplicity of perspectivism, no starting-point of sufficient confidence remains for the identification, let alone reconstruction of irony. This is what happens in *Tristram Shandy*; this is the consequence of the wholly ironic context that Sterne has contrived. Where truth and uncertainty have become relative, the notions of 'norm' and, therefore, of 'opposite' and 'reversal' lose their hierarchical significance. Irony then stems not from the contrast to absolute expectations, but from the interaction of elements with each other, and these are in themselves shifting. If, as Lionel Trilling has observed in regard to the concepts of sincerity and authenticity, ' "the whole" is seen as "confused" rather than as orderly and rational, as, in George Eliot's words, peremptory and absolute, the human relation to it need not be fixed and categorical; it can be mercurial and improvisational'.[48]

The outcome is an irony so total and engulfing that it consumes itself, destroying whatever it has just created. However, by withholding the accolade of truth to any one meaning, it leaves all meanings at the level of potentiality. Or there may be no meaning beneath the chaotic surface, no reality behind the appearances. And there is no way of ever knowing for sure. This is the essence of the modern ironic dilemma that *Tristram Shandy* has captured with bewildering brilliance. Its irony may be characterised in the adjectives I have suggested: immanent, intrinsic, conceptual, ontological, progressive; or it may be designated as 'romantic'.

9 In Search of a Theory

'– to define – is to distrust'
Tristram Shandy, vol. 3, ch. 33

1

'Toward a Definition of Romantic Irony in English Literature':[1] the title of Stuart Sperry's article alludes to the predicament faced sooner or later by all who write about romantic irony, that is to say, the necessity, but the infeasibility of the task of definition. Without definition the phenomenon remains inchoate; yet no succinct definition is adequate to its complexity.

The increasing attention that romantic irony has recently been attracting has resulted in a number of attempted definitions. Sperry's own suggestion, '*indeterminacy*', 'a kind of irresolution', which he links to 'the beginnings of that fragmentation and skepticism we see on all sides of us today' (p. 5), has the advantage of steering between limiting specificity and unserviceable vagueness. Some of the more picturesque definitions unfortunately fall into the latter trap: Ricarda Huch's charming phrase, 'ein geistiges Fliegenkönnen'[2] ('the spiritual ability to fly'); the generous sweep of René Bourgeois' 'le sens du jeu'[3] ('the sense of play'); or Vladimir Jankélévich's grandiose verdict: 'une ivresse de la subjectivité transcendentale'[4] ('an intoxication of transcendental subjectivity'). Though apposite, none of these is of much practical help. Many of the more substantive definitions are equally unsatisfactory because they are either too partial or too restrictive. For instance, David Simpson claims that

English romantic irony, broadly put, consists in the studied avoidance on the artist's part of determinate meanings, even at

225

such times as he might wish to encourage his reader to *produce* such meanings for himself; it involves the refusal of closure, the incorporation of any potentially available 'metacomment' within the primary language of the text, the provision of a linguistic sign which moves towards or verges on a 'free' status, and the consequent raising to self-consciousness of the authoritarian element of discourse, as it effects both the author-reader relation and the intentional manipulation, from both sides, of the material through which they communicate.[5]

This proposition, though challenging and tenable up to a point, is so imbued with contemporary theories of reading and of language as to be less than luminescent to the uninitiated. Culler's account, while stemming from a similar critical approach, is considerably more incisive and illuminating; citing Flaubert's *Bouvard et Pécuchet* as a prime example, he describes romantic irony as 'the posture of a work which contains within itself an awareness of the fact that while pretending to give a true account of reality it is in fact fiction and that one must view with an ironic smile the act of writing a novel in the first place'.[6] This is a valid position, except in its exclusive concentration on only one aspect of the phenomenon. Morton L. Gurewitch's hypothesis that romantic irony 'blends a romantic ardor with an anti-romantic animus'[7] is rather naïve in its implicit separation of the romantic from the ironical component. Even that most thoroughly scholarly investigation by Ingrid Strohschneider-Kohrs finally comes up with a definition that is brief and acceptable, but reductive in its formalism: 'Mittel der Selbstrepräsentation der Kunst'[8] ('the means whereby art represents itself'). Martin Walser elaborates somewhat fancifully on that sparse formula without amending its substance: 'Das Bewusstsein des Bewusstseins, das andauernde Selbstbewusstsein also, die Transzendental-Präsenz also, ist dann die Desillusions-Technik der Romantiker geworden. Beim Dichten immer dazudichten, dass man dichte'[9] ('The consciousness of consciousness, the unremitting self-consciousness, the presence of the transcendental then became the Romantics' technique of disillusionment. In the act of writing always to write in that one in writing'). Most recently Anne K. Mellor has offered the best crisp summary in English: 'Romantic irony, then, is a mode of consciousness or a way of thinking about the world that finds a corresponding literary mode',[10] and she has backed this statement with a competent exposition of that 'way of thinking'. The weakness of her paradigm, however, stems from its exclusive dependence on Friedrich Schlegel, whom she explicates and illustrates, but does not query or develop.

The greatest challenge in grappling with romantic irony is to try to get away from Schlegel's cryptic terminology so as to evolve not so much a portable definition as a robust understanding of the phenomenon in its bewildering ramifications. Such an endeavour must take as its point of departure not the postulates of German Romantic theory but the actuality of romantic irony as it becomes manifest in the works of some of its outstanding exponents. By delineating the differences between their irony and that of traditional ironists, the relationship between the two modes can be brought out, and with it the specific character of romantic irony.

Fundamental distinctions can be drawn between traditional, classical irony and romantic, modern irony. Traditional irony is an irony of discrimination that springs from the security of knowledge held with assurance. Buttressed by faith in the existence of truths and absolute standards, it is an expression of moral judgement as well as of social values. Among the possible alternatives facing him, the traditional ironist is able to distinguish sharply between what he considers 'true' and what he regards as 'false'. His confidence in his knowledge is rooted in the solidity of the ethical framework and in the widespread acceptance of norms held to be sound. His world possesses the coherence of firm contours, and he himself maintains a steady perspective on it; in saying the opposite to what he means, he knows what he means, and what he wants to attain. From the vantage-point of his detachment, and with a slightly supercilious sense of his moral and intellectual superiority over the masses, the traditional ironist uses irony as a means of sceptical evaluation and as a weapon for clarification, seeking to elicit and establish the truth by an argumentation *per contrarium*. His irony is generally local and concrete, focused on contraries that can be resolved. Such stable irony is akin to satire in so far as it is a means to an end, though the ironist always harbours a deeper scepticism about the human condition than the satirist, together with an awareness that its innate ambivalence may in part defy resolution. His mask must, however, remain fairly transparent and his irony finite if they are to achieve the purpose for which they are designed. For the mask and the rhetoric of irony are the visible manifestations of a vision of the universe, from which they must not be divorced. Irony is never merely a figure of speech; all irony, whether traditional or romantic, originates in a vision of the universe, though that vision is quite different in the two modes. Beneath his ambiguities and equivocations, the traditional ironist aspires to an affirmation of certainty.

Socratic irony is a good example of traditional irony at its most subtle. Often regarded as a dialectical tool and a method of inductive polemics, it far exceeds these circumscribed limits in its reach. Whether Socratic irony is deemed 'a war upon Appearance waged by a man who knows Reality',[11] or whether its essence lies 'in Socrates' commitment to the process of intellectual self-enquiry combined with a skepticism concerning the ultimate conclusions it might yield'[12] is largely immaterial. What matters is the staunch commitment to the worth of the process and, beyond that, to the validity of the vision inspiring it. The pretence of ignorance and the mocking assertions of the contrary to what Socrates believed are intended as provocations to uncover falsehoods. In this sense Socrates' systematic irony represents an oblique profession of faith in the efficacy of rational enquiry as well as in the authenticity of the standards upheld. The teasing method of ironical rhetoric peculiar to Socrates springs not from a doubting state of mind but from strongly held convictions, from the urge to attain truth and, what is more, to lead others towards that truth.

The unceasing questions of romantic irony, by contrast, are less a pursuit of enlightenment that an assent to, indeed an affirmation of continuing doubt. For romantic irony is an irony of uncertainty, bent primarily on the perplexities of searching. Alert to the plurality of all meaning and the relativity of every position, the romantic ironist probes an open-ended series of contradictions which bound into a chaos of contingencies instead of coming to rest in a state of resolution or comprehension. In the context of a changing, disjointed world of shifting values, his quest is for transcendental certainty, even while he may question its existence. His irony is therefore pervasive and infinite, absorbing everything in its exponential progression. It is not a perspective on a situation, but a presence within each situation. So its effect is one of kinetic, relativistic perspectivism. Irony is not used to differentiate the true from the false because for the romantic ironist all options may be true, or false; nor can he manipulatively say the opposite to what he means because he cannot be sure of any meaning. Thus whereas the traditional ironist, who accepts authority and has a hold on knowledge, exposes the disparity between appearance and reality, the romantic ironist, who suspects that each successive reality may be as illusory as the previous one, subjects appearance and reality alike to an unrelenting ontological scrutiny. And the greater the gaps in the knowledge held, the more radical the doubts, and the larger and deeper the spaces occupied by irony. In short, far from *using* irony, as the traditional ironist does, the romantic ironist *is* ironic. His irony is the instrument for registering the obdurate paradoxicality of a universe in eternal flux.

2

The divergence between traditional and romantic irony is thus as much a matter of ontology and epistemology as of literary technique. The form that the discourse takes devolves from the underlying philosophic vision. But it is in the discourse itself that the difference between the two modes becomes fully apparent.

In narration this can most cogently be expressed in terms of the narrative stance. The dynamics of the tripartite relationship between the narrator, the narrative, and the reader are distinctively at variance in the two kinds of irony. Traditional irony resides in the space between the narrative and the reader who is able to reconstruct the intended covert meaning with the aid of clues deliberately planted by the knowing narrator who acts as an invisible guide because he wants his irony to be understood. The narrator's stance is impersonal and detached; he functions as an extraneous observer, purposefully uncovering subversive implications which are brought to the reader's attention through indirect but unmistakable signals. The presentation of Casaubon's feelings in *Middlemarch*, cited in the first chapter, is a fine instance of such irony. The narrator, while maintaining his aesthetic distance, is in collusion with the reader, behind the protagonists' backs, so to speak. The irony is transparent in that the words carry meanings other than those on the surface, and it is finite in application and stable in that there is no further demolition of the reconstructed meaning.

Romantic irony, on the other hand, is situated primarily in the space between the narrator and his narrative. The discreet, assured chronicler of traditional irony is replaced in romantic irony by a self-conscious, searching narrator who openly stands beside his story, arranging it, intruding into it to reflect on his tale and on himself as a writer. He portrays himself in the act of writing alongside his story as an integral part of his narrative, operating not from behind the scenes, but groping his way across the stage in the presence of his protagonists and his readers. So the romantic ironist assumes a prominence in the text that is the antithesis of the reticent role of the traditional ironist. The distance between the mask and the persona of the narrator is significantly foreshortened to the point where the mask takes possession of the persona. The sense of a dissembling that is meant to be seen through has vanished, and so has the consistent texture of traditional irony. With the romantic ironist the mask merges with the persona in a displacement likely to generate disorientation. The narrator abdicates his controlling, directing function, or at least appears or pretends to do so, becoming in effect a narrative gamesman[13] who delights in sporting with his creation, exploiting it as a medium for displaying the fireworks of his creativity. While traditional irony is *between* the lines, romantic irony is *in* the lines.

One immediate result of this shift of emphasis is a drastic reduction in the status of the story. While the created, finished product and the effects it achieves attract most interest in such works as *Pride and Prejudice, Middlemarch,* and *Effi Briest,* it is the actual business of story-telling that demands greatest attention in *Tristram Shandy, Don Juan,* or *Jacques le fataliste.* The romantic ironist has forgone that supremacy over the world and over his story that enables the traditional ironist to order, to explain, and to resolve. The romantic ironist's self-conscious embroilment in the strategies of narration is at the expense of his narrative. An important mutation occurs here in the art of narration. Not only is linear plot replaced by associative arabesque; in fact, classical aesthetic theory, which held that writers should adapt their style to their tale, is inverted when manner takes precedent over matter. The insistence on the essentially fictional, illusory nature of art furthers this transference. The prominence and space given to the narrated situation declines in proportion to that devoted to the narrative situation. In the *Flegeljahre* and in *Don Juan* the two are roughly equal, but in *Jacques le fataliste* and certainly in *Tristram Shandy* it is on the tactics of narration rather than on the stories narrated that the spotlight falls. With the romantic ironist narration usurps the centre of the stage, dislodging the story from its customary privileged place. Classical narrative expectations are overturned when narration asserts its autonomy in this way. Literature as product yields to literature as process.

This shift of focus has far-reaching consequences for the reader. The traditional ironist looks outwards to his narrative and also to his listeners; through a network of oblique but comprehensible signals he maintains a tacit rapport with the reader to whom the ironic countermeaning is to be communicated. The stance of the romantic ironist, on the contrary, is introverted; his gaze is directed inwards onto the work he is creating and onto himself as its creator. The reader, even when he is specifically addressed, is no more than an audience of the creative spectacle at best, and at worst merely an eavesdropper. For although the romantic ironist assumes an audible and visible role in his intrusive running commentary on his narration, he has a tenuous connection to the reader despite his vociferous presence because of his overriding interest in himself and in the problems of writing. This entails another fundamental alteration in the entire narrative set-up. The contract between narrator and reader loses its reliability as the basis for communication. Once perspective is converted into perspectivism, the reader is deprived of his sense of assurance *vis-à-vis* the narrative. The signals that he catches from the mercurial narrator may be loud and manifold, but they are inevitably conflicting and confusing since the narrator himself has no firm position or clear insight. So in romantic irony 'the meaning is not simply "reversed" in any determinate and identifiable sense; it is unsettled'.[14] It is 'unsettled' through the reciprocal suspicion of narrator and reader. On the one hand, the unreliable narrator implies that it is the reader who is unreliable; on the other, the reader comes to query the narrator's competence and to doubt his knowledge. The resultant irony is wholly different in nature to that engendered by a mutually trusting narrator and reader whose shared intelligence is contrasted with the ignorance of the protagonists. In place of the reader's participation in knowledge, as is the case in traditional irony, in romantic irony he is, by devious manoeuvres, made to realise the unattainability of truth and the prevalence of paradox. It is the reader who becomes the disconcerted victim of irony, whereas in traditional irony he is a party to the whisperings and snickerings at the expense of the protagonists, the duped objects on whom he preys in concert with the narrator.

Because of these divergences in narrative disposition and in the underlying vision of the universe, the discourse of romantic irony is a palpable depature from that of traditional irony. The ironic discourse of such contemporary writers as Barthelme, Kafka, Beckett, Borges, or Nabokov has been characterised as one 'that invites its own ironies upon itself, through the deliberate introduction into both story and discourse of gaps, contradictions, and absurdities'.[15] It contrasts with that of, say, Balzac, Austen, or George Eliot, where irony 'was controllable only at the price of introducing a highly coercive and manipulative discourse' (p. 86). The phrase 'only at the price of', together with the adjective 'coercive', contains a value judgement that is hardly warranted. However, the essential distinction between the two modes of discourse is legitimate and important. Almost equally important is the fact that the specification of twentieth century irony is apposite to romantic irony without need of modification or qualification. The close similarity between the discourse engendered by the irony known as 'romantic' and that intrinsic to many modernist texts is the surface stylistic manifestation of the kinship between them. Like its modern descendant, romantic irony emanates from an open sense of self which is projected into images of hovering identity and which finds its aesthetic format in the eschewal of enclosure. The literary structures of romantic as of modern irony are nurtured by the perception of art as a self-generating dynamic process. The consciousness of its own mainsprings is incorporated into the composition and determines its intrinsic form.

The transformation wrought in fiction by romantic irony has a wider significance that extends far beyond the disposition and tactics of narration into the approach to representation in the arts in general. A bold postulate has recently been put forward in the field of art history which has a direct relevance in this context. In *Absorption and Theatricality*, Michael Fried documents and analyses 'a major shift in the relationship between painting and beholder'[16] in mid-eighteenth century French painting. He chooses the terms 'absorption' and 'theatricality' to indicate two disjunctive positions. By 'absorption' he means the representation of a group of figures hermetically engrossed in whatever they are doing and hence perfectly oblivious to anything extraneous, including the beholder's presence. This corresponds in effect to the situation in traditionally ironic narrative. 'Theatricality', by contrast, denotes the primacy of dramatic and expressive considerations and 'the accomplishment of an ontologically prior relationship, at once literal and fictive, *between painting and beholder*' (p. 76; italics are Fried's). The thrust for theatricality entailed 'the fracturing of perspectival unity, which makes it virtually impossible for the beholder to grasp the scene as a single instantaneously apprehensible whole' (p. 134). The parallelism in presupposition and in impact to romantic irony in narration is quite striking, as is the timing of this shift during the 'pivotal period':

> starting around the middle of the eighteenth century in France, the beholder's presence before the painting came increasingly to be perceived by critics and theorists as something that had to be accomplished or at least powerfully affirmed by the painting itself; and more generally that the existence of the beholder, which is to say the primordial convention that paintings are made to be beheld, emerged as problematic for painting as never before. (p. 93)

Such a perception is animated by the same self-consciousness of art as an illusory theatrical play with its own possibilities and with its audience as romantic irony. What is more, it produced in painting a paradox closely akin to that implicit in narration:

> the recognition that paintings are made to be beheld and therefore presuppose the existence of a beholder led to the demand for the actualization of his presence: a painting, it was insisted, had to attract the beholder, to stop him in front of itself, and to hold him there in a perfect trance of involvement. At the same time, taking Diderot's writings as the definitive formulation of a conception of painting that up to a point was widely shared, it was only by negating the beholder's presence that this could be achieved: only by establishing the fiction of his absence or nonexistence could his actual placement before and enthrallment by the painting be secured. This paradox

directs attention to the problematic character not only of the painting-beholder relationship but of something still more fundamental – the *object*-beholder (one is tempted to say object-'subject') relationship which the painting-beholder relationship epitomizes. (pp. 103–4; italics are Fried's)

The outcome of romantic irony in narrative is equally contradictory. To all appearances the reader is actively invited, indeed cajoled and coerced, into energetic participation in the making as well as in the reading of the narrative. But in reality his efforts are neutralised by the teasing mistrust of which he is the victim; the multiple invocations to the reader are no more than a disarming strategy. He remains an outsider to the transactions between the narrator and his narrative on which the text pivots. He has ultimately a lesser stake in the dynamics of romantic irony than in traditional irony where the confiding narrator, though sparing of explicit appeals, counts on him for comprehension. Thus traditional irony may be said to depend on the reader's relationship to the text, while romantic irony hinges on the narrator's orientation towards his own construct.

If the shift in narrative is in many ways similar to that in painting, it differs in one important respect. 'Absorption' and 'theatricality' represent in Fried's terminology opposing poles with no intermediate possibilities between the two. This is not the case with traditional and romantic irony in fiction. It would no doubt be satisfying to be able to systematise the two modes as either/or alternatives, but such a clear-cut schema would be misleading. When the extreme examples of each type, say *Pride and Prejudice* and *Tristram Shandy*, are juxtaposed, the contrast is so conspicuous as to suggest a mutually exclusive antithesis. It is true also that in the majority of texts one mode or the other predominates. But this does not amount to the 'absolute split' that Booth claims when he argues that:

it is important to recognize the absolute split between works designed to be reconstructible on firm norms shared by authors and readers, and those other 'ironic' works that provide no platform for reconstruction. In one kind all or most of the ironies are resolved into relatively secure moral or philosophical perceptions or truths; in the other, all truths are dissolved in an ironic mist.[17]

Much closer to the mark than 'absolute split' is Sperry's phrase: 'innumerable gradations'[18] 'between the historical prevalence of specific or corrective irony and the whole line of development that leads to the all-pervading ironies of Beckett and Genet'. 'Innumerable gradations' indicates a sliding scale which is in fact as valid in the typological as in the historical context in which it is here applied. The change from 'stable' to 'unstable', from traditional to romantic irony, chronologically and typologically, consists in a process of relativisation, a shift from a steady perspective to a paradoxical perspectivism. It is the degree and intensity of ambivalence that is at variance. This is revealed primarily in the stance of the ironic narrator and in his handling of the dialectical tensions inherent in the irony. In *Pride and Prejudice* the tensions are dissipated through the elucidation of the misunderstandings. In *Madame Bovary* they turn on the vexatory image of Emma, the outcome of the dissonant oscillation between perspective and viewpoint, and the source of fluctuating attitudes on the part of the narrator and the reader alike. In *Don Juan* the dialectic is exploited for structural purposes, particularly in the alternation between the text's fictional and metafictional levels. In the *Flegeljahre* and in *Jacques le fataliste* it is immanent in both subject and form: it is portrayed in the contrast between the twins and between Jacques and his master, and it also shapes the arabesque patterns of these texts. Its most complete incarnation is in *Tristram Shandy*, where the indeterminate relationship between the actual and the fictive narrator opens up vast spaces of dubiety, while the compelling preponderance of a highly suspect but unassailable first-person narrating voice removes any assured vantage ground from which to direct a definitive interpretation. In all these works except *Pride and Prejudice*, the dialectical tensions remain unresolved, but the movement from the almost total certainties of *Pride and Prejudice* to the almost total uncertainties of *Tristram Shandy* is one of 'gradation' rather than 'split'. When the quantitative balance between resolvable and unresolvable ambivalence reaches a certain point, the proportions are so decisively altered as to consummate a qualitative transformation. The metamorphosis in the conceptualisation of irony in the late eighteenth and early nineteenth century marks the crucial turning-point where the qualitative transformation is voiced and asserted. But in literary practice the lines of demarcation between traditional and romantic irony are too fluid to be subordinated to any rigorous paradigm. It is perhaps a fitting hallmark of irony that it should be so resistant to schematisation.

3

In the light of this theory of romantic irony, some commonly held beliefs about it can be dispelled as fictions.

First, the thesis that it is 'ein historisches Phänomen'[19] ('a historical phenomenon'). Through the name attached to it by Hettner it has come to be associated with a specific period of literary history. Not without some justification either, since it was the leading theoretician of German Romanticism, Friedrich Schlegel, who identified the phenomenon, recognised its importance, and delineated its characteristics. It was, moreover, at a particular phase in history, roughly contemporaneous with its cognitive formulation, that this kind of irony became widespread and prominent in fiction. Yet it is a curious reflection of its jumbled time-schema that the opening volumes of *Tristram Shandy* appeared within five years of Dr Johnson's *Dictionary*. Despite some such inconsistencies in its upsurge, romantic irony does have a historical constituent, but it would be erroneous to insist on its historicity, and quite wrong to envisage it along purely historical lines.

Many critics have indeed made passing reference to the tendency of romantic irony to surpass its conventional historical boundaries. Strohschneider-Kohrs cautiously concedes: 'das von der Romantik konzipierte Prinzip der künstlerischen Ironie und die mit dieser Konzeption hervorgehobene Möglichkeit der Kunst trägt eine gewisse Antizipation von Problemen der modernen Kunst in sich'[20] ('the principle of artistic irony as conceived by the Romantics and the potential for art brought out in this conception includes a certain anticipation of problems of modern art'). Muecke resorts to a slightly evasive witticism: 'To study Romantic Irony is to discover how modern Romanticism could be, or, if you like, how Romantic Modernism is.'[21] Muecke's cardinal example of romantic irony in the modern period is Thomas Mann's *Doktor Faustus* (1947). One could just as well cite James Joyce's *Ulysses* (1922), André Gide's *Les Faux-monnayeurs* (1926; *The Coiners*), Samuel Beckett's *Molloy* (1951), Italo Svevo's *La Coscienza di Zeno* (1920; *Confessions of Zeno*), Saul

Bellow's *Herzog* (1964), almost any of the fictions of Jorge Luis Borges, Max Frisch's *Mein Name sei Gantebein* (1964; *A Wilderness of Mirrors*) or *Der Mann erscheint im Holozän* (1979; *Man in the Holocene*), Delmore Schwartz's story, 'In Dreams Begin Responsibilities' (1948), or such very recent works as Stanislaw Lem's *Doskonale próżnia* (1974; *A Perfect Vacuum*), E. L. Doctorow's *Loon Lake* (1980), Gilbert Sorrentino's *Mulligan Stew* (1979), Juan Benet's *Una meditácion* (1970; *A Meditation*), or Italo Calvino's *Se una notte d'inverno un viaggiatore* (1979; *If on a Winter's Night a Traveler*). This is a random sample of twentieth-century fictions that draw heavily on practices central to romantic irony. The continuing relevance, indeed the crucial importance, of this kind of irony to modern fiction is cogent evidence of its transcendence of the limits of historicity.

Equally telling is its existence before the cultural segment called Romanticism. Friedrich Schlegel and the Romantics were themselves fully aware of the historical antecedents on which they based their perception of irony. It is no coincidence that *Don Quixote* held pride of place among their reading. Tieck published a new German translation of Cervantes' novel in 1799–1801, and even if the Romantics did misread[22] certain aspects of *Don Quixote*, they were the first to appraise adequately the teasing ambivalences it insinuates into the narrator-reader relationship. *Don Quixote* was indisputably the foremost model to the Romantics of uses of irony other than those habitual among the Augustans. They also idolised Shakespeare, not only for the spontaneous originality of his genius, but specially for that imaginative perspectivism that enabled him to transport himself into every situation and every character with a mobility that never ceased to astonish them. It is for this quality that Shakespeare is granted an irony that is romantic in its stance, though Schlegel still asserted: 'Cervantes ist doch romantischer als Shakespeare'[23] ('Cervantes is even more romantic than Shakespeare'). The sporadic occurrence of an irony akin to romantic irony before the Romantic period and its frequent recurrence thereafter vitiates the argument that it is predominantly a historical phenomenon. It must be accorded archetypal as well as historical status. It encompasses a typological approach to the manipulation of fictional illusion together with an open-ended querying epistemology and an ontology that embraces an order of disorder quite distinct from orderliness. Such an approach becomes pre-eminent at an identifiable historical period, but it is by no means confined to that period. To disregard the archetypal dimension of romantic irony is to forfeit an element of momentous significance for an understanding of the art of narration and, above all, for the devices and structures of modern fiction.

Any enquiry into the historicity of romantic irony must needs beg another question: if romantic irony is not to be associated solely with the Romantic period, how appropriate is its name? To put it more bluntly, should it be deemed a misnomer? It is well to recall at this juncture that this name was not in fact accepted usage among the originators of the concept, but was popularised only later by mid-nineteenth century scholars. The Romantics themselves, with an intuitive sense of its wider implications, chose to refer to it as 'artistic' irony. They would, however, emphatically have affirmed the integral function of such irony within the metaphysical and aesthetic edifice they built. Irony was the essential dynamic force in a progressive process in which the work of art was to be de-constructed and re-constructed into a closer approximation of the ideal. Irony is thus one of the major instruments of Romantic idealism: 'sie erscheint als eines ihrer "Mittel", ist erkennbar als ein inneres agens, eine der Bedingungen romantisch-poetischer Möglichkeit'[24] ('it appears as one of its "means", it is recognisable as an inner activating force, one of the conditions for the romantic-poetic endeavour'). What is more, a number of other cardinal tenets of Romanticism, such as the supremacy of the subjective vision, the belief in the transcendental nature of art and in the artist's divine creative powers, and the consequent explosion of self-consciousness have a direct bearing on the crystallisation of the new concept of irony. So it is a facet of the philosophical, aesthetic, and literary re-orientation that is at the core of the Romantic movement. It is no coincidence that an innovative perception of irony and new uses of irony in fiction came into the forefront at that time. In this sense, therefore, there is a certain aptness in the name 'romantic' irony. Yet it has also proved an unfortunate misnomer in so far as it has fostered too exclusive an identification of this type of irony with a limiting period concept. The irony normally described as romantic irony represents an aesthetic category independent of the Romantic movement. Its name has, regrettably, contributed to the underestimation of the phenomenon it denotes by triggering an automatic association that has resulted in a failure to appreciate to the full its importance beyond the Romantic period.

Partly because of the misleading implications of its name, romantic irony has acquired the reputation of being a peculiar caprice of a few esoteric writers at the turn of the eighteenth into the nineteenth century, resistant to common comprehension and of slight relevance anyway. Such a view of romantic irony is a grave misconception. There is admittedly no denying the intricacy of the concept nor the often rebarbative formulation of ideas by its sponsors from Friedrich Schlegel to Kierkegaard. But these objections do not impugn the worth of the ideas in themselves, although they make them less accessible. What is ultimately at issue in romantic irony is nothing other than the authority of the invented fictional world both unto itself and in relation to the world of our experience. The authenticity of the self-contained illusion remains intact in traditional irony, whereas it is incessantly undermined and questioned in romantic irony. A progressive deconstruction of illusion takes place: first it is broken within the fiction by the impulse to self-representation in mirror images and in those labyrinthine arabesques so favoured by Romantic and modern narrators. The illusion becomes controversial at a second level through the continual arousal of the reader's awareness of the text's standing as fiction. This has a strangely contradictory impact: for the pretence of realism is heightened when the contingencies of the known world appear to be faithfully noted as they beset the narrative; but at the same time the sense of artifice is strongly reinforced through the reader's realisation of the games that are being played. Taken far enough, as in *Tristram Shandy,* such games can finally draw the entire text into an ironic state of relativity. In the transition from traditional irony to romantic irony, irony within the framework of the fiction is transmuted into an irony of the fiction which may then be potentiated into an irony of fictional irony – and of the fictionality of existence. It is a process that starts with ambiguity, edges from ambivalence to paradox, and ends in an alienating derangement of the text and of the world. So romantic irony, far from being the remote preserve of a small coterie of specialists roaming the byways of the late eighteenth and early nineteenth century, must be of urgent concern to all who travel the highways of fiction and of life.

Notes

Preface

1. *The Contours of European Romanticism* (London: Macmillan, 1979 and Lincoln: University of Nebraska Press, 1980) pp. 17–39.
2. George Wilhelm Friedrich Hegel, 'Über Solgers nachgelassene Schriften und Briefwechsel', *Sämtliche Werke*, Jubiläumsausgabe, ed. H. Glockner (Stuttgart: Frommans Verlag, 1930) vol. xx, p. 161.
3. This is the customary basis for considerations of romantic irony. See for example: Ingrid Strohschneider-Kohrs, *Die romantische Ironie in Theorie und Gestaltung*, 2nd rev. edn (Tübingen: Niemeyer, 1977); Anne K. Mellor, *English Romantic Irony* (Cambridge, Mass.: Harvard University Press, 1980).

Chapter 1   Beware of Irony

1. Lionel Trilling, *Sincerity and Authenticity* (Cambridge, Mass.: Harvard University Press, 1971) p. 120.
2. H. W. Fowler, *A Dictionary of Modern English Usage* (Oxford and New York: Oxford University Press, 1965) pp. 305–6.
3. C. Hugh Holman (ed.), *A Handbook to Literature*, 3rd rev. edn (Indianapolis and New York: Bobbs-Merrill, 1972) p. 279.
4. M. H. Abrams, *A Glossary of Literary Terms*, 3rd edn (New York: Holt, Rinehart & Winston, 1971) p. 80.
5. Charles I. Glicksberg, *The Ironic Vision in Modern Literature* (The Hague: Martinus Nijhoff, 1969) p. 14.
6. Reprinted in Robert Wooster Stallman (ed.), *Critiques and Essays in Criticism* (New York: Ronald Press, 1949) pp. 85–104; p. 103.
7. Morton D. Zabel (ed.), *Literary Opinion in America*, 2nd rev. edn (New York: Harper & Row, 1951) pp. 729–41.
8. See Robert Coles, *Irony in the Mind's Life. Essays on Novels by James Agee, Elizabeth Bowen, and George Eliot* (New York: New Directions, 1974).
9. See Cyrus Hamlin, 'Platonic Dialogue and Romantic Irony: Prolegomenon to a Theory of Literary Narrative', *Canadian Review of Comparative Literature*, iii (1976) 25: 'my definition of irony, . . . as a fundamental principle of discontinuity in the structure of literary language'.

240

10. Northrop Frye, *Anatomy of Criticism* (New York: Atheneum, 1969), p. 114.

11. Geoffrey, H. Hartman, *Criticism in the Wilderness* (New Haven, Conn. and London: Yale University Press, 1980) p. 278.

12. Norman Knox, 'On the Classification of Ironies', *Modern Philology*, lxx (1972) 53–62.

13. Douglas C. Muecke, *Irony* (London: Methuen, and New York: Barnes & Noble, 1970) p. 49.

14. A. E. Dyson, *The Crazy Fabric. Essays in Irony* (London: Macmillan, and New York: St Martin's Press, 1965) pp. 220–3.

15. Douglas C. Muecke, *The Compass of Irony* (London: Methuen, 1969) p. 159.

16. Alan Wilde, *Horizons of Assent: Modernism, Postmodernism, and the Ironic Imagination* (Baltimore and London: The Johns Hopkins University Press, 1981) pp. 9–10. Italics are the author's.

17. For the early history of 'irony' see George G. Sedgewick, *Of Irony, Especially in Drama* (Toronto: Toronto University Press, 1948) and Alan Reynolds Thompson, *The Dry Mock: A Study of Irony in Drama* (Berkeley: University of California Press, and Cambridge: Cambridge University Press, 1948).

18. Trilling, *Sincerity and Authenticity*, p. 120.

19. See Norman Knox, *The Word 'Irony' and Its Contexts 1500–1755* (Durham, N. Carolina: Duke University Press, 1961).

20. David Worcester, *The Art of Satire* (Cambridge, Mass.: Harvard University Press, 1940; reprinted New York: Russell & Russell, 1960).

21. Dyson, *The Crazy Fabric*, p. 2.

22. Thompson, *The Dry Mock*, p. 257.

23. Catherine Kerbrat-Orecchioni, 'L'ironie comme trope', *Poétique*, xli (1980) 109. Italics are the author's.

24. Beda Allemann uses the terms 'Spannungsfeld' and 'Spielraum' in his essay 'Ironie als literarisches Prinzip' in Albrecht Schaefer (ed.), *Ironie und Dichtung* (Munich: Beck, 1970) p. 30.

25. Frye, *Anatomy of Criticism*, p. 40.

26. William Empson, *Seven Types of Ambiguity* (London: Chatto & Windus, 1953) p. 1.

27. 'Die Kunst des ironischen Autors liegt darin, diese schwebende Zwischenlage auf geradezu seiltänzerische Manier einzuhalten.' Allemann, in *Ironie und Dichtung*, p. 21.

28. Wayne C. Booth, *A Rhetoric of Irony* (Chicago and London: University of Chicago Press, 1974) p. 256.

29. Trilling, *Sincerity and Authenticity*, p. 120.

30. See Harald Weinrich, *Linguistik der Lüge* (Heidelberg: Schneider, 1966) pp. 61–5.

31. Beda Allemann, *Ironie und Dichtung*, 2nd rev. edn (Pfullingen: Neske, 1969) p. 13.

32. E. D. Hirsch, Jr., *Validity in Interpretation* (New Haven, Conn. and London: Yale University Press, 1967) p. 86. Italics are the author's.

33. Hirsch, *Validity in Interpretation*, p. 66.

34. Gérard Genette, *Narrative Discourse* (Ithaca, N.Y.: Cornell University Press, 1980) p. 77. Italics are the author's.

35. See Victor Brombert, 'Opening Signals in Narrative', *New Literary History*, xi (1980) 489–502.
36. Trilling, *Sincerity and Authenticity*, p. 2.
37. Anthony Close, *The Romantic Approach to 'Don Quixote'* (Cambridge: Cambridge University Press, 1978).
38. See Walter Jackson Bate, *The Burden of the Past and the English Poet* (London: Chatto & Windus, 1971); Harold Bloom, *The Anxiety of Influence* (New York: Oxford University Press, 1973).
39. Knox, *The Word 'Irony'*, p. 55.
40. P. Gifford, 'Socrates in Amsterdam: The Uses of Irony in *La Chute*', *Modern Language Review*, lxxiii (1978) 511.
41. Muecke, *Irony*, p. 30.
42. Cf. Muecke, *The Compass of Irony*, p. 53: 'Let us then define irony . . . as ways of speaking, writing, acting, behaving, painting, etc. in which the real or intended meaning presented or evoked is intentionally quite other than, and incompatible with, the ostensible or pretended meaning'; and Booth, *A Rhetoric of Irony*, p. 91: 'Whether a given word or passage or work *is* ironic depends, in our present view, not on the ingenuity of the reader, but on the intentions that constitute the creative act.' Italics are the author's.
43. D. H. Green, *Irony in the Medieval Romance* (Cambridge, London, and New York: Cambridge University Press, 1979) p. 9.

Chapter 2   The Metamorphosis of Irony

1. Johann Wolfgang von Goethe, *Werke* (Weimar: Böhlau, 1890) 2. Abteilung, vol. i, p. xii.
2. Ernst Behler, *Klassische Ironie, Romantische Ironie, Tragische Ironie* (Darmstadt: Wissenschaftliche Buchgesellschaft, 1972) p. 9.
3. *Lyceumsfragment*, no. 42, *Kritische Ausgabe*, vol. ii, ed. Hans Eichner (Munich-Vienna-Paderborn: Schöningh, 1967) p. 152. Cited subsequently as *KA*.
4. *Literary Notebooks 1797–1801*, ed. Hans Eichner (Toronto and London: Toronto University Press, 1957) no. 1309, p. 137. Cited subsequently as *LN*.
5. *LN*, no. 1959, p. 193.
6. *KA*, vol. ii, pp. 368–70.
7. *KA*, vol. ii, p. 370.
8. *Philosophische Lehrjahre, KA,* vol. xviii, part 2, ed. Ernst Behler (Munich-Vienna-Paderborn: Schöningh, 1963) p. 668.
9. *Lyceumsfragment*, no. 42, *KA*, vol. ii, p. 152.
10. Marburger Handschriften, Heft iii, p. 52. Cited by Strohschneider-Kohrs, *Die romantische Ironie*, p. 32.
11. *LN*, no. 500, p. 64. Italics are the author's.
12. *Über die Unverständlichkeit, KA,* vol. ii, p. 370.
13. *LN*, no. 696, p. 82.
14. *LN*, no. 1068, p. 114: 'Die Paradoxie ist für die Ironie die *conditio sine qua non*, die Seele, Quell und Princip.'
15. *Lyceumsfragment*, no. 42, *KA*, vol. ii, p. 153.

16. *Ideen*, no. 69, *KA*, vol. ii, p. 263.
17. *Lyceumsfragment*, no. 108, *KA*, vol. ii, p. 160.
18. *Athenäaumsfragment*, no. 51, *KA*, vol. ii, p. 172.
19. *Philosophische Lehrjahre*, *KA*, vol. xviii, part 1, p. 85.
20. *LN*, no. 1682, p. 168.
21. *Lyceumsfragment*, no. 108, *KA*, vol. ii, p. 160.
22. *Lyceumsfragment*, no. 42, *KA*, vol. ii, p. 152.
23. *Athenäumsfragment*, no. 116, *KA*, vol. ii, p. 182.
24. *Philosophische Lehrjahre*, *KA,* vol. xviii, part 2, p. 628.
25. See the interpretations by Strohschneider-Kohrs, *Die romantische Ironie*, p. 228 ff.; and Peter Szondi, 'Friedrich Schlegel und die romantische Ironie', *Euphorion*, xlviii (1954) 397–411; reprinted in *Satz und Gegensatz* (Frankfurt: Insel, 1964), pp. 5–24.
26. Allemann, *Ironic und Dichtung*, p. 22.
27. *LN*, no. 501, p. 64: 'Shakesp[eare] ist in der Liebe, in Fant[asie] und Sent[imentalität] bis zur Ironie gekommen; also die seinige durchaus romantisch. Nicht so die des Ariosto, – '; no. 705, p. 83: 'Romantische Ironie ist wohl allen rh[etorischen] D[ramen] nothwendig?'; no. 709, p. 84: 'Auch Petrarcha hat romantische Ironie. – '; no. 712, p. 84: '*Absolute* S[entimentalität] und *absolute* F[antasie] führt auch ohne Universalp[oesie] zu R[omantischem], aber doch erst mit dieser durch Trennung und Gegensatz zu absolut R[omantischem] oder zur romantischen Ironie.'
28. Novalis, *Allgemeines Brouillon*, no. 445, *Schriften*, ed. Paul Kluckhohn and Richard Samuel (Darmstadt: Wissenschaftliche Buchgesellschaft, 1968) vol. iii, p. 326.
29. Hegel, *Vorlesungen über die Ästhetik, Sämtliche Werke*, vol. xii (1927) pp. 102.
30. Hermann Hettner, *Schriften zur Literatur,* ed. Jürgen Jahn (Berlin: Aufbau, 1959) p. 52.
31. Hettner, *Geschichte der deutschen Literatur im 18. Jahrhundert*, ed. Georg Witkowski (Leipzig: List, 1928) vol. ii, p. 252.
32. Rudolf Haym, *Die romantische Schule*, 3rd rev. edn (Berlin: Weidemann, 1914) p. 296.
33. Adam Müller, 'Ironie, Lustspiel, Aristophanes', *Kritische, ästhetische und philosophische Schriften,* ed, Walter Schroeder and Werner Siebert (Berlin: Luchterhand, 1967) vol. i, p. 238: 'bist Du mit Freiheit, mit Bewusstsein, mit Ironie von der einen Seite der Menschheit, von der *tragischen*, auf die andere, die *komische* Seite hinübergetreten?'. Italics are the author's.
34. Müller, *Kritische, ästhetische und philosophische Schriften*, vol. 1, p. 234: 'Verlangen Sie eine deutsche Übersetzung des Wortes, so weiss ich Ihnen keine bessre zu geben, als Offenbarung der Freiheit des Künstlers oder des Menschen'.
35. Karl Wilhelm Ferdinand Solger, *Erwin,* ed. Wolfhart Henckmann (Munich: Fink, 1971) pp. 437–8.
36. Solger, *Vorlesungen über Ästhetik*, ed. Karl Wilhelm Ludwig Heyse (Leipzig, 1829; reprinted Darmstadt: Wissenschaftliche Buchgesellschaft, 1962) p. 247: 'Die echte Ironie setzt das höchste Bewusstsein voraus'.
37. Solger, *Erwin*, p. 392: 'den Standpunkt der Ironie'.
38. *Erwin*, p. 392.
39. *Erwin*, p. 394.

40. Solger, *Vorlesungen über Ästhetik*, p. 245: 'Die Ironie ist keine einzelne, zufällige Stimmung des Künstlers, sondern der innerste Lebenskeim der ganzen Kunst'.

41. Hegel, *Grundlinien der Philosophie, Sämtliche Werke*, vol. vii, p. 219. Italics are the author's. Trans. T. M. Knox (Oxford: Clarendon, 1942) pp. 102–3; italics added to correspond to the German.

42. Hegel, *Vorlesungen über die Ästhetik, Sämtliche Werke*, vol. xii (1928) p. 102.

43. Hegel, *Vorlesungen über die Ästhetik, Sämtliche Werke*, vol. xii (1928) p. 104.

44. Hegel, *Vorlesungen über die Geschichte der Philosophie, Sämtliche Werke*, vol. xviii (1928) p. 63; 'Die Ironie ist das Spiel mit Allem; dieser Subjektivität ist es mit Nichts mehr Ernst'.

45. Hegel, *Vorlesungen über die Ästhetik, Sämtliche Werke*, vol. xii, p. 103.

46. Hegel, *Vorlesungen über die Ästhetik, Sämtliche Werke*, vol. xii, p. 221.

47. Søren Kierkegaard, *The Concept of Irony*, trans. Lee M. Capel (Bloomington and London: Indiana University Press, 1965) p. 279.

48. Kierkegaard is referring to the fable of the fox and the crow.

49. Bate, *The Burden of the Past*, p. vii.

50. Arthur O. Lovejoy, *The Great Chain of Being* (Cambridge, Mass.: Harvard University Press, 1936) p. 297.

51. Michel Foucault, *The Order of Things* (New York: Pantheon Books, 1970) specially pp. 206–48. The French title is *Les Mots et les choses* (Paris: Gallimard, 1966).

52. Immanuel Kant, *Kritik der reinen Vernunft, Werke*. ed. Wilhelm Weischedel (Darmstadt: Wissenschaftliche Buchgesellschaft, 1966) vol. ii, p. 25.

53. Foucault, *The Order of Things*, p. 120. Italics are the author's.

54. Foucault, *The Order of Things*, p. 118.

55. Norman Kretzmann, 'The Main Thesis of Locke's Semantic Theory', in H. Parret (ed.), *History of Linguistic Thought and Contemporary Linguistics* (Berlin and New York: de Gruyter, 1976) p. 331.

56. Kretzmann, 'The Main Thesis of Locke's Semantic Theory', in Parret, *History of Linguistic Thought*, p. 331.

57. Foucault, *The Order of Things*, p. 118.

58. Foucault, *The Order of Things*, p. 304.

59. Ian Hacking, 'Is Locke the Key?', review of Hans Aarsleff, *From Locke to Saussure: Essays on the Study of Language and Intellectual History* (Minneapolis: University of Minnesota Press, 1982) in *New York Review of Books*, 24 June 1982, p. 37. Hacking dissents from Aarsleff, and would answer his title question largely in the negative.

60. Etienne Bonnot de Condillac,. 'Discours préliminaire' to the *Cours d'études pour l'instruction du Prince de Parme* (1775), *Oeuvres philosophiques de Condillac*, ed. George L. Roy (Paris: Presses universitaires, 1947) vol. i, p. 403 b.

61. Heinrich Bosse, 'The Marvellous and Romantic Semiotics', *Studies in Romanticism*, xiv (1975) 225. I am indebted to David Wellbery of Stanford University for directing my attention to this article, and for other helpful suggestions about eighteenth-century language theory.

62. Ian Hacking, *Why Does Language Matter to Philosophy?* (Cambridge: Cambridge University Press, 1975) p. 18.

63. William Wordsworth, *Preface to the 'Lyrical Ballads', Poetical Works*, ed. E. de Selincourt (Oxford: Clarendon Press, 1944) vol. ii, p. 400.

64. Wordsworth, *Poetical Works*, vol. ii, p. 387.

65. Wordsworth, *Poetical Works*, vol. ii, p. 395.

66. Anne K. Mellor's *English Romantic Irony* redresses this misconception by showing the presence of irony in Byron, Coleridge, Keats, Carlyle, and Lewis Carroll.

67. *Athenäumsfragment*, no. 116, *KA*, vol. ii, p. 182.

68. Ian Watt, *The Rise of the Novel* (Berkeley and London: University of California Press, 1957) p. 176.

69. Robert Alter, *Partial Magic. The Novel as a Self-Conscious Genre* (Berkeley and London: University of California Press, 1975) p. xv.

70. Bernhard Heimrich, *Fiktion und Fiktionsironie in Theorie und Dichtung der deutschen Romantik* (Tübingen: Niemeyer, 1968).

71. See Franz Stanzel, *Die typischen Erzählsituationen im Roman* (Wiener Beiträge zur englischen Philologie, no. 63, Wien-Stuttgart: Braumüller, 1955 and 1963); trans. James P. Pusack, *Narrative Situations in the Novel* (Bloomington: Indiana University Press, 1971).

72. Victor Lange, 'The Reader in the Strategy of Fiction', in Ronald G. Popperwell (ed.), *Expression, Communication and Experience in Literature and Language* (London: Modern Humanities Research Association, 1973) pp. 91–3.

73. Wolfgang Iser, *Der implizite Leser. Kommunikationsformen des Romans von Bunyan bis Beckett* (Munich: Fink, 1972); *The Implied Reader. Patterns of Communication in Prose Fiction from Bunyan to Beckett* (Baltimore and London: The Johns Hopkins University Press, 1974) p. 78.

74. Victor Lange, 'Erzählformen im Roman des achtzehnten Jahrhunderts', in Volker Klotz (ed.), *Zur Poetik des Romans* (Darmstadt: Wissenschaftliche Buchgesellschaft, 1969) pp. 32–47.

75. The term 'characterized' to denote fictive readers represented within a fiction is suggested by W. Daniel Wilson (in 'Readers in Texts', *PMLA*, xcvi [1981] 848–63) as preferable to 'fictitious' or 'contrived' because it is less ambiguous. Wilson's categories: 'characterized', 'implied', and 'real' reader are not so useful in practice because not all fictive readers by any means are 'characterized', and 'implied' readers are an extraordinarily elusive breed. I prefer to distinguish simply between 'fictive' and 'actual'; the 'fictive' reader/writer is internal and contrived, while the 'actual' reader/writer is external and real.

76. See Wayne C. Booth, 'The Self-Conscious Narrator in Comic Fiction before *Tristram Shandy*', *PMLA*, lxvii (1952) 163–85.

Chapter 3   Jane Austen: *Pride and Prejudice*

1. Howard S. Babb, *Jane Austen's Novels: The Fabric of Dialogue* (Columbus, Ohio: Ohio State University Press, 1962) p. 13.

2. Jane Austen, *Pride and Prejudice* in *The Novels of Jane Austen*, ed. R. W. Chapman (London: Oxford University Press, 3rd edn, 6th impression, 1952) vol. ii, p. 31. All subsequent references are to this edition, and will cite the volume and chapter numbers of the original edition (e.g. vol. 1, ch. vii) as well as the page of this edition.

3. Genette, *Narrative Discourse*, p. 123.
4. Reuben A. Brower, *The Fields of Light. An Experiment in Critical Reading* (New York: Oxford University Press, 1951) p. 164.
5. Marvin Mudrick, *Jane Austen: Irony as Defense and Discovery* (Princeton, N.J.: Princeton University Press, 1952) p. 31.
6. Mudrick, *Jane Austen*, p. 113.
7. Booth, *A Rhetoric of Irony*, pp. 1–2.
8. Mudrick, *Jane Austen*, p. 95.
9. Barbara Hardy, *A Reading of Jane Austen* (New York: New York University Press, 1976) p. 88.
10. Virginia Woolf, *The Common Reader*, First Series (London: Hogarth Press, 1925), p. 174.
11. Norman Page, *The Language of Jane Austen* (Oxford: Blackwell, 1972) p. 8.
12. Brower, *The Fields of Light*, p. 173.
13. Jane Nardine, *Those Elegant Decorums: The Concept of Propriety in Jane Austen's Novels* (Albany, N.Y.: State University of New York Press, 1973) p. 5.
14. David Daiches, *The Novel and the Modern World* (Chicago: Chicago University Press, rev. edn, 1965) esp. pp. 2–6.
15. John Bayley, *The Uses of Division. Unity and Disharmony in Literature* (London: Chatto & Windus, 1976) p. 22.
16. Alistair M. Duckworth, *The Improvement of the Estate: A Study of Jane Austen's Novels* (Baltimore and London: The Johns Hopkins University Press, 1971) p. 140.
17. See Page, *The Language of Jane Austen*, chapter 2, 'The Best Chosen Language', pp. 55–80; and Babb, *Jane Austen's Novels*, especially chapter 1.
18. Darrel Mansell, *The Novels of Jane Austen* (London: Macmillan, 1973) p. 106.
19. Karl Kroeber, *Styles in Fictional Structure: The Art of Jane Austen, Charlotte Brontë, George Eliot* (Princeton, N.J.: Princeton University Press, 1971) p. 15.
20. Hardy, *A Reading of Jane Austen*, p. 80.
21. Northrop Frye, *The Secular Scripture: A Study of the Structure of Romance* (Cambridge, Mass.: Harvard University Press, 1976) p. 171.
22. Brower, *The Fields of Light*, pp. 180–1.
23. Booth, *A Rhetoric of Irony*, p. 200.
24. R. W. Chapman (ed.), *Jane Austen's Letters to Her Sister Cassandra and Others* 2nd edn (London: Oxford University Press, 1952) p. 299.
25. Mudrick, *Jane Austen*, p. 31.
26. Mary Lascelles, *Jane Austen and Her Art* (Oxford: Clarendon Press, 1939) p. 174.

Chapter 4   Gustave Flaubert: *Madame Bovary*

1. Gustave Flaubert, *Madame Bovary*, ed. Edouard Maynial (Paris: Garnier, 1947) p. 3. All subsequent references are to this edition.
2. Jean Rousset, *Forme et signification* (Paris: Corti, 1962) p. 113.
3. 'Pas un mot de trop'. Flaubert, letter to Louise Colet, 2 January 1854; *Oeuvres complètes*, vol. xii (Paris: Conard, 1927) p. 2.

4. 'Tout est de *tête'*. Flaubert, letter to Louise Colet, 6 April 1853; *Oeuvres complètes*, vol. xi (1926) p. 156. Italics are the author's.

5. Enid Starkie, *The Making of the Master* (London: Weidenfeld & Nicolson, 1967), p. 293.

6. Jonathan Culler, *Flaubert. The Uses of Uncertainty* (London: Elek and Ithaca, N.Y.: Cornell University Press, 1974) p. 111.

7. Victor Brombert, *The Novels of Flaubert* (Princeton, N.J.: Princeton University Press, 1966) p. 41.

8. Jean-Paul Sartre, *L'idiot de la famille* (Paris: Gallimard, 1971) vol. ii, p. 1202: 'il dit "nous" pour se contraindre à se faire solidaire des railleurs et à présenter son personnage *du dehors* dans tout son opacité'. Italics are the author's.

9. Cecil Jenkins, 'Flaubert and the "Autonomy" of the Novel', *The Listener*, 14 April 1966, p. 537.

10. Genette, *Narrative Discourse*, p. 221.

11. Flaubert, letter to Louise Colet, 16 January 1852; *Oeuvres complètes*, vol. xi, p. 345.

12. cf. Heimrich, *Fiktion und Fiktionsironie,* p. 42.

13. Albert Thibaudet, *Gustave Flaubert* (Paris: Gallimard, 1935) p. 97.

14. R. J. Sherrington, *Three Novels by Flaubert. A Study of Techniques* (Oxford: Clarendon Press, 1970) p. 89

15. Culler, *Flaubert*, p. 122.

16. For Flaubert's systematic use of a network of names with ironic undertones see Alfred G. Engstrom, 'Flaubert's Correspondence and the Ironic and Symbolic Structure of *Madame Bovary'*, *Modern Philology*, xlvi (1949) 481–4.

17. Anthony K. Thorlby, *Gustave Flaubert and the Art of Realism* (New Haven, Conn. and London: Yale University Press, 1957) p. 40.

18. See Georges Poulet, *The Metamorphoses of the Circle*, trans. Carley Dawson and Elliot Coleman (Baltimore. The Johns Hopkins University Press, 1966) pp. 249–65. Also A. A. Mendilow, *Time and the Novel* (London: Peter Nevill, 1952 and New York: Humanities Press, 1965) p. 127.

19. Brombert, *The Novels of Flaubert,* p. 73.

20. See Joseph Frank, 'Spatial Form in Modern Literature' in *The Widening Gyre* (New Brunswick, N.J.: Rutgers University Press, 1963) pp. 14–15.

21. Matthew Arnold, 'Count Leo Tolstoy', *The Works of Matthew Arnold*, vol. iv (London: Macmillan, 1903) p. 203.

22. Alison Fairlie, *Flaubert: 'Madame Bovary'* (London: Edward Arnold, 1962) p. 14.

23. Letter to Louise Colet, 6 April 1853; *Oeuvres complètes*, vol. xii, p. 155.

24. Marcel Proust, 'A propos du "style" de Flaubert', *La Nouvelle revue française*, xiv (1920) 84: 'A mon avis, la chose la plus belle de l'*Education Sentimentale*, ce n'est pas une phrase, mais un blanc' ('In my opinion, the most beautiful thing in *Sentimental Education* is not a phrase, but a blank').

25. See D. L. Demorest, *L'expression figurée et symbolique dans l'oeuvre de Gustave Flaubert* (Paris: Conard, 1931; Geneva: Slatkine, 1967); Robert Goodhand, 'Emma Bovary, the Baker's Paramour', *Rice University Studies*, lix (1973) analyses the references to farming, wheat, miller, flour, baker, and bread as a symbolic and ironic configuration of Emma's life; Lilian R. Furst, 'The Role of Food in *Madame Bovary'*, *Orbis Litterarum*, xxxiv (1979) 53–65.

26. 'La moindre virgule dépend du plan général' ('The slightest comma devolves from the overall plan'). Flaubert, letter to Louise Colet, 26 August 1853; *Oeuvres complètes*, vol. xi, pp. 321–2. That claim is substantiated by a sentence as simple as that at the close of the second chapter when Charles is thinking about the sudden death of Héloïse: 'Elle l'avait aimé, après tout' (p. 21; 'She had loved him, after all'). That pausing comma, followed by the feeble, concessive adverbial phrase seriously undermines the force of the previous assertion, thereby concluding the whole grotesque episode of Charles' first marriage on a suitably ironic anti-climax.

27. The term is Genette's; in *Narrative Discourse*, p. 189, he applies it to *Madame Bovary*.

28. John Porter Houston, *Fictional Technique in France 1802–1927* (Baton Rouge, La.: Louisiana State University Press, 1972) pp. 67–8.

29. Benjamin F. Bart, 'Art, Energy, and Aesthetic Distance', in Benjamin F. Bart (ed.), *'Madame Bovary' and the Critics* (New York: New York University Press, 1966) p. 89.

30. Brombert, *The Novels of Flaubert*, p. 83.

31. Benjamin F. Bart, *Flaubert* (Syracuse, N.Y.: Syracuse University Press, 1967) p. 318.

32. Rainer Warning, 'Irony and the "Order of Discourse" in Flaubert', *New Literary History*, xiii (1982) 266.

33. Houston, *Fictional Technique in France*, p. 66.

34. Rousset, *Forme et signification*, p. 121.

35. Rousset, *Forme et signification*, pp. 117–22.

36. Sherrington, *Three Novels by Flaubert*, p. 128.

37. Thibaudet, *Gustave Flaubert*, p. 108.

38. Stephen Ullmann, *Style in the French Novel* (Cambridge: Cambridge University Press, 1957) p. 118. Chapter 2 is on 'Reported Speech and Internal Monologue in Flaubert'.

39. Genette, *Narrative Discourse*, p. 172.

40. Leo Spitzer, 'Pseudo-objektive Motivierung', *Zeitschrift für französische Sprache und Literatur*, xlvi (1923) 374.

41. Culler, *Flaubert*, p. 202.

42. Culler, *Flaubert*, p. 77.

43. Culler, *Flaubert*, p. 232.

44. Harry T. Levin, *The Gates of Horn* (New York: Oxford University Press, 1966) pp. 246–69.

45. Rousset, *Forme et signification*, p. 126.

46. Letter to Mlle. Leroyer de Chantepie, 18 March 1857; *Oeuvres complètes*, vol. xiv (1927) p. 164.

47. Culler, *Flaubert*, p. 110.

Chapter 5   George Gordon Byron: *Don Juan*

1. Virginia Woolf, *A Writer's Diary*, ed. Leonard Woolf (London: Hogarth Press, and New York: Harcourt Brace and World, 1954) p. 4, diary entry of 9 August 1918.

2. George Gordon Byron, *Don Juan*, ed. Leslie A. Marchand (Boston: Houghton Mifflin, 1958) canto 1, stanzas ccxxii and ccxxiii, p. 59. All subsequent page references are to this edition, and all italics are the author's.

3. M. K. Joseph, *Byron the Poet* (London: Gollancz, 1964) p. 191.

4. John Wain, 'Byron: The Search for Identity', originally published in *The London Magazine*, v. no. 7 (July 1958) 45; reprinted in *Essays and Ideas* (London and Toronto: Macmillan, 1963), p. 87, and in Paul West (ed.), *Byron: A Collection of Critical Essays* (Englewood Cliffs, N.J.: Prentice Hall, 1963) p. 158.

5. Mellor, *English Romantic Irony*, p. 31.

6. Mellor, *English Romantic Irony*, p. 54.

7. See Leo Weinstein, *The Metamorphoses of Don Juan*, Stanford Studies in Literature, xviii (Stanford University Press, 1959) ch. 8, esp. pp. 79–82.

8. W. H. Auden, 'The Life of a That There Poet', review of Leslie A. Marchand, *Byron: A Biography*, *The New Yorker*, 26 April 1958, p. 146; reprinted in E. E. Bostetter (ed.), *Twentieth Century Interpretations of 'Don Juan'* (Englewood Cliffs, N.J.: Prentice Hall, 1969) p. 18.

9. Joseph, *Byron the Poet*, p. 186.

10. T. S. Eliot, 'Byron' in *On Poetry and Poets* (London: Faber & Faber, and New York: Farrar, Straus & Giroux, 1957) p. 234.

11. Byron, letter of 12 October 1820, *Byron's Letters and Journals*, ed. Leslie A. Marchand (London: John Murray, 1977) vol. vii, p. 202. All subsequent references to Byron's letters are to this edition, and all italics are the author's.

12. Karl Kroeber, *Romantic Narrative Art* (Madison and London: University of Wisconsin Press, 1960) p. 159.

13. Joseph, *Byron the Poet*, p. 155.

14. Byron, letter of 25 December 1822, *Byron's Letters and Journals*, vol. x (1980) p. 68.

15. Paul Graham Trueblood, *The Flowering of Byron's Genius: Studies in Byron's 'Don Juan'* (New York: Russell & Russell, 1962) p. 1.

16. Kroeber, *Romantic Narrative Art*, p. 162.

17. Ernest J. Lovell, Jr., 'Irony and Image in *Don Juan*', in Clarence D. Thorpe, Carlos Baker and Bennett Weaver (eds), *The Major English Romantic Poets: A Symposium in Reappraisal* (Carbondale, Ill.: Southern Illinois University Press, 1957) p. 137; reprinted in Bostetter, *Twentieth Century Interpretations of 'Don Juan'*, p. 26.

18. George Ridenour, *The Style of 'Don Juan'* (New Haven, Conn. and London: Yale University Press, 1960) p. 12.

19. T. S. Eliot, *On Poetry and Poets*, p. 237.

20. Kernan, *The Plot of Satire*, p. 205.

21. Truman Guy Steffan, *Byron's 'Don Juan'*, vol. i: *The Making of a Masterpiece* (Austin: University of Texas Press, and Edinburgh: Nelson, 1957), p. 278.

22. Roger B. Salomon, 'Mock-Heroes and Mock-Heroic Narrative: Byron's *Don Juan* in the Context of Cervantes', *Studies in the Literary Imagination*, ix, no. 1 (Spring 1976) 74.

23. Salomon, 'Mock-Heroes and Mock-Heroic Narrative', *Studies in the Literary Imagination*, ix, no. 1 (Spring 1976) 75.

24. See Ridenour, *The Style of 'Don Juan'*; Jerome McGann, *'Don Juan' in Context* (Chicago and London: University of Chicago Press, 1976); Joseph,

Byron the Poet; John D. Jump, *Byron* (London and Boston: Routledge & Kegan Paul, 1972); Ronald Bottrall, 'Byron and the Colloquial Tradition in English Poetry', *Criterion*, xviii (1939) 204–24; Lovell, 'Irony and Image in *Don Juan*', in Thorpe, Baker and Weaver (eds.), *The Major English Romantic Poets*; A. B. England, *Byron's 'Don Juan' and Eighteenth Century Literature: A Study of Some Rhetorical Continuities and Discontinuities* (Lewisburg, Pa.: Bucknell University Press, and London: Associated University Presses, 1975).

25. Peter Conrad, *Shandyism: The Character of Romantic Irony* (Oxford: Blackwell, 1978) p. 59.
26. Richmond P. Bond, *English Burlesque Poetry 1700–1750* (Cambridge, Mass.: Harvard University Press, 1932) p. 3.
27. Elizabeth Boyd, *'Don Juan': A Critical Study* (New Brunswick, N.J.: Rutgers Univ. Press, 1945; reprinted New York: Humanities Press, 1975) p. 148.
28. Maurice Bowra, *The Romantic Imagination* (London: Oxford University Press, 1961) p. 173.
29. See Salomon, 'Mock-Heroes and Mock-Heroic Narrative', *Studies in the Literary Imagination*, ix, no. 1 (Spring 1976) 71 ff. for astute comments on the problem of genre in *Don Juan.*
30. England, *Byron's 'Don Juan',* p. 93.
31. McGann, *'Don Juan' in Context,* p. 60.
32. Letter to John Murray, 29 June 1819, *Byron's Letters and Journals,* vol. vi (1976) p. 168.
33. Letter to John Murray, 12 August 1819, *Byron's Letters and Journals,* vol. vi (1976) pp. 207–8.
34. Woolf, *A Writer's Diary*, p. 3, diary entry of 9 August 1918.
35. Woolf, *A Writer's Diary*, p. 3, diary entry of 9 August 1918.
36. McGann, *'Don Juan' in Context,* p. 93 ff.
37. England, *Byron's 'Don Juan'*, pp. 17 and 80.
38. England, *Byron's 'Don Juan'*, p. 169. England develops this interpretation extensively.
39. Brian Wilkie, 'Byron and the Epic of Negation', *Romantic Poets and Epic Tradition* (Madison and London: University of Wisconsin Press, 1965) especially pp. 211–24.
40. Ridenour, *The Style of 'Don Juan'*, p. 109.
41. Mellor, *English Romantic Irony*, p. 72. Italics are the author's.
42. Improvisation is not to be equated with non-correction. The variorum edition, edited by Truman Guy Steffan and Willis W. Pratt (Austin: University of Texas Press, and Edinburgh: Nelson, 1957), has shown that Byron was a far more careful writer than had previously been supposed.
43. William Hazlitt, 'Lord Byron' in *The Spirit of the Age, Complete Works*, centenary edition, ed. P. P. Howe (London and Toronto: Dent, 1932) vol. xi, p. 75, fn.
44. Bate, *The Burden of the Past*, pp. 107–8.
45. Salomon, 'Mock-Heroes and Mock-Heroic Narrative', *Studies in the Literary Imagination*, ix, no. 1 (Spring 1976) 83.
46. *Medwin's Conversations of Lord Byron*, ed. Ernest J. Lovell, Jr. (Princeton, N.J.: Princeton University Press, 1966) p. 138.

47. See Joseph, *Byron the Poet,* Appendix C: 'Proportion of Narrative to Comment/Digression in *Don Juan*'. According to Joseph's reckoning, the proportion of comment/digression ranges from a low of 15.4% in canto 16 (the ghost!) to a high of 71.9% in canto 12.
48. William J. Calvert, *Byron: Romantic Paradox* (Chapel Hill: University of North Carolina Press, 1935; reprinted New York: Russell & Russell, 1962) p. 194.
49. Letter to John Murray, 12 August 1819, *Byron's Letters and Journals,* vol. vi (1976) p. 208.
50. England, *Byron's 'Don Juan',* p. 186.
51. Bostetter, *Twentieth Century Interpretations of 'Don Juan',* p. 1.
52. Salomon, 'Mock-Heroes and Mock-Heroic Narrative', *Studies in the Literary Imagination,* ix, no. 1 (Spring 1976) 85.
53. Ridenour, *The Style of 'Don Juan'*: 'The myth of the Fall, then, is an important means of organizing the apparently contradictory elements of *Don Juan.*' (p. 21).
54. Michael G. Cooke, *The Blind Man Traces the Circle: On the Patterns and Philosophy of Byron's Poetry* (Princeton, N.J.: Princeton University Press, 1969) p. 173.
55. Cooke, *The Blind Man Traces the Circle,* p. 132.
56. Wilkie, *Romantic Poets and Epic Tradition,* p. 223.
57. Wilkie, *Romantic Poets and Epic Tradition,* p. 224.
58. Friedrich Schlegel, *Lyceumsfragment,* no. 42, *KA,* vol. ii, p. 152.

Chapter 6   Jean Paul: *Flegeljahre*

1. See Wulf Köpke, *Erfolglosigkeit, Zum Frühwerk Jean Pauls* (Munich: Fink, 1977) pp. 252–3. The derivation from Rousseau accounts for the customary French pronunciation of the first element, while the second retains its native German sound.
2. Jean Paul Friedrich Richter, letter to Paul Emil Thieriot, 20 January 1802, *Sämtliche Werke,* ed. Eduard Berend, section III, vol. iv (Berlin: Akademie, 1960), p. 129.
3. *Selberlebensbeschreibung, Sämtliche Werke,* section II, vol. iv (Weimar: Böhlau, 1934) p. 92.
4. *Bemerkungen über den Menschen, Sämtliche Werke,* section II, vol. v (Weimar: Böhlau, 1936) p. 59.
5. *Vorschule der Ästhetik, Werke,* ed. Norbert Miller, vol. v (Munich: Hanser, 1963), p. 57. The *Vorschule* has been translated by Margaret R. Hale under the title *Horn of Oberon* (Detroit: Wayne State University Press, 1973).
6. Wulf Köpke, 'Zusammensetzungen mit "Selbst" bei Jean Paul', *Jahrbuch der Jean Paul Gesellschaft,* viii (1973) 107: 'mit der Kenntnis und Einschätzung des Selbst, mit Selbsttäuschung, mit der eigenen Schriftstellerei und mit dem Komplex der Vernichtung des Selbst'.
7. Jean Paul Friedrich Richter, *Werke,* ed. Norbert Miller, vol. iii (Munich: Hanser, 1969) no. 46, p. 241. All subsequent references to the *Flegeljahre* are to this edition, and all italics are Jean Paul's. The number of the chapter as well as the page is given for the sake of convenience.

8. Ulrich Profitlich, *Eitelkeit. Eine Untersuchung zum Romanwerk Jean Pauls* (Berlin and Zurich: Gehlen, 1969) p. 33.

9. *Vorschule der Ästhetik,* #34, *Werke,* ed. Norbert Miller, vol. v, p. 133.

10. Wolfdietrich Rasch, *Die Erzählweise Jean Pauls* (Munich: Hanser, 1961). Reprinted in Jost Schillemeit (ed.), *Interpretationen,* vol. iii, *Deutsche Romane von Grimmelshausen bis Musil* (Frankfurt: Fischer, 1966) p. 83. All references to the Rasch monograph are to the reprint in *Interpretationen.*

11. Wolfgang Kayser, 'Wer erzählt den Roman?' in Klotz (ed.), *Zur Poetik des Romans,* pp. 197–216.

12. *Flegel* means a lout, a boor, a scamp, a rascal; *Flegelei* denotes rudeness, bad behaviour; hence the *Flegeljahre* are the troublesome, turbulent years of adolescence.

13. Eliza Buckminster Lee, *Walt and Vult, or The Twins* (Boston: Munroe, and New York: John Wiley, 1846) p. vii.

14. For a highly illuminating discussion of Jean Paul's handling of footnotes see Walter Rehm, 'Jean Pauls vergnügtes Notenleben oder Notenmachen und Notenlesen', *Jahrbuch der deutschen Schillergesellschaft,* iii (1959) 244–337. For a brief analysis of the footnotes in the *Flegeljahre* see Dorothea Berger, *Jean Paul Friedrich Richter* (New York: Twayne, 1972) pp. 100–2.

15. Margarete Schieder, *Die Humoristen-Gestalten in Jean Pauls Romanen mit besonderer Berücksichtigung der Schoppe-Gestalt* (Köln, Diss., 1969) p. 191.

16. Karl August Johann Friedrich Frey, *Jean Pauls 'Flegeljahre': Materialien und Untersuchungen* (Berlin: Mayer & Muller, 1907) p. 218: ' "Man verstehe kein Wort, man sehe nichts" ' (' "Not a word can be understood, and there is nothing to be seen" ').

17. Burkhardt Lindner, 'Autonomisierung der Literatur als Kunst, klassisches Werkmodell und auktoriale Erzählweise', *Jahrbuch der Jean Paul Gesellschaft,* x (1975) 107.

18. Eduard Berend, introduction to Jean Paul, *Sämtliche Werke,* section I, vol. x (Weimar: Böhlau, 1927) p. xli.

19. Wilhelm Dilthey, 'Jean Paul', *Von deutscher Dichtung und Musik* (Leipzig and Berlin: Teubner, 1933) p. 453.

20. Friedrich Theodor Vischer, 'Eine Schrift über Jean Paul', *Kritische Gänge,* ed. Robert Vischer, 2nd edn (Munich: Meyer & Jessen, 1922) vol. ii, p. 428.

21. Clemens Brentano sub-titled his novel *Godwi,* published anonymously 1800–1802, 'Ein verwildeter Roman' ('A novel run wild'). Uwe Schweikert refers to this formula when he comments: 'Man kann zu jener Zeit geradezu von einem "Verwildern" des Romans sprechen' ('One can indeed speak of the novel's "running wild" at that time'), *Jean Pauls 'Komet': Selbstparodie der Kunst* (Stuttgart: Metzler, 1971), p. 112.

22. See Karl Konrad Polheim, *Die Arabeske. Ansichten und Ideen aus Friedrich Schlegels Poetik* (Munich–Paderborn–Vienna: Schöningh, 1966).

23. Friedrich Schlegel, *Anthenäumsfragment,* no. 421, *KA,* vol. ii, p. 246: 'Ein eignes Phänomen ist es; ein Autor, der die Anfangsgründe der Kunst nicht in der Gewalt hat, nicht ein Bonmot ausdrücken, nicht eine Geschichte gut erzählen kann' ('It is a curious phenomenon; an author who has not mastered the elements of his art, who cannot shape a neat phrase or tell a story well').

24. Rudolf Alexander Schröder, *Gesammelte Werke* (Frankfurt and Berlin: Sukrkamp, 1952) vol. ii, p. 697: 'Wenn er [der Leser] die Spreu vom Weizen gesondert hat, wird er sich der verbleibenden reichen Ernte doppelt erfreuen. Er braucht ja nur das Ganze in seine gesonderten Eidyllien zu zerlegen, um dann jedes einzelne rein zu geniessen. Darf er sich doch auch sagen, dass das, was er aufgibt, ein in bezug auf Jean Paul im Grunde Unwesentliches sei.' ('When he [the reader] has separated the wheat from the chaff, he can take double pleasure in the remaining rich harvest. He need only dissect the whole into its individual idylls in order then to enjoy each one. He can also tell himself that what he sacrifices is basically inessential to Jean Paul.')

25. Hermann Meyer, 'Jean Pauls *Flegeljahre*' in *Zarte Empirie* (Stuttgart: Metzler, 1963) pp. 57–112. Reprinted in Uwe Schweikert (ed.), *Jean Paul* (Darmstadt: Wissenschaftliche Buchgesellschaft, 1974). All references are to this reprint.

26. Peter Horst Neumann, *Jean Pauls 'Flegeljahre'* (Göttingen: Vandenhoeck & Ruprecht, 1966).

27. 'Vorrede' to the *Selberlebensbeschreibung, Sämtliche Werke*, section II, vol. iv, #7, p. 363.

28. *Selberlebensbeschreibung, Sämtliche Werke,* section II, vol. iv, #53, p. 365.

29. Letter to Friedrich von Oertel, 6 April 1799, *Sämtliche Werke,* section III, vol. iii (Berlin: Akademie, 1959) p. 177.

30. Rasch, in Schillemeit (ed.), *Interpretationen*, vol. iii, p. 93.

31. Rasch, in Schillemeit (ed.), *Interpretationen*, vol. iii, p. 92.

32. Burkhardt Lindner, *Jean Paul: Scheiternde Aufklärung und Autorrolle* (Darmstadt: Agora, 1976) p. 150.

33. Lindner, 'Autonomisierung der Literatur als Kunst', *Jahrbuch der Jean Paul Gesellschaft,* x (1975) 98.

34. Rehm, 'Notenleben', *Jahrbuch der deutschen Schillergesellschaft,* iii (1959) 303.

35. Rasch, in Schillemeit (ed.), *Interpretationen*, vol. iii, p. 114.

36. Rüdiger Scholz, *Welt und Form des Romans bei Jean Paul* (Bern and Munich: Francke, 1973) p. 243.

37. Jean Paul attached great importance to the names given to characters; he insisted in the *Vorschule der Ästhetik* (#74, *Werke*, ed. Norbert Miller, vol. v, p. 270): 'Sogar die Kleinigkeit des Namen-Gebens ist kaum eine' ('Even the minor matter of giving names is hardly a minor one').

38. *Hoppelpoppel* is untranslatable. According to Grimms *Deutsches Wörterbuch* (Leipzig: Hirsel, 1877), it is derived from the verb *hoppen* or *hoppeln*, which means to move forwards in little irregular leaps, like a rabbit. *Hoppelpoppel* normally refers to what is otherwise called *Bauernfrühstück*, i.e. scrambled eggs with ham and fried potatoes, and so has come to denote a raggle-taggle mixture.

39. Meyer, 'Jean Pauls *Flegeljahre*' in Schweikert (ed.), *Jean Paul*, p. 237.

40. Strohschneider-Kohrs, *Die romantische Ironie*, p. 406.

41. *Vorschule der Ästhetik,* #37 *Werke*, ed. Norbert Miller, vol. v, p. 148.

42. It has often been pointed out that Jean Paul used the term 'Humor' to describe a stance similar to, though not wholly consonant with Schlegel's conception of irony. By contrast, 'Ironie' denoted for Jean Paul a Swiftian, satirical stance; in his *Vorschule der Ästhetik,* #37 (*Werke*, ed. Norbert Miller,

vol. v, pp. 148–54), which is almost contemporaneous with the *Flegeljahre*, he characterises irony as cold, objective, and intellectual. His admiration goes to what he calls 'Laune' ('whimsy') which is endowed with the qualities peculiar to his own writing, namely, subjectivity, imagination, and 'feurige Sprachfülle' ('fiery abundance of language'). However, the difference between Jean Paul and Schlegel is primarily terminological, and Jean Paul's narratives offer striking examples of what Schlegel called 'Ironie'. See Behler, *Klassische Ironie, Romantische Ironie, Tragische Ironie,* pp. 108–10; Strohschneider-Kohrs, *Die romantische Ironie,* p. 148 ff.; René Wellek, *A History of Modern Criticism* (New Haven, Conn. and London: Yale University Press, 1955) vol. ii, p. 108.

43. Anne Louise-Germaine Necker de Staël, *De L'Allemagne,* ed. Jean de Pange and Simone Balayé (Paris: Hachette, 1958–60) vol. iii, p. 284.

44. 'Noten und Abhandlungen zum *Westöstlichen Divan*', *Werke,* Hamburger Ausgabe, ed. Erich Trunz (Munich: Beck, 1976) vol. ii, p. 185.

45. *Romantische Schule, Werke,* ed. Ernst Elser (Leipzig and Vienna: Bibliographisches Institut, n.d.) vol. v, p. 330. Jean Paul's language was considered so difficult and peculiar that, in consultation with the author, Carl Reinhold compiled a *Wörterbuch zu Jean Paul (Dictionary to Jean Paul),* of which, however, only one volume – devoted to *Levana* – appeared in Leipzig in 1809.

46. *Biographische Belustigungen,* 'Vorrede zum satirischen Appendix' (1796), *Sämtliche Werke,* section I, vol. v (Weimar: Böhlau, 1930) p. 328.

47. Meyer, 'Jean Pauls *Flegeljahre'* in Schweikert (ed.), *Jean Paul,* p. 215.

48. *Palingenesien, Sämtliche Werke,* section I, vol. vii (Weimar: Böhlau, 1931) p. 324.

49. *Sämtliche Werke,* section I, vol. xvi (Weimar: Böhlau, 1938) pp. 167–264.

50. *Sämtliche Werke,* section I, vol. xvi, p. 212.

51. Peter Michelsen, *Laurence Sterne und der deutsche Roman des 18. Jahrhunderts,* 2nd edn. (Göttingen: Vandenhoeck & Ruprecht, 1972) p. 321.

52. See Meyer, 'Jean Pauls *Flegeljahre'* in Schweikert (ed.) *Jean Paul,* pp. 250–63. Even Meyer, after minute scrutiny, has to concede the lack of connection in most instances.

53. Frey, *Jean Pauls 'Flegeljahre',* p. 220.

54. See especially Eva Anne Baratta, *Surrealistische Züge im Werke Jean Pauls* (Bonn: Bouvier, 1972) p. 50 and *passim.*

55. Michelsen, *Laurence Sterne und der deutsche Roman des 18. Jahrhunderts,* p. 332.

56. Friedrich Schlegel, *Philosophische Lehrjahre,* IV, no. 15, *KA,* vol. xviii, part 1, p. 198.

57. Heinrich Bosse, in 'Der offene Schluss der *Flegeljahre',* *Jahrbuch der Jean Paul Gesellschaft,* ii (1967) 73–84, argues that it is the relationship of the twins that is at the centre of the plot and that their final break-up marks the completion of the novel. This thesis is convincing as far as it goes, but it leaves many loose ends, notably the narrator.

58. Uwe Schweikert, *Jean Paul* (Stuttgart: Metzler, 1970) p. 46.

59. cf. Jean Paul, *Vorschule der Ästhetik, Werke,* ed. Norbert Miller, vol. v, p. 447: 'Sie [die Dichtkunst] ist kein platter Spiegel der Gegenwart, sondern der Zauberspiegel der Zeit, welche nicht ist. Jenes Etwas, dessen Lücke unser Denken und unser Anschauen entzweit und trennt, dieses Heiligste

zieht sie durch ihre Zauberei vom Himmel näher herab.' ('It [the art of poetry] is no flat mirror of the present, but a magic mirror of a time that is not in being. The ineffable something, whose absence divides and disrupts our thinking and our perceiving, this most sacred thing draws it down from heaven more nigh to us through its magic.')

60. Hans Keith, *Spiegel und Spiegelung bei Jean Paul. Studien zu Sein und Schein in Persönlichkeit und Werk Jean Pauls* (Diss., Erlangen: Müller, 1965) p. 33.
61. Walter Harich, *Jean Paul* (Leipzig: Haesserl, 1925) p. 627.
62. Meyer, 'Jean Pauls *Flegeljahre*', in Schweikert (ed.) *Jean Paul*, p. 254.
63. Uwe Schweikert, *Jean Pauls 'Komet': Selbstparodie der Kunst*, p. 121.
64. Walter Höllerer, in Jean Paul, *Werke*, ed. Norbert Miller, vol. iii, p. 839.
65. Solger, *Vorlesungen über Ästhetik*, p. 241.
66. Walter Benjamin, 'Der Begriff der Kunstkritik in der deutschen Romantik', *Gesammelte Schriften,* ed. Rolf Tiedemann and Hermann Schweppenhäuser (Frankfurt: Suhrkamp, 1955) vol. ii, p. 489.
67. The phrase 'eine gewissermassen meta-ironische Konzeption' was coined by Heimrich, *Fiktion und Fiktionsironie,* p. 118.

Chapter 7   Denis Diderot: *Jacques le fataliste et son maître*

1. Denis Diderot, *Jacques le fataliste et son maître*, ed. Yvon Belaval (Paris: Gallimard, 1973) p. 35. All subsequent references are to this edition.
2. Arthur M. Wilson, *Diderot* (New York: Oxford University Press, 1972) p. 667.
3. Thomas Kavanagh, *The Vacant Mirror: a Study of Mimesis through Diderot's 'Jacques le fataliste'*, Studies on Voltaire and the Eighteenth Century, no. 104 (Banbury, Oxon.: The Voltaire Foundation, 1973) p. 23.
4. Herbert Dieckmann, 'Diderot et le lecteur', *Mercure de France*, cccxxix (1957) 648.
5. Francis Prunier, *L'Unité secrète de 'Jacques le fataliste'* (Paris: Minard, 1970) p. 17: 'Ce n'est pas un hasard, si la première page de *Jacques le fataliste* invoque le hasard, comme seul principe d'explication: l'ironie de ce départ ne doit pas égarer le lecteur.' ('It is not by chance that the first page of *Jacques le fataliste* invokes chance as the sole explanatory principle: the irony of this start must not mislead the reader.')
6. Aram Vartanian, '*Jacques le fataliste*: Journey into the Ramifications of a Dilemma', in John N. Pappas (ed.), *Essays on Diderot and the Enlightenment in Honor of Otis Fellows* (Geneva: Droz, 1974) p. 332.
7. Critics are divided as to Diderot's own attitude to fatalism when he was writing *Jacques le fataliste*. Prunier takes the extreme view that this is 'un livre *masqué*' (*L'Unité secrète de 'Jacques le fataliste'*, p. 322; 'a *masked* book'; italics are the author's) in which Diderot could at last put forward all his own arguments in favour of fatalism, which he had had, out of discretion, to suppress or refute in his articles. The contrary position is taken by Georges May (in 'Le Fatalisme et *Jacques le fataliste*' in *Thèmes et figures du Siècle des Lumières*. Mélanges offerts à Roland Mortier, ed. Raymond Trousson [Geneva: Droz, 1980] pp. 161–76): by reference to two books on fatalism published shortly before *Jacques le fataliste*, i.e. Prémontval's *Du Hazard sous*

l'empire de la Providence, Pour servir de préservatif contre la doctrine du Fatalisme moderne (1755) and Jacques Rochette's *Le Fatalisme, ou Collection d'anecdotes, pour prouver l'influence du sort sur l'histoire du coeur humain* (1769) May speculates that parody of currently fashionable fatalism could have been one factor in Diderot's composition of *Jacques le fataliste.* A more interesting hypothesis is advanced by Rainer Warning (*Illusion und Wirklichkeit in 'Tristram Shandy' und 'Jacques le fataliste'* [Munich: Fink, 1965] p. 86), namely that Diderot could conceive fate not in empirical reality but only in the fictive realm of invented novels which he consequently satirised in the name of realism. The standard analysis of the topic by Robert J. Loy (*Diderot's Determined Fatalist* [New York: King's Crown Press, 1950] pp. 128–60) heads towards compromise, as do such major studies of Diderot as Arthur Wilson's, and Lester G. Crocker's *Diderot's Chaotic Order* (Princeton, N.J.: Princeton University Press, 1974). Ambivalence on Diderot's own part would seem a likely basis for his ironical approach.

8. Strohschneider-Kohrs, *Die romantische Ironie*, p. 255.
9. F. Schlegel, *Lyceum*, no. 26, *KA*, vol. ii, p. 149.
10. Stephen Werner, *Diderot's Great Scroll: Narrative Art in 'Jacques le fataliste'.* Studies on Voltaire and the Eighteenth Century, no. 128 (Banbury, Oxon.: The Voltaire Foundation, 1975) p. 16.
11. Leo Spitzer, 'The Style of Diderot', *Linguistics and Literary History* (Princeton, N.J.: Princeton University Press, 1948) p. 166.
12. Huguette Cohen, *La Figure dialogique dans 'Jacques le fataliste'.* Studies on Voltaire and the Eighteenth Century, no. 67 (Banbury, Oxon.: The Voltaire Foundation, 1976) p. 18.
13. Schlegel, *LN*, no. 1459, p. 150: 'Jacques von Diderot ist nicht sowohl ein Roman als eine Persifflage dagegen' ('Diderot's Jacques is not so much a novel as a persiflage on it'). Many critics have interpreted *Jacques le fataliste* primarily as a satirical novel: Ronald Grimsley ('L'ambiguité dans l'oeuvre romanesque de Diderot' in *Cahiers de l'Association internationale des études françaises*, xiii [Paris: Belles Lettres, 1961] p. 227) sees it as a mockery of the idea of fatalism; Vivienne Mylne (*The Eighteenth Century French Novel: Techniques of Illusion* [Manchester; Manchester University Press, and New York: Barnes & Noble, 1965] p. 216 and Rainer Warning (*Illusion und Wirklichkeit*, especially pp. 84–9) emphasise the satire on the contemporary class of heroic adventure novels.
14. Yvon Belaval, introduction to Gallimard edition of *Jacques le fataliste*, p. 32.
15. Robert Mauzi, 'La Parodie romanesque dans *Jacques le fataliste*', *Diderot Studies*, vi (1964) 97.
16. Schlegel, *Ideen*, no. 69, *KA*, vol. ii, p. 263.
17. Loy, in *Diderot's Determined Fatalist*, arrives at 158, while Erich Köhler, in ' "Est-ce que l'on sait où l'on va?" ': L'unité structurale de *Jacques le fataliste et son maître* de Diderot', *Philologica Pragensia*, xiii (1970), makes it 180.
18. For example, Georges May (in 'Le Maître, la chaîne et le chien dans *Jacques le fataliste*' in *Cahiers de l'Association internationale des études françaises*, xiii, pp. 269–82) has argued for an 'ordre secret' in the intertwining of the themes of the master, the chain and the dog; Loy (in *Diderot's Determined Fatalist*, pp. 60–67) has carefully worked out the time sequence as eight days; Werner has championed the centrality of the 'grand rouleau' (in

Diderot's Great Scroll), and Prunier has pleaded for the 'unité secrète de *Jacques le fataliste*'. These attempts to ferret out an 'organisation cachée' ('hidden order'), as Per Nykrog has called it (in 'Les étapes des amours de Jacques', *Orbis Litterarum*, supplement no. 3 [1963] 113), are clearly in refutation of the older view that *Jacques le fataliste* was no more than a muddled 'enchevêtrement de récitis héteroclites' ('tangle of ill-assorted tales') because Diderot was lamentably 'incapable de composer' ('inept at composition'). This view of Pierre Castex and Paul Surer (in *Manuel des études litteraires françaises*, XVIIIè siècle [Paris: Hachette, 1944] p. 97) is now dismissed as patently untrue; but the excessive emphasis on the orderliness of the work's disposition must arouse an equal unease.

19. Cohen, *La Figure dialogique*, p. 61.
20. *Jacques le fataliste et son maître*, edited with a commentary by Simone Lecointre and Jean Le Galliot (Paris: Bordas, 1974), p. 202.
21. Benjamin, 'Der Begriff der Kunstkritik in der deutschen Romantik', *Gesammelte Schriften*, vol. ii, p. 489.
22. Heimrich, *Fiktion und Fiktionsironie*, pp. 74–5.
23. Alter, *Partial Magic*, pp. 63–4. The phrase 'intelligence du Récit' is taken from Roland Barthes, *Le Degré zéro de l'écriture* (Paris: Editions du Seuil, 1953) pp. 46–7.
24. Friedrich Ernst Daniel Schleiermacher, *Vorlesungen über die Ästhetik*, *Sämtliche Werke*, ed. H. Ritter (Berlin: Reimer, 1839) Abt. 3, vol. iv, p. 83.
25. Stephen Mautner, 'The Story of the Compromised Author: Parabasis in Friedrich Schlegel and Denis Diderot', *Comparative Literature Studies*, xvi (1979) 31.
26. Roger Kempf, *Diderot et le roman, ou le démon de la présence* (Paris: Editions du Seuil, 1964) p. 34.
27. Siegried Jüttner discusses the tension between 'Leserfreiheit' ('reader's freedom') and 'positive Leserlenkung' ('positive direction of the reader') in 'Experimentell-exploratorisches Erzählen: Zur Analyse des *Jacques le fataliste et son maître* von Diderot', *Romanische Forschungen* xc (1978) 192–225, and especially 207.
28. Warning, *Illusion und Wirklichkeit*, p. 112.
29. Werner, *Diderot's Great Scroll*, p. 23.
30. Sharon L. Kabelac, 'Irony as a Metaphysic in *Le Neveu de Rameau*', *Diderot Studies*, iv (1971) 111.
31. Cohen, *La Figure dialogique*, p. 160.
32. Cohen, *La Figure dialogique*, p. 32.
33. Werner, *Diderot's Great Scroll*, p. 94.

Chapter 8   Laurence Sterne, *Tristram Shandy*

1. Laurence Sterne, *Tristram Shandy*, ed. Howard Anderson (New York and London: Norton, 1980) vol. 5, ch. xxxii, p. 236. All subsequent references are to this edition, and all italics are the author's. Volume and chapter numbers are included for the sake of convenience.
2. William Kenrick in the *Monthly Review*, appendix to no. xxi (1759) 561. Reprinted in the Norton edition of *Tristram Shandy*, p. 471.

3. *Tristram Shandy* pp. 108, 122, 184, 268, 449. The other footnotes with their first-person references to 'my father' or their parody of scholarly pedantry are made to come from Tristram's pen.

4. Booth, *Rhetoric of Fiction*, p. 240.

5. Richard A. Lanham, *'Tristram Shandy': the Games of Pleasure* (Berkeley and London: University of California Press, 1973) p. 28.

6. Victor Lange, 'Erzählformen im Roman des achtzehnten Jahrhunderts', in Klotz (ed.), *Zur Poetik des Romans*, p. 43.

7. Henri Fluchère, *Laurence Sterne: de l'homme à l'oeuvre* (Paris: Gallimard, 1961); trans. Barbara Bray, *Laurence Sterne: From Tristram to Yorick* (London: Oxford University Press, 1965) p. 337. References are to the English translation.

8. John Preston, *The Created Self: The Reader's Role in Eighteenth Century Fiction* (London: Heinemann and New York: Barnes & Noble, 1970) p. 187.

9. Fluchère, *Laurence Sterne*, p. 55.

10. William Bowman Piper, *Laurence Sterne* (New York: Twayne, 1965) p. 17.

11. 'The Comic Syntax of *Tristram Shandy*', in Howard Anderson and John S. Shea (eds), *Studies in Criticism and Aesthetics 1600–1800* Minneapolis: University of Minnesota Press, 1967), p. 322.

12. A. E. Dyson, 'Sterne: the Novelist as Jester', *Critical Quarterly*, iv (1962) 311.

13. Fluchère, *Laurence Sterne*, p. 56.

14. Preston, *The Created Self*, p. 199.

15. Lowry Nelson, Jr., 'The Fictive Reader and Literary Self-Reflexiveness', in Peter Demetz, Thomas Greene and Lowry Nelson, Jr. (eds), *The Disciplines of Criticism* (New Haven, Conn. and London: Yale University Press, 1968) p. 181.

16. Nelson, 'The Fictive Reader' in *Disciplines of Criticism*, p. 182.

17. Howard Anderson, *'Tristram Shandy* and the Reader's Imagination', *PMLA*, lxxxvi (1971) 969.

18. Helene Moglen, *The Philosophical Irony of Laurence Sterne* (Gainesville: University of Florida Press, 1975) p. 40.

19. John Traugott, *Tristram Shandy's World: Sterne's Philosophical Rhetoric* (Berkeley and London: University of California Press, 1954) p. xiii.

20. Virginia Woolf, 'Phases of Fiction', originally published in *Granite and Rainbow*, reprinted in *Collected Essays*, ed. Leonard Woolf (London: Chatto & Windus, 1966) vol. ii, p. 92.

21. Howard Anderson, *'Tristram Shandy* and the Reader's Imagination', *PMLA*, lxxxvi (1971) 970.

22. Dyson, *Crazy Fabric*, p. 33.

23. J. Paul Hunter, 'Response as Reformation: *Tristram Shandy* and the Art of Interruption', *Novel*, iv (1971) 146.

24. Conrad, *Shandyism*, p. 163.

25. Conrad, *Shandyism*, p. 102.

26. Traugott, *Tristram Shandy's World*, p. 125.

27. See Dieter A. Berger, 'Das gezielte Missverständnis: Kommunikationsprobleme in Laurence Sternes *Tristram Shandy*', *Poetica* v (1972) 329–47.

28. Sigurd Burckhardt, *'Tristram Shandy*'s Law of Gravity', *English Literary History*, xxviii (1961) 78.

29. See for example Andrew Wright, 'The Artifice of Failure', *Novel*, ii (1969) 212–20; Dietrich Rolle, *Fielding und Sterne: Untersuchungen über die Funktion des Erzählers* (Münster: Aschendorff, 1963).
30. See Lanham, *Games of Pleasure*, p. 46. Italics are the author's.
31. Burckhardt, '*Tristram Shandy*'s Law of Gravity; *English Literary History*, xxviii (1961) 80.
32. Samuel Taylor Coleridge, *Miscellaneous Criticism*, ed. Thomas Middleton Raysor (London: Constable, and Bambridge, Mass.: Harvard University Press, 1936) p. 126. Italics are the author's.
33. E. M. Forster, *Aspects of the Novel* (London: Arnold, 1927) p. 146.
34. Schlegel, *LN*, No. 1356, p. 142.
35. Alter, *Partial Magic*, p. 30.
36. Mendilow, *Time and the Novel*, p. 161.
37. See Fluchère, *Laurence Sterne*, pp. 105–8, and Theodore Baird, 'The Time-Schema in *Tristram Shandy* and a Source', *PMLA*, li (1936) 803–20.
38. Booth, 'The Self-Conscious Narrator in Comic Fiction before *Tristram Shandy*', *PMLA*, lxvii (1952) 185.
39. Preston, *The Created Self*, p. 133.
40. Virginia Woolf, 'The *Sentimental Journey*', *Collected Essays*, vol. i, p. 95.
41. Dyson, *Crazy Fabric*, p. 35.
42. Coleridge, *Miscellaneous Criticism*, p. 118.
43. Ben Reid coined the phrase: 'The Sad Hilarity of Sterne', *Virginia Quarterly Review*, xxxii (1956).
44. *Modern Philology*, xlviii (1951) 172–83.
45. Dyson, 'Sterne: the Novelist as Jester', *Critical Quarterly*, iv (1962) 316.
46. Moglen, *The Philosophical Irony of Laurence Sterne*, p. 6.
47. Rolle, *Fielding und Sterne*, p. 147.
48. Trilling, *Sincerity and Authenticity*, p. 121.

Chapter 9   In Search of a Theory

1. *Romantic and Modern: Revaluations of a Literary Tradition*, ed. George Bornstein (Pittsburgh: University of Pittsburgh Press, 1977) pp. 3–28.
2. Ricarda Huch, *Die Blütezeit der Romantik* (Leipzig: Haessel, 1926) p. 278.
3. René Bourgeois, *L'ironie romantique* (Grenoble: Presses universitaires, 1974) p. 245.
4. Vladimir Jankélévich, *L'ironie* (Paris: Flammarion, 1964) p. 17.
5. David Simpson, *Irony and Authority in Romantic Poetry* (London: Macmillan, and Totowa, N. J.: Rowman & Littlefield, 1979) p. 190. Italics are the author's.
6. Culler, *Flaubert*, p. 202.
7. Morton L. Gurewitch, *European Romantic Irony*, Diss., Columbia Univ., 1957 (London and Ann Arbor, Michigan: University Microfilms International) p. 3.
8. Strohschneider-Kohrs, *Die romantische Ironie*, p. 70.
9. Martin Walser, *Selbstbewusstein und Ironie* (Frankfurt: Suhrkamp, 1981) pp. 51–2.
10. Mellor, *English Romantic Irony*, p. 24.

11. Sedgewick, *Of Irony, Especially in Drama*, p. 13.
12. Sperry, 'Toward a Definition of Romantic Irony in English Literature', in *Romantic and Modern*, p. 6.
13. Barbara Hardy, *Tellers and Listeners* (London: Athlone Press, 1975) p. 9. Hardy calls Cervantes, Fielding, Sterne, Diderot, Joyce, Beckett and Nabokov 'narrative gamesmen'.
14. Simpson, *Irony and Authority*, p. 193.
15. Robert Scholes, *Semiotics and Interpretation* (New Haven, Conn. and London: Yale University Press, 1982), p. 86.
16. Michael Fried, *Absorption and Theatricality. Painting and Beholder in the Age of Diderot* (Berkeley and London: University of California Press, 1980) p. 66.
17. Booth, *A Rhetoric of Irony,* p. 151.
18. Sperry, 'Toward a Definition of Romantic Irony in English Literature', in *Romantic and Modern*, p. 25.
19. Strohschneider-Kohrs, *Die romantische Ironie*, p. 1.
20. Strohschneider-Kohrs, *Die romantische Ironie*, p. 434.
21. Muecke, *The Compass of Irony*, p. 182.
22. See Anthony Close, *The Romantic Approach to 'Don Quixote'*.
23. Marburger Handschrift, Heft iii, p. 74; cited by Strohschneider-Kohrs, *Die romantische Ironie*, p. 79, fn. 279.
24. Strohschneider-Kohrs, *Die romantische Ironie*, p. 39.

Selected Bibliography

On Irony

Allemann, Beda, *Ironie und Dichtung.* 2nd rev. edn (Pfullingen: Neske, 1969).
Allemann, Beda, 'Ironie als literarisches Prinzip', in Albrecht Schaefer (ed.), *Ironie und Dichtung* (Munich: Beck, 1970) pp. 11–33.
Behler, Ernst, *Klassische Ironie, Romantische Ironie, Tragische Ironie* (Darmstadt: Wissenschaftliche Buchgesellschaft, 1972).
Benjamin, Walter, 'Der Begriff der Kunstkritik in der deutschen Romantik', *Gesammelte Schriften,* ed. Rolf Tiedemann and Hermann Schweppenhäuser (Frankfurt: Suhrkamp, 1955) vol. ii, pp. 420–528.
Booth, Wayne C., *A Rhetoric of Irony* (Chicago and London: University of Chicago Press, 1974).
Bourgeois, René, *L'ironie romantique* (Grenoble: Presses universitaires, 1974).
Brooks, Cleanth, 'Irony as a Principle of Structure', in Morton D. Zabel (ed.), *Literary Opinion in America,* 2nd rev. edn (New York: Harper & Row, 1951) pp. 729–41; an expanded version of 'Irony and "Ironic" Poetry', *College English,* ix (1948) 231–7.
Conrad, Peter, *Shandyism. The Character of Romantic Irony* (Oxford: Blackwell, 1978).
De Man, Paul 'The Rhetoric of Temporality: Irony' in Charles S. Singleton (ed.), *Interpretation: Theory and Practice* (Baltimore and London: The Johns Hopkins University Press, 1969) pp. 191–209.
Dyson, A. E., *The Crazy Fabric. Essays in Irony* (London: Macmillan, and New York: St. Martin's Press, 1965).
Empson, William, *Seven Types of Ambiguity* (London: Chatto & Windus, 1953).
Friedemann, Käte, 'Die romantische Ironie', *Zeitschrift für Ästhetik,* iii (1919) 270–82.
Frye, Northrop, *Anatomy of Criticism* (Princeton, N.J.: Princeton University Press, 1957).
Gifford, P., 'Socrates in Amsterdam: The Uses of Irony in *La Chute*', *Modern Language Review,* lxxiii (1978) 499–512.
Glicksberg, Charles I., *The Ironic Vision in Modern Literature* (The Hague: Martinus Nijhoff, 1969).
Green, D. H., 'On Recognising Medieval Irony', in A. P. Foulkes (ed.), *The Uses of Criticism* (Bern: Herbert Lang, 1976) pp. 11–55.
Green, D. H., *Irony in the Medieval Romance* (Cambridge: Cambridge University Press, 1979).
Gurewitch, Morton L., *European Romantic Irony* (Diss.: Columbia University,

1957; London and Ann Arbor, Michigan: University Microfilms International).

Hamlin, Cyrus, 'Platonic Dialogue and Romantic Irony: Prolegomenon to a Theory of Literary Narrative', *Canadian Review of Comparative Literature*, iii (1976) 5–26.

Hass, Hans-Egon and Mohrlüder Gustav-Adolf (eds.), *Ironie als literarisches Phänomen* (Cologne: Kiepenhauer & Witsch, 1973).

Haym, Rudolf, *Die romantische Schule,* 3rd rev. edn (Berlin: Weidemann, 1914).

Hegel, Georg Wilhelm Friedrich, *Grundlinien der Philosophie, Sämtliche Werke*, ed. H. Glockner (Stuttgart: Fromanns Verlag, 1928) vol. vii.

Hegel, Georg Wilhelm Friedrich, *Vorlesungen über die Ästhetik, Sämtliche Werke,* vol. xii.

Hegel, Georg Wilhelm Friedrich, *Vorlesungen über die Geschichte, Sämtliche Werke,* vol. xviii.

Heimrich, Bernhard, *Fiktion und Fiktionsironie in Theorie und Dichtung der deutschen Romantik* (Tübingen: Niemeyer, 1968).

Hettner, Hermann, *Schriften zur Literatur*, ed. Jürgen Jahn (Berlin: Aufbau, 1959).

Hettner, Hermann, *Geschichte der deutschen Literatur im achtzehnten Jahrhundert,* ed. Georg Witkowski (Leipzig: List, 1928).

Hutchens, Eleanor N., 'The Identification of Irony', *English Literary History*, xxvii (1960) 352–63.

Immerwahr, Raymond, 'The Subjectivity or Objectivity of Friedrich Schlegel's Poetic Irony', *Germanic Review*, xxvi (1951) 173–91.

Immerwahr, Raymond, 'Romantic Irony and Romantic Arabesque prior to Romanticism', *The German Quarterly*, xlii (1969) 665–84.

Jankélévich, Vladimir, *L'ironie romantique* (Paris: Flammarion, 1964).

Kerbrat-Orecchioni, Cathérine, 'L'ironie comme trope', *Poétique*, xli (1980) 108–27.

Kierkegaard, Søren, *The Concept of Irony*. Trans. Lee M. Capel (Bloomington and London: Indiana University Press, 1965).

Knox, Norman, *The Word 'Irony' and Its Contexts 1500–1755* (Durham, North Carolina: Duke University Press, 1961).

Knox, Norman, 'On the Classification of Ironies', *Modern Philology*, lxx (1972) 53–62.

Mellor, Anne K. *English Romantic Irony* (Cambridge, Mass.: Harvard University Press, 1980).

Muecke, Douglas C., *The Compass of Irony* (London: Methuen, 1969).

Muecke, Douglas C., *Irony* (London: Methuen, and New York: Barnes & Noble, 1970).

Müller, Adam, *Kritische, ästhetische und philosophische Schriften,* ed. Walter Schroeder and Werner Siebert (Berlin: Neuwied, 1967).

Perkins, Robert L., 'Hegel and Kierkegaard: Two Critics of Romantic Irony', *Review of National Literatures*, i (1970) 232–54.

Prang, Helmut, *Die romantische Ironie* (Darmstadt: Wissenschaftliche Buchgesellschaft, 1972).

Richter, David H., 'The Reader as Ironic Victim', *Novel*, xiv (1981) 135–51.

Schlegel, Friedrich, *Literary Notebooks 1797–1801*, ed. Hans Eichner (Toronto and London: Toronto University Press, 1957).

Schlegel, Friedrich, *Kritische Ausgabe* (Munich-Vienna-Paderborn: Schöningh); vol. ii, ed. Hans Eichner, 1967; vol. xviii, ed. Ernst Behler, 1963.

Sedgewick, George G., *Of Irony, Especially in Drama* (Toronto: Toronto University Press, 1948).

Simpson, David, *Irony and Authority in Romantic Poetry* (London: Macmillan, and Totowa, N.J.: Rowman & Littlefield, 1979).

Solger, Karl Wilhelm Ferdinand, *Vorlesungen über Ästhetik*, ed. Karl Wilhelm Ludwig Heyse (Leipzig, 1829; reprinted Darmstadt: Wissenschaftliche Buchgesellschaft, 1962).

Solger, Karl Wilhelm Ferdinand, *Erwin*, ed. Wolfhart Henckmann (Munich: Fink, 1971).

Sperry, Stuart M., 'Toward a Definition of Romantic Irony in English Literature', in George Bornstein (ed.), *Romantic and Modern: Revaluations of a Literary Tradition*. Festschrift for Carlos Baker (Pittsburgh: University of Pittsburgh Press, 1977) pp. 3–28.

Strohschneider-Kohrs, Ingrid, *Die romantische Ironie in Theorie und Gestaltung*, 2nd rev. edn (Tübingen: Niemeyer, 1977).

Strohschneider-Kohrs, Ingrid, 'Zur Poetik der deutschen Romantik: Die romantische Ironie', in Hans Steffen (ed.), *Die deutsche Romantik, Poetik, Formen und Motive* (Göttingen: Vandenhoeck & Ruprecht, 1976) pp. 75–97.

Suleiman, Susan, 'Interpreting Ironies', *Diacritics*, vi (1976) 15–21.

Szondi, Peter, 'Friedrich Schlegel und die romantische Ironie', *Euphorion*, xlviii (1954) 397–411; reprinted in *Satz und Gegensatz* (Frankfurt: Insel, 1964) pp. 5–24.

Thompson, Alan Reynolds, *The Dry Mock: A Study of Irony in Drama* (Berkeley: University of California Press, and Cambridge: Cambridge University Press, 1948).

Walser, Martin, *Selbstbewusstsein und Ironie* (Frankfurt: Suhrkamp, 1981).

Warren, Robert Penn, 'Pure and Impure Poetry', Mesures lecture, Princeton University, 1942; reprinted in Robert Wooster Stallman (ed.), *Critiques and Essays in Criticism* (New York: Ronald Press, 1949) pp. 85–104.

Watt, Ian, 'The Ironic Tradition in Augustan Prose from Swift to Johnson', in *Restoration and Augustan Prose*. Papers delivered at the Third Clark Library Seminar, 14 July 1956 (Los Angeles: William Andrews Clark Memorial Library, 1956) pp. 19–46.

Wilde, Alan, *Horizons of Assent: Modernism, Postmodernism, and the Ironic Imagination* (Baltimore and London: The Johns Hopkins University Press, 1981).

Wright, Andrew, 'Irony and Fiction', *Journal of Aesthetics and Art Criticism*, xii (1953) 111–18.

Other Relevant Works

Aarsleff, Hans, *The Study of Language in England 1780–1860* (Princeton, N.J.: Princeton University Press, 1967).

Alter, Robert, *Partial Magic. The Novel as a Self-Conscious Genre* (Berkeley and London: University of California Press, 1975).

Bate, Walter Jackson, *The Burden of the Past and the English Poet* (London: Chatto & Windus, 1971).

Berkeley, George, *Treatise Concerning the Principles of Human Understanding, Works*, ed. Alexander Campbell Fraser (Oxford: Clarendon Press, 1871) vol. i.

Bosse, Heinrich, 'The Marvellous and Romantic Semiotics', *Studies in Romanticism*, xiv (1975) 211-34.

Condillac, Etienne Bonnot de, *Essai sur l'origine des connaissances humaines, Oeuvres philosophiques*, ed. Georges L. Roy (Paris: ,Presses universitaires, 1947) vol. i.

Condillac, Etienne Bonnot de, *Cours d'études pour l'instruction du Prince de Parme, Oeuvres philosophiques*, vol. i.

Fichte, Johann Gottlieb, *Grundlagen der gesamten Wissenschaftslehre* (Tübingen: Cotta, 1802).

Foucault, Michel, *Les Mots et les choses* (Paris: Gallimard, 1966). Trans. *The Order of Things* (New York: Pantheon Books, 1970).

Fried, Michael, *Absorption and Theatricality. Painting and Beholder in the Age of Diderot* (Berkeley and London: University of California Press, 1980).

Genette, Gérard, 'Discours du récit', in *Figures*, III (Paris: Editions du Seuil, 1972) pp. 67-278. Trans. Jane E. Lewin, *Narrative Discourse. An Essay in Method* (Ithaca, N.Y.: Cornell University Press, 1980).

Hacking, Ian, 'Is Locke the Key?', Review of Hans Aarsleff, *From Locke to Saussure: Essays on the Study of Language and Linguistic History* (Minneapolis: University of Minnesota Press, 1982) in *New York Review of Books*, 24 June 1982, 36-8.

Herder, Johann Gottfried, *Abhandlung über den Ursprung der Sprache, Sämtliche Werke*, ed. Bernhard Suphan (Berlin: Weidemann, 1891) vol. v.

Iser, Wolfgang, *Der implizite Leser. Kommunikationsformen des Romans von Bunyan bis Beckett* (Munich: Fink, 1972). *The Implied Reader. Patterns of Communication in Prose Fiction from Bunyan to Beckett* (Balimore and London: The Johns Hopkins University Press, 1974).

Kant, Immanuel, *Kritik der reinen Vernunft*, ed. Wilhelm Weischedel (Darmstadt: Wissenschaftliche Buchgesellschaft, 1966).

Kayser, Wolfgang, 'Wer erzählt den Roman?' in Volker Klotz (ed.), *Zur Poetik des Romans*. Wege der Forschung no. 305. (Darmstadt: Wissenschaftliche Buchgesellschaft, 1969) pp. 197-216.

Kernan, Alvin B., *The Plot of Satire* (New Haven, Conn., and London: Yale University Press, 1965).

Kretzmann, Norman, 'The Main Thesis of Locke's Semantic Theory' in H. Parret (ed.), *History of Linguistic Thought and Contemporary Linguistics* (Berlin and New York: de Gruyter, 1976) pp. 331-47.

Lange, Victor 'Erzählformen im Roman des achtzehnten Jahrhunderts', *Anglia*, lxxxvi (1958) 129-44; reprinted in Volker Klotz (ed.), *Zur Poetik des Romans*. Wege der Forschung, no. 305. (Darmstadt: Wissenschaftliche Buchgesellschaft, 1969) pp. 32-47.

Lang, Victor, 'The Reader in the Strategy of Fiction', in Ronald G. Popperwell (ed.), *Expression, Communication and Experience in Language and Literature*. Proceedings of the XII Congress of the International Federation for Modern Languages and Literatures (London: Modern Humanities Research Association, 1973) pp. 86-102.

Locke, John, *An Essay Concerning Human Understanding*, ed. Alexander Campbell Fraser (Oxford: Clarendon Press, 1894).

Trilling, Lionel, *Sincerity and Authenticity* (Cambridge, Mass.: Harvard University Press, 1971).

Weinrich, Harald, *Linguistik der Lüge* (Heidelberg: Schneider, 1966).

Wellek, René, *A History of Modern Criticism*, vol. ii, *The Romantic Age* (New Haven, Conn. and London: Yale University Press, 1955).

Wilson, W. Daniel, 'Readers in Texts', *PMLA*, xcvi (1981) 848–63.

Worcester, David, *The Art of Satire* (Cambridge, Mass.: Harvard University Press, 1940; reprinted New York: Russell & Russell, 1960).

Jane Austen, *Pride and Prejudice*

Babb, Howard S., *Jane Austen's Novels: The Fabric of Dialogue* (Columbus: Ohio State University Press, 1962).

Brower, Reuben A., *The Fields of Light. An Experiment in Critical Reading* (New York: Oxford University Press, 1951) pp. 164–81.

Butler, Marilyn, *Jane Austen and the War of Ideas* (Oxford: Clarendon Press, 1975).

Duckworth, Alistair M., *The Improvement of the Estate: A Study of Jane Austen's Novels* (Baltimore and London: The Johns Hopkins University Press, 1971).

Halliday, E. M., 'Narrative Perspective in *Pride and Prejudice*', *Nineteenth Century Fiction*, xv (1960) 65–71.

Halperin, John (ed.), *Jane Austen Bicentenary Essays* (Cambridge: Cambridge University Press, 1975).

Hardy, Barbara, *A Reading of Jane Austen* (New York: New York University Press, 1976).

Harmsel, Henriette Ten, *Jane Austen: A Study In Fictional Conventions* (The Hague: Mouton, 1964).

Kroeber, Karl, *Styles in Fictional Structure: The Art of Jane Austen, Charlotte Brontë, George Eliot* (Princeton, N.J.: Princeton University Press, 1971).

Lascelles, Mary, *Jane Austen and Her Art* (Oxford: Clarendon Press, 1939).

Litz, A. Walton, *Jane Austen. A Study of Her Artistic Development* (New York: Oxford University Press, 1965).

Mansell, Darrel, *The Novels of Jane Austen* (London: Macmillan, 1973).

Mudrick, Marvin, *Jane Austen: Irony as Defense and Discovery* (Princeton, N.J.: Princeton University Press, 1952).

Nardine, Jane, *Those Elegant Decorums: The Concept of Propriety in Jane Austen's Novels* (Albany: State University of New York Press, 1973).

Page, Norman, *The Language of Jane Austen* (Oxford: Blackwell, 1972).

Van Ghent, Dorothy, *The English Novel* (New York: Holt, Rinehart & Winston, 1953) pp. 105–23.

Watt, Ian (ed.), *Jane Austen. A Collection of Critical Essays* (Englewood Cliffs, N.J.: Prentice-Hall, 1963).

Wright, Andrew H., *Jane Austen's Novels. A Study in Structure* (London: Chatto & Windus, 1964).

Gustave Flaubert, *Madame Bovary*

Bart, Benjamin F., *Flaubert* (Syracuse, N.Y.: Syracuse University Press, 1967).

Bart, Benjamin F., 'Art, Energy, and Aesthetic Disease', in Benjamin F. Bart (ed.), *'Madame Bovary' and the Critics* (New York: New York University Press, 1966) pp. 73–105.

Brombert, Victor, *The Novels of Flaubert* (Princeton, N.J.: Princeton University Press, 1966).

Culler, Jonathan, *Flaubert. The Uses of Uncertainty* (London: Elek, and Ithaca, N.Y.: Cornell University Press, 1974).

Demorest, D. L., *L'expression figurée et symbolique dans l'oeuvre de Gustave Flaubert* (Paris: Presses modernes, 1931; reprinted Geneva: Slatkine, 1967).

Fairlie, Alison, *Flaubert: 'Madame Bovary'* (London: Edward Arnold, 1962).

Furst, Lilian R., 'The Role of Food in *Madame Bovary*', *Orbis Litterarum*, xxxiv (1979) 53–65.

Genette, Gérard, 'Silences de Flaubert', *Figures* I (Paris: Editions du Seuil, 1966) pp. 223–43.

Goodhand, Robert, 'Emma Bovary, the Baker's Paramour', *Rice University Studies*, lix (1973) 37–41.

Houston, John Porter, *Fictional Technique in France 1802–1927* (Baton Rouge, La.: Lousiana State University Press, 1972).

Jenkins, Cecil 'Flaubert and the "Autonomy" of the Novel', *The Listener*, 14 April 1966.

Levin, Harry T., *The Gates of Horn* (New York: Oxford University Press, 1966) pp. 246–69.

Proust, Marcel, 'A propos du "style" de Flaubert', *La Nouvelle revue française*, xiv (1920) 72–90. Nenden, Liechtenstein: Kraus reprint, 1968.

Rousset, Jean, *Forme et signification* (Paris: Corti, 1962) pp. 109–33.

Sartre, Jean-Paul, *L'idiot de la famille* (Paris: Gallimard, 1971).

Sherrington, R. J., *Three Novels by Flaubert. A Study of Techniques* (Oxford: Clarendon Press, 1970).

Starkie, Enid, *The Making of the Master* (London: Weidenfeld & Nicolson, 1967).

Thibaudet, Albert, *Gustave Flaubert* (Paris: Gallimard, 1935).

Thorlby, Anthony K., *Gustave Flaubert and the Art of Realism* (New Haven, Conn., and London: Yale University Press, 1957).

Ullmann, Stephen, *Style in the French Novel* (Cambridge: Cambridge University Press, 1957).

Warning, Rainer, 'Irony and the "Order of Discourse" in Flaubert', *New Literary History*, xiii (1982) 253–86.

George Gordon Byron, *Don Juan*

Auden, W. H., 'The Life of a That There Poet', *The New Yorker*, 26 April 1953, 135–42; reprinted in Edward E. Bostetter (ed.), *Twentieth Century Interpretations of 'Don Juan'* (Englewood Cliffs. N.J.: Prentice-Hall, 1969) pp. 16–20.

Bloom, Harold, *The Visionary Company* (Garden City, N.Y.: Doubleday, 1961, and London: Faber & Faber, 1962) pp. 251–64.

Bottrall, Ronald, 'Byron and the Colloquial Tradition in English Poetry', *Criterion*, xviii (1939) 204–24; reprinted in M. H. Abrams (ed.), *English Romantic Poets* (New York: Oxford University Press, 1960) pp. 210–27.

Bowra, C. M., *The Romantic Imagination* (London: Oxford University Press, 1950) pp. 149–73.

Boyd, Elizabeth, *'Don Juan'. A Critical Study* (New Brunswick, N.J.: Rutgers University Press, 1945; reprinted New York: Humanities Press, 1975).

Bush, Douglas, *Mythology and the Romantic Tradition in English Poetry* (Cambridge, Mass.: Harvard University Press, 1937).

Calvert, William J., *Byron: Romantic Paradox* (Chapel Hill: University of North Carolina Press, 1935; reprinted New York: Russell & Russell, 1962).

Cooke, Michael G., *The Blind Man Traces the Circle: On the Patterns and Philosophy of Byron's Poetry* (Princeton, N.J.: Princeton University Press, 1969).

Eliot, T. S., 'Byron', *On Poetry and Poets* (London: Faber & Faber, and New York: Farrar, Straus & Giroux, 1957), pp. 223–39.

England, A. B., *Byron's 'Don Juan' and Eighteenth Century Literature: A Study in Some Rhetorical Continuities and Discontinuities* (Lewisburg, Pa.: Bucknell University Press, and London: Associated University Presses, 1975).

Gardner, Helen, *'Don Juan'*, *The London Magazine*, v, no. 7 (July 1958) 58–65.

Joseph, M. K., *Byron the Poet* (London: Gollancz, 1964).

Jump, John D., *Byron* (London and Boston: Routledge & Kegan Paul, 1972).

Kroeber, Karl, *Romantic Narrative Art* (Madison, Wisc. and London: University of Wisconsin Press, 1960) pp. 135–67.

Leavis, F. R., 'Byron's Satire', *Revaluation* (London: Chatto & Windus and New York: W. W. Norton, 1936) pp. 148–53; reprinted in Paul West (ed.), *Byron. A Collection of Critical Essays* (Englewood Cliffs, N.J.: Prentice-Hall, 1963) pp. 83–7.

Lovell, Ernest J., Jr., 'Irony and Image in *Don Juan*', in Clarence D. Thorpe, Carlos Baker and Bennett Weaver (eds.), *The Major English Romantic Poets: A Symposium in Reappraisal* (Carbondale, Ill.: Southern Illinois University Press, 1957), pp. 129–48.

Marchand, Leslie A., *Byron's Poetry: A Critical Introduction* (Boston: Houghton Mifflin, 1965, and London: Murray, 1966).

McGann, Jerome, *Fiery Dust: Byron's Poetic Development* (Chicago and London: University of Chicago Press, 1968).

McGann, Jerome, *'Don Juan' in Context* (Chicago and London: University of Chicago Press, 1976).

Ridenour, George, *The Style of 'Don Juan'* (New Haven, Conn. and London: Yale University Press, 1960).

Ridenour, George, 'The Mode of Byron's *Don Juan*', *PMLA*, lxxix (1964) 442–6.

Rutherford, Andrew, *Byron: A Critical Study* (Stanford, Ca.: Stanford University Press, 1961).

Rutherford, Andrew, *Byron: The Critical Heritage* (London: Routledge & Kegan Paul, and New York: Barnes & Noble, 1970).

Salomon, Roger B., 'Mock-Heroes and Mock-Heroic Narrative: Byron's *Don Juan* in the Context of Cervantes', *Studies in the Literary Imagination,* ix, no. 1 (Spring 1976) 69–86.

Steffan, Truman Guy, *Byron's 'Don Juan'*, vol. 1: *The Making of a Masterpiece* (Austin: University of Texas Press, and Edinburgh: Nelson, 1957).

Trueblood, Paul Graham, *The Flowering of Byron's Genius: Studies in Byron's 'Don Juan'* (New York: Russell & Russell, 1945, 1962).

Wain, John, 'Byron, the Search for Identity', *The London Magazine*, v. no. 7, (July

1958) 44–57; reprinted in *Essays on Literature and Ideas* (London and Toronto: Macmillan, 1963) pp. 85–102.

Weinstein, Leo, *The Metamorphoses of Don Juan* (Stanford, Ca.: Stanford University Press, 1959).

Wilkie, Brian, 'Byron and the Epic of Negation', *Romantic Poets and Epic Tradition* (Madison, Wisc. and London: University of Wisconsin Press, 1965) pp. 188–226.

Jean Paul, *Flegeljahre*

Arnold, Heinz Ludwig (ed.), *Text + Kritik: Jean Paul* (Munich: Boorberg Verlag, 1974).

Bacmeister, Gisela, ' "Hoppelpoppel oder das Herz" und seine Bedeutung im Gefüge der *Flegeljahre*', in Albrecht Goetze and Günther Pflaum (eds.), *Vergleichen und verändern*. Festschrift für Helmut Motekat (Munich: Huber, 1970) pp. 140–6.

Baratta, Eva Anne, *Surrealistische Züge im Werke Jean Pauls* (Bonn: Bouvier, 1972).

Berend, Eduard, 'Die Namengebung bei Jean Paul', *PMLA*, lvii (1942) 820–50.

Berger, Dorothea, *Jean Paul Friedrich Richter* (New York: Twayne, 1972).

Böckmann, Paul, 'Die humoristische Darstellungsweise Jean Pauls', in Hans Werner Seiffert and Bernhard Zeller (eds), *Festgabe für Eduard Berend* (Weimar: Böhlau, 1959) pp. 38–53.

Bosse, Heinrich, 'Der offene Schluss der *Flegeljahre'*, *Jahrbuch der Jean Paul Gesellschaft*, ii (1967) 73–84.

Frey, Karl A. J. F., *Jean Pauls 'Flegeljahre': Materialien und Untersuchungen*. Palaestra no. 61 (Berlin: Mayer & Muller, 1907).

Harich, Walter, *Jean Paul* (Leipzig: Haessel, 1925).

Jäger, Gustav, 'Jean Pauls poetischer Generalbass: Bemerkungen zur musikalischen Struktur seiner Romane', in Hans Werner Seiffert and Bernhard Zeller (eds), *Festgabe für Eduard Berend* (Weimar: Böhlau, 1959) pp. 54–73.

Keith, Hans, *Spiegel und Spiegelung bei Jean Paul. Studien zu Sein und Schein in Persönlichkeit und Werk Jean Pauls* (Erlangen: Müller, 1965).

Kommerell, Max, *Jean Paul* (Frankfurt: Klostermann, 1923).

Köpke, Wulf, 'Zusammensetzungen mit "Selbst" bei Jean Paul', *Jahrbuch der Jean Paul Gesellschaft*, viii (1973) 100–22.

Köpke, Wulf, *Erfolglosigkeit. Zum Frühwerk Jean Pauls* (Munich: Fink, 1977).

Lindner, Burkhardt, 'Autonomisierung der Literatur als Kunst, klassisches Werkmodell und auktoriale Erzählweise', *Jahrbuch der Jean Paul Gesellschaft*, x (1975) 85–107.

Lindner, Burkhardt, *Jean Paul. Scheiternde Aufklärung und Autorrolle* (Darmstadt: Agora, 1976).

Mayer, Gerhart, 'Die humorgeprägte Struktur von Jean Pauls *Flegeljahre*', *Zeitschrift für deutsche Philologie*, lxxxviii (1964) 409–26.

Meyer, Hermann, 'Jean Pauls *Flegeljahre*', in *Zarte Empirie* (Stuttgart: Metzler, 1963) pp. 57–112.

Michelsen, Peter, *Laurence Sterne und der deutsche Roman des achtzehnten*

Jahrhunderts. Palaestra, no. 232 (Göttingen: Vandenhoeck & Ruprecht, 2nd edn, 1972).

Neumann, Peter Horst, *Jean Pauls 'Flegeljahre'.* Palaestra no. 245 (Göttingen: Vandenhoeck & Ruprecht, 1966).

Profitlich, Ulrich, *Eitelkeit. Eine Untersuchung zum Romanwerk Jean Pauls* (Berlin and Zurich: Gehlen, 1969).

Rasch, Wolfdietrich, *Die Erzählweise Jean Pauls. Metaphernspiele und dissonante Strukturen* (Munich: Hanser, 1961); reprinted in Jost Schillemeit (ed.), *Interpretationen,* vol. iii, *Deutsche Romane von Grimmelshausen bis Musil* (Frankfurt: Fischer Bücherei, no. 716, 1966) pp. 82–117.

Rehm, Walter, 'Jean Pauls vergnügtes Notenleben oder Notenmachen und Notenlesen', *Jahrbuch der deutschen Schillergesellschaft,* iii (1959) 224–337.

Schieder, Margarete, *Die Humoristen-Gestalten in Jean Pauls Romanen mit besonderer Berücksichtigung der Schoppe-Gestalt* (Diss.: Cologne, 1969).

Schweikert, Uwe, *Jean Paul.* Sammlung Metzler, no. 91 (Stuttgart: Metzler, 1970).

Schweikert, Uwe, *Jean Pauls 'Komet': Selbstparodie der Kunst* (Stuttgart: Metzler, 1971).

Schweikert, Uwe (ed.), *Jean Paul.* Wege der Forschung, no. 336 (Darmstadt: Wissenschaftliche Buchgesellschaft, 1974).

Scholz, Rüdiger, *Welt und Form des Romans bei Jean Paul* (Bern and Munich: Francke Verlag, 1973).

Wölfel, Kurt, 'Ein Echo das sich selber ins Unendliche nachhalt', *Jahrbuch der Jean Paul Gesellschaft,* i (1966) 17–52.

Denis Diderot, *Jacques le fataliste et son maître*

Catrysse, Jean, *Diderot et la mystification* (Paris: Nizet, 1970).

Cohen, Huguette, *La Figure dialogique dans 'Jacques le fataliste'.* Studies on Voltaire and the Eighteenth Century, no. 62 (Banbury, Oxon.: The Voltaire Foundation, 1976).

Crocker, Lester G., *Diderot's Chaotic Order* (Princeton, N.J.: Princeton University Press, 1974).

Dieckmann, Herbert, 'Diderot et le lecteur', *Mercure de France,* cccxix (1957) 620–48.

Fredman, Alice G., *Diderot and Sterne* (New York: Columbia University Press, 1955).

Grimsley, Ronald, 'L'ambiguité dans l'oeuvre romanesque de Diderot', *Cahiers de l'Association internationale des études françaises,* xiii (Paris: Belles Lettres, 1961) pp. 223–37.

Jüttner, Siegfried, 'Experimentell-exploratorisches Erzählen: Zur Analyse des *Jacques le fataliste et son maître* von Diderot', *Romanische Forschungen,* xc (1978) 195–225.

Kabelac, Sharon L., 'Irony as a Metaphysic in *Le Neveu de Rameau',* *Diderot Studies,* iv (1971) 97–112.

Kavanagh, Thomas, *The Vacant Mirror: A Study of Mimesis through Diderot's 'Jacques le fataliste'.* Studies on Voltaire and the Eighteenth Century, no. 104 (Banbury, Oxon.: The Voltaire Foundation, 1973).

Kempf, Roger, *Diderot et le roman, ou le démon de la présence* (Paris: Editions du Seuil, 1964).

Köhler, Erich, 'Zur strukturellen Einheit von *Jacques le fataliste*', *Romanistisches Jahrbuch*, xvi (1965) 126–48.

Köhler, Erich, ' "Est-ce que l'on sait où l'on va?" ': L'unité structurale de *Jacques le fataliste et son maître* de Diderot', *Philologica Pragensia,* xiii (1970) 186–202.

Loy, Robert J., *Diderot's Determined Fatalist* (New York: King's Crown Press, 1950).

Mautner, Stephen, 'The Story of the Comprised Author: Parabasis in Friedrich Schlegel and Denis Diderot', *Comparative Literature Studies*, xvi (1979) 21–32.

Mauzi, Robert, 'La parodie romanesque dans *Jacques le fataliste*', *Diderot Studies*, vi (1964) 81–132.

May, Georges, 'Le maître, la chaine et le chien dans *Jacques le fataliste*', *Cahiers de l'Association internationale des études françaises,* xiii (Paris: Belles Lettres, 1961) pp. 269–82.

May, Georges, 'Le Fatalisme et *Jacques le fataliste*', in Raymond Trousson (ed.), *Thèmes et figures du Siècle des Lumières.* Mélanges offertes à Roland Mortier (Geneva: Droz, 1980) pp. 161–76.

Mylne, Vivienne, *The Eighteenth Century French Novel: Techniques of Illusion* (Manchester: Manchester University Press, and New York: Barnes & Noble, 1965).

Nykrog, Per, 'Les étapes des amours de Jacques', *Orbis Litterarum*, supplement, no. 3 (1963) 113–26.

Prunier, Francis, *L'Unité secrète de 'Jacques le fataliste'* (Paris: Minard, 1970).

Spitzer, Leo, 'Pseudo-objektive Motivierung', *Zeitschrift für französische Sprache und Literatur,* xlvi (1923) 359–85.

Spitzer, Leo, 'The Style of Diderot', *Linguistics and Literary History* (Princeton, N.J.: Princeton University Press, 1948) pp. 135–91.

Vartanian, Aram, '*Jacques le fataliste*: Journey into the Ramifications of a Dilemma', in John N. Pappas (ed.), *Essays on Diderot and the Enlightenment in Honor of Otis Fellows* (Geneva: Droz, 1974) pp. 325–47.

Warning, Rainer, *Illusion und Wirklichkeit in 'Tristram Shandy' und 'Jacques le fataliste'* (Munich: Fink, 1965).

Werner, Stephen, *Diderot's Great Scroll: Narrative Ar in 'Jacques le fataliste'.* Studies on Voltaire and the Eighteenth Century, no. 128 (Banbury, Oxon.: The Voltaire Foundation, 1975).

Wilson, Arthur M., *Diderot* (New York: Oxford University Press, 1972).

Laurence Sterne, *Tristram Shandy*

Anderson, Howard, 'Associationism and Wit in *Tristram Shandy*', *Philological Quarterly*, xlviii (1969) 27–41.

Anderson, Howard, '*Tristram Shandy* and the Reader's Imagination', *PMLA*, lxxxvi (1971) 966–73.

Berger, Dieter A., 'Das gezielte Missverständnis: Kommunikationsprobleme in Laurence Sternes *Tristram Shandy, Poetica*, v (1972) 329–47.

Booth, Wayne C., 'Did Sterne Complete *Tristram Shandy*?', *Modern Philology*, xlviii (1951) 172–83.

Booth, Wayne C., 'The Self-Conscious Narrator in Comic Fiction before *Tristram Shandy*', *PMLA*, lxvii (1952) 163–85.

Burckhardt, Sigurd, '*Tristram Shandy*'s Law of Gravity', *English Literary History*, xxviii (1961) 70–88.

Cash, Arthur Hill and John Stedmond (eds.), *The Winged Skull* (London: Methuen, and Kent, Ohio: Kent State University Press, 1971).

Dyson, A. E., 'Sterne: the Novelist as Jester', *Critical Quarterly*, iv (1962) 309–19.

Fietz, Lothar, 'Fiktionsbewusstsein und Romanstruktur in der Geschichte des englischen und amerikanischen Romans', in Helmut Kreuzer (ed.), *Gestaltungsgeschichte und Gesellschaftsgeschichte*. Festschrift für Fritz Martini (Stuttgart: Metzler, 1969) pp. 115–31.

Fluchère, Henri, *Laurence Sterne: de l'homme à l'oeuvre* (Paris: Gallimard, 1961). Trans. Barbara Bray, *Laurence Sterne: From Tristram to Yorick* (London: Oxford University Press, 1965).

Hunter, J. Paul, 'Response as Reformation: *Tristram Shandy* and the Art of Interruption', *Novel*, iv (1971) 132–46.

Lanham, Richard A., '*Tristram Shandy*': the Games of Pleasure* (Berkeley and London: University of California Press, 1973).

Moglen, Helene, *The Philosophical Irony of Laurence Sterne* (Gainesville, Fl.: University of Florida Press, 1975).

Nelson, Lowry, Jr., 'The Fictive Reader and Literary Self-Reflexiveness', in Peter Demetz, Thomas Greene and Lowry Nelson, Jr. (eds.), *The Disciplines of Criticism* (New Haven, Conn. and London: Yale University Press, 1968) pp. 173–91.

Parish, Charles, 'The Nature of Mr. Tristram Shandy, Author', *Boston University Studies in English*, v (1961) 74–90.

Piper, William Bowman, *Laurence Sterne* (New York: Twayne, 1965).

Preston, John, *The Created Self: The Reader's Role in Eighteenth Century Fiction* (London: Heinemann, and New York: Barnes & Noble, 1970).

Reid, Ben, 'The Sad Hilarity of Sterne', *Virginia Quarterly Review*, xxxii (1956) 107–30.

Rolle, Dietrich, *Fielding und Sterne: Untersuchungen über die Funktion des Erzählers* (Münster: Aschendorff, 1963).

Russell, H. K., '*Tristram Shandy* and the Technique of the Novel', *Studies in Philology*, xlii (1945) 581–95.

Thomsen, Christian W., *Das Groteske im englischen Roman des achtzehnten Jahrhunderts* (Darmstadt: Wissenschaftliche Buchgesellschaft, 1974).

Traugott, John, *Tristram Shandy's World: Sterne's Philosophical Rhetoric* (Berkeley and London: University of California Press, 1954; reprinted New York: Russell & Russell, 1970).

Traugott, John (ed.), *Laurence Sterne. A Collection of Critical Essays* (Englewood Cliffs, N.J.: Prentice-Hall, 1968).

Watt, Ian, 'The Comic Syntax of *Tristram Shandy*', in Howard Anderson and John S. Shea (eds), *Studies in Criticism and Aesthetics 1600–1800*. In Honor of Samuel Holt Monk (Minneapolis: University of Minnesota Press, 1967) pp. 315–31.

Wright, Andrew, 'The Artifice of Failure', *Novel*, ii (1969) 212–20.

Index

Abrams, Meyer H., 2, 240
Allemann, Beda, 29, 241, 243
Alter, Robert, 245, 257, 259
Anderson, Howard, 257, 258
Arbuthnot, John, 8
Ariosto, 100
Aristotle, 107
Arnauld, Antoine, 39
Arnold, Matthew, 83, 247
Auden, Wystan Hugh, 98, 249
Austen, Jane, x, 8, 14, 18, 19,
    49–67, 76, 83, 86, 91, 96, 99,
    102, 111, 112, 115, 119, 123,
    137, 145, 232, 245–6
  Pride and Prejudice, 18, 19, 49–67,
    71, 72, 73, 75, 76, 78, 83,
    92, 93, 94, 95, 116, 120, 129,
    132, 133–4, 136, 137, 145,
    154, 155, 156, 159, 162, 169,
    171, 175, 182, 183, 184,
    185–6, 191, 195, 198, 200,
    203, 205–6, 208, 212, 213,
    216, 219, 230, 234, 235, 245–6

Babb, Howard S., 245, 246
Baird, Theodore, 259
Balzac, Honoré de, 232
Baratta, Eva Anne, 254
Bart, Benjamin F., 85, 248
Barthelme, Donald, 232
Barthes, Roland, 257
Bate, Walter Jackson, 111, 242, 244,
    250
Bayley, John, 246
Beckett, Samuel, 2, 14, 27, 200,
    232, 235, 236, 245, 260
Behler, Ernst, 242, 254
Belaval, Yvon, 255, 256

Bellow, Saul, 237
Benet, Juan, 237
Benjamin, Walter, 156, 157, 179,
    255, 257
Berend, Eduard, 130, 251, 252
Berger, Dieter A., 258
Berger, Dorothea, 252
Berkeley, George, 41
Blake, William, 43
Bond, Richmond P., 250
Booth, Wayne C., ix, 1, 4, 5, 14,
    58, 191, 234, 241, 242, 245,
    246, 258, 259
  A Rhetoric of Irony, 1, 4, 5, 241,
    242, 246
Borges, Jorge Luis, 232, 237
Bosse, Heinrich, 152, 244, 254
Bottrall, Ronald, 250
Bourgeois, René, 225, 259
Bowra, Maurice, 250
Boyd, Elizabeth, 250
Brentano, Clemens, 252
Brombert, Victor, 70, 242, 247, 248
Brooks, Cleanth, 3, 156
Brower, Reuben A., 246
Burckhardt, Sigurd, 258, 259
Byron, George Gordon, x, 8, 18,
    43, 93–120, 124, 134, 137, 245,
    248–51
  Childe Harold's Pilgrimage, 116
  Don Juan, 8, 18, 19, 93–120, 124,
    133, 135, 136, 151, 155, 156,
    157, 159, 162, 179, 181, 182,
    191, 194, 207, 211, 219, 230,
    235, 248–51

Calvert, William J., 251
Calvino, Italo, 237

Camus, Albert, 18
  La Chute, 18, 20, 242
Carlyle, Thomas, 126, 245
Carroll, Lewis, 245
Castex, Pierre, 257
Cervantes Saavedra, Miguel de, ix,
  27, 29, 208, 237, 260
  Don Quixote, 20, 48, 90, 146, 167,
  237
Cicero, 24
Close, Anthony, 242, 260
Cohen, Huguette, 256, 257
Coleridge, Samuel Taylor, 43, 109,
  207–8, 218, 245, 259
Coles, Robert, 240
Condillac, Etienne Bonnot de, 41,
  244
Conrad, Peter, 250, 258
Cooke, Michael G., 118, 251
Crocker, Lester G., 256
Culler, Jonathan, 89, 90, 226, 247,
  248, 259

Daiches, David, 246
Dante, Alighieri, 29
Demorest, Don Louis, 247
Diderot, Denis, ix, x, 18, 29, 48,
  96, 99, 111, 159–87, 233,
  255–7
  Jacques le fataliste et son maître, 18, 19,
  99, 159–87, 197, 219, 230,
  231, 235, 255–7
Dieckmann, Herbert, 162, 255
Dilthey, Wilhelm, 252
Doctorow, E. L., 237
Dostoyevsky, Fyodor Mikhailovich,
  14, 19
Duckworth, Alistair M., 246
Dyson, Anthony Edward, 5, 217,
  222, 241, 258, 259

Eliot, George, 16–18, 223, 232, 240,
  246
  Middlemarch, 16–18, 19, 229, 230
Eliot, Thomas Stearns, 3, 99, 249
Empson, William, 13, 241
England, A. B., 250, 251
Engstrom, Alfred, 247

Fairlie, Alison, 247
Fichte, Johann Gottlieb, 30, 38–9,
  41, 47, 138, 142
Fielding, Henry, 6, 8, 14, 100, 109,
  198, 260
Flaubert, Gustave, x, 8, 69–92, 95,
  96, 99, 102, 111, 112, 115, 137,
  226, 246–8
  Bouvard et Pécuchet, 8, 226
  Madame Bovary, 69–92, 94, 95, 96,
  99, 108, 114, 116, 119, 120,
  129, 132, 134, 136, 155, 156,
  159, 162, 175, 182, 183, 198,
  200, 203, 212, 213, 219, 235,
  246–8
Fluchère, Henri, 258, 259
Fontane, Theodor, 18
  Effi Briest, 18, 230
Forster, Edward Morgan, 208, 259
Foucault, Michel, 244
Frank, Joseph, 247
Frey, Karl, A. J., 152, 252, 254
Fried, Michael, 232–4, 260
Frisch, Max, 237
Frye, Northrop, ix, 3, 4, 241, 246
  Anatomy of Criticism, 3, 241

Genet, Jean, 235
Genette, Gérard, 52, 241, 246, 247,
  248
Gide, André, 236
Gifford, P., 20, 242
Glicksberg, Charles I., 240
Goethe, Johann Wolfgang von, 19,
  23, 47, 126, 146, 242
Goodhand, Robert, 247
  Grande Encyclopédie, 37, 39
Green, Dennis Howard, 242
Grimsley, Ronald, 256
Gurewitch, Morton L., 226, 259

Hacking, Ian, 42, 244
Hamlin, Cyrus, 240
Hardy, Barbara, 246, 260
Harich, Walter, 255
Hartman, Geoffrey H., 241
Haym, Rudolf, 30, 243
Hazlitt, William, 111, 114, 250

Hegel, Georg Wilhelm Friedrich, 30, 31–3, 34, 35, 240, 243, 244
Heimrich, Bernhard, 45, 157, 179, 247, 255, 257
Heine, Heinrich, 146
Herder, Johann Gottfried, 41
Hettner, Hermann, 30, 236, 243
Hirsch, Eric Donald, 19, 241
Höllerer, Walter, 255
Horace, 107
Houston, John Porter, 84, 248
Huch, Ricarda, 225, 259
Hugo, Victor, 43
Humboldt, Wilhelm von, 41
Hunter, J. Paul, 258

Iser, Wolfgang, 47, 245

Jankélévich, Vladimir, 225, 259
Jenkins, Cecil, 247
Jean Paul (Richter, Johann Paul Friedrich), x, 96, 111, 121–57, 208, 251–5
  Flegeljahre, 121–57, 179, 181, 182, 191, 204, 207, 230, 235, 251–5
  Vorschule der Ästhetik, 121, 123, 124, 253
Johnson, Samuel, 23, 34, 48, 49, 97, 137, 141, 236
Joseph, M. K., 249, 251
Joyce, James, 222, 236, 260
Jump, John D., 250
Jüttner, Siegfried, 257

Kabelac, Sharon L., 257
Kafka, Franz, 2, 8, 14, 27, 200, 232
Kant, Immanuel, 37–8, 39, 47, 244
Kavanagh, Thomas, 255
Kayser, Wolfgang, 252
Keats, John, 245
Keith, Hans, 255
Kempf, Roger, 257
Kenrick, William, 257
Kerbrat-Orecchioni, Cathérine, 241
Kernan, Alvin, 249
Kierkegaard, Søren 30, 33–5, 239, 244
Knox, Norman, 5, 7, 20, 241, 242

Köhler, Erich, 256
Köpke, Wulf, 250
Kretzmann, Norman, 244
Kroeber, Karl, 101, 246, 249

Lancelot, Claude, 39
Lange, Victor, 47, 245, 258
Lanham, Richard, 191–2, 207, 258, 259
La Rochefoucauld, François, 6
Lascelles, Mary, 246
Lem, Stanislaus, 237
Levin, Harry T., 248
Lindner, Burkhardt, 252, 253
Locke, John, 40, 41, 205, 244, 245
Lovejoy, Arthur, O., 244
Lovell, Ernest, J., Jr., 249, 250
Loy, Robert J., 256

Mann, Thomas, 236
Mansell, Darrel, 246
McGann, Jerome, 250
Mautner, Stephen, 257
Mauzi, Robert, 256
May, Georges, 255, 256
Mellor, Anne K., 226–7, 240, 244, 249, 250, 259
Mendilow, Adam Abraham, 209, 247
Meyer, Hermann, 132, 253, 254, 255
Michelsen, Peter, 254
Moglen, Helene, 199, 222, 258, 259
Montesquieu, Charles-Louis de Secondat, 8, 102
Mudrick, Marvin, 246
Muecke, Douglas, C., ix, 1, 4, 5, 20, 236, 241, 242, 260
  The Compass of Irony, 1, 4, 241, 242, 260
Müller, Adam, 25, 30, 31, 243
Mylne, Vivienne, 256

Nabokov, Vladimir, 2, 18, 232, 260
Nardine, Jane, 246
Nelson, Lowry, Jr., 198, 258
Neumann, Peter Horst, 132, 152, 253

Novalis (Hardenberg, Friedrich von), 30, 43, 243
Nykrog, Per, 257

Orwell, George, 19

Page, Norman, 246
Petrarch, 25, 29
Piper, William Bowman, 258
Plato, 24, 118
Polheim, Karl Konrad, 252
Pope, Alexander, 109
Poulet, Georges, 247
Preston, John, 196, 258, 259
Profitlich, Ulrich, 252
Proust, Marcel, 61, 247
Prunier, Francis, 255

Quintilian, 7, 23, 24

Rasch, Wolfdietrich, 252, 253
Rehm, Walter, 252, 253
Reid, Ben, 259
Richards, Ivor Armstrong, 3
Ridenour, George, 117, 249, 250, 251
Rolle, Dietrich, 222, 259
Rousseau, Jean-Jacques, 100, 102, 121, 251
Rousset, Jean, 246, 248

Salomon, Roger, B., 103, 249, 250, 251
Sartre, Jean-Paul, 70, 247
Satire, 8–11, 60, 79–81, 102–3, 217, 227
Schieder, Margarete, 252
Schlegel, August Wilhelm, 30, 43
Schlegel, Friedrich, ix, x, 24–30, 31, 33, 34, 38, 43, 44–5, 47, 48, 118, 119, 132, 137, 151, 168, 186, 227, 236, 237, 239, 242, 243, 251, 252, 254, 256, 257, 259
Schleiermacher, Friedrich Ernst Daniel, 257
Scholes, Robert, 260
Scholz, Rüdiger, 253
Schröder, Rudolf Alexander, 253

Schwartz, Delmore, 237
Schweikert, Uwe, 252, 253, 254, 255
Sedgewick, George G., 241, 260
Shakespeare, William, 29, 237
Shelley, Percy Bysshe, 43
Sherrington, R. J., 247, 248
Simpson, David, 225–6, 259, 260
Smollett, Tobias, 47, 100
Socrates, 2, 24, 29, 168, 228
Socratic irony, 4, 7, 228
Solger, Karl Wilhelm Friedrich, 25, 30, 31, 33, 240, 243, 244
Sorrentino, Gilbert, 237
Southey, Robert, 109
Sperry, Stuart M., 225, 235, 260
Spitzer, Leo, 173, 248, 256
Staël, Anne-Louise-Germaine Necker de, 43, 100, 146, 254
Stanzel, Franz, 245
Starkie, Enid, 247
Steffan, Truman Guy, 249, 250
Stendhal (Beyle, Henri), 18, 43
    Le Rouge et le noir, 18
Sterne, Laurence, ix, x, 29, 48, 96, 111, 133, 136, 186, 189–223, 258–60
    Tristram Shandy, x, 18, 45, 47, 48, 189–223, 230, 231, 234, 235, 236, 239, 257–9
Strohschneider-Kohrs, Ingrid, 226, 236, 240, 242, 243, 253, 254, 256, 259, 260
Surer, Paul, 257
Svevo, Italo, 236
Swift, Jonathan, 6, 8, 9–10, 102, 253
    A Modest Proposal, 9
    A Tale of a Tub, 8
    Gulliver's Travels, 8, 9–10, 19, 102
Szondi, Peter, 243

Thibaudet, Albert, 247, 248
Thompson, Alan Reynolds, 241
Thorlby, Anthony K., 247
Tieck, Ludwig, 25, 29, 157, 237
Traugott, John, 258
Trilling, Lionel, 1, 6, 15, 223, 240, 241, 242, 259

Trueblood, Paul Graham, 249

Ullmann, Stephen, 248

Vartanian, Aram, 164, 255
Virgil, 93, 106, 107
Vischer, Friedrich Theodor, 252
Voltaire (Arouet, François-Marie),
　6, 8

Wain, John, 249
Walser, Martin, 226, 259
Warning, Rainer, 85, 86, 248, 256,
　257
Warren, Robert Penn, 3

Watt, Ian, xi, 195, 245
Weinrich, Harald, 241
Weinstein, Leo, 249
Wellek, René, 254
Werner, Stephen, 256, 257
Wilde, Alan, 6, 241
Wilkie, Brian, 250, 251
Wilson, Arthur, M., 255
Wilson, Daniel, W., 245
Woolf, Virginia, 93, 108, 157, 200,
　214, 246, 248, 250, 258, 259
Worcester, David, 241
Wordsworth, William, 43, 108, 244
Wright, Andrew, 259

Young, Edward, 36